THE POLITICAL ECONOMY OF
DEMOCRATIC TRANSITIONS

THE POLITICAL ECONOMY OF DEMOCRATIC TRANSITIONS

Stephan Haggard and Robert R. Kaufman

PRINCETON UNIVERSITY PRESS   PRINCETON, NEW JERSEY

Library of Congress Cataloging-in-Publication Data

Haggard, Stephan.
The Political economy of democratic transitions / Stephan Haggard
and Robert R. Kaufman.
p.   cm.
Includes bibliographical references and index.
ISBN 0-691-02974-1 (cloth : alk. paper). — ISBN 0-691-02775-7
(pbk. : alk. paper)
1. Democracy—Economic aspects.
2. Authoritarianism—Economic aspects.   3. Economic
policy—Political aspects.   4. Democracy—Cross-cultural studies.
5. Authoritarianism—Cross-cultural studies.   6. Economic
policy—Cross-cultural studies.   I. Kaufman, Robert R.   II. Title.
JC423.H29   1995
338.9—dc20
94-49595
CIP

This book has been composed in Times Roman

Princeton University Press books are printed on acid-free paper
and meet the guidelines for permanence and durability of the
Committee on Production Guidelines for Book Longevity of the
Council on Library Resources

Printed in the United States of America by Princeton Academic Press

1 3 5 7 9 10 8 6 4 2
(Pbk.)
1 3 5 7 9 10 8 6 4 2

To Our Children

LISSA AND MATTHEW KAUFMAN AND KIT HAGGARD

Contents

Figures and Tables

FIGURES

TABLES

Preface and Acknowledgments

THIS BOOK has had a long gestation. We first met at a series of workshops organized by Miles Kahler at the Lehrman Institute in the fall of 1984 that led to his volume on *The Politics of International Debt* (Cornell University Press, 1985). In late May 1985, we met again at a conference on the political economy of stabilization sponsored by the Yale Center for International and Area Studies and the Institute for Social and Policy Studies and organized by Colin Bradford.

That meeting initiated a long and fruitful collaboration among us and a group of close colleagues and friends: Thomas Callaghy, Miles Kahler, Joan Nelson, and Barbara Stallings. That collaboration, funded generously by the Ford and Rockefeller Foundations, produced *Fragile Coalitions* (Transaction Books for the Overseas Development Council, 1989) and *Economic Crisis and Policy Choice* (Princeton University Press, 1990), both edited by Joan Nelson. Our first written collaboration was a contribution to a project on developing country debt directed by Jeffrey Sachs for the National Bureau of Economic Research. Surviving the experience reasonably well, we went on to edit *The Politics of Economic Adjustment* (Princeton University Press, 1992). In addition to essays by Kahler, Stallings, and Nelson, we were fortunate to work with John Waterbury and Peter Evans on that project.

Still not tired of one another's intellectual company, we began to discuss a more extended study on the political economy of democratic transitions. Work on the project began during leaves in 1991 and 1992 funded by individual research and writing grants from the John D. and Catherine T. MacArthur Foundation. We are grateful to the foundation for providing the resources that allowed us to make significant headway in initiating this project.

During part of this period, Haggard and Steven B. Webb from the World Bank co-directed a collective research project on economic adjustment in new democracies, to which Kaufman contributed a study of Mexico. The results of this project were published as *Voting for Reform: Economic Adjustment in New Democracies* (Oxford University Press, 1994), co-edited by Haggard and Webb. Steve Webb deserves special thanks, as does the excellent team of scholars that contributed to our understanding of Poland, Chile, Senegal, Nigeria, Thailand, Turkey, and Spain. Tony Dunn at the Council on Foreign Relations and Johannes Linn at the World Bank helped Haggard to obtain the Council on Foreign Relations International Affairs Fellowship which funded his work at the World Bank; Vittorio Corbo, director of the Macroeconomics and Growth Division at the time, was kind enough to invite a political scientist into his division. Kaufman would like to thank his co-authors on the Mexico portion of the project, Carlos Bazdresch and Blanca Heredia, for their valuable collaboration as well as for the general education they provided about that complex political system.

Kaufman spent his leave during 1991 and 1992 at the Institute for Latin American and Iberian Studies at Columbia University. He would like to thank Douglas A. Chalmers, the director, assistant directors Marc Chernik and Katie Roberts Hite, and other members of the staff for welcoming him to the Institute and providing a supportive and stimulating environment in which to work. In July 1994, he worked on final revisions of the manuscript as a scholar-in-residence at the Bellagio Study and Conference Center of the Rockefeller Foundation.

During the time that this manuscript evolved, Haggard also had the pleasure of working on three other projects that assisted his thinking on these issues. Robert Dohner collaborated in a study on the politics of adjustment in the Philippines, part of a larger project on the political feasibility of adjustment organized by Christian Morrisson of the OECD Development Centre. Haggard was also able to interview a number of Korean policymakers and scholars in connection with a joint research project on Korean macroeconomic policy sponsored by the Harvard Institute for International Development (HIID) and the Korean Development Institute (KDI). Susan Collins, Richard Cooper, Chungsoo Kim, Ban Ho Koo, David Lindauer, Dwight Perkins and Sung-tae Ro collaborated in that project. Haggard also co-authored the conclusion to John Williamson's study on *The Political Economy of Policy Reform* (Institute for International Economics, 1993), a project that brought together a number of policymakers and scholars involved in particular reform episodes. Haggard's move to the Graduate School of International Relations and Pacific Studies at the University of California, San Diego, in 1992 provided him a stimulating new home in which to finish this project; teaching a course with Susan Shirk and Matthew Shugart on institutions was particularly instructive.

Kaufman benefited from his collaborative work with Barbara Stallings, which resulted in a co-edited book, *Debt and Democracy in Latin America* (Westview Press, 1989), and a study of the role of political parties, published in *The Macroeconomics of Populism* (MIT Press, 1991), edited by Rudiger Dornbusch and Sebastian Edwards. His understanding of the politics of democratic transitions has also been advanced through collaboration on the project on Economic Liberalization and Democratic Consolidation, directed by Laurence Whitehead and sponsored by the Social Science Research Council. Comments on a paper presented at the University of Bologna, Forli, Italy, in Spring 1992, were particularly helpful. He would also like to acknowledge the help of Eric Hershberg, staff director for the SSRC.

A number of individuals read the manuscript in draft form and have given us both criticism and encouragement. Luiz Carlos Bresser Pereira, Katrina Burgess, Tom Callaghy, Douglas Chalmers, T. J. Cheng, David Collier, Jorge Dominguez, Kent Eaton, Geoffrey Garrett, Barbara Geddes, Peter Gourevitch, Carol Graham, Howard Handleman, Peter Katzenstein, Sylvia Maxfield, Marcilio Marques Moreira, Molly O'Neal, Adam Przeworski, Garry Rodan, Matthew Shugart, Eduardo Silva, Van Whiting, Eliza Willis, and Carol Wise read the entire manuscript and offered extensive comments. Other individuals read portions of the manuscript and provided us with insights on particular issues and countries or assisted us in other ways. Our thanks to Lisa Anderson, Henri Barkey, Peter Beck, Kiren Chaudhry, Scott Christensen, Yun-han Chu, Ruth Collier, Larry Diamond, Rick Doner, Jeff Frieden, Martin Garguilo, Eric Hershberg, Kevin Hewison, Paul Hutchcroft, Ted James, Jan Kubik, Joohee Lee, Barbara Lewis, Arend Lijphart, Chung-in Moon, Manuel Montes, Joan Nelson, Daniel Nielson, Greg Noble, Ziya Öniş, Süleyman Özmucur, Leigh Payne, Shelley Rigger, Hector Schamis, Michael Shafer, Denise Stanley, Evelyne Huber Stephens, Nick van de Walle, John Waterbury, and Ed Winckler. Edwin Chan, Michelle Chang, William Clark, Michael Cripps, Enrique Delamonica, Todd Eisenstadt, and Daniel Nielsen provided us with research assistance.

Parts of this manuscript have been presented before colloquia and seminars where we received extensive comments and criticism. We would like to thank the following individuals and institutions: Jon Fox of the Political Science Department at MIT; Paul Boeker and Colleen Morton of the Institute of the Americas, La Jolla; David Trubek and Jeff Cason of the Global Studies Research Program and the MacArthur Scholars Workshop at the University of Wisconsin, Madison; Thomas Biersteker, Dietrich Rueschemeyer, and Hector Schamis of the Watson Institute, Brown University; Colin Bradford of the Development Centre of the Organization for Economic Cooperation and Development, Paris; Leslie Armijo, Thomas Biersteker, and Abraham Lowenthal, organizers of the workshop on political and economic liberalization at the University of Southern California; Jonathan Hartlyn, Evelyne Huber Stephens, and John Stephens of the University of North Carolina; members of the Political Economy Seminar, Rutgers University; Peter Evans and Jim Rauch, co-chairs of a working group on ideas, institutions, and economic growth; Larry Diamond and Marc Plattner of the *Journal of Democracy*; and Peter Berger and Robert Hefner of the Institute for the Study of Economic Culture.

Spouses always receive expressions of thanks, whatever their actual role in the completion of research projects. In this case, though, Nancy Gilson and Laura Schoen genuinely deserve gratitude, having suffered patiently not only through this book, but through our earlier collaborations as well. Nancy and Laura carried a double burden: not only did each provide support and encouragement for her husband, but each had to put up with the intrusions of his co-author as well. So far, remarkably enough, marriages and friendships have survived very well, despite long and expensive phone conversations, frequent absences for conferences and consultations, sleepless nights, and mood swings.

Finally, this book is dedicated to our children, Lissa and Matthew Kaufman and Kit Haggard: the next generation of democrats and the one after that.

August 1994

THE POLITICAL ECONOMY OF
DEMOCRATIC TRANSITIONS

The Political Economy of Democratic Transitions

IN THE last two decades, the developing world has experienced political and economic changes of epochal proportions. In the political sphere, the most remarkable development has been the widespread trend away from authoritarian rule toward democracy. The dictatorships of southern Europe were among the first to fall, the casualties of both internal divisions and external political pressures. Beginning in the late 1970s, Latin American militaries started to withdraw from power. Over the course of the next decade, political transitions began in a number of Asian countries as well, including Korea, Taiwan, Thailand, the Philippines, Turkey, and Pakistan. What Samuel Huntington has called the "third wave" of democratization crested in the late 1980s with the stunning collapse of Communist governments in Eastern Europe and the Soviet Union, and increasing pressure on authoritarian regimes in Africa and the Middle East.[1]

The economic transformation of the developing world has been no less dramatic. External shocks at the beginning of the decade hit many countries harder than the Great Depression and contributed to recession and macroeconomic instability throughout the 1980s; in some cases, these problems persisted well into the 1990s. The response to these shocks has been a profound shift in development strategy, away from state-led, inward-oriented models of growth toward emphasis on the market, private ownership, and greater openness to trade and foreign investment.[2] The pace of economic liberalization has varied across countries, but the broad direction of change is unmistakable.

The coincidence of these historical events raises long-standing questions about the relationship between economic and political change. What role have economic crises played in the near-global wave of political liberalization and democratization? Can new democracies manage the daunting political challenges posed by economic crises and reform efforts? Under what economic and institutional conditions is democracy most likely to be consolidated?

[1] Samuel P. Huntington, *The Third Wave: Democratization in the Late Twentieth Century* (Norman: University of Oklahoma Press, 1991).

[2] For a summary view of the main policy changes initiated in the 1980s, see John Williamson, ed., *Latin American Adjustment: How Much Has Happened?* (Washington, D.C.: Institute for International Economics, 1990); Olivier Blanchard et al., *Reform in Eastern Europe* (Cambridge, Mass.: MIT Press, 1992).

Neither liberal theories of modernization that originated in the 1950s nor the more pessimistic dependency perspective of subsequent decades has provided fully satisfactory answers to these questions. Modernization theory postulated a positive correlation between capitalist development and democratization and thus failed to anticipate the "new authoritarianism" that swept through the relatively industrialized Latin American countries.[3] Nor could it account for the economically successful authoritarian capitalism that persisted for long periods of time in East Asia. Closer scrutiny of both democratic and authoritarian regime transitions also called into question the weight given to socioeconomic variables in Marxist and dependency writing and in the literature on "bureaucratic-authoritarianism."[4] By the beginning of the 1980s, most analyses of regime change had turned away from economic explanations of any kind, emphasizing instead the autonomy of purely political processes.[5]

Although this attention to "the political" constitutes an important corrective to earlier intellectual trends, it is a mistake to relegate the economic and political realms to separate spheres of analysis; economic conditions and policy, as well as the nature of political institutions, shape the prospects for democracy. The purpose of this book is to build on the substantial literature on democratic transitions and economic reform to construct a political economy of democratic transitions.

We explore three questions, each of which is relevant to a different phase in the transition from authoritarianism to consolidated democratic rule. The first is the way economic conditions affect the capacity of ruling elites to determine the *timing* and *nature* of their withdrawal (Part One, chapters 1 through 4). The second is the way in which the economic and institutional legacies of the transition affect economic policymaking in new democratic regimes (Part Two, chapters 5 through 8). Finally, we explore the conditions under which market-oriented reform and democracy can be reconciled and consolidated (Part Three, chapters 9 through 11). Before turning

---

[3] Guillermo O'Donnell, *Modernization and Bureaucratic-Authoritarianism: Studies of South American Politics* (Berkeley, Calif.: Institute of International Studies, 1973); David Collier, ed., *The New Authoritarianism in Latin America* (Princeton, N.J.: Princeton University Press, 1979).

[4] Criticisms of the socioeconomic approach to regime change can be found in Collier, *The New Authoritarianism,* especially David Collier, "Overview of the Bureaucratic-Authoritarian Model," pp. 3–19; Albert O. Hirschman, "The Turn to Authoritarianism in Latin America and the Search for Its Economic Determinants," pp. 61–99; and José Serra, "Three Mistaken Theses Regarding the Connection between Industrialization and Authoritarian Regimes," pp. 99–165; and in Juan Linz and Alfred Stepan, eds., *The Breakdown of Democratic Regimes: Crisis, Breakdown and Reequilibration* (Baltimore: Johns Hopkins University Press, 1978), pp. 11–13.

[5] Guillermo O'Donnell, Philippe Schmitter, and Laurence Whitehead, eds., *Transitions from Authoritarian Rule: Prospects for Democracy* (Baltimore: Johns Hopkins University Press, 1986).

to these specific questions, we outline our broad analytic orientation and the theoretical structure that guides our enterprise.

THE THEORETICAL ORIENTATION

The course of both regime change and economic policymaking is ultimately determined by the strategic choices of key actors—the supporters and opponents of the incumbent government—as constrained by economic circumstances and existing institutions. In some recent literature on democratic transitions, however, "choice" has received greater emphasis than "constraint." The most influential study in this vein is by Guillermo O'Donnell and Philippe Schmitter, who build on earlier work by Dankwart Rustow and Juan Linz.[6] They identify actors primarily according to their political strategies, such as their inclination to support or oppose the regime, to form alliances, or to bargain with adversaries ("hardliners" vs. "softliners"). O'Donnell and Schmitter do not deny the importance of economic factors or more enduring forms of political organization. Nonetheless, they highlight "the high degree of indeterminacy embedded in situations where unexpected events *(fortuna),* insufficient information, hurried and audacious choices, confusion about motives and interests, plasticity and even indefinition of political identities, as well as the talents of specific individuals *(virtù)* are frequently decisive in determining outcomes."[7]

The approach pioneered by O'Donnell and Schmitter offers a counterweight to the structural biases in previous analyses of regime change, and directs attention to the way institutions are continually reshaped by purposive human agency. In its game-theoretic form, as in the penetrating essays by Adam Przeworski, a choice-based approach achieves both elegance and deductive rigor.[8] Yet such approaches fail to address the factors that shape actors' political preferences, the conditions under which these

[6] Guillermo O'Donnell and Philippe C. Schmitter, *Tentative Conclusions about Uncertain Democracies,* pt. 4 of O'Donnell, Schmitter, and Whitehead, eds., *Transitions from Authoritarian Rule.* See also Dankwart Rustow, "Transitions toward Democracy: Toward a Dynamic Model," *Comparative Politics* 2 (1970): 337–63; Juan Linz, *Crisis, Breakdown and Reequilibration* (Baltimore: Johns Hopkins University Press, 1978); Giuseppe di Palma, *To Craft Democracies: An Essay on Democratic Transitions* (Berkeley: University of California Press, 1990); John Higley and Richard Gunther, *Elites and Democratic Consolidation in Latin America and Southern Europe* (New York: Cambridge University Press, 1992); Terry Lynn Karl, "Dilemmas of Democratization in Latin America," *Comparative Politics* 23 (1990): 1–21; Terry Lynn Karl and Philippe Schmitter, "Modes of Transition in Latin America, Southern and Eastern Europe," *International Social Science Journal* 43 (1991): 269–84.

[7] O'Donnell and Schmitter, *Tentative Conclusions,* p. 5.

[8] Adam Przeworski, *Democracy and the Market: Political and Economic Reforms in Eastern Europe and Latin America* (New York: Cambridge University Press, 1991).

preferences change, and even the identity of the pivotal actors. To leave such questions open, while at the same time dismissing the utility of more conventional institutional and social categories as O'Donnell and Schmitter appear to do,[9] is virtually to forgo the possibility of generalization. One is left with little middle ground between relatively abstract models of strategic choice and detailed case studies.

There are also strong empirical reasons to reevaluate these purely political approaches. Some conclusions about the weak causal significance of economic factors, including those of O'Donnell and Schmitter, were reached before the impact of the crisis of the 1980s could be fully assessed. It is now more apparent that political conflicts associated with severe economic crisis contributed directly to the collapse of incumbent authoritarian regimes in a number of countries. Moreover, our concern is not limited to the determinants of regime change alone; we are also interested in the performance and prospects of the new democratic regimes that have emerged in the last two decades. Issues of policy reform and growth constitute the most salient questions on the political agenda of these new democratic governments, and successful economic adjustment is likely to affect whether they are consolidated.

At the broadest theoretical level, our analysis is guided by three working assumptions which, though widely shared in current work in political economy, appear to have been jettisoned in much of the recent writing on democratic transitions and consolidation. First, although we reject the strong claim that social interests and relations determine the prospects for democracy, we assume that the economic-cum-social structure constitutes an essential point of departure for understanding politics, including the politics of regime change.[10] The analysis of socioeconomic structure is crucial for identifying politically relevant groups and their policy preferences, and for understanding political alignments and conflicts.

Second, we assume that the opportunities for political elites to mobilize political support or opposition will depend on how economic policy and performance affect the income of different social groups. Both aggregate

[9] See O'Donnell and Schmitter, *Tentative Conclusions,* p. 4.

[10] For political economy approaches to democratization, see Jeffrey Frieden, *Debt, Development, and Democracy: Modern Political Economy and Latin America, 1960–1985* (Princeton, N.J.: Princeton University Press, 1991) and Dietrich Rueschemeyer, Evelyne Huber Stephens, and John Stephens, *Capitalist Development and Democracy* (Chicago: University of Chicago Press, 1992). Rueschemeyer, Stephens and Stephens provide a comprehensive review of the modernization literature on democratization, pp. 12–39. One issue we do not address is the question of the role of ethnic homogeneity and heterogeneity in transition processes. In sharp contrast to the choice-based approach, this literature begins precisely with the assumption that organized social groups constitute the building blocks for any theoretical analysis of regime change and stability. See, for example, Donald Horowitz, *A Democratic South Africa? Constitutional Engineering in a Divided Society* (Berkeley: University of California Press, 1991).

economic performance and the distributive consequences of policy are crucial to politics everywhere, affecting the chances of both incumbents and oppositions. Economic crises, such as those that struck the developing world in recent decades, affect not only the preferences of different social actors among a given set of policies, but also their preferences among different institutional arrangements and their capacity to maintain or change those institutions.

Finally, we argue that it is impossible to derive political or policy outcomes from economic cleavages and interests without consideration of the institutional context in which groups operate. It is a central theme of this book that generalizations about the relationship between group interests, economic policy, and democracy are undertheorized when they fail to take into account the way politics is structured by representative institutions and the state itself.[11]

GENERAL CONCEPTS AND ARGUMENTS

We build our analysis around several core propositions about the relationship between economic policy and performance, political institutions, and the stability of authoritarian and democratic political regimes. The first point is that all regimes in mixed economies rest on some explicit or implicit bargain between political leaders and key support groups. Economic conditions will determine how stable and robust that bargain is. Good times generate support. Economic crisis, by contrast, creates incentives for the private sector to defect from that bargain, increases the likelihood of political protest "from below," and reduces the capacity of ruling elites to manage the resulting distributive conflicts. Failure to avoid economic crisis or to adjust quickly to it therefore increases the probability that opposition will be directed not just at the government but at the fundamental rules of the game.

We do not mean to imply that there is a deterministic relationship between crisis and regime change. Authoritarian rulers in power at the beginning of the "third wave" of democratization faced a variety of international and domestic pressures for political reform that were not directly related to economic performance. Democracies, by contrast, often draw on reservoirs of legitimacy and support during periods of crisis that authoritarian regimes lack.[12] We argue, however, that the inability to avoid or adjust successfully to economic crisis increases the probability that authori-

---

[11] For example, Rueschemeyer, Stephens, and Stephens conclude their major study of the role of class forces in democratization by underlining the critical role of political parties in the transition process. *Capitalist Development and Democracy*, p. 282.

[12] Juan J. Linz and Alfred Stepan, *Problems of Democratic Transition and Consolidation: Southern Europe, South America and Eastern Europe* (unpublished ms.), pp. 83–84.

tarian regimes will be transformed and reduces the capacity of authoritarian leaders to control the process of political change, including the terms on which they exit. Similarly, we expect that the prospects for the consolidation of democracy will be better when the government is able to successfully administer its economic inheritance.

What, then, determines the capacity of governments to manage the economy effectively? We argue that for both authoritarian and democratic regimes, the answers are to be found in the nature of political institutions. We focus particular attention on two variables: the constitution of executive authority and the nature of the representative institutions that mediate between contending political and social groups and the government.

Economic Crisis and the Politics of Adjustment

It is important to begin by clarifying the nature of the political problems posed by economic crises and the way variations in institutional arrangements affect political responses to them. In our usage, crises have two components. First, they are characterized by a sharp deterioration in aggregate economic performance, indicated by slowed growth and accelerating inflation. Not all groups lose during periods of low growth or high inflation, and some may gain; crises always have distributive implications that are important for understanding the specifics of any case. The main challenge for political elites, however, springs from the fact that a sharp deterioration in aggregate economic performance cuts across social strata and affects the income of a wide array of social groups.

A second aspect of a crisis is that the economic deterioration is not self-correcting. Crises may be triggered by temporary external shocks or overlap with cyclical fluctuations, but they imply that prevailing policy approaches cannot be sustained without continued economic deterioration. Crises thus pose challenges both to policy and to the coalition of interests that benefited from the policy status quo.

The appropriate adjustment strategy in the face of crisis is the subject of both uncertainty and heated debate, and we make no judgment about the precise policy course required in any particular setting. We do assume, however, that in times of economic crisis, investment and growth will not resume without policy change. In countries facing high inflation and severe balance-of-payments problems, fiscal and exchange rate adjustments are likely to be necessary conditions of stabilization. Where the state has intervened extensively in markets, some liberalization, including through trade and price reform, is also likely to be a component in shifting the structure of incentives. These expectations do not imply an endorsement of "orthodoxy"; there are a variety of possible adjustment paths, and a number of ways in which the state can continue to intervene fruitfully to correct market failures and promote equity.[13] However, there is growing evidence that stable macroeconomic policy and attention to the significance of relative prices and trade are important determinants of long-term growth.[14]

The distributive effects of initiating and sustaining these policy changes constitute the heart of the politics of adjustment. We assume that at least some politically influential groups benefited from the policy regime and institutional arrangements that existed prior to the crisis; thus economic policy adjustments necessarily generate political opposition from some quarters. However, as we have already noted, failure to adjust also has serious, even regime-threatening, political costs. Balancing the political risks of adjustment against those of attempting to maintain the status quo is the core dilemma that governments face in situations of economic crisis.[15]

The Initiation and Consolidation of Economic Reforms

In analyzing the politics of adjustment, we distinguish between the initiation and consolidation of reform.[16] At the onset of reform, potential beneficiaries face high uncertainty about future payoffs and substantial barriers to collective action. Those who have gained from past policies, on the other hand, are certain about their preferences, feel the pain of adjustment immediately, and have typically overcome collective action problems.

In these circumstances, we argue that centralized executive authority is important for overcoming policy stalemates. The successful initiation of reform depends on rulers who have personal control over economic decision-making, the security to recruit and back a cohesive "reform team," and the political authority to override bureaucratic and political opposition to policy change.[17]

---

[13] The World Bank's recent report on *The East Asian Miracle* (New York: Oxford University Press for the World Bank, 1993), is indicative of a subtle shift in thinking on these issues. For a critique, see Albert Fishlow et al., *Miracle or Design? The World Bank's East Asian Miracle Study* (Washington D.C.: Overseas Development Council, 1994).

[14] For evidence on the role of macroeconomic policy in long-term growth, see Stanley Fischer, "The Role of Macroeconomic Factors in Growth," *Journal of Monetary Economics* 3 (1993): 485–513. On the role of trade in long-term growth—though not necessarily trade policy or exports—see Ross Levine and David Renelt, "A Sensitivity Analysis of Cross-Country Growth Regressions," *American Economic Review* 82 (1992): 942–63.

[15] Joan Nelson, ed., *Economic Crisis and Policy Choice: The Politics of Adjustment in the Third World* (Princeton, N.J.: Princeton University Press, 1990).

[16] Stephan Haggard and Robert R. Kaufman, "Introduction," in *The Politics of Economic Adjustment* (Princeton, N.J.: Princeton University Press, 1992).

[17] For a more extended discussion of this theme, see John Waterbury, "The Heart of the Matter? Public Enterprise and the Adjustment Process," in *The Politics of Economic Adjustment;* John Williamson and Stephan Haggard, "The Political Conditions for Economic Reform," in John Williamson, ed., *The Political Economy of Policy Reform* (Washington: Institute for International Economics, 1993), pp. 572–73, 578–82.

Such discretionary authority is two-edged; if unchecked over the longer run, it can undermine effective economic management by creating uncertainty. In the short run, however, centralization of authority has been crucial for economic reform in both authoritarian and democratic regimes. In military and one-party regimes, centralized authority has derived from rulers' personal control over the coercive and party apparatus. In democracies, it has been based on special constitutional provisions and emergency powers, mandates claimed by newly elected governments during their "honeymoons," and powers delegated to the executive by legislators.

The consolidation of economic reform rests on conditions that are different from, and in certain respects antithetical to, those associated with the initiation phase. First, expectations about government intentions are most likely to be stabilized if the potential for predatory or arbitrary behavior on the part of the executive is reduced through the evolution of checks on executive discretion and the delegation of authority to policy-making agencies. Second, reforms must eventually appeal to a new coalition of beneficiaries. No reform can be consolidated in the absence of the organization of such groups and the establishment of effective networks of support and communication between them and state authorities.

There are a variety of representative mechanisms that might achieve these objectives, including the types of corporatist arrangements that are characteristic of the small European social democratic states and which have received attention in some parts of Latin America.[18] We argue, however, that political parties are of particular importance for understanding the consolidation of economic reform. In authoritarian regimes, parties serve as instruments of both control and cooptation. In democracies, parties legislate and serve to organize the stable bases of support that are required to sustain policy initiatives.

In sum, we argue that the ability of both authoritarian and democratic leaders to maintain power is partly a function of economic performance, which in turn is dependent on the conduct of economic policy. Institutions affect the coherence of policy both in the initiation phase, when executive authority is an asset, and during the consolidation phase when success rests on building bases of social support.

The book examines the interaction between institutions, economic policy, performance, and stability during three distinct phases of the transition process. Part One examines the "late authoritarian" period. The key question we address with respect to this phase is the timing and terms of authori-

---

[18] Philippe Schmitter, "Interest Intermediation and Regime Governability in Contemporary Western Europe and North America," in S. Berger, ed., *Organizing Interests in Western Europe* (New York: Cambridge University Press, 1981), p. 287–330; Peter Katzenstein, *Small States in World Markets: Industrial Policy in Europe* (Ithaca, N.Y.: Cornell University Press, 1985).

tarian withdrawals, and particularly the extent to which outgoing leaders are capable of controlling the transition. Part Two looks at the early democratic period. We are interested both in the coherence and effectiveness of economic management, and in the effects of economic performance on emergent political cleavages, conflicts, and institutions. The third phase, and the subject of Part Three, is still unfolding: the consolidation and routinization of democratic politics. We ask how the long-run prospects for democracy are affected by development strategy and economic performance, and conversely, how democratic institutions influence the prospects for growth.

ECONOMIC POLICY AND POLITICAL STABILITY IN AUTHORITARIAN REGIMES

Authoritarian regimes do not permit fully competitive elections and rely on intimidation, manipulation, and cooptation to restrict the activity of independent interest groups and political oppositions. As Linz argues, however, they do tolerate limited forms of political contestation. To survive, they must accommodate the interests of some constituency; they are accountable to *someone*, if only the military establishment or other sectors within the state elite.[19] As we have suggested, they are arguably more dependent than democracies on their capacity to deliver material resources to key supporters, and it is for this reason that economic performance can be pivotal in dislodging them.

Military Governments

Authoritarian regimes in middle-income countries that are led by the military have generally had shorter political life-spans than those ruled by dominant parties. In contrast to dominant-party regimes, military-backed governments are "regimes of exception"; they lack both a long-term rationale for remaining in power and the organizational channels for building stable bases of support. Military governments have used elections to legitimate their authority and have created official parties to compete in those elections; however, parties that are creatures of the military have difficulty in maintaining loyalty and support over time. In the absence of a dominant party, the military establishment itself constitutes the most important institutional framework for the recruitment of political leaders and the delib-

[19] Juan J. Linz, "Totalitarian and Authoritarian Regimes," in Fred Greenstein and Nelson Polsby, eds., *Handbook of Political Science*, vol. 3 (Reading, Mass.: Addison-Wesley, 1975). See also Susan Shirk's concept of "reciprocal accountability" in *The Political Logic of Economic Reform in China* (Berkeley: University of California Press, 1993), pp. 70–91.

eration of policy issues. This enhances the likelihood that the officer corps will be divided by factionalism and by cross-cutting alliances with competing civilian interests.

Among military-backed governments, the capacity to respond to economic crisis varies with the cohesion of the military establishment. As we have just noted, factionalism is commonplace in military regimes, particularly those that have governed for long periods of time. Factional divisions undermine the capacity for governments to provide sustained backing for a unified policy team; policy stalemate and further economic deterioration tend to open fatal wounds in the regime. Allies in the private sector defect and broader oppositions mobilize from below. This opposition, in turn, widens conflicts among military elites themselves over the costs of staying in power. Military governments facing such manifest difficulties typically seek to negotiate their exit from power, although under conditions of internal division and political isolation.

We offer no general explanation for the sources of military cohesion. Factionalism has been relatively muted in some military establishments, however, and this can affect their responses to economic crisis. Cohesion is greatest where personalist rulers have gained control over both the government and the military establishment, including particularly control over recruitment and promotion within the officer corps. It can also be affected by the perception of external threats, or by a shared sense of purpose during the early stages of authoritarian takeovers. Where factionalism is limited or controlled, governments have a greater opportunity to survive the destabilizing effects of economic crisis and to undertake far-reaching economic reforms. Although even relatively cohesive military governments have eventually been impelled to yield to democratic oppositions, they have been able to negotiate transfers of power under relatively favorable economic and political conditions.

A central argument of the book is that military regimes that are able to exit in favorable economic conditions generally do so on terms that are different from those that exit during crises. In these "non-crisis" transitions, ruling elites are less isolated politically than those exiting during times of crisis, and are more likely to enjoy either explicit or tacit support. As a result, they are in a better position to impose an institutional framework that maintains their prerogatives, favors the chances of their political allies, and restricts the freedom of maneuver of incoming democratic governments.

Dominant Party Regimes

Unlike military regimes, dominant-party authoritarian governments are characterized by a greater separation of political and coercive functions.

This separation has several important implications. First, although dominant parties often become centers of bureaucratic privilege, they also provide rulers with a means of recruiting and coordinating subordinates within the state apparatus. Conversely, because the military establishment is less directly involved in such activities, it is less likely to be politicized and less prone to mount coups. Finally, dominant parties provide a mechanism for coopting and controlling social groups and managing elections.

The most distinctive feature of dominant-party regimes relative to military ones is their political resiliency in the face of both economic downturns and periods of growth. Because they possess greater political resources for the management of political conflict, they are more likely to persist through economic crises, even when they are unable to adjust effectively; this is the case with many of the Middle Eastern and African regimes, as well as the Communist regimes, most of which only fell when their *external* support collapsed.

As with military regimes, there is a high degree of variation among dominant-party governments with respect to economic management; some of the worst performing economies in the world have been in single-party regimes. Among the middle-income capitalist economies that are the subject of this volume, however, the two dominant-party regimes that we analyze—Mexico and Taiwan—have had more success both in initiating economic reforms and in constructing a political coalition to sustain them. These dominant party regimes were also more likely than their military counterparts to manage the political pressures that stem from economic *success*. The dominant party provided rulers with a means to manage political reform and the opening of the economy without losing control of the political system.

ECONOMIC POLICY AND PERFORMANCE IN NEW DEMOCRACIES

The key difference between authoritarian regimes and their democratic successors is that the rules of the latter guarantee opposition groups the right to challenge incumbent rulers and policies, and to replace those rulers through competitive elections. Such competition assumes broad suffrage rights, free speech and association, and guarantees of basic civil liberties.[20] Democratic transitions can be considered to have occurred when authoritarian governments are forced to yield power to ones that operate within this set of rules.

[20] We assume that it is analytically useful to distinguish these political dimensions of democracy from other social rights, although the latter are certainly no less important from a normative point of view. See Robert Dahl, *Polyarchy: Participation and Opposition* (New Haven, Conn.: Yale University Press, 1971), chap. 1, pp. 1–16.

New democratic governments face distributive pressures from groups reentering the political arena, and uncertainty about the loyalty of groups associated with the old order. The severity of these challenges and the capacity to respond will depend on the economic legacy of the old regime and the nature of the political institutions that emerge during the transition. Two variables are useful in accounting for differences among new democracies in economic policy and performance, and in analyzing the prospects for consolidation. The first is whether the transition occurs during an economic crisis, or in a setting in which adjustment problems have already been confronted by authoritarian regimes and performance is good. The second variable is the extent of fragmentation and polarization within the newly established party system. In some, but not all cases, these two variables are related: economic crisis contributes to the fragmentation and polarization of the party system, which in turn undermines the capacity to manage the economy effectively.

Crisis transitions are characterized by a rapid disintegration of the coalitional foundations of the authoritarian regime and strong reactions against the policy orientation of the outgoing government. New democratic governments taking office in such contexts face both opportunities and difficulties in framing and implementing coherent economic policy. On the one hand, economic circumstances provide opportunities for executives to seize the initiative and launch wide-ranging economic reforms. On the other hand, the changed political circumstances associated with a transition to democratic rule permit groups to press demands for relief on the government, demands that can impede both the initiation and the consolidation of reforms.

In non-crisis transitions, by contrast, distributive demands on the government are constrained by the relative strength of parties and social groups aligned with, or sympathetic to, the economic project of the outgoing authoritarian government. Not only will such a coalition seek continuity of policy; it will also seek to protect its gains by establishing institutional rules that favor policy continuity, including limits on political competition.

Economic management in new democracies is not simply a function of these socioeconomic variables; much depends on how interests are aggregated. We pay particular attention to how the party systems that emerge following authoritarian rule influence the mobilization of political demands, operating on the assumption that this in turn will affect the prospect for both economic reform and the consolidation of democracy. We argue that fragmented and polarized party systems heighten partisan rivalries, magnify conflicts among organized interests, and weaken the capacity of the executive to initiate reform. These very failings can increase the incentives for reformist executives to bypass representative institutions and the normal constitutional process altogether. Even if they succeed at initiating reform, however, the continuity and credibility of policy in such systems is jeopardized by the difficulty of forging stable electoral, legislative, and bureaucratic majorities, by ideological polarization between government and opposition, and by the resulting exacerbation of political business cycles.

Effective economic policy is more likely in cohesive party systems in which fragmentation is limited and polarization muted. This party configuration might occur when transitions restore pre-authoritarian constitutions that favor two-party or moderate multiparty competition, or where historical patterns of party fragmentation and polarization have been transformed under authoritarian auspices. Initiation of radical reforms may also be quite difficult in such centrist party systems because of vested interests and strong incentives toward policy incrementalism. In crisis situations, however, such systems can provide important resources for reformist executives that fragmented and polarized party systems lack. These include institutional incentives to dampen extremist claims and as a result, greater ease both in reaching policy compromises and in building stable bases of political support. These factors are particularly important for consolidating economic reform over the long run.

MARKET REFORMS AND THE CONSOLIDATION OF DEMOCRACY

Democratic consolidation is a process through which acceptance of a given set of constitutional rules becomes less directly contingent on immediate rewards and sanctions and increasingly widespread and routinized. In Philippe Schmitter's characterization, it is the transformation of the institutional arrangements and understandings that emerged at the time of the transition "into relations of cooperation and competition that are reliably known, regularly practiced, and voluntarily accepted by those persons or collectivities . . . that participate in democratic governance."[21]

There is no single route to stable democratic capitalism and no single

---

[21] Philippe Schmitter, "Consolidation and Interest Systems," in Larry Diamond and Gary Marks, eds., *Comparative Perspectives on Democracy: Essays in Honor of Seymour Martin Lipset*; *American Behavioral Scientist* 35, 4 and 5 (March/June 1992), p. 424.

For Valenzuela, consolidation is indicated by the elimination of tutelary powers and reserved domains of authority protected by threats of a return to authoritarian rule, by the absence of major discrimination in the electoral process, and by the acceptance of elections as the only legitimate route to power. J. Samuel Valenzuela, "Consolidation in Post-Transition Settings," in Scott Mainwaring, Guillermo O'Donnell, and J. Samuel Valenzuela, eds., *The New South American Democracies in Comparative Perspective* (Notre Dame, Ind.: University of Notre Dame Press, 1992), p. 69.

type of consolidated democracy. Successful consolidation does imply, however, the transformation of the discretionary style of executive decision-making that characterizes the initiation of reforms in both the crisis and the non-crisis democracies. Strong executives may be important for resolving the collective action problems associated with severe economic crisis, but ultimately they must be accountable to, and checked by, representative institutions. In crisis transitions, this has implied a need to move beyond reliance on executive decrees and plebiscitary appeals. In non-crisis cases, it has implied eliminating nondemocratic restrictions on participation imposed by authoritarian predecessors.

The consolidation of democracy and the consolidation of economic reform are closely related, but have different political foundations. Democracy is a decision-making system in which there is a degree of uncertainty concerning substantive outcomes. Democracy provides opportunities for competing interests to contest and change policies, including economic ones. But democracies are unlikely to become institutionalized if broad assumptions underlying the management of the economy lack widespread support or are subject to continuous challenge.

In part, the resolution of this tension hinges on whether reform leads to sustained and equitable growth; this question looms especially large for democratic governments coming to power under crisis conditions. To date, most new democracies have been able to survive policy stalemates and poor economic performance for a considerable period of time. But survival is not the same as consolidation. We argue that prolonged stagnation can undermine the social foundations and institutional vitality of democratic regimes even when they do not actually collapse; if severe crises continue or recur, there is no reason to believe that such democracies will survive at all.

Democratic consolidation depends not only on economic performance, but on how representative institutions structure distributive outcomes. In some cases, corporatism or differences in the constitution of executive authority, particularly the difference between presidential and parliamentary rule, are salient in this regard. However, we again place particular emphasis on the way party systems structure contestation over economic issues. For reasons already implied, fragmented and polarized party systems pose particular difficulties. On the other hand, there is a variety of alternative party systems that can organize stable support from the beneficiaries of market-oriented policies while providing compensation to groups that are harmed.[22] These include two-party systems and moderate multi-party systems dominated by either center-right or center-left coalitions.

[22] John Ruggie, building on Karl Polanyi, has labeled such arrangements the "compromise of embedded liberalism"; "International Regimes, Transactions, and Change: Embedded Liberalism in the Postwar Economic Order," *International Organization* 36 (1982): 379–415.

THE EMPIRICAL APPROACH: SELECTING CASES

Though our study considers evidence from a wide range of experiences, the analysis is built around a comparison of twelve countries: in Latin America, Argentina, Bolivia, Brazil, Chile, Peru, Mexico, and Uruguay; in Asia, Korea, Taiwan, the Philippines, Thailand, and Turkey. Like any set of cases selected for purposes of comparative analysis, this one is subject to the question, why these and not others? In an ideal world, it would be desirable to have either the entire universe of new democracies, or a random sampling from different regions. In fact, the selection was partly governed by practical considerations concerning the existence of quality monographic work, the availability of quantitative data, the opportunity for useful comparisons, and our own prior research. The conclusions drawn from this particular group of countries must therefore be assessed against evidence drawn from other cases and regions.

Nevertheless, there are a number of reasons that these cases provide a plausible sample for cross-national comparison. First, the sample includes most of the major middle-income developing countries that have undergone democratic transitions in recent years, and with the partial exception of Mexico and Taiwan, consists *only* of countries that have undergone democratic transitions.[23] Were we primarily interested in the determinants of democratic transitions per se, it would have been a mistake to exclude countries that remained authoritarian; there would be no variance on the dependent variable. In chapter 1, where we consider the effects of crisis on authoritarian governments more generally, we do draw on evidence from a wider array of cases. However, our primary concern is not with whether a transition occurs, but rather with variations in the transition process and in the characteristics of the new democratic governments that emerge from it.

Other broad commonalities among the cases facilitate comparison. All of the countries but Bolivia are middle-income capitalist countries[24] and all are characterized by declining agrarian populations, substantial industrialization, sizeable middle and working classes and "popular sectors," and substantial differentiation between business elites and politico-military organizations. Bolivia, which is poorer and more rural than the other countries, nevertheless resembles other Latin American cases in terms of the historic patterns of conflict among popular-sector groups, economic elites, and the military establishment; it was included because it represents an important example of successful stabilization within a democratic political

---

[23] Peru and Thailand experienced reversions to authoritarian rule in the early 1990s; we discuss these developments in chaps. 6 and 7.

[24] As defined by the World Bank, *World Development Report 1992* (Washington, D.C.: The World Bank, 1992).

context. We would expect that these relatively complex and diversified industrializing societies have different political dynamics than either poor agrarian ones or rich oil exporters. A growing, though still modest body of work, has sought to theorize about democratization in Africa and the Middle East, and we have referenced this work at several points in our analysis.[25] However, the extent of actual democratization in these two regions is extremely limited, and to include a wider range of cases would have further complicated our task.

Our cases also invite comparison with the countries of Eastern Europe, and particularly with the more developed ones: Poland, Hungary and the Czech Republic. Several interesting comparative studies have emerged attempting such comparisons, particularly with the large Latin American countries.[26] In our judgment, the advantages of including these cases were outweighed by important structural differences, including their socialist economic structure, the unique role of external political forces in the transition, and the more profound nature of the economic transformation. In the conclusion, however, we offer some brief observations on how our findings might be of relevance to understanding socialist transitions.

Despite the broad similarities among the countries we have chosen, there are also important variations in the sample as well. The most important for our analytic purposes are economic. All of the developing countries in the study faced international shocks in the 1980s, though to differing degrees. Moreover, their economic performance has varied quite substantially, from the sustained high growth of Taiwan and Thailand to the highly erratic performance of Argentina and Bolivia. As we have argued, differences in economic performance play an important causal role in Parts One and Two of the book; however, we also seek to explain these differences in the post-transition period.

The inclusion of both Latin American and Asian cases also allows us to assess patterns of democratization and economic adjustment among countries that have pursued different development strategies, and to build on a growing literature of cross-regional comparisons.[27] In many Latin Ameri-

---

[25] See Ellis Goldberg, Resat Kasaba, and Joel S. Migdal, eds., *Rules and Rights in the Middle East: Democracy, Law, and Society* (Seattle: University of Washington Press, 1994); Thomas Callaghy and John Ravenhill, eds., *Hemmed In: Responses to Africa's Economic Decline* (New York: Columbia University Press, 1993).

[26] See particularly Luiz Bresser Pereira, José María Maravall, and Adam Przeworski, *Economic Reforms in New Democracies* (Cambridge: Cambridge University Press, 1993); Joan Nelson, ed., *A Precarious Balance,* vol. 1, *Democracy and Economic Reforms in Eastern Europe,* and vol. 2, *Democracy and Economic Reforms in Latin America* (Washington, D.C.: Overseas Development Council, 1994); Barbara Geddes, "The Leninist Legacy in Eastern Europe," unpublished ms., University of California at Los Angeles, n.d.

[27] See, for example, Stephan Haggard, *Pathways from the Periphery: The Politics of Growth in the Newly Industrializing Countries* (Ithaca, N.Y.: Cornell University Press, 1990)

can countries, Turkey, and to some extent the Philippines, the crisis of the 1980s took place against the backdrop of an effort to move to a secondary phase of import substitution, concentrated in the capital-intensive consumer durables and capital goods industries. This strategy relied on state-owned enterprises that showed increasing financial weaknesses over time, Keynesian macroeconomic policies that showed a persistent inflationary bias, and highly protected industrial sectors. Though there are cases of export success among the Latin American countries, particularly Brazil, incentives were generally biased against exports. Both industrial and macroeconomic policy contributed to persistent balance-of-payments problems and an increasing reliance on external debt.

The Southern Cone countries—Chile, Argentina, and Uruguay—-constitute important variations on this general pattern, because of the attempts in the 1970s under military rule to dismantle the regulatory and protectionist policies of earlier decades. The attempt to impose neoliberal models was far from complete, but involved massive coercion against unions and public-sector workers, as well as extensive protests from import-substituting industrialists. By the end of the 1970s, the viability of these experiments was undermined by unsustainable exchange-rate and fiscal policies and unregulated private-sector borrowing, producing severe financial crises and forcing new rounds of adjustment.

Korea, Taiwan, and Thailand, finally, began processes of democratization facing quite different sets of economic challenges. In Korea and Taiwan, "strong" authoritarian governments spearheaded shifts in the 1960s toward industrialization based on the aggressive promotion of labor-intensive manufactured exports, followed during the 1970s by efforts to diversify their industrial bases through both secondary import substitution and export "deepening." In the 1970s, a number of Southeast Asian countries, including Thailand, followed suit.

These strategies established a context for political reform that was quite distinct from that in Latin America, Turkey, and the Philippines. Korea and Thailand were hit hard by external shocks, and all three countries faced adjustment challenges in the 1980s. Korea and Thailand shared with their Latin American counterparts concerns with rising levels of indebtedness. Other adjustment problems were different, however, including rising wage levels that threatened international competitiveness, declining agricultural sectors, and in Korea and Taiwan, trade surpluses that jeopardized macroeconomic stability and brought strong external pressure for greater market opening. Nonetheless, in all three cases conservative macroeconomic policies and a strong export capacity provided greater resilience than their Latin

---

and Gary Gereffi and Don Wyman, eds., *Manufacturing Miracles: Paths of Industrialization in Latin America and East Asia* (Princeton, N.J.: Princeton University Press, 1990).

American counterparts enjoyed. The ability of new democratic governments to sustain this policy thrust is a major focus of our attention in Part Two.

Finally, the sample contains a wide variation with respect to political institutions. A comparison of military and party-dominant systems is a central aspect of our analysis of authoritarian regimes. The new democracies include both presidential and parliamentary systems, as well as systems that vary with respect to a variety of other institutional features that are of interest to us, including party systems, electoral rules, and the powers of the executive.

The findings from small-n comparisons are heavily dependent on the cases chosen, and the risks of selection bias are high. However, our sample is actually quite large relative to the universe of cases, and includes a substantial portion of all newly democratic middle-income countries. Moreover, it encompasses significant variation in both the economic and political variables that are of interest to us.

ORGANIZATION OF THE VOLUME

The organization of the volume largely follows the arguments summarized in the preceding sections, although there are some differences in the sequence of topics in order to enhance the clarity of the presentation. Part One (chapters 1 through 4) examines the response of military regimes to economic crisis and their capacity to manage the terms of political transition. Chapter 1 provides an overview of the analytic issues. Chapter 2 examines cases in which deteriorating economic performance hastened the withdrawal of military regimes: Argentina, Bolivia, Brazil, Peru, the Philippines, and Uruguay. In chapter 3, we explore the experience of the four non-crisis cases in which military governments were able to undertake successful adjustment prior to the transition: Chile, Korea, Turkey, and the more ambiguous case of Thailand, where the transition is difficult to identify. Chapter 4 provides a systematic comparison of the institutional and policy legacies of these crisis and non-crisis transitions.

Part Two focuses on the political economy of adjustment in new democracies. Chapter 5 extends the discussion of "crisis" and "non-crisis" transitions, and elaborates our arguments about the effect of economic conditions and the party system on economic policy choice. Chapters 6 and 7 provide an empirical examination of the crisis and non-crisis cases respectively. Chapter 8 examines the dominant-party regimes of Mexico and Taiwan. Combining the analytic concerns of Parts One and Two, the chapter analyzes both the capacity of these dominant parties to manage the economy and their distinctive capacity to dictate the pace of political change.

Part Three turns to issues of the consolidation of democratic and market institutions. Chapter 9 examines the effect of economic conditions on the stability of democratic rule. Chapter 10 explores how alternative institutional arrangements might lead to stable social compromises that reconcile democracy and the market. Chapter 11 offers some brief concluding observations on both theory and the future of democracy.

Part One

THE POLITICAL ECONOMY OF AUTHORITARIAN WITHDRAWALS

CHAPTER ONE

The Political Economy of Authoritarian Withdrawals

SEVERAL different factors might account for the dramatic increase in the number of authoritarian withdrawals during the 1970s and 1980s. The wide geographic spread of the movement toward democracy suggests that international pressures played an important role. Diplomatic pressures from the Western European democracies and the lure of membership in the European Community were significant in the southern European transitions, and contributed to limiting the Turkish military's stay in power in the early 1980s. In the Caribbean, Central and South America, and the Philippines, American influence mattered.[1] The United States' encouragement of constitutional government reflected the attempt to counter leftist threats through political reform, a strategy that dates to the Alliance for Progress. Most of the transitions at the end of the decade occurred among Eastern European states that could no longer count on the military and political backing of their Soviet patrons.

The "contagion effect," discussed in work by Laurence Whitehead, has been another international source of pressure on authoritarian regimes. Successful democratic opposition in one country has an impact on the perceptions and behavior of actors in neighboring countries or in those with strong cultural links.[2] Developments in Spain resonated throughout Latin America and the "people power" revolution in the Philippines challenged other Asian dictatorships. Events in Poland and East Germany had implications for other Eastern European regimes and the Soviet Union; their collapse, in turn, was debated virtually everywhere.

The structural changes associated with long-term economic growth constitute still a third influence at work. In southern Europe, the East Asian newly industrializing countries, and Eastern Europe, economic development resulted in the emergence of more complex, literate, middle-class societies that demanded increased political participation. Economic success thus arguably contributed to the demise of authoritarianism.

Given the myriad of forces that have worked to destabilize incumbent

[1] See Abraham Lowenthal, ed., *Exporting Democracy: Themes and Issues* (Baltimore: Johns Hopkins University Press, 1991).

[2] Laurence Whitehead, "The International Dimension of Democratization: A Survey of the Alternatives," paper presented at the International Political Science Association Congress, Buenos Aires, 21–25 July, 1991.

authoritarian rulers over the past several decades, our emphasis on the role of economic crisis requires justification. As Samuel Huntington has argued, specific transitions from authoritarianism to democracy are overdetermined: each is attributable to different combinations of causes, none of which is either necessary or sufficient to explain democratic transitions in general.[3] Why, then, should we focus intensively on economic crisis and adjustment as catalysts of political change?

One reason is that economic crisis *did* appear to accelerate, if not cause, the collapse of authoritarian regimes in a number of countries. This was particularly true in Latin America and Africa, where the shocks of the 1980s were profound. Where poor economic performance played a role in authoritarian withdrawals, it is important to specify clearly how economic deterioration affected political transformation. How did crisis affect the power relations among supporters of the regime and anti-regime opponents? Why were some regimes more vulnerable than others to the pressures created by these shifts?

A second reason to examine the impact of economic crisis is that even where it was not solely responsible for the transition itself, it had powerful effects on the *terms* on which authoritarian governments withdrew. Authoritarian governments able to avoid crises or adjust effectively were better positioned to resist pressures to leave office and maintained greater control over the timing and conditions of their exit. As we will suggest in Part Two, the differences between crisis and non-crisis transitions thus had an important impact on the institutional characteristics of incoming democratic governments.

This chapter provides an overview of the challenges economic crises pose to authoritarian regimes and the cross-national variation in responses to those challenges. We focus particularly on the withdrawal of military regimes, the typical form authoritarian rule took in middle-income capitalist societies, reserving the discussion of the more unusual dominant-party regimes to chapter 8. In the first section, we discuss the way economic factors, including both the level of development and short-run performance, affect the stability of authoritarian regimes. We begin with the general proposition that in relatively differentiated middle-income countries, the probability of a democratic transition increases during periods of economic distress.

Though the empirical evidence reviewed in the second section suggests that this hypothesis is plausible, the relationship is not a deterministic one; there are a number of anomalous cases in which democratic transitions occurred in the absence of economic crises. In the third section, we outline

---

[3] Samuel Huntington, *The Third Wave: Democratization in the Late Twentieth Century* (Norman: Oklahoma University Press, 1991), p. 38.

the institutional factors that made military regimes more or less vulnerable to economic crisis, emphasizing organizational and other sources of cohesion and factionalism, and provide an overview of how the general argument applies to the case studies that follow in chapters 2 and 3.

ECONOMIC DEVELOPMENT AND THE STABILITY OF AUTHORITARIAN REGIMES

The Lipset Hypothesis

Virtually all of the theoretical discussion of the effect of economic factors on regime type has focused on the question raised over thirty years ago by Seymour Martin Lipset: whether a high *level* of development is a precondition for the emergence and maintenance of democratic rule.[4] Notwithstanding the controversy it has generated, there are both theoretical and empirical reasons why the Lipset hypothesis is plausible.[5] As Robert Dahl has suggested, the diffusion of skills and organizational resources associated with high levels of economic development expands the range of groups with capacities to influence politics. "A modern dynamic pluralist society disperses power, influence, authority and control away from any single center toward a variety of individuals, groups, associations and organizations."[6] Such developments, in turn, increase the costs of repression relative to those of toleration, and thus the chances that authoritarian rulers will acquiesce to pressures for political liberalization and democratic reform when they arise.

Empirically, the correlation initially observed by Lipset between measures of economic development and democracy has remained one of the strongest findings in political science.[7] With some important exceptions, such as India, very poor countries tend to be authoritarian; very rich countries are overwhelmingly democratic.

Predictably, however, there is wide variation in regime type among middle-income countries that are neither very rich nor very poor. Hunt-

---

[4] Seymour Martin Lipset, "Some Social Requisites of Democracy: Economic Development and Political Legitimacy," *American Political Science Review* 53 (1959): 69–105.

[5] For a review of these hypotheses, see Alex Hadenius, *Democracy and Development* (New York: Cambridge University Press, 1992), pp. 77–82.

[6] Robert Dahl, *Democracy and Its Critics* (New Haven: Yale University Press, 1989), p. 252.

[7] For comprehensive reviews of the literature and presentation of new empirical findings, see Hadenius, *Democracy and Development*; Larry Diamond, "Economic Development and Democracy Reconsidered," *American Behavioral Scientist* 35 (1992): 450–99; John F. Helliwell, "Empirical Linkages Between Democracy and Economic Growth," *British Journal of Political Science,* 24 (1994): 225–48.

ington has suggested that such middle-income countries occupy a "zone of transition or choice, in which traditional forms of rule become increasingly difficult to maintain and new types of political institutions are required to aggregate the demands of an increasingly complex society. . . ."[8] As he points out, the recent wave of democratic transitions has occurred primarily among these middle-income countries.

But prior to the recent wave of democratic transitions, these same "transitional" countries had spawned new forms of *authoritarian* rule. The well-known work of Guillermo O'Donnell found that bureaucratic-authoritarian installations occurred in the most developed Latin American countries, not the least developed.[9] In a recent cross-national study, Lipset, Seong, and Torres found an "N-curve" relationship between authoritarianism and economic development. The probability of nondemocratic regimes *increased* with development in a middle range of countries (per capita income between $2,346 and $5,000 in 1980), but *decreased* with development among lower- and upper-income countries.[10]

In short, the relationship between level of development and regime type seems indeterminate among middle-income countries, which have been characterized by both authoritarian and democratic rule. A certain threshold of national income may constitute an important condition for democratic rule. But the level of economic development cannot tell us anything about the dynamics of democratic transitions or why they occur when they do.

Economics and Politics: The Equation in the Short Run

An alternative hypothesis is that the stability of authoritarian regimes depends both on the overall level of development *and* on economic conditions in the short run.[11] Authoritarian regimes vary according to which segments of the population are given preference, but all are responsive to the economic interests and demands of at least some sectors of their societies. Inclusionary authoritarian regimes such as Peru's initially mobilized mass support from above. Some authoritarian regimes, such as those in Central America and Africa, are based on highly personalistic ties between rulers and traditional social elites or clients. More typical of our

---

[8] Huntington, *The Third Wave*, p. 201.

[9] Guillermo O'Donnell, *Modernization and Bureaucratic-Authoritarianism: Studies in South American Politics* (Berkeley, Calif.: Institute of International Studies, 1973).

[10] S. M. Lipset, K. R. Seong, and J. C. Torres, "A Comparative Analysis of Social Requisites of Democracy," unpublished paper, Hoover Institution, Stanford University, 1991; Diamond, "Economic Development and Democracy Reconsidered."

[11] See also John Londregan and Kenneth Poole, "Poverty, the Coup Trap and the Seizure of Executive Power," *World Politics* 42 (1990): 151–83.

sample of middle-income countries are "bureaucratic-authoritarian" re-gimes based around a military-technocrat alliance, an economic reform program, and support from some portions of the modern private sector, both domestic and foreign.

Whatever the nature of the underlying "authoritarian bargains," poor economic performance—whether the result of external shocks, bad policy, or both—means a reduction in the resources available to political elites for sustaining bases of support. The effort to control inflation or to undertake structural reforms can further weaken the government's hand. Stabilization of inflation and balance-of-payments adjustment typically involve policies that reduce aggregate income in the short run. Though these stabilization measures are likely to be the most difficult politically, structural adjustment measures also have costs, since governments are typically unable to compensate for the withdrawal of rents from previously privileged groups.

In some cases, authoritarian rulers may be able to weather economic distress by forcing the costs of adjustment onto excluded groups, yet there are significant constraints in attempting to do so. Authoritarian governments cannot appeal to broad principles of democratic legitimation. Coercion is also costly, and generally either ineffective or counterproductive in securing the confidence of the private sector. To survive, such governments must sustain bases of support; they are therefore accountable even if that accountability is not always institutionalized and is focused on a relatively narrow range of interests.

We can examine the effects of economic crises on the stability of military regimes by tracing the interests and likely political responses of three sets of political and economic actors: private-sector business groups; middle-class and popular-sector organizations; and military and political elites who control the state and the main instruments of coercion.

First, deteriorating economic performance disrupts the "authoritarian bargains" that rulers typically forge with some portion of the private sector. The specific bases of business support depend, of course, on the structure of the economy, the resources available to specific groups, and the political project of the government. In our sample of countries, authoritarian regimes have rested on a wide variety of coalitional foundations, including import-substituting industrialists in most Latin American countries, financial and agro-export elites in Chile, and export-oriented manufacturing firms in Korea and Taiwan. Yet in all mixed-economy middle-income countries, business elites are pivotal actors because they control both existing assets and the flow of investment that is crucial to continued growth. Even where authoritarian governments restrict the formal political access of such groups, political leaders nonetheless seek their cooperation and support.

In military regimes, this cooperation is secured in three ways: by promising protection against perceived threats to private property; by pursuing broad development strategies that favor certain sectors; and by providing more particularistic favors or rents. Economic crisis and corresponding pressures for policy adjustment weaken the ability of the government to deliver in all three of these areas, and thus encourage a reassessment of the overall political bargain.

The initial reactions of the private sector to poor economic performance typically focus on changes in specific policies or government personnel. But if private sector actors believe that authoritarian governments are unwilling or unable to change policies detrimental to their individual and collective interests, if they lose "confidence," they can quickly recalculate the costs associated with democratization; this is particularly likely where there are opportunities to ally with "moderate" oppositions. On purely self-interested grounds, crises can push business groups to view democracy as the system most likely to provide them with opportunities to defend their interests.

The defection of private-sector groups poses particularly serious challenges to military regimes; the private sector is well placed to play an organizational and financial role within the opposition. But more important is the fact that loss of private-sector confidence confronts the government with bleak prospects for future investment and growth. It is possible to coerce individuals, and even to seize their assets, but it is difficult to force them to invest.

Middle- and lower-income groups, by contrast, are more vulnerable to political repression, and in all the countries in our sample, repressive tactics were used to "manage" public protests against deteriorating economic conditions. But military governments have relied on material rewards to win support or deflect opposition from these groups as well, and economic crisis clearly weakens the government's ability to do so. In several cases, rulers actively bid for the allegiance of portions of the popular sector through public employment, large-scale public works projects, and consumer subsidies. Even in harshly antilabor regimes, material payoffs have played an important role. In both Korea and Taiwan, for example, the political control of labor was a component of export-led growth strategies. But this growth strategy resulted in a steady improvement of living standards that bought the government the acquiescence, if not support, of some segments of labor. Even in the Southern Cone countries of Latin America, arguably the most labor-repressive of all authoritarian regimes, governments used exchange-rate policy, partial indexation, and other forms of compensation to limit the deterioration of workers' incomes.

The primary political weapon of mass-based groups and social movements in authoritarian settings is the mobilization of protest: strikes, street demonstrations, or where opportunities exist, referenda and electoral campaigns. These protests are frequently directed at political targets, but it would be misleading to interpret their origins and popularity as purely political. Such movements often have their origins in reaction to particular economic grievances: unemployment; inflation in the prices of staples, fuel, and transportation; declining real wages.[12] More importantly, these conditions provide opportunities for the political leaders of the opposition to draw in new adherents by linking economic circumstances to the exclusionary nature of the political order.[13]

Most crucial to the survival of military regimes, finally, is the continuing loyalty of the politico-military elite itself: the heads of the armed forces, strategic segments of the state apparatus, and in some cases, the individuals who control the machinery of the ruling party. We follow O'Donnell and Schmitter, Przeworski, and others in arguing that, except in cases of military defeat and foreign occupation, the proximate cause for the exit of authoritarian regimes can almost always be found in splits within this elite.[14] The crucial question for our purposes is the extent and manner in which economic conditions play a role in creating these divisions.

O'Donnell and Schmitter argue that the emergence of divisions between "hardliners" and "softliners" reflects preferences and assessments of risk that are not systematically related to economic conditions.[15] Agencies or individuals involved in earlier acts of repression, for example, are more inclined to adopt a "hardline" position against political liberalization than are officers who are less exposed to future reprisals. Similarly, willingness to support the use of coercion in response to protest may also reflect purely political assessments about the efficacy of coercion in deterring the escalation of protest or the possibilities of reaching agreement with a moderate opposition.

[12] This is not to suggest that all grievances are economic, particularly among middle-class groups. Because of their access to communications and organizational resources, white-collar groups, particularly within the liberal professions, play an especially important role in anti-government protests. These groups do not always favor democracy, but arbitrary governmental authority can pose threats not only to their careers but to professional norms, such as the integrity of the law or of universities. Except during periods of intense polarization, they are thus inclined to press for constitutionalism. Their incorporation into popular democratic movements is often pivotal to the process of political transition, in part because it affects the government's calculus concerning the use of coercion.

[13] For a useful discussion of the way these mobilizations can be affected by the strength of the union movement and past relationships to the party and the incumbent regime, see J. Samuel Valenzuela, "Labor Movements in Transitions to Democracy: A Framework for Analysis," *Comparative Politics,* 21 (1989): 445–73.

[14] See Guillermo O'Donnell and Philippe Schmitter, *Tentative Conclusions about Uncertain Democracies,* pt. 4 of O'Donnell, Schmitter, and Laurence Whitehead, eds., *Transitions from Authoritarian Rule* (Baltimore: Johns Hopkins University Press, 1986), pp. 15–17. Przeworski, *Democracy and the Market: Political and Economic Reforms in Eastern Europe and Latin America* (New York: Cambridge University Press, 1991), chap. 2, pp. 51–94.

[15] Ibid.

Even where economic crises are not the *source* of factional conflicts between hard and softliners, however, they are likely to widen them. In the first instance, economic downturns affect the loyalty of the military-political elite directly by reducing the ability of the government to deliver material benefits. Like any other component of the public sector, military establishments are threatened by adjustment measures: devaluations which increase the cost of foreign procurement, reductions of pay, and budget cuts. Opponents to adjustment measures may thus find important allies from within the armed forces themselves.

The changes in the interests of the major actors that we have outlined ultimately affect the course of political change through their influence on the strategic interactions between the politicians who constitute the leadership of the opposition and authoritarian elites. As these dynamics have been well charted by O'Donnell and Schmitter and by Przeworski, we need not reiterate them in detail.[16] We have already noted how the widening disaffection with the regime presents new opportunities for opposition politicians to mobilize support. There may be divisions within the opposition; we discuss their effects in more detail in the case studies. But from the perspective of the authoritarian leadership, the defection of private-sector groups and the widening of popular-sector protest increase both the cost of coercion and the risk that it will prove ineffective. It is precisely under such conditions that the splits we have noted within the regime begin to have strategic importance for the transition process. "Softliners" begin to calculate that the corporate interests of the ruling elite are best guarded by conciliation, rather than further repression. Even when the objective is a "broadened dictatorship" rather than a transition to democratic rule, the division within the government between softliners and hardline defenders of the status quo provides the opportunity for the opposition to press for broader political reforms.

ECONOMIC CRISIS AND AUTHORITARIAN WITHDRAWALS: EMPIRICAL PATTERNS

The relevance of short-term economic performance to authoritarian withdrawals can be gauged in a preliminary way by a survey of twenty-seven democratic transitions occurring between 1970 and 1990. Transitions are defined here as the first year of a competitively elected government; the two exceptions are Brazil, in which the opposition came to power through the electoral college, and Thailand, where the prime minister was selected by legislators not all of whom had been elected.

---

[16] See O'Donnell and Schmitter, *Tentative Conclusions,* pp. 15–36; and Przeworski's discussion of the hardliner-softliner dynamic in *Democracy and the Market,* pp. 51–88.

As Table 1.1 shows, these transitions occurred under a wide range of conditions, including relatively strong economic growth. Nevertheless, in a substantial majority of the cases, the years preceding the transition were marked by declining growth, increasing inflation, or both. Twenty-one of the twenty-seven countries experienced declining growth prior to the transition; among the remaining cases, long-term growth rates were very low in El Salvador and Ghana, and had declined by historic standards in Brazil. Two-thirds of the transitions were also preceded by increasing inflation. In Argentina and Uruguay, inflation was very high, although it had declined somewhat relative to the earlier period.

Only in Korea, Chile, and Turkey did transitions occur during periods of high and rising rates of growth and declining rates of inflation. Thailand presents a somewhat ambiguous case, since growth slowed somewhat in the early 1980s. However, overall economic conditions remained highly favorable in Thailand throughout the 1980s; growth rates were among the highest in the world and inflation decreased. For these reasons, we do not consider Thailand a crisis case.

On the other hand, although yearly growth rates improved slightly in some other countries prior to transitions, in most instances they remained very low. Brazil, which we classify as a case of crisis-induced transition, experienced a brief economic upswing in the year prior to the transition, but this had been preceded by several years of severe recession. Moreover, the outgoing regime had failed to confront a number of pressing adjustment issues and inflation accelerated substantially prior to the change in regime.

The inferences that can be drawn from these data about the causal relationship between economic conditions and regime change are limited by the fact that the table does not include countries in which regimes survived severe economic shocks. There is surprisingly little cross-national statistical work on the economic determinants of regime change, however. One recent exception is a study by Mark Gasiorowski,[17] which uses a pooled time-series technique to explore the relationship between economic conditions, measured in terms of growth and inflation, and transitions to and from democracy. Gasiorowski finds little effect of growth on democratization, but argues that in the 1980s high inflation had a statistically significant effect on the probability that authoritarian regimes would transit to democracy.

To clarify theoretical expectations, it is useful to consider those regimes that did not democratize in response to economic crises. During the 1970s and 1980s, these survivors consisted mainly of authoritarian regimes in Africa and the Middle East, and until 1989, the Communist regimes of

---

[17] Mark Gasiorowski, "Economic Crisis and Political Regime Change: An Event History Analysis," unpublished ms., Department of Political Science, Louisiana State University, October 1993.

TABLE 1.1

Economic Performance prior to Democratic Transitions

	GDP Growth		
	Avg. Performance, Transition Year and Two Previous Years (A)	Avg. Performance, Five Previous Years (B)	A − B
Honduras, 1982	−0.5	7.6	−8.1
Romania, 1990	−4.3	2.9	−7.2
Philippines, 1986	−3.2	3.9	−7.1
Ecuador	6.3	13.2	−7.0
Bolivia, 1982	−1.5	4.4	−6.6
Portugal, 1976	1.3	7.4	−6.1
Argentina, 1983	−3.2	2.4	−5.6
Uruguay, 1985	−2.4	2.0	−4.4
Hungary, 1990	−2.3	1.8	−4.1
Spain, 1977	2.5	6.2	−3.7
Nicaragua, 1990	−4.6	−0.9	−3.5
Greece, 1974	4.3	7.7	−3.4
Thailand, 1973	6.3	9.2	−2.9
Nigeria, 1979	2.6	5.3	−2.7
Senegal, 1978	0.1	2.5	−2.4
Thailand, 1983	5.8	7.8	−2.0
Argentina, 1973	3.2	4.4	−1.2
Poland, 1989	2.2	3.1	−0.9
Guatemala, 1986	0.0	0.6	−0.6
Peru, 1980	3.5	4.1	−0.6
Czechoslovakia, 1989	1.7	2.2	−0.5
Turkey, 1974	6.5	6.9	−0.4
Brazil, 1985	3.3	3.1	0.2
El Salvador	−0.9	−1.2	0.3
Turkey, 1983	4.3	3.0	1.3
Korea, 1988	11.7	8.5	3.2
Chile, 1990	6.3	3.9	2.4
Ghana, 1979	3.3	−1.9	5.2
Paraguay, 1989	5.7	0.1	5.6

TABLE 1.1 *(continued)*

	Inflation		
	Avg. Performance, Transition Year and Two Previous Years (A)	Avg. Performance, Five Previous Years (B)	A − B
Brazil, 1985	188.7	75.5	113.2
Poland, 1989	112.2	34.1	78.1
Bolivia, 1982	69.7	10.1	59.6
Ghana, 1979	81.3	26.4	54.9
Peru, 1980	61.2	24.3	36.9
Argentina, 1973	51.4	19.7	31.7
Portugal, 1976	22.2	7.7	14.5
Greece, 1974	15.6	2.1	13.5
Hungary, 1990	20.5	7.1	13.4
Uruguay, 1985	58.9	45.6	13.3
Guatemala, 1986	19.7	7.7	12.0
Philippines, 1986	24.7	13.8	10.9
Spain, 1977	18.8	9.9	8.9
Turkey, 1974	14.3	7.5	6.8
Thailand, 1973	6.9	2.5	4.4
Honduras, 1982	12.2	7.9	4.3
Paraguay, 1989	23.6	19.5	4.1
Romania, 1990	2.7	1.7	1.0
Nigeria, 1979	15.7	16.0	−0.3
Czechoslovakia, 1989	0.5	1.9	−1.4
El Salvador, 1984	12.2	14.4	−2.2
Ecuador, 1979	11.7	14.1	−2.4
Thailand, 1983	7.2	9.8	−2.6
Korea, 1988	4.3	7.3	−3.0
Chile, 1990	19.2	23.5	−4.3
Argentina, 1983	204.4	211.2	−6.8
Senegal, 1978	5.3	13.9	−8.6
Turkey, 1983	32.9	51.7	−18.8

Source: International Monetary Fund, *International Financial Statistics*, various issues. Comparable data for inflation in Nicaragua is not available.

Note: Country names in italics are those of cases discussed in this volume.

Eastern Europe. The survival of authoritarianism in these regions was attributable in part to the continued backing of external patrons. Regimes in the more advanced Eastern European states collapsed quickly once Soviet support was withdrawn. Authoritarian regimes in poor countries have arguably been kept alive by the unwillingness of external donors to sever the aid tie, usually for strategic as well as humanitarian reasons. One important source of political pressure on the poorer African countries in the early 1990s was the evaporation of a strategic justification for continued support, and a greater willingness to link assistance to political reform.[18]

The failure of democracy to take root in poorer countries, however, also reflects structural conditions that were highlighted by Lipset in his original analysis. In particular, the capacity of rulers in very poor countries to prolong their domination was facilitated by the relative weakness of organized interests. Highly dependent private sectors and geographically dispersed rural cultivators lacked the independence or organization to launch sustained protest against declining economic conditions. In these societies, economic hardship was often associated with social violence, palace coups, and the deterioration of central control over population and territory.[19] But into the early 1990s, predatory personalist rulers were surprisingly adept at resisting reform and clinging to office through continued access to external aid, repression, and careful maintenance of select patronage relations.[20]

A plausible hypothesis that combines economic conditions in both the long and short run is that authoritarian regimes are more vulnerable to economic downturns in middle-income capitalist countries. In such societies, wealth holders are more sharply differentiated from the political elite. Social groups hold substantial and independent organizational and material resources that are crucial to regime stability. The middle and working classes are politically relevant and there are lower barriers to collective action on the part of urbanized low-income groups. Countries fitting this description are also more likely to have prior histories of party politics, labor mobilization, and civic association. In both southern Europe and Latin America, these political traditions provided the basis for political mobilization during periods of crisis.

---

[18] See Joan M. Nelson with Stephanie Eglington, *Encouraging Democracy: What Role for Conditional Aid?* (Washington D.C.: Overseas Development Council, 1992), pp. 15–18.

[19] See Londregan and Poole, "Poverty, the Coup Trap and the Seizure of Executive Power."

[20] For reviews of the constraints on democratization in Africa, see Robert H. Jackson and Carl G. Rosberg, "Democracy in Tropical Africa: Democracy versus Autocracy in African Politics," *Journal of International Affairs* 38 (1985): 293–305; Larry Diamond, "Introduction: Roots of Failure, Seeds of Hope," in Diamond, Juan Linz, and Seymour Martin Lipset, eds., *Democracy in Developing Countries: Africa* (Boulder, Colo.: Lynne Riener, 1988), pp. 1–32; Thomas M. Callaghy and John Ravenhill, eds., *Hemmed In: Responses to Africa's Economic Decline* (New York: Columbia University Press, 1993).

VARIATIONS IN RESPONSES: THE INSTITUTIONAL
BASES OF MILITARY RULE

Neither these socioeconomic factors associated with level of development, nor short-term economic conditions, are fully able to explain the pattern of regime change; institutions also mattered (Figure 1.1). First, the distinction between military regimes and dominant-party systems appears to play some role in accounting for variations in the stability of authoritarian rule. One-party states outside of Eastern Europe showed considerable durability and substantial ability to control the pace of political liberalization. In Latin America, the Stroessner regime in Paraguay, based on an alliance between the military and the dominant Colorado party, was not forced from power until 1990. Mexico's ruling party continued to dominate the political landscape even in the face of crisis; we discuss that case in more detail in Chapter 8. One-party systems in Africa began to face more severe challenges in the early 1990s, in part as a result of declining external support. Nonetheless, single-party structures in countries such as Zambia arguably contributed to the surprising longevity of authoritarian rule in the face of secular economic decline and severe external shocks.[21] In Eastern Europe, Communist regimes survived the declining economic performance of the 1980s, and some, including Poland and Romania, weathered acute crises.

Military regimes in middle-income countries generally appeared more vulnerable to economic shocks. These governments faced strong challenges from civil society, yet lacked the mediation of a dominant party. Severe economic difficulties played an important role in virtually all of the Latin American transitions except Chile and were important in the collapse of the Marcos regime in the Philippines. However, some military regimes were able either to avoid crisis or to engage in successful economic adjustments that served to prolong authoritarian rule. Among the cases in this category are four that will be discussed in more detail in subsequent chapters: Korea, Chile, Turkey, and Thailand.

The differences between "successful" and "unsuccessful" regimes was partly fortuitous: some rulers were simply more skilled than others in manipulating the rivalries within the opposition and the ruling coalition itself. The more successful military governments also appeared to share some common institutional features, however, particularly mechanisms that reduced factionalism within the government and increased cohesion. We

---

[21] For a discussion of this factor in Africa during earlier decades, see Ruth Berins Collier, *Regimes in Tropical Africa: Changing Forms of Supremacy, 1945–1975* (Berkely, Los Angeles, and London: University of California Press, 1982). For an excellent discussion of the current period, see Michael Bratton and Nicolas van de Walle, "Neopatrimonial Regimes and Political Transitions in Africa," *World Politics* 46 (July 1994): 453–89.

FIGURE 1.1

The Political Economy of Authoritarian Withdrawals

	Economic Crisis	No Economic Crisis
I. POLITICAL CHALLENGES TO THE REGIME	Political demands overlap with: 1. Economically motivated mass protest 2. Defection of business elites 3. Internal division of military-political elites over material benefits	Primarily political demands for liberalization
II. POLITICAL OUTCOMES Military-dominant, low cohesion	Internal divisions raise cost of coercion; government fails to control either elite defection or mass protest Regime unable to adjust to crisis Regime collapses; outgoing elites unable to influence structure of new regime (Argentina, Bolivia, Brazil, Peru, Uruguay, the Philippines)	Military-business-political coalition remains stable; regime controls terms of the transition (Thailand)
Military-dominant, high cohesion	Government adjusts to crisis, reasserts authority internally, represses opposition, regains business loyalty Survives crisis, exerts control over terms of the transition (Chile 1981–82, Korea 1980)	Regime exerts strong control over terms of the transition (Chile 1990, Korea 1987, Turkey 1983)
Dominant party	Government adjusts to crisis, exerts strong control over terms terms of liberalization; transition ambiguous (Mexico)	Regime exerts strong control over terms of liberalization; transition ambiguous (Taiwan)

can see this most clearly by beginning with a discussion of those divided military governments that proved vulnerable to crisis.

Vulnerable Regimes

Military governments that had difficulty adjusting were characterized by uncertain or divided control over the bureaucracy and the main instruments of economic policy, as well as economic teams that were politically weak or internally divided. To a certain extent, these divisions reflected disagreements over the technical diagnosis of daunting economic problems. More typically, they reflected political, economic, and ideological conflicts within the military establishment itself.

One important source of conflict lay in the division of labor between the military officers holding political office and those who remained in charge of military personnel and procurement. The interests of these two groups were especially likely to diverge during periods of economic crisis, when the military as *government* faced unpopular policy choices that had consequences for the armed forces as an *institution*.[22] The most durable arrangement for managing such conflicts was a fusion of military and political authority in the head of state.[23] But this pattern was approximated only in Chile and Korea among the countries considered in this volume; we return to these cases below.

In other cases, the military high command retained independence with regard to appointments and promotion, yet was excluded from day-to-day political decision-making. This arrangement created a potential center for opposition to government authority. In Bolivia, reformist officers complained of "political interference" and corruption, and played a key role in the return to civilian rule. Conflicts between military presidents and the military command also contributed to the overthrow of Velasco in Peru and Viola in Argentina. The Philippines constitutes a somewhat different case, since Marcos did not come from the military. However, the military split over the merits of Marcos's rule, and it was that split which proved fatal for the government.

Collegial participation in political decisions through juntas and ruling councils that represented the different service branches constituted one institutional way of resolving tensions between the military government and the high command. In Brazil and Uruguay, this arrangement contributed to more orderly transfers of political authority and the maintenance

[22] See Alfred Stepan, *The Military in Politics: Changing Patterns in Brazil* (Princeton, N.J.: Princeton University Press, 1971).

[23] Karen L. Remmer, *Military Rule in Latin America* (Boulder, Colo., San Francisco, and Oxford: Westview Press, 1991), pp. 37–41.

of military cohesion. But collegial rule could not fully overcome a variety of other divisions that tended to emerge within military governments over time, divisions that were typically exacerbated by crises.[24]

In general, these conflicts were rooted in the expansion of military roles and diversification into other specialized political, economic, or policy functions. These new roles provided officers opportunities to build independent organizational and political bases and weakened hierarchical lines of authority within the military chain of command. The resulting cleavages took a number of forms. In some cases, the autonomy of local commanders increased as a result of sustained internal war or drug-control operations, as in Bolivia. Elsewhere, the involvement of officers in the management of state enterprises and other governmental agencies also generated the potential for conflict, as well as the organizational base for alliances between officers and civilian groups opposing reform efforts; this pattern was visible in a number of Latin American and African countries.

Programmatic disagreements were most pronounced in the bureaucratic-authoritarian regimes, particularly in Latin America, that had come to office with quite explicit political-economic projects. Military factions opposing such projects typically had their own institutional bases of power in the armed forces or the state sector, and could count on powerful allies in the private sector or civilian political class as well. Within the Brazilian military, this generated fierce factional struggles throughout the 1960s and 1970s over how long to hold power and on what terms, and over competing models of economic development. In Argentina and Uruguay, opponents of the neoliberal policies of the mid-1970s had important bases of support in the planning and intelligence agencies and in the state enterprise sector.[25]

These various divisions within the military elite made it more difficult for governments to provide consistent and coherent backing for the risky policy adjustments required to establish credibility among important eco-

---

[24] In Argentina, the heads of the three branches of the armed forces were incorporated directly into a junta and a Legislative Advisory Council. But reciprocal veto powers made the government unwieldy and contributed to the fragmentation of the state apparatus. "As the guerilla threat was exterminated, internal splits reemerged over economic policy, political strategy, and the power and autonomy of the repressive apparatus." Maria Susana Ricci and J. Samuel Fitch, "Ending Military Regimes in Argentina: 1966–1973 and 1976–1983," in Louis W. Goodman, Johanna S. R. Mendelson,and Juan Rial, eds., *The Military and Democracy; the Future of Civil-Military Relations in Latin America* (Lexington, Mass.: Lexington Books, D. C. Heath, 1990), p. 59.

[25] Ibid., pp. 55–75. In Uruguay, military officials in control of the Banco de la Republica and ESCMACO provided important sources of support for opposition to technocrats in the Finance Ministry. See Howard Handelman, "Military Authoritarianism and Political Change," in Howard Handelman and Thomas G. Sanders, eds., *Military Government and the Movement toward Democracy in South America* (Bloomington: Indiana University Press, 1981), pp. 215–37.

nomic actors, including foreign creditors. As a result the economic policy-making apparatus either fragmented into warring factions or cycled between teams with contradictory programs. These weaknesses, in turn, contributed to a further decline in the credibility of government programs and a further deepening of the economic crisis.

As in Latin America and the Philippines, extensive factionalism also pervaded the armed forces in Thailand; rapid and relatively successful economic adjustment in that country thus constitutes somewhat of an anomaly in comparison with these other cases. We attribute this exceptionalism to the fact that military factionalism was counterbalanced by other institutional features of the regime, including both a unifying monarchy and a cohesive technocratic elite that enjoyed substantial prestige and independence. The technocrats did not prevent the military from making several important policy mistakes in the late 1970s, but the regime did avoid the severe macroeconomic disequilibria that generated serious political difficulties in the crisis cases. As in the other non-crisis cases discussed below, this in turn permitted military-backed governments to exert considerable control over the pace of political reform. Despite an extensive political liberalization and gradual transition, the military never fully relinquished its role in the polity in the 1980s, and launched another coup against the parliamentary system in 1991.

In all of the other factionalized military regimes, escalating economic crisis made the management of other political pressures more difficult. Some military regimes sought to build support through controlled electoral openings. However, where government parties were weak, even controlled elections posed hazards for authoritarian rulers.[26] In the absence of dominant parties, such rulers were impelled to forge links to notables or politicians with uncertain loyalty in order to orchestrate electoral victories. In situations of economic crisis, as opportunities for patronage declined, such links became more problematic, while the opportunities expanded for anti-regime electoral oppositions to exploit economic grievances for broader political ends. This was particularly apparent in Bolivia, Brazil, and the Philippines, where electoral contests crystallized opposition and served to undermine authoritarian rule.

Divisions within the government also affected the way economic elites weighed the risks of opening the political system to democratic oppositions. Where internal dissent was high, and again particularly where that dissent centered to some extent on the conduct of economic policy, private-sector groups were more likely to lose faith in the capacity of the regime

---

[26] Perhaps the most consistent voice for this perspective is Bolivar Lamounier. See for example "*Authoritarian Brazil* Revisited: The Impact of Elections on the Abertura," in Alfred Stepan, ed., *Democratizing Brazil: Problems of Transition and Consolidation* (New York: Oxford University Press, 1989), pp. 43–83.

to manage the economic crisis. As a result, they were more inclined to support political reforms aimed at altering the system of representation.

As suggested above, finally, cleavages within the elite also expanded the political space for mass democratic oppositions by lowering the risks of anti-regime protest. If it is known that some forces within the government dissent from the authoritarian status quo, repressive responses become less likely, and a crucial space is opened for oppositions to initiate anti-government protests. Under extreme conditions, repressing opposition initiatives may prove impossible because key portions of the military are unwilling to respond to orders to use force; this was most dramatically the case in the Philippines and East Germany.

Cohesive Military Regimes

Three military regimes present full or partial exceptions to the foregoing pattern of internal division; each was able to exert substantial influence over the timing and terms of the democratic transition. Two of these, Chile and Korea, faced economic and political challenges in the early 1980s, and a third—Turkey—seized power in the midst of a deep economic, political, and social crisis. In all of these cases, governments did not leave power until they had made extensive adjustments in the economy and deep changes in the structure of the political system, in effect *creating* bases of support for the institutional and political changes initiated during the authoritarian period.

The precise reasons for these exceptional patterns hinge on a variety of case-specific factors, but in all three the capacity of the military establishment to contain internal divisions played an important role in the outcome. Three factors worked to mitigate these divisions: the fusion of political and military authority; a greater specialization of military roles; and the length of time in power.

Chile and Korea had by far the most cohesive military establishments of the countries considered here. One characteristic of each case, as already noted, was a fusion of military and political authority in the head of state. This reduced the ambiguity about lines of authority, allowing the top political-military leader not only to control appointments and personnel decisions within the military, but to exercise dual control—through both military and civilian chains of command—over military personnel seconded to the government itself. This factor, as we shall see in more detail in chapter 3, was crucial for the survival of the Pinochet regime in Chile. An equivalent structure existed in Korea, buttressed by executive control over a pervasive intelligence apparatus, even though Park Chung Hee and Chun Doo Hwan ruled nominally as civilians.

A variety of factors also encouraged the insulation of the corporate hierarchies and the maintenance of loyalty to the central command. In Chile, the governing responsibilities of the Chilean military expanded substantially under Pinochet. But ironically, the socialization of the military to a narrow definition of mission during several decades of democratic government resulted in strong obedience to the chain of command, which in turn facilitated Pinochet's control over the military establishment.

In Korea, the threat from the north provided strong incentives for the maintenance of corporate unity within the armed forces. In the immediate wake of the Park assassination, a portion of the military elite was quickly able to reestablish internal discipline and to reassert its authority over the political system as a whole, surviving the worst economic difficulties the country had faced in twenty years.

In both cases, concentrated executive authority and dependable support from the military establishment allowed the government to provide unambiguous backing to coherent and powerful teams of economic technocrats. In Korea, Chun Doo Hwan gave unwavering support to his reform team. In Chile, Pinochet's support for the "Chicago boys" is well known. Notwithstanding some important reshuffling of the policymakers during the shocks of the early 1980s, the two regimes' support for technocratic elites continued through the end of their rule.

Turkey presents a more ambiguous institutional picture. Unlike either Chile or Korea, the military establishment had been characterized by political factionalism and struggles over patronage; in this respect, it was closer to the typical Latin American military establishments than to Chile or Korea. One implication was that even following the military coup the economic technocrats assembled under Özal had less extensive control over the bureaucracy, important segments of which were opposed to the reform effort; on some issues, the military itself proved recalcitrant.

Unlike other military governments, however, internal division within the Turkish armed forces was held in check by the relatively limited tenure and purpose of the military intervention. During the escalating political crisis of 1979–80, competing factions of "moderates" and "radicals" drew together in the face of paralysis of civilian government and near–civil war conditions; in exchange for the moderates' backing for intervention, radicals agreed to hold to a preannounced timetable for withdrawal. This unity of purpose almost certainly would have eroded had the military remained in power over a long period; this in fact had been the experience in comparable cases of "collegial" military government in Uruguay, Argentina, and Brazil. However, during the short period of military rule that ensued, the incoming government was able to sustain the institutional support necessary to undertake harshly repressive measures against opposition and to back important adjustment measures that had been initiated, but had failed, under the ousted democratic government.

Successful economic management did not ensure the indefinite survival of these regimes. Even in good times, most rulers were eventually forced to respond in some measure to democratic forces based in the domestic working and middle classes and to foreign pressures, and all had in any case made some commitment to exit politics. However, in each of these regimes, as well as in Thailand, the capacity to engineer economic recoveries or sustain strong economic performance permitted incumbent elites to exert greater control over changes in the political rules of the game and the economic policy choices of successor governments. In short, the different transition paths we have outlined here had important ramifications for the nature of their successor governments.

Political changes occurring under favorable economic conditions differed in at least three important ways from those that occurred during crisis; these differences are addressed in detail in chapter 4. First, transitions in good times were more likely to be characterized by the persistence and/or the reconstruction of cooperative relations between the incoming democratic government and the private sector. In regimes unable to adjust to crisis, the defection of business groups from the ruling coalition left outgoing political and military authorities isolated vis-à-vis broad, but heterogeneous democratic oppositions. New democratic governments faced the difficult—and sometimes impossible—task of reestablishing private-sector confidence. Where economic crisis was avoided or successfully managed, relatively strong center-right blocs continued to play an important role on the political scene, providing support for continuity with some capacity to veto departures from previous economic policies.

Successful adjustment and/or avoidance of crisis also limited the role played by middle-class and professional groups in populist antiauthoritarian coalitions. Where regimes had been unable to adjust, middle-class groups were more likely to join with the popular sector around distributive demands as well as political reform. In the non-crisis cases, middle-class groups sometimes joined mass movements for political democracy, but adopted more conservative positions on economic issues. This reinforced continuity in economic policy and tended to leave groups on the left more isolated.

Finally, even where rightist blocs accepted the necessity of democratization, successful economic performance increased their capacity to influence the rules of political competition, particularly those providing guarantees for the interests of business and military elites and those regulating the entry of mass-based groups into the political process.

CHAPTER TWO

Economic Crisis and Authoritarian Withdrawal

IN ARGENTINA, Bolivia, Brazil, Peru, Uruguay, and the Philippines, democratic transitions occurred in the context of severe economic difficulties that contributed to opposition movements. In all of these cases, authoritarian rulers sought to dictate the limits of political reform through repression, the manipulation of political institutions, or by preserving an explicit veto over the political agenda and the range of groups allowed to participate in politics. However, the political conflicts unleashed by economic crises substantially reduced their capacity to achieve these objectives. With the partial exception of the Brazilian case, no outgoing military government was able to exercise a significant influence over the terms of the transition or the organization of its democratic successor. In Argentina, the Philippines, and Bolivia, outgoing rulers were unable to shield themselves fully from reprisals for offenses committed during their tenure in office.

We are cautious in the causal weight we place on the role of economic crisis. The military foundations of these regimes made indefinite rule improbable, and internal divisions within the government increased their vulnerability. In the absence of crisis, however, they would probably have left office later and on terms exhibiting greater continuity with the authoritarian order.

We do not attempt to retell the histories of these authoritarian withdrawals in detail. Our objectives, rather, are twofold. We analyze how mounting economic difficulties encouraged opposition within the private sector and contributed to the mobilization of broader social and electoral movements. Second, we highlight the way these political challenges created economic policy dilemmas that widened existing splits among authoritarian elites, divisions that affected the timing of the transition and the terms under which the military withdrew from office.

THE SOURCES AND POLICY DYNAMICS OF ECONOMIC CRISIS

To understand how economic crises became politicized, it is necessary to specify more clearly both the nature of the crisis and the typical policy responses to it. The economic problems of the six countries varied in nature and intensity, but there are several common features that provide the basis for comparison.[1] The onset of the crisis was typically signaled by a serious deterioration in the balance of payments and pressure on reserves and the exchange rate. The balance-of-payments problems reflected both past domestic policy mistakes and external shocks, most notably the sudden withdrawal of external lending associated with the debt crisis. The consequence was weakened control over macroeconomic policy. Governments had relied heavily on external borrowing to finance fiscal as well as current-account deficits; when capital inflows dried up, they had few choices but to rely on the inflation tax. A weakening balance-of-payments position was thus accompanied by widening fiscal deficits, accelerating inflation, and the distributional conflicts that accompany such macroeconomic instability.

Eventually, and usually after considerable hesitation, governments responded with devaluations, the imposition of trade and exchange controls, and some attempt to tighten fiscal and monetary policy. Whether such adjustment programs were fully implemented or abandoned, the combination of external shocks, balance-of-payments adjustment efforts, and general uncertainty contributed to a marked slowdown in economic activity, an increase in unemployment and a deterioration in real wages. Economic policy became the focal point both for intra-elite conflict and for mass mobilization.

Balance-of-Payments Crises

Table 2.1 charts macroeconomic trends in each of the six crisis cases, focusing on the period prior to the authoritarian withdrawal. Peru, and then Bolivia, were the first of the six countries under discussion here to fall into major debt crises.[2] These crises were characterized by a freeze on external financing and tense, inconclusive negotiations with the IMF and external creditors. In the wake of the first oil shock, the Velasco and then the

---

[1] For comparative discussions of most of the cases included here, see Joan Nelson, ed., *Economic Crisis and Policy Choice: The Politics of Adjustment in the Third World* (Princeton, N.J.: Princeton University Press, 1990); Jeffrey D. Sachs, ed., *Developing Country Debt and the World Economy* (Chicago: University of Chicago Press, 1989); and Jeffrey D. Sachs and Susan M. Collins, eds., *Developing Country Debt and Economic Performance*, vol. 2, *Country Studies: Argentina, Bolivia, Brazil, and Mexico*, and vol. 3, *Country Studies: Indonesia, Korea, Philippines, and Turkey* (Chicago: University of Chicago Press, 1989).

[2] On Peru, see Barbara Stallings, "Politics and Economic Crisis: A Comparative Study of Chile, Peru, and Colombia," in Nelson, *Economic Crisis and Policy Choice*, pp. 157–268; Rosemary Thorp, "Peruvian Adjustment Policies, 1978–1985," in Rosemary Thorp and Laurence Whitehead, eds., *Latin American Debt and the Adjustment Crisis* (London: Macmillan, 1987), pp. 208–38. On Bolivia, see Malloy and Gamarra, *Revolution and Reaction: Bolivia, 1964–1985* (New Brunswick, N.J.: Transaction Books, 1988); Juan Antonio Morales and Jeffrey Sachs, "Bolivia's Economic Crisis," in Sachs and Collins, *Developing Country Debt and Economic Performance*, 2:157–268.

TABLE 2.1

Economic Trends and Authoritarian Withdrawal: The Crisis Cases

	Argentina							
	1976	*1977*	*1978*	*1979*	*1980*	*1981*	*1982*	*1983*
GDP Growth	−0.2	6.4	−3.2	7.0	1.5	−6.6	−14.9	3.0
Inflation	444.0	176.0	175.5	159.5	100.8	104.5	164.8	343.8
Fiscal Deficit/GDP	−7.1	−2.8	−3.2	−2.6	−3.5	−9.1	−7.5	−12.7
Current Account/GDP	1.2	2.2	2.8	−0.5	−3.1	−3.8	−4.1	−3.8
Investment/GDP	27.1	27.2	23.9	22.6	22.7	18.3	16.9	17.3
Real Wage	−32.7	−1.5	−1.8	14.9	11.8	−10.6	−10.4	25.5

	Bolivia							
	1975	*1976*	*1977*	*1978*	*1979*	*1980*	*1981*	*1982*
GDP Growth	6.6	6.1	4.2	3.4	0.2	−1.4	1.0	−4.4
Inflation	8.0	4.5	8.1	10.4	19.7	47.2	32.1	123.5
Fiscal Deficit/GDP	na	na	na	na	na	−5.5	−4.6	−25.0
Current Account/GDP	−5.3	−1.9	−3.6	−8.8	−9.0	−0.1	−7.6	−2.8
Investment/GDP	24.4	21.2	20.8	24.7	20.8	15.4	13.3	12.5
Real Wage	na	na	na	0.4	−1.4	−5.5	−8.7	−27.7

	Brazil							
	1978	*1979*	*1980*	*1981*	*1982*	*1983*	*1984*	*1985*
GDP Growth	5.0	6.8	9.2	−4.4	0.7	−3.4	5.0	8.3
Inflation	38.7	52.7	82.8	105.6	97.8	142.1	197.0	226.9
Fiscal Deficit/GDP	−2.78	na	−2.4	−2.4	−2.6	−4.1	−4.8	−11.2
Current Account/GDP	−3.5	−4.7	−5.5	−4.5	−5.8			

TABLE 2.1 (*continued*)

	Philippines							
	1979	*1980*	*1981*	*1982*	*1983*	*1984*	*1985*	*1986*
GDP Growth	6.3	5.2	3.9	2.9	0.9	−6.0	5.3	−7.8
Inflation	17.5	18.2	13.1	10.2	10.0	50.3	23.1	0.8
Fiscal Deficit/GDP	−0.1	−1.4	−4.3	−4.5	−2.0	−1.9	−1.9	−5.0
Current Account/GDP	−5.1	−5.9	−5.9	−8.6	−8.3	−4.1	−0.1	3.2
Investment/GDP	31.0	29.1	27.6	28.2	30.1	22.5	15.8	16.3
Real Wage	−11.3	−11.0	21.3	9.0	1.9	3.4	2.6	−2.8

	Uruguay							
	1978	*1979*	*1980*	*1981*	*1982*	*1983*	*1984*	*1985*
GDP Growth	5.3	6.2	6.0	1.9	−9.4	−5.9	−1.5	0.3
Inflation	44.5	66.8	63.5	34.0	19.0	49.2	55.3	72.2
Fiscal Deficit/GDP	−0.9	na	0.0	−1.5	−9.1	−3.9	−5.2	−2.2
Current Account/GDP	−2.5	−4.9	−7.0	−4.1	−2.5	−1.2	−2.7	−2.5
Investment/GDP	16.0	17.3	17.3	15.4	14.4	14.3	12.1	11.4
Real Wage	−3.6	−8.1	−0.4	7.5	−0.6	−20.7	−15.9	−4.2

Sources: All data except real wage growth, International Monetary Fund, *International Financial Statistics Yearbook,* various issues; real wage data for Latin America, Economic Commission for Latin America, *Economic Survey of Latin America and the Caribbean,* various issues; real wage data for the Philippines, World Bank, *The Philippines: An Opening for Sustained Growth* (Washington D.C.: The World Bank Report #11061-PH, April 1, 1993), vol. 3, Table E.2, p. 47.

Note: GDP Growth: annual growth in gross domestic product: Inflation: annual percent change in consumer price index: Fiscal Deficit/GDP or Surplus/GDP, fiscal deficit or surplus as a share of GDP: Current Account/GDP: current account surplus/deficit as a share of GDP: Investment/GDP: investment as a share of GDP. Real wage: annual real wage growth. Series are not strictly comparable across countries. For Argentina, manufacturing wages; for Bolivia, national average minimum wage growth; for Brazil, manufacturing wages in São Paulo; for Peru, private-sector manual workers in Lima; for Uruguay, national average wages; for Philippines, unskilled labor in Manila.

Bermudez governments in Peru did undertake a series of stabilization initiatives, but these met serious resistance both from within the military and from highly mobilized popular-sector groups; as a result, they were never fully implemented. In Bolivia, a cycle of coups and countercoups within the military after 1978 prevented coherent policies of any sort. In both countries, profound political uncertainties were clearly a contributing factor in prolonging and deepening the economic crisis.

In the other countries, the domestic policy choices of the 1970s became increasingly unsustainable in the face of adverse trends in the terms of trade and the declining availability of external credit. In the Philippines, and in

Brazil under Planning Minister Antonio Delfim Neto, governments gambled on countercyclical responses to the second oil shock, but widening fiscal deficits, inflation, and sharp increases in external indebtedness soon forced both to change course. During 1979, Delfim's heterodox experiment combined extensive government investment in the agricultural and energy sectors with a maxidevaluation in December. By the end of 1980, however, sharp deterioration in reserves forced a turn toward very tight monetary and credit policy. When the Mexican crisis broke in August 1982, the government moved reluctantly, and in the face of substantial public protest, toward acceptance of an IMF program.[3]

The Philippines declared a moratorium on debt service in October 1983, initiating a prolonged period of acrimonious negotiations with creditors.[4] With the end of external financing, the emergence of domestic shortages and hoarding, and an expansive monetary policy, the import-dependent economy slid into the worst recession in its postwar history. Inflation accelerated to record levels. Yet due to impending elections, the Marcos government delayed serious adjustments until the second half of 1984.[5]

Argentina and Uruguay ran into similar problems, but the source was somewhat different: the controversial effort to use a preannounced rate of nominal devaluation, the *tablita,* as an "anchor" for inflation expectations.[6] Inflation did decline somewhat after the adoption of the *tablita* in both cases, but continued to outpace exchange-rate depreciation. The result was high domestic interest rates and large capital inflows, followed by declining confidence in the government's capacity to sustain an increasingly overvalued exchange rate, capital flight, and forced devaluation.

Argentina's problems became evident with the failure of several financial-industrial conglomerates in late 1980. Difficulties spread rapidly to other sectors. In February 1981, shortly before the scheduled change of government to a new president, Roberto Viola, massive capital flight forced

---

[3] Albert Fishlow, "A Tale of Two Presidents: The Political Economy of Crisis Management," and Edmar L. Bacha and Pedro S. Malan, "Brazil's Debt: From Miracle to the Fund," both in Alfred Stepan, ed., *Democratizing Brazil: Problems of Transition and Consolidation* (New York and Oxford: Oxford University Press, 1989), pp. 83–120 and 120–43.

[4] For an analysis of the Philippine debt crisis, see Robert S. Dohner and Ponciano Intal, Jr., "The Marcos Legacy: Economic Policy and Foreign Debt in the Philippines," in Sachs and Collins, *Developing Country Debt and Economic Performance,* 3:371–614.

[5] See Stephan Haggard, "The Political Economy of the Philippine Debt Crisis," in Nelson, *Economic Crisis and Policy Choice,* pp. 215–57.

[6] See Nicolas Ardito Barletta, Mario I. Blejer, and Luis Landau, eds., *Economic Liberalization and Stabilization Policies in Argentina, Chile, and Uruguay* (Washington, D.C.: The World Bank, 1984); Joseph Ramos, *Neoconservative Economics in the Southern Cone of Latin America, 1973–1983* (Baltimore: Johns Hopkins University Press, 1986); I. M. D. Little et al., *Boom, Crisis and Adjustment: the Macroeconomic Experience of the Developing Countries* (New York: Oxford University Press for the World Bank, 1993), pp. 219–63.

the outgoing team to devalue. The neoliberal model of trade and capital-account liberalization quickly unraveled. Viola represented factions within the military establishment that had opposed this policy experiment from the beginning. With heavily indebted private firms clamoring for relief, he moved to reverse some of the orthodox measures of his predecessors, raising tariff barriers and easing the flow of credit and subsidies to the private sector. In December 1982, he was replaced in a coup that returned neoliberals to office, but throughout this period, budget deficits remained very large, with estimates ranging from an annual average of 12.7 to 16.4 percent of GDP for the 1980–84 period.[7] Argentina fell into a cycle of devaluation, widening fiscal deficits, and an inflation that had accelerated to an annual rate of more than 340 percent by the time Alfonsín took office.

Developments in Argentina had major consequences for Uruguay's economy. Although the military had also adopted the *tablita* in 1978, Uruguay's currency remained cheap in terms of the Argentine peso, and as a result, Argentine capital flowed into Uruguay's banking, real estate, and construction sectors. The Argentine devaluations during 1981 reversed this flow, contributing to an almost immediate collapse of the construction sector and a steep decline in manufacturing activity.[8] The military elite, by that point in the midst of complex internal debates over how to respond to its defeat in the plebiscite of 1980, delayed exchange-rate corrections for over a year. By November 1982, however, the government was forced to accept a major devaluation, which was followed in 1983 by a devastating decline in real wages and a resurgence of inflation.[9]

Government Responses: Elite Division and Policy Drift

These changes in the economic situation posed difficult predicaments for authoritarian governments. The hardship associated with stabilization programs carried obvious political risks, but postponing corrective action threatened a loss of confidence among important business elites and foreign creditors, and thus even more painful economic dislocation over the longer run. Coherent and sustained policy responses to such dilemmas were impeded not only by mounting protests against the government, but by sharp internal divisions within the military and political elite.

In the Philippines in 1984, Marcos did adopt an extremely tough stabi-

---

[7] Rudiger Dornbusch and Juan Carlos de Pablo, "Debt and Macroeconomic Instability in Argentina," in Sachs, *Developing Country Debt and the World Economy,* pp. 37–56.

[8] Economic Commission for Latin America, "The Evolution of the Economy and Economic Policy in Uruguay between 1981 and 1984," *Economic Survey of Latin America and the Caribbean 1984* (Santiago: ECLA, 1984), pp. 643–47.

[9] Ibid., p. 624.

lization program that succeeded in cutting inflation and halting the peso's slide. But this came only after a significant delay and under intense pressure from both external creditors and important segments of the domestic private sector that were becoming increasingly disenchanted with the government's economic mismanagement.[10] Because of divisions within the Marcos government, the stabilization program did not address some of the more profound structural problems in the economy, and had the effect of exacerbating the recession, which was a substantial source of Marcos' political difficulties both inside and outside the ruling circle in 1984 and 1985. When he took the fateful decision to call snap elections for February 1986, the country was still mired in a deep recession.[11] In Brazil, the attempts to impose austerity measures met with strong opposition from within the military, as well as from business and labor groups; the government failed to meet the conditions attached to the IMF package negotiated at the end of 1982.[12]

In Peru, Argentina, Bolivia, and Uruguay, divisions within the military were even more pronounced; in the first three cases, the unraveling of military rule began with internal coups d'état. Bolivia represents the extreme case in this regard, with no fewer than three coups and six presidents between the overthrow of General Banzer in 1978 and the eventual establishment of a civilian government in 1982. Opposition to stabilization programs was only one factor in the intense, highly personalist struggles for public power and resources during this period, but it clearly played an important role at several points. In 1979 rumors of a possible IMF agreement contributed to the overthrow of Banzer's immediate successor, General Pereda. During one of the two brief civilian interludes that began at the end of 1979, the Lydia Gueiler administration signed an IMF agreement, but a wave of crippling strikes ensued, leading to an overthrow of her government in April of the following year.[13] Until 1985, no government, either military or civilian, was capable of arresting the economy's decline.

In all of these cases, two specific policy issues posed the most acute policy and political dilemmas for the governments in power: exchange-rate management and fiscal policy. In the 1970s, the inflow of foreign capital

---

[10] For more details on the politics of the stabilization effort, see Robert Dohner and Stephan Haggard, *The Political Feasibility of Adjustment in the Philippines* (Paris: OECD, 1994).

[11] See Stephan Haggard, "The Political Economy of the Philippine Debt Crisis," pp. 243–44.

[12] Bolivar Lamounier and Alkimar R. Moura, "Economic Policy and Political Opening in Brazil," in Jonathan Hartlyn, and Samuel Morley, eds., *Latin American Political Economy: Financial Crisis and Political Change* (Boulder, Colo.: Westview Press, 1986), pp. 165–96.

[13] Laurence Whitehead, "Bolivia's Failed Democratization, 1977–1980," in Guillermo O'Donnell, Philippe C. Schmitter, and Laurence Whitehead, eds., *Transitions from Authoritarian Rule: Prospects for Democracy* (Baltimore and London: Johns Hopkins University Press, 1986), pt. 2, *Latin America,* p. 65.

had supported (and in some cases contributed to) overvalued local currencies. Appreciation of the local currency had become an important means through which incumbent regimes attempted to control inflation, sustain incomes in the large non-traded goods sector, and provide benefits to favored importers and consumers.[14] Governments were thus inclined to undertake devaluations only when confronted with escalating capital flight, substantial deterioration in the level of reserves, and strong pressure from creditors.

When needed devaluations are postponed, their economic and political consequences become more disruptive. In Argentina and Uruguay, devaluations drove a number of firms to bankruptcy; those that had contracted dollar-denominated debt directly or were dependent on imports were hit particularly hard. Devaluations were also followed by a sharp deterioration in real wages; efforts to offset declining worker incomes with public relief added to the fiscal strain. Outside of Argentina and Uruguay, most external debt was contracted through the public sector. As a result, the cutoff of external borrowing and devaluations compounded preexisting fiscal difficulties.[15]

Barry Ames's discussion of the dilemmas faced by the Brazilian military regime illustrates some of the political implications of such fiscal crises.[16] After the cautious political opening initiated in 1974, the Geisel administration sought to broaden its base of support by expanding expenditures on agriculture, education, and welfare at the expense of spending on the military itself. In 1979, Figueireido turned in a more redistributive direction by introducing wage legislation that heavily favored low- and middle-income workers. As the recession of 1981 hit, however, these plans were scuttled, in part due to sharp protest from higher-paid workers. In 1982, Figueireido was forced to retreat from his spending strategy entirely. Social expenditures were reduced in favor of increases aimed at the regime's traditional sources of support, the military and regional elites. Spending on public works grew in an effort to offset growing unemployment. During the 1982 state-level elections, the first direct election for governors in twenty years, the government party lost heavily in the industrial states that had been the initial target of social welfare and wage policies. Meanwhile, the

[14] This is a theme of Jeffry A. Frieden, *Debt, Development, and Democracy* (Princeton, N.J.: Princeton University Press, 1991).

[15] For an overview of fiscal issues, see William R. Easterly, "Fiscal Adjustment and Deficit Financing During the Debt Crisis," World Bank Policy, Planning and Research Working Paper No. 138, January 1989. On the effect of budget cuts on investment, see Luis Serven and Andres Solimano, *Striving for Growth after Adjustment: The Role of Capital Formation* (Washington, D.C.: The World Bank, 1993).

[16] Barry Ames, *Political Survival: Politicians and Public Policy in Latin America* (Berkeley: University of California Press, 1987), pp. 181, 201.

military began to protest about its own level of budgetary support, which remained extremely low as a percent of GDP. A number of key officers began to argue that the armed forces would do better under civilian rule.[17]

Faced with such tradeoffs and the crushing difficulty of making large, short-term fiscal adjustments, most regimes relied heavily on the inflation tax, hoping that the costs could be passed on to more politically vulnerable sectors of the population. Increased inflation usually, though not always, resulted in declines in real wages and hit hard at the poor, who held a disproportionate share of their total assets in cash.

Deteriorating economic conditions affected the prospects for regime change through the reactions of key social groups and the military establishment itself. In the following sections, we focus more closely on the reactions of two sets of actors outside the government: business groups and popular-sector organizations. As the economic crisis escalated, mounting opposition from these groups widened preexisting divisions within the ruling elite, the crucial precipitating ingredient in leading to the withdrawal or collapse of authoritarian orders.

THE DEFECTION OF BUSINESS ELITES

The economic deterioration described in the preceding section had ruinous implications for major portions of the private sector. In most countries, to be sure, particular sectors had faced difficulties prior to the crisis. Import-substituting industries were badly squeezed by the neoliberal policies of the Southern Cone regimes, Peruvian business was necessarily concerned about the populist rhetoric and policy of the first phase of military rule, and Philippine business grumbled about the favors granted to Marcos cronies. Except in Peru, however, conflicts between governments and the private sector were muted by the perception that the regime had provided a favorable business climate,[18] and in all of the cases, the overall expansion of the economy tended to reduce the demands for changes in policy or political structure.

[17] Alfred Stepan, *Rethinking Military Politics: Brazil and the Southern Cone* (Princeton, N.J.: Princeton University Press, 1988), p. 72.

[18] In Howard Handelman's interviews with Uruguayan business elites in the late 1970s, for example, he suggests that "the official position of large manufacturers, as expressed by the CIU and in my interviews held with corporate leaders, has been very supportive of the government's economic policy. Industrial spokesmen credit the current regime with 'creating a better business atmosphere,' lessening bureaucratic regulation and red tape, developing a more favorable tax structure, easing imports of raw materials, and bringing 'labor peace.'" "Economic Policy and Elite Pressure," in Howard Handelman and Thomas G. Sanders, eds., *Military Government and the Movement toward Democracy in South America* (Bloomington: Indiana University Press, 1981), p. 271.

In contrast, the downturns of the late 1970s and early 1980s cut a much wider path across the economy, with activity declining sharply in many sectors that had gained from earlier booms. For the first time, large, but highly leveraged financial-industrial conglomerates (grupos) were seriously threatened with collapse, and in Argentina and Brazil, two of the largest such conglomerates (Sesestin and Matarazzo) declared bankruptcy. In all of the countries, heavily indebted commercial and manufacturing firms suffered from high real interest rates and from the shocks of devaluation. Slowed or negative growth rates in the manufacturing sector typically led the decline in GDP.

The decline of manufacturing raises the question of how sectoral differences might be related to active opposition to the regime. Jeffry Frieden, in particular, has argued that the politicization of business depends on both economic exit options and the political alternatives. Thus, he suggests, business opposition to continued authoritarian rule in Latin America was more prevalent among import-substituting firms with fixed assets than among financial groups and other sectors with liquid assets, since the latter had the option of capital flight.[19]

This argument is empirically plausible, especially in the South American countries that Frieden examines. In Argentina and Brazil, the leaders of the Federation of Industries of São Paulo (FIESP) and the Industrial Union of Argentina (UIA), the major industrial associations in each country, were highly visible critics of government policy, complaining of high interest rates and favoritism toward the banking sector. Although these sectoral cleavages were important, however, their significance in the process of regime change should not be overestimated. The deepening crisis affected firms of all sizes and sectors, leading to public expressions of concern throughout the business community. As Frieden himself points out, for example, the Brazilian banking community had become seriously alarmed by the financial distress of their industrial clients by 1983 and began to call publicly for policy changes.[20] But even in situations where the private sector preferred to maintain a low political profile—a common phenomenon in all our cases—declining confidence and diminishing investment opportunities themselves posed a threat to political stability, since they confronted the leadership with bleak prospects for future growth.

As crises deepened, the politically salient fact was the relative uniformity of business reactions across economic sectors; authoritarian governments could not be assured of the active support of *any* segment of the business community. Generalized business concerns over the long-term

---

[19] Jeffry Frieden, *Debt, Development, and Democracy* (Princeton, N.J.: Princeton University Press, 1991), p. 33.
[20] Ibid., p. 132.

capacity to manage the economy began to outweigh fears about the potential risks associated with democratization. Aside from demands for specific policy changes, three types of grievance undermined the authoritarian bargain: concerns about the security of basic property rights; complaints about personalist and predatory behavior on the part of political elites; and opposition to technocratic control of economic decision-making. The relative emphasis attached to each of these grievances varied depending on the nature of the authoritarian "project," as well as the government's response to the crisis itself. We distinguish between business responses to the populist regime in Peru, in which concern about property rights dominated, the personalist dictatorships in the Philippines and Bolivia, and the bureaucratic-authoritarian regimes of Brazil, Argentina, and Uruguay.

Military Populism in Peru

The populist orientation of the Peruvian military made it unique among the governments we are studying, since serious tensions characterized its relations with the private sector since its inception in 1968. Although business leaders were deeply concerned about the signs of popular unrest that had become evident prior to 1968, radical factions within the military also appeared to pose a threat to private property. Nonetheless, an aggressive policy of import substitution and subsidies provided the basis for an uneasy accommodation between the government and industrial and mining interests, and after the settlement of the disputes over the International Petroleum Company expropriation in 1969, foreign banks became active lenders to the country.

This accommodation broke down with the balance-of-payments crisis of 1974–75, and the authoritarian bargain quickly unraveled. The government briefly moved more to the left, attempting to attract popular-sector support by launching an amibitious initiative on "social ownership." Fearing even more radical redistributive initiatives, business responded with a media campaign against the government, which was in turn met in 1974 by a crackdown on the press.

As class conflicts escalated in 1975, a more conservative military faction seized control of the government and sought to regain private-sector support in order to stabilize the economy and repair relations with external creditors. Concerned about the radicalization of increasingly independent popular-sector organizations, most business associations responded positively, but cautiously. With populist currents still strong within the military establishment, the end of authoritarian government was increasingly viewed as a prerequisite for the protection of private property. The commercial and industrial associations generally welcomed the military-sponsored stabilization program, at least rhetorically, and supported decisions to put down leftist opposition with force. But the price of their collaboration was a commitment by the military to accept a timetable for the transfer of political power to moderate opposition leaders.[21]

Bolivia and the Philippines: Predatory States

In Bolivia and the Philippines, governments were in principle more favorably disposed to the principle of private property, but were headed by personalist rulers who exercised a high degree of discretionary power.[22] In both of these otherwise very different political settings, business opposition crystallized against networks of favoritism that excluded significant private-sector interests.

In the Philippines, the assassination of Marcos's long-time political opponent, Benigno Aquino, in August 1983 focused private-sector opposition to the regime. Aquino came from one of the Philippines' most prominent families, and his murder, for which the Marcoses were widely believed to be responsible, shocked all segments of the business and political elite. Even before the Aquino assassination, however, several prominent members of the Makati Business Club, the main vehicle of the non-crony private sector, had begun to organize and speak out against economic mismanagement, the increasing weight of the cronies, and the predatory behavior of the government.[23] Drawing on academic analysis that made explicit links between authoritarianism, cronyism, and poor economic performance, these portions of the private sector played a crucial role in forging a centrist anti-Marcos coalition that included opposition politicians, academics, the Church, and the middle classes.[24]

The private sector also played an important role in the Bolivian transi-

[21] Julio Cotler, "Military Intervention and 'Transfer of Power to Civilians,'" in O'Donnnell, Schmitter and Whitehead, *Transitions from Authoritarian Rule,* pt. 3, *Comparative Perspectives,* pp. 163–68.

[22] For an excellent theoretical discussion of the nature of predatory rule in the Philippines, see Paul D. Hutchcroft, "Oligarchs and Cronies in the Philippine State: The Politics of Patrimonial Plunder," *World Politics* 43 (April 1991): 414–50.

[23] The most eloquent spokesman was Jaime Ongpin. See his "Report on the Economic Crisis," *Business Day* (Manila), August 13 and 14, 1984. Another source of business views is *MBC [Makati Business Club] Economic Papers,* various issues.

[24] The most influential analysis of the crisis was done by a collective of economists at the University of the Philippines. Emmanuel De Dios, ed., *An Analysis of the Philippine Economic Crisis* (Quezon City: University of the Philippines, 1984). For an analysis of the political context at the time, see Stephan Haggard, "The Political Economy of the Philippines Debt Crisis," pp. 245–48; Mark Turner, *Regime Change in the Philippines,* Department of Political and Social Change Monograph no. 7, Australian National University (Canberra, 1987).

tion. Prior to the extreme corruption of the García Meza administration (1980–81), the major private-sector organization, the Bolivian Federation of Private Entrepreneurs (CEPB) had been more ambivalent about democracy than about military rule. The Banzer dictatorship had been good for business, protecting it from the left and contributing directly to more coherent private sector organization. On the other hand, as Malloy and Gamarra argue, the instability of the early 1980s "demonstrated that the military was unable to formulate a policy to deal with the increasingly grave economic crisis, and furthermore had a distinct statist bent that was also at odds with what at least some segments of the private sector saw as their long-term interests."[25] In particular, there was a concern that the public sector was becoming parasitic.[26] The behavior of the García Meza government would clinch this perception. But as early as August 1981, when "institutionalist" officers came back into power, the CEPB assumed the initiative in calling for the restoration of the 1980 Congress and the selection of Siles Suazo as president, even though Siles had been the most left-leaning of the three major candidates in the 1979 elections.

Bureaucratic-Authoritarianism: Argentina, Brazil, and Uruguay

In Brazil, Argentina, and Uruguay, the economic crises of the early 1980s occurred under antipopulist, bureaucratic-authoritarian regimes that had previously received substantial backing from business interests.[27] The collaboration was especially close in Brazil, where major industrial and financial firms reaped large profits from public contracts, subsidies, and joint ventures with state-owned firms. Calls for political reform did surface among São Paulo business leaders in the late 1970s, but this had little resonance within the private sector as a whole.[28] Big business was also inclined favorably toward military rule in Argentina and Uruguay, where the regime was credited with restoring a positive business climate after a

---

[25] James M. Malloy and Eduardo Gamarra, *Revolution and Reaction,* p. 129.

[26] Catherine M. Conaghan, "Retreat to Democracy: Business and Political Transition in Bolivia and Ecuador," in Diane Ethier, ed., *Democratic Transition and Consolidation in Southern Europe, Latin America, and Southeast Asia* (London: Macmillan, 1990), pp. 73–90, and "Capitalists, Technocrats, and Politicians: Economic Policy-Making and Democracy in the Central Andes," Working Paper no. 109, May 1988, Kellogg Institute.

[27] See Guillermo A. O'Donnell, *Modernization and Bureaucratic-Authoritarianism* (Berkeley: Institute of International Studies, University of California, 1973); David Collier, ed., *The New Authoritarianism in Latin America* (Princeton, N.J.: Princeton University Press, 1979).

[28] See Leigh Payne, *Brazilian Industrialists and Democratic Change* (Baltimore: Johns Hopkins University Press, 1994), pp. 57–61.

dangerous period of class polarization and conflict. Trade liberalization was a point of contention in both countries, but liberalization did not go as far as it had in Chile, and the largest industrial companies continued to receive public protection and subsidies, usually with the backing of particular segments of the military.[29]

Serious strains between government and business began to surface following the devaluations and tightened macroeconomic policies of the early 1980s. In Argentina during 1981 and 1982, bankruptcies of major industrial and financial firms led to increasingly insistent calls for relief by the UIA and to bitter public criticisms by the heads of major firms.[30] Charles Gillespie catalogues how one business sector after another in Uruguay had been alienated by the early 1980s: ". . . manufacturers for the domestic market by tariff cuts, exporters by overvalued exchange rates from 1978, petty commerce by the massive contraction of real earnings, construction by the military's refusal to mitigate the slump that had begun in 1981 with countercyclical policies, and practically everyone . . . by the high interest rate policy and the unwillingness to help firms that had taken on heavy debts in order to invest."[31] In Brazil, the first signs of business disaffection came as early as 1977, when a number of prominent São Paulo industrialists launched a campaign of public criticism of the "statization" of the Brazilian economy. Dissatisfaction became much more widespread in the early 1980s, however, as growth rates turned negative. Some indicators of the trend can be gleaned from periodic surveys of entrepreneurial opinion conducted by *Exame,* a leading business journal. In 1983, the Figuereido government received the worst ratings recorded in the four-year series: only 13 percent of over six hundred respondents ranked the administration as

---

[29] Joseph Ramos, *Neoconservative Economics in the Southern Cone of Latin America, 1973–1983* (Baltimore: Johns Hopkins University Press, 1986), pp. 109–37. Maria Susana Ricci and J. Samuel Fitch, "Ending Military Regimes in Argentina: 1966–1973 and 1976–1983," in Louis W. Goodman, Johanna S. R. Mendelson, and Juan Rial, eds., *The Military and Democracy; the Future of Civil-Military Relations in Latin America* (Lexington, Mass.: D. C. Heath, 1990), pp. 55–75; Howard Handelman, "Economic Policy and Elite Pressure," in Handelman and Sanders, *Military Government and the Movement toward Democracy in South America* (Bloomington: Indiana University Press, 1981), p. 254.

[30] In early 1981, one major group of business leaders declared in a public letter that "the economy was now worse than it was in March 1976 when the Armed Forces took power." *Latin America Weekly Report* (hereafter *LAWR*) 81-02, January 9, 1981, p. 10. These complaints mounted even under the relatively friendly Viola administration, as powerful Cabinet figures delayed proposed bailouts of heavily indebted public firms, ibid., 81-33, August 21, 1981, p. 1. In 1982, the bankruptcy of Celulosa Argentina, the country's largest paper and pulp company, was publicly ascribed by its managers to the military regime, with the "death blow" applied by the austerity policies of the Galtieri administration; ibid., 82-07, February 12, 1982, p. 4.

[31] Charles G. Gillespie, "Uruguay's Transition from Collegial Military-Technocratic Rule," in O'Donnell, Schmitter, and Whitehead, *Transitions from Authoritarian Rule,* pt. 2, *Latin America,* p. 180.

"excellent" or "good," whereas 43 percent considered it "bad" or "very bad." Planning Minister Antonio Delfim Neto fared even more poorly. In 1983, 60 percent of the respondents gave him strongly negative ratings, whereas in 1980, 69 percent had ranked him as "good" or "excellent."[32] For the first time as well, press reports about business financing for moderate opposition parties began to surface during the early 1980s.[33]

The immediate target of business criticism in Argentina, Brazil, and Uruguay was the austere credit and fiscal policies that the military governments were forced to pursue in the early 1980s, policies that had also been criticized by unions and other popular-sector groups then reentering the political arena.[34] Underlying these protests over specific policies was a much deeper skepticism about the capacity of the military establishment to overcome internal divisions and to provide a stable and coherent economic project of any sort. In Uruguay, the prestige of the military establishment had never been very high. Doubts increased substantially following revelations of widespread corruption within the officer corps during the bruising internal succession struggle in 1981. Gregorio Alvarez, the victor in that struggle, was perceived as an opportunist without a clear economic or political vision.[35]

In Brazil and Argentina, increasingly erratic policy behavior reflected division and uncertainty among military and political elites. In Argentina, the Viola administration promised a sharp turn away from the neoliberal policies pursued under Videla, then backed away from many of the relief measures initially proposed by his minister of industry, Eduardo Oxenford.[36] Viola himself was replaced by a coup d'état that brought a far more orthodox team back to power at the end of 1981. In Brazil, the Figuereido administration got caught in a cycle of stop-go measures: a turn from austerity to expansionism under Delfim in 1979 and 1980, a bruising fiscal and monetary retrenchment in 1981, a slight easing in 1982, and a series of partially implemented IMF agreements in 1983 and 1984.[37]

With economic problems mounting, business elites began to reevaluate

---

[32] Quoted in Glaucio Ary Dillon Soares, "Elections and the Redemocratization of Brazil," in Paul W. Drake and Eduardo Silva, eds., *Elections and Democratization in Latin America, 1980–1985* (University of California, San Diego: Center for Iberian and Latin American Studies, 1986), p. 294. See also *LAWR* 81-90, February 27, 1981, p. 8.

[33] Ibid.

[34] In both Peru and Bolivia, it should be noted, the main business organizations *supported* stabilization initiatives during the transition period; this was broadly true in the Philippines as well.

[35] Howard Handelman, "Military Authoritarianism and Political Change," in Handelman and Sanders, *Military Government and the Movement Toward Democracy,* pp. 215–36.

[36] Maria Susana Ricci and J. Samuel Fitch, "Ending Military Regimes in Argentina: 1966–1973 and 1976–1983," in Goodman, Mendelson, and Rial, *The Military and Democracy,* pp. 55–75.

[37] Lamounier and Moura, "Economic Policy and Political Opening in Brazil."

the costs and benefits of the technocratic decision-making style that characterized authoritarian rule. Business groups had complained periodically about their lack of access to the remote technocrats who conducted macroeconomic policy, but such concerns had been offset by particularistic benefits and the fact that governments were willing to repress popular-sector challenges. The private sector's gradual disaffection did not reflect a democratic epiphany, but a pragmatic response to changing circumstances. With authoritarian governments increasingly unable to deliver their side of the bargain, "voice" began to appear increasingly important to business groups, even if it meant reopening the arena to the previously excluded popular sector.[38]

ECONOMIC CRISIS AND POPULAR MOBILIZATION

Under most of the authoritarian regimes we have discussed, portions of the popular sector experienced periods of substantial income loss even prior to the macroeconomic crises discussed in the preceding sections. The initial years of the "Peruvian experiment" represent an exception, but in Argentina, Bolivia, Brazil, the Philippines, and Uruguay, the demobilization of the union movement was a deliberate feature of authoritarian governments' political and economic strategies. Partly as a consequence of these policies, the living standards of the working class lagged well behind those of upper-income groups or even deteriorated in absolute terms. Given that these results could be traced in part to systematic exclusion from political participation and the denial of civil and political liberties, labor groups had few reasons to defend the regime and many incentives to oppose it.

The recessions of the mid-1970s or early 1980s, however, led to devastating income losses not only to poorer urban households but to the somewhat better-off unionized and white-collar workers as well, particularly in the public sector. These groups faced increased risk of unemployment, reduction in public services and transfers, and sharp declines in real wages. Trends in real wages suggest the magnitude of the crises (see Table 2.1). In all of the Latin American countries, there is at least one year during the transition period when real wages drop by more than 10 percent. Workers in the Philippines appeared to fare somewhat better during the crisis of the mid-1980s, but this overlooks the long-term decline in real wages in the Philippines that began in the 1960s, as well as sharp declines in living standards in 1979–80. In 1986, the year of the transition, real wages were only 10 percent higher than they had been in 1978.

---

[38] See Sylvia Maxfield, "National Business, Debt-Led Growth, and Political Transition in Latin America," in Barbara Stallings and Robert R. Kaufman, eds., *Debt and Democracy in Latin America* (Boulder, Colo., San Francisco, and London: Westview Press, 1989), pp. 75–91.

These changes had somewhat contradictory political implications for the behavior of popular-sector groups. Unlike business elites, white- and blue-collar workers controlled no investment resources vital to the regime and were hampered by significant collective action problems. Precisely because of the slack in labor markets, organized labor found it difficult to maintain solidarity during periods of economic downturn. However, the sharp fall in income also provided incentives for the leaders of social movements, trade union organizations, and parties to organize protest, and the increasing tensions among military and business groups opened new opportunities for them to do so.[39] We distinguish between two distinct, but often related forms of collective action: strikes aimed at economic demands, especially through union activity in the workplace; and broader political mobilization and demonstrations against the regime.

Strikes

The reentry of labor onto the political scene during a period of acute crisis creates a number of pressures on incumbent governments. Labor mobilization raises suppressed distributional issues, both through wage negotiations and through the broader support that strikes receive from leftist political movements. Labor mobilization also has second-order economic effects. Wage concessions by management can contribute to broader inflationary pressures, which in turn further heighten distributional conflicts. Equally if not more important is the fact that independent union activity and strikes in authoritarian settings always carry political as well as economic significance, since they confront authoritarian leaders with difficult choices between extended and costly repression and loss of political control.

Table 2.2 displays ILO data for strike activity in Peru, Brazil, and the Philippines during the crisis period and years of political transition, the three countries for which there are comparable data.[40] Strike activity moves in the expected direction, escalating as economic conditions deteriorate. The political significance of these figures, however, varied with the level of prior organization and the political role of the labor movement in each country.

In the Philippines, strikes escalated during the crisis of 1984 and 1985 as the government stabilization program imposed high costs on labor. The labor movement itself was weakly organized, however, split between pro-

---

[39] On the variation in forms of collective action from country to country see J. Samuel Valenzuela, "Labor Movements in Transitions to Democracy: A Framework for Analysis," *Comparative Politics* 21 (1989): 445–73.

[40] The ILO provides no comparable data for Argentina, Uruguay, and Bolivia, but in Argentina and Uruguay strike activity was almost totally suppressed anyway until at least the final year of the transition.

TABLE 2.2

Strike Activity during Transitions

	Peru			Brazil	The Philippines		
	No.	Workers Involved (000s)	Man-Days Lost (000s)	No.	No.	Workers Involved (000s)	Man-Days Lost (000s)
1974	570	362.7	1676.6				
1975	779	617.1	2533.6				
1976	440	258.1	852.7				
1977	234	406.5	817.9				
1978	364	1398.4	4518.1				
1979	653	841.1	1676.3				
1980	739	481.5	2239.9	81	62	20.9	105.3
1981				79	260	98.6	795.7
1982				126	158	53.8	1670.0
1983				312	155	33.6	581.3
1984				534	282	65.3	1907.8
1985				843	371	111.3	2457.7
1986				1493	581	169.5	3637.9
1987				na	436	89.6	1907.7

Source: International Labour Organization, *Year Book of Labour Statistics* (Geneva: International Labour Organization); various issues.

and anti-Marcos factions.[41] The political effectiveness of the more militant leftist unions was limited by their unwillingness to reach a workable political compromise with the more conservative mainstream opposition that finally united around Corazon Aquino in 1985. As a result, union organizations, and the left more generally, played a surprisingly small role in the mass protests that contributed to bringing down the regime.

In Peru, strike activities reflected the growing influence of left political forces within labor organizations originally sponsored by the regime itself. The upsurge of labor militancy beginning in the early 1970s had complex implications for the military establishment and its relations with other political forces. Within the military, it placed the more radical officers associated with the Velasco regime on the defensive and contributed eventually to the coup of August 1975 that placed the more moderate Morales Bermúdez in power. The turn away from populism after 1975 eroded previous bases of support for the regime, however. Groups that had previously been encouraged and even fostered by the military stepped up their

[41] See Virginia Teodosio, "Tripartism and the Imperatives of Development in the Philippines," (Ph.D. diss., University of Sydney, 1987), pp. 224–52.

political activity, and thus ironically increased pressures for political liberalization. A massive general strike in July 1977 was the pivotal event in pushing a wavering military establishment to hold elections for a Constituent Assembly.[42] Strike activity peaked in 1978, the year of the election and the trough of the mid-1970s recession.

In Brazil, the labor movement reentered the scene in 1978 and 1979 when wildcat stoppages culminated in an industry-wide strike throughout the São Paulo automobile and metalworking districts. These were years of strong growth rather than recession, but it was also a period of escalating inflation, and the strikes were initially triggered by revelations that the government had manipulated the price data on which wage adjustments were based. Industry-wide bargaining ceased after 1981, the result of a tough government crackdown on the labor movement as well as the recession. But the number of plant-level strikes tripled during the early 1980s.[43] In a system based on the repression of union movements this inevitably implied a confrontation with political authorities. In 1982 and 1983, activists within the union movement succeeded in negotiating contract settlements that far exceeded the guidelines set by the labor tribunals. Their success in doing so was widely viewed as an important political victory for anti-regime militants vis-à-vis both the government and the officialist union leadership. In July 1983, labor protest against the government's IMF stabilization program led to the first explicitly political strike since 1964, a one-day work stoppage in São Paulo and Rio Grande de Sul.[44]

Political Mobilization: Electoral Movements and Direct Action Campaigns

In the Philippines, Brazil, and Bolivia, oppositions exploited elections that military governments staged in order to legitimate their rule; electoral campaigns became a focal point for anti-regime activity. In all six countries, moreover, "direct action" campaigns—anti-regime protests, general strikes, and demonstrations—also figured prominently in the authoritarian withdrawals.[45] This popular upsurge occurred at different points in the

---

[42] Evelyne Stephens, "The Peruvian Military Government, Labor Mobilization, and the Political Strength of the Left," *Latin American Research Review* 18 (1983): 57–93.

[43] Margaret E. Keck, "The New Unionism in the Brazilian Transition," in Stepan, *Democratizing Brazil*, p. 267. Maria Hermínia Tavares de Almeida, "Unions, Economic Crisis and High Inflation: Brazil and Argentina in Comparison," Série Política Comparada 2, Departamento de Ciência Política, Universidad de São Paulo, n.d.

[44] Margaret Keck, "The New Unionism in the Brazilian Transition," p. 276.

[45] Guillermo O'Donnell and Philippe C. Schmitter, *Tentative Conclusions about Uncertain Democracies*, pt. 4 of O'Donnell, Schmitter, and Whitehead, *Transitions from Authoritarian Rule*, pp. 53–56.

process of transition, but tended to culminate in "climactic moments" that, because of the size and timing of demonstrations and the difficulties they posed for the regime, proved important for the process of political change; these are summarized in Table 2.3.

The role of mass protest in authoritarian withdrawal was perhaps most dramatic in the Philippines, where the massive "people's power" movement against electoral fraud, organized in part with the support of the Catholic Church, dealt a death blow to the Marcos government.[46] In Bolivia a decade earlier, a small but well-publicized hunger strike by miners' wives triggered a wave of popular protests that undermined the authority of the Banzer government and unraveled his attempt to manipulate the transition. In Uruguay, Brazil, and Peru, huge street demonstrations and protest rallies broke serious logjams in elite negotiations over political reform. In Argentina, the military temporarily staved off public protest through its disastrous Malvinas adventure, but a general strike in March 1982 exposed the isolation of a besieged regime that already faced serious internal divisions.[47]

As we argued in chapter 1, the agenda of the direct action campaigns was in the first instance political: the freeing of political prisoners, broader space for political parties to operate, electoral reforms, and an acceleration of electoral timetables. However, just as it is misleading to ignore the political content of economic strike activity, it would be wrong to overlook the profound economic grievances that motivated political protest. Political mobilization occurred during periods of deep economic distress, usually during or just after sharp declines in real wages. In all cases, opposition political elites drew on economic as well as political themes in making their appeals; demands for political change were closely connected to perceptions that existing institutional structures were detrimental to long-term material interests. In some cases, including Brazil, the term "democratization" became virtually synonymous with economic revival.

THE WITHDRAWAL FROM POWER

As we argued in chapter 1, the survival of authoritarian regimes ultimately depends on the capacity of rulers to retain the loyalty of the elites that directly control coercive, administrative, and political resources. In Brazil and the Philippines, these elites included civilian officials who occupied electoral offices, but the most important group in all cases was the military

---

[46] The literature on the events of February 1986 is large. A succinct summary stressing the American role is Stanley Karnow, *In Our Image: America's Empire in the Philippines* (New York: Ballantine Books, 1989), pp. 411–34.

[47] William C. Smith, *Authoritarianism and the Crisis of the Argentine Political Economy* (Stanford, Calif.: Stanford University Press, 1991), p. 256; Ricci and Fitch, "Ending Military Regimes in Argentina: 1966–1973 and 1976–1983."

TABLE 2.3
Popular-Sector Mobilization

Argentina
March 30, 1982. General strike organized by CGT is accompanied by demonstrations throughout the country. Thousands are arrested, but it is the first major mass demonstration since 1976. The government launches the Malvinas invasion in April.

Brazil
Early 1984. Campaign for direct election of the president in 1985 ("direitas ja," or "direct elections now") draws mass rallies in all the major cities of Brazil, organized by opposition parties, unions, and social movements. Millions of citizens mobilize in the largest mass rallies in Brazilian history.

Bolivia
January 1978. Strikes and demonstrations organized by the miners' union protesting political prisoners and repression of union movement constitute the largest protest mobilization since the beginning of the Banzer dictatorship in 1971. Strikes are joined by rural unions, implying a loss of control over critical rural voters as well as union members. The scheduled election, aimed at reinforcing Banzer's authority, slips out of control and he is forced from power.

November and December 1979. Widespread strikes against an IMF program weaken the interim democratic government of Lydia Gueiler; military re-seizes control under García Meza in July 1980.

Peru
July 1977. National strike organized by the left parties, independent unions, and radical social movements protests the military government, IMF negotiations, and austerity, climaxes a wave of strike activities and demonstrations organized during the preceding two years. Demonstrations are repressed, but in August, the government announces that elections for a Constituent Assembly will be held in June 1978.

Uruguay
November 1983. Mass rally organized by political parties, unions, and social movements demands release of political prisoners and restoration of electoral democracy. An estimated 400,000 citizens participate out of a total national population of less than three million. Rally climaxes a series of monthly rallies and demonstrations beginning in May 1983, the first since the military takeover in 1973.

Philippines
February 1986. Massive "people power" demonstrations in Manila, with support from the Catholic Church, protest Marcos's claims of electoral victory in his contest with Corazon Aquino and protect dissident military factions from armed reprisal. Within days, Marcos is forced from office.

itself. An important characteristic of those regimes that collapsed in the face of economic crisis was that the allegiance of some key political and military elites had been problematic for some time, creating serious internal divisions within the government. Military leaders harbored reservations about the overall economic project, about the viability of long-term repression, or about the effects of continued political intervention on the integrity of the military as an institution. In the Philippines, military concerns included increasing corruption, declining military budgets, and doubts about the capacity of the Marcos government effectively to manage a widening rural insurgency. In the Latin American countries, the growing strength of the secret police and intelligence apparatus and the threat of eventual reprisals for military conduct of, or complicity in, repression and torture constituted additional worries. In most cases, these doubts had been present since the inception of the regime itself. But divisions deepened as the economic and political crisis worsened and the costs of continuing repression rose relative to the risks of negotiating a change of political regime. Hardliners became increasingly isolated and softliners either took control of the transition process, or, in the Philippines and Argentina, the regime simply collapsed.

The result of these internal defections was that the military lost control over the timing of its withdrawal. As we will argue in more detail in chapter 4, divisions within the military and the existence of a manifest economic crisis also made it much more difficult to control the conditions of withdrawal. First, the crisis served to erode support for the government's particular development model; in contrast to the countries in which withdrawal occurred in relatively favorable conditions, the outgoing elite could count on little social support for a continuation of its policies. Second, internal divisions and lack of social support also made it difficult to exercise control over the *political* terms of the transition, for example, by excluding groups or otherwise controlling entry into the political arena. Finally, the weakened position of the military made it difficult to guard its own prerogatives, or even to protect itself against reprisals.

The Philippines

We look first at the Philippines, where collapse came with dramatic suddenness in February 1986; the process of military defection was compressed into a tense and dramatic week.[48] The ouster of the Marcoses came

---

[48] Compelling journalistic accounts include Monina Allery Mercado, ed., *People Power: An Eyewitness History of the Philippine Revolution of 1986* (Manila: Reuter Foundation, 1986), and Patricio Mamot, *People Power* (Quezon City: New Day, 1986). A good analytic introduction is Anne Mackenzie, "People Power or Palace Coup: the Fall of Marcos," in Turner, *Regime Change in the Philippines,* pp. 1–57.

in the wake of an effort to reassert control and to counter mounting criticism from abroad by calling snap elections in November 1985 for February 1986. Marcos calculated that the factionalized opposition would not be able to unite effectively behind one candidate. The combination of patronage politics and outright fraud would guarantee an adequate margin of victory, and the continuing loyalty of the military would in any case allow the government to repress any short-term protests that might emerge. However, with assistance from the Catholic Church the factions headed by Corazon Aquino and Salvador Laurel respectively managed to unite. Vote counting was closely scrutinized both by the foreign press and by a citizens' poll-watching organization.

Most crucially, the military establishment did not hold. Defense Minister Enrile and Lieutenant General Ramos had been encouraging the reformist movement within the military as part of an internal power struggle against Marcos crony, General Fabian Ver.[49] When Marcos had himself certified as the victor by shifting the vote counting to the controlled legislature, the hostile response from the media, both domestic and foreign, and the Church was overwhelming. Only massive coercion could have sustained the tainted electoral verdict. The final straw came when Enrile and Ramos went into open revolt against Marcos, with support from the Catholic Church and ultimately from hundreds of thousands of middle-class supporters, who surrounded Camp Aguinaldo where Ramos and Enrile were headquartered. The combination of military defection and massive public support not only undermined the ability of Marcos to reassert control, but finally pushed the wavering Reagan administration to recognize that the situation was untenable.[50]

The question of the degree of continuity between the Marcos and Aquino governments is the subject of substantial debate.[51] On the one hand, the facts that key military officers played a crucial role in the transition, and that large segments of the middle and business class had supported Aquino, resulted in some important elements of continuity. The crony "model" was thoroughly discredited, but the broad private-sector and elite backing for Aquino meant that neither the import-substituting approach to industrialization nor the highly skewed pattern of land tenure would be fundamentally challenged. Moreover, the politicization of the military was an enduring legacy of the Marcos era. Given that portions of the military saw themselves as key players in Aquino's political triumph, they quickly became disgruntled when she failed to address either their material or their

---

[49] David Wurfel, *Filipino Politics: Development and Decay* (Ithaca, N.Y.: Cornell University Press), pp. 289–91.

[50] See Karnow, *In Our Image*, pp. 411–34.

[51] For an optimistic early assessment, see Patricio Mamot, *The Aquino Administration's Baptism by Fire* (Manila: National Book Store, 1987); for a "continuist" position, see Hutchcroft, "Oligarchs and Cronies in the Philippine State."

political concerns. During her presidential term Aquino would confront five coup attempts, and though they were all beaten back, the military, increasingly in league with Marcos associates, did constrain the government.[52]

On the other hand, the swift collapse of the government in a period of weak economic performance set in motion political changes that conform to the general pattern that we have outlined. Marcos and his family were forced to flee, Marcos's associates were purged from the upper ranks of the military, the judiciary, and the civil service, and the political system was thrown open to a variety of new political forces. The government even adopted a conciliatory stance toward the insurgency, using the lure of democracy to undermine continued support for the armed struggle.

Argentina, Bolivia, and Peru: Military Coups against Military Governments

In Argentina, Bolivia, and Peru, the internal struggles leading to the withdrawal of the regime occurred over a more extended period of time. Economic and political crises contributed to military coups that eventually replaced hardline governments with ones more willing to acquiesce to the transfer of authority to civilians. Regime collapse was most chaotic in Argentina and Bolivia, leaving the least opportunity for outgoing military elites to influence the structure of the new political order. In both cases, a series of military leaders attempted to extend the life of the regime (following the departures of Videla and Banzer respectively), but were unable to retain the support of rival military factions, and were quickly overthrown. General García Meza, the longest-lived of the Bolivian military leaders, managed to hang on for over a year after an extraordinarily bloody coup d'état in July 1980. But with the military splintering rapidly into warring factions, he was soon overthrown by an "institutionalist" group that turned authority over to the civilian Congress originally elected in 1980.

In Argentina, General Viola had begun a "dialogue" with conservative politicians over a new constitutional framework, but in December 1981, after only nine months in office and in the context of a rapidly deteriorating economy, he was ousted in a palace coup. General Galtieri, Viola's successor, briefly rallied contending factions around the Malvinas adventure, but was displaced in another coup d'état only eight months later when that enterprise collapsed in defeat. By 1983, the navy and air force had withdrawn from the ruling junta entirely, leaving only a caretaker army-backed government under General Bignone. After an unsuccessful attempt to

---

[52] See the intriguing analysis by Criselda Yabes, *The Boys from the Barracks: the Philippine Military after EDSA* (Manila: Anvil Publishing, 1991).

negotiate an amnesty with opposition politicians, Bignone presided over the election of a civilian president.

The Peruvian military withdrew from power in a more orderly fashion. A Constituent Assembly elected in 1977 negotiated the transfer of power with the outgoing military government of Morales Bermúdez, setting the stage for a transitional period that ended with general elections in 1980. By the time of the elections, the economy had entered a brief period of recovery, stimulated by the 1979 increase in oil prices and the fact that Peru's new trans-Andean oil pipeline was up and running. As in Argentina and Bolivia, however, the decisive turning points in the process of authoritarian withdrawal occurred when economic crisis and civilian political opposition had seriously weakened the commitment of military leaders to the original authoritarian project.

The first of these came in August 1975, when a coup d'état displaced Velasco. In the context of a rapidly deteriorating economic situation, the incoming Morales Bermúdez government promised to begin a "second phase" of the revolution and initiated a tentative dialogue with business groups, American Revolutionary Popular Alliance (APRA) leaders and other moderate civilian politicians. As the crisis persisted, the successor government ended its two-year effort to mediate between conflicting factional forces by acquiescing to the Constituent Assembly elections of 1977. This event was at least as important as the 1980 elections themselves,[53] for it decisively shifted the momentum to the regime's civilian opponents. The government lifted all major restrictions on party activity, public assembly, and the media; committed itself to a definite timetable for elections; and transferred management of the economy to technocrats linked closely to the industrial and financial elite.

Negotiated Withdrawals: Uruguay

In Uruguay and Brazil, reformist factions within the military had begun to gain influence prior to the economic crisis; withdrawals in both countries were thus negotiated by military governments that had already made commitments to political liberalization. Furthermore, although the military establishments in these two countries were divided, they remained more cohesive than those in the Philippines, Argentina, Bolivia, or Peru. Nonetheless, crisis did influence the decision to withdraw from power. Crises weakened the position of diehards wishing to prolong the life of the regime, in part by undercutting their claims to superior economic management. Growing economic difficulties also reinforced the view of softliners that

[53] Cotler, "Military Interventions and 'Transfer of Power to Civilians' in Peru," p. 171.

the interests of the military lay in withdrawal from power, pushing them toward a pace of concessions faster than they had originally intended.[54]

In Uruguay, three important steps marked the road to the election of a new civilian government in 1985. The first, in 1980, was the surprising rejection by plebiscite of a new constitution intended to ratify military control. The plebiscite took place during a year of relatively strong economic performance, and indicated the regime's lack of legitimacy even in good times. Yet the implications of the plebiscite for political change were highly inconclusive. A power struggle after the plebiscite resulted in the selection of a new military president, Gregorio Alvarez, who promised elections in 1985. But Alvarez was widely suspected of harboring continuist ambitions and his hardline adversaries retained strong command positions within the military establishment.[55] For the next three years, the military government sought to retain many of the restrictive provisions of the defeated 1980 Constitution: continued authority for the National Security Council, the right to search homes, the right to declare a "state of subversion," and the right to hold suspects for fifteen days without trial.[56]

Unlike during the plebiscite, subsequent military efforts to pursue these objectives occurred in the context of sharply deteriorating economic conditions. In November 1982, pro-military candidates were overwhelmingly defeated in primary elections held within the *Colorado* and *Blanco* parties in order to select leaders who could negotiate with government authorities. The victories of the anti-military opposition in both traditional parties represented a severe setback to continuists within the government. The victories occurred during a year in which manufacturing output had declined over 16 percent and only days after a run on the peso forced the Central Bank to devalue the currency and reverse the government's anti-inflation policy. "Economic discontent," states Charles Gillespie, "must have played a large part in the growth of opposition to the regime."[57]

---

[54] See John Markoff and Silvio R. Duncan Baretta, "Economic Crisis and Regime Change in Brazil: the 1960s and the 1980s," *Comparative Politics* 22 (1990): 421–45.

[55] According to the astonishing logic of hardline Interior Minister Manuel Nuñez, the defeat in the plebiscite indicated that "the people preferred the status quo." Quoted in Howard Handelman, "Prelude to Elections: The Military's Legitimacy Crisis and the 1980 Constitutional Plebiscite in Uruguay," in Drake and Silva, *Elections and Democratization in Latin America,* p. 202. Alvarez's promise of elections and civilian government was made in a system where civilian presidents remained nominally in authority between 1973 and 1981, and should be evaluated in this context.

[56] For a discussion of the bargaining over military prerogatives, see David Pion-Berlin, "Crafting Allegiance: Civilian Control and the Armed Forces in Uruguay, Argentina, and Chile," unpublished ms., University of California, Riverside, September 1992.

[57] Charles G. Gillespie, "Activists and Floating Voters: The Unheeded Lessons of Uruguay's 1982 Primaries," in Drake and Silva, *Elections and Democratization in Latin America*, p. 216.

Survey results cited by Gillespie show a sharp last-minute shift of opinion that resulted in the decisive defeat of pro-regime candidates by those favoring a full and rapid transition to electoral democracy.

Even after two successive defeats at the polls, the military's insistence on retaining special political powers stalled negotiations on an electoral transfer for nearly two more years; it was only in August 1984 that agreements between party negotiators and the military elite cleared the way for the transition to go forward. These agreements could not have been reached without a series of well-timed maneuvers on the part of Colorado and leftist party leaders who agreed to negotiate without the participation of the Blancos. By this time, however, the political equation had shifted in significant ways. Mass rallies and demonstrations began to increase during the second half of 1983, a year in which real wages plunged by almost 20 percent. The enormous turnout for the mass rally of November 1983, involving close to one-sixth of the entire Uruguayan population, had an especially strong effect within the military establishment, leading both the commander in chief and the commander of the Montivedeo division to resume talks on their own with party leaders.

Events continued to spin out of control over the next several months, with widening opposition from students, unions, the press, and an array of new social movements. In January 1984, the more radical portions of the labor movement staged a successful general strike, and in June, there was a massive "civil strike" sponsored by all active political forces. Clearly on the defensive, the Alvarez government at last decided to scale back its objectives substantially, concentrating primarily on protecting itself against reprisals and isolating its most vocal opponent, Wilson Ferreira of the Blanco party. To accomplish the latter goal, it freed the imprisoned leader of the leftist Broad Front in March, and began in April to negotiate its exit with him and the Colorado leaders.

The agreements reached in August, following shortly after the June civic strike, did prohibit Ferreira's presidential candidacy. To win these concessions, however, the military was forced to accept an opening of the electoral arena to the forces of the political Left and to abandon virtually all of the claims to continued authority that it had been making since 1980. The military also failed to extract clear guarantees of immunity from future prosecutions, although it was subsequently successful in resisting judicial proceedings. "Only in Argentina," writes Howard Handelman, "did the armed forces command suffer a greater loss of political authority than in Uruguay."[58]

---

[58] Pion-Berlin, "Crafting Allegiance," p. 10; Handelman, "Economic Policy and Elite Pressure," p. 202.

Negotiated Withdrawals: Brazil

In Brazil, a controlled political opening had been the goal of the government since 1974. The decision to initiate the opening followed the first oil shock, which caused a substantial drop in growth from the extraordinary double-digit highs of 1971–73 and gave rise to a widespread perception that the "Brazilian miracle" had ended. Until the 1980s, however, political reforms moved forward in the context of continued economic expansion, financed by external debt. Annual growth rates through the second half of the 1970s averaged over 7 percent, approximately the same as in the late 1960s.

The gradualism of the political liberalization during this period reflected both the continuing influence of hardliners within the security apparatus and the general staff, and the preferences of more moderate officers themselves.[59] The hardliners pressed periodically for tougher enforcement of censorship and for selective repression designed to keep opponents off balance. Softliners sought to retain control of the reforms by forging alliances with conservative regional politicians and by manipulating electoral laws to preserve the official party's control of the Federal Congress and state governments.[60] Thus, although Figueiredo had come to office in 1979 promising that the next president would be a civilian, it was assumed that he would be selected through an electoral college controlled by the military and its political allies.

As in Uruguay, however, the recession of the early 1980s produced a sharp change in the context in which these intra-elite differences played themselves out.[61] In the 1982 gubernatorial elections, opposition candidates swept to victory in all of the large states of the industrialized southeast, capturing unprecedented control over local police forces and state patronage resources.[62] As the depression deepened during the following year, business criticism and labor militancy were accompanied by food riots and increasing crime in the major cities of the south. In early 1984, opposition party leaders organized a series of mass demonstrations across the country. These protests, called the "direct elections now" (*direitas ja*) campaign,

---

[59] For a general description of this process, see Thomas Skidmore, "Brazil's Slow Road to Democratization; 1974–1985," in Stepan, *Democratizing Brazil*, pp. 5–43.

[60] Frances Hagopian, "The Politics of Oligarchy: The Persistence of Traditional Elites in Contemporary Brazil" (Ph.D. dissertation, Massachusetts Institute of Technology, 1986).

[61] See Luciano Martins, "The 'Liberalization' of Authoritarian Rule in Brazil," in O'Donnell, Schmitter, and Whitehead, *Transitions from Authoritarian Rule*, pt. 2, *Latin America*, pp. 90–91; Glaucio Ary Dillon Soares, "Elections and the Redemocratization of Brazil," pp. 291–97.

[62] The winners included the radical populist Leonel Brizola, one of the prime targets of the 1964 coup, who was elected as governor of Rio de Janeiro.

demanded abandonment of the electoral college and direct election of the next president.

These developments had two effects on the military elites and their civilian allies. For moderate military officers, efforts to repress such protests implied an unacceptable expansion of the role of hardline security forces within the state apparatus. In late 1981, their concern grew after revelations that security forces had planned to explode a bomb at a convention center in Rio de Janeiro and to use the incident as a pretext for a crackdown on opponents of the regime. The plot failed, but it widened the already substantial gap between hardliners and softliners within the armed forces.

At the same time, relations between military moderates and their civilian political allies were seriously strained by the outcome of the 1982 gubernatorial elections and by the campaign for direct election of the president in 1984. As evidence of support for the opposition mounted, the leaders of the official party distanced themselves from the military government, calling for a faster pace of political reform. Government-controlled legislative majorities eventually managed to defeat the constitutional amendment demanded in the "direitas ja" campaign, but the military-civilian alliance had been fatally damaged. In 1985, a breakaway faction of the official party joined the opposition Party of the Brazilian Democratic Movement (PMDB) in the electoral college to select opposition leader Tancredo Neves as the president elect, marking the first time since the 1960s that the military elites had failed to dictate the presidential succession.

To a much greater extent than the other crisis transitions, Brazilian democratization exhibited strong political and institutional continuities. The military establishment itself also retained important institutional prerogatives and continued to control portions of the state apparatus for the rest of the decade. Moreover, the regional political bosses who had reentered electoral politics in the 1970s expanded their control over important centers of patronage. Neves himself belonged to a center-right segment of the opposition that was reasonably acceptable to the military elite. When he died unexpectedly in April 1985, he was replaced by José Sarney, leader of the breakaway official party.

However, the transition also led to major changes that had not been planned or viewed as acceptable prior to the economic crisis. The military's role in "arbitrating" presidential politics and influencing economic policy, though still important, was more circumscribed under the New Republic than at any time since the Vargas era. Even more significantly, grass-roots opposition movements weakened the corporatist pillars of the old order. Industrial unions, left parties, and rural social movements reentered the Brazilian system with unprecedented independence. Thus, notwithstanding the continuing influence of the old political oligarchies, the transition brought with it a significant shift in the balance of political forces.

CONCLUSION

The transitions discussed in this chapter varied substantially in terms of the extent to which ruling elites negotiated with opposition forces and the types of agreements reached. These variations have generated a number of useful distinctions in the literature, including between "pacted transitions" and "rupturas."[63] However, we have emphasized two common features of these transitions. First, economic crises resulted in loss of social support for the government, reflected in both the defection of private-sector allies and an upsurge of popular protest; second, these political pressures deepened preexisting divisions within the ruling elite. Military and other elites usually remained powerful, but their capacity to restrict or regulate the behavior of formerly excluded groups declined significantly after the transition. We elaborate these points later on, in chapter 4, but turn first to a discussion of the non-crisis cases.

[63] See Terry Lynn Karl, "Dilemmas of Democratization in Latin America," *Comparative Politics* 23 (1990): 1–22 Terry Lynn Karl and Philippe Schmitter, "Modes of Transition in Latin America, Southern and Eastern Europe," *International Social Science Journal* 53 (1991): 269–84.

CHAPTER THREE

Surviving Crises, Withdrawing in Good Times

THE CRISIS CASES discussed in the previous chapter support the hypothesis that economic shocks can hasten the demise of authoritarian regimes. In this chapter, we explore cases that constitute anomalies from the perspective of a purely economic explanation of regime change. Why were some regimes able to survive severe economic challenges? What were the characteristics of transitions that occurred under comparatively good economic conditions?

We begin by examining two countries, Chile and Korea, where authoritarian regimes survived economic challenges in the late 1970s and early 1980s. The Pinochet regime in Chile experienced a wrenching crisis in 1982, at least as severe as the ones that contributed to the collapse of comparable bureaucratic-authoritarian regimes in Argentina, Uruguay, and Brazil. Yet Pinochet stayed in power until almost the end of the decade. In 1979–80, Korea also confronted economic difficulties that, though mild by Latin American standards, contributed to serious political unrest. As in Chile, however, the military reasserted its hegemony over the political system, and it was not until 1987, in the midst of an unprecedented economic boom, that the Chun Doo Hwan government relinquished power.

Our explanation for the survival of these regimes emphasizes institutional characteristics that strengthened the hand of the military. In contrast to those regimes that fell in the face of adversity, internal cleavages in the Chilean and Korean militaries were either limited or quickly muted. Military cohesion provided the government greater leeway in using coercion and closed off opportunities for the formation of coalitions between softliners and moderate opposition forces. The absence of serious intra-elite divisions also provided the political basis for a more coherent response to economic difficulties; in both cases, economic teams received strong executive support and were able to initiate and sustain effective adjustment efforts.

The second part of this chapter focuses on transitions that occurred in good economic times; in addition to the "delayed" transitions in Chile and Korea, Turkey and Thailand stand out in this regard. The fact that these authoritarian governments withdrew when economic circumstances were favorable is an important reminder that short-term conditions are not the only factors at work in understanding authoritarian withdrawals. In all four cases, long-term socioeconomic changes, international political pressures, and domestic demands for political reform played a role. A consistent contrast with the crisis cases, however, is the relative political strength of authoritarian rulers vis-à-vis the opposition during the transition process. Favorable economic conditions reduced the incentives for economic elites to defect. Not only were private-sector supporters less likely to bolt, but the regime retained broader bases of support as well. As we will show in more detail in the following chapter, these political advantages associated with effective adjustment and favorable economic conditions enabled outgoing elites to exercise substantial influence over the new political order.

SURVIVING CRISIS: PINOCHET'S CHILE

The dynamics of the economic crisis that hit Chile during the early 1980s are strikingly similar to those in Argentina and Uruguay. As in these two countries, a major source of economic difficulties was the attempt to use the exchange rate as a nominal anchor to control inflationary expectations. The Chilean government began to experiment with preannounced devaluations in 1976. Three years later, it introduced a fixed exchange rate in conjunction with a drastic reduction in tariffs. Given that fiscal discipline was far tighter in Chile than in Argentina and Uruguay, these policies arguably stood a better chance of reducing domestic inflation to world levels. However, in part because of a decision to index wages, domestic prices increased more rapidly than international ones, the real exchange rate appreciated, and it became increasingly costly to sustain the fixed nominal rate.[1]

The onset of the crisis was signaled in late 1981 by a drastic deterioration in the balance of payments, a diminished flow of external credit, and a number of domestic bank failures. During 1982, the current-account deficit jumped to over 14 percent of GDP, more than double the annual average of the preceding five years (see Table 3.1). The government was forced into a major devaluation, which in turn triggered more bankruptcies and a virtual collapse of the financial system. In 1982, unemployment increased to over 25 percent and GDP dropped by 14.2 percent, the worst performance in the entire region.[2]

The enormity of this collapse led to a series of ad hoc steps to halt the free fall of the economy. In January 1983, in a stunning and ironic reversal of earlier efforts to liberalize the financial sector, the government nationalized most of the new financial-commercial conglomerates that had emerged

[1] On the role of exchange-rate policy, see Sebastian Edwards and Alejandra Cox Edwards, *Monetarism and Liberalization: The Chilean Experiment* (Cambridge, Mass.: Ballinger, 1987), pp. 53–92, 109–34.

[2] Genaro Arriagada, *Pinochet: The Politics of Power* (Boston: Unwin Hyman, 1988), p. 51.

TABLE 3.1

Economic Crisis and Adjustment in Chile, 1979–1985

	1979	1980	1981	1982	1983	1984	1985
GDP Growth	8.3	7.8	5.6	−14.2	−0.7	6.3	2.4
Inflation	33.4	35.1	19.7	9.9	27.3	19.9	30.7
Fiscal Deficit/GDP	4.8	5.4	2.6	−1.0	−2.6	−3.0	−2.4
Current Account/GDP	−5.7	−7.1	−14.5	−9.5	−5.7	−11.0	−8.8
Investment/GDP	17.8	21.0	22.7	11.3	9.8	13.6	13.7
Real Wage	8.3	9.0	9.1	−0.2	−10.7	0.1	−3.8

Source: The World Bank, *World Tables 1993* (Washington, D.C.: The World Bank, 1994); International Monetary Fund, *International Financial Statistics Yearbook,* various issues; Economic Commission on Latin America, *Economic Survey of Latin America and the Caribbean,* various issues.

Note: For definitions of the first five variables, see Table 2.1. Real Wage: real wage for nonagricultural workers.

during the 1970s, again taking direct control of a large portion of the Chilean economy. Over the next two years, Pinochet appointed and then dismissed a series of six finance ministers, including his original corps of "Chicago boys," and temporarily reversed the trade liberalization that had been a hallmark of the reign of the "Chicago boys."[3]

The Social and Political Response

The crisis also triggered a political response not unlike that in the Philippines and other South American countries.[4] Beginning in May 1983, protests spearheaded by the copper workers' union produced the first mass demonstrations since 1973. Even more dangerous to the regime was the appearance of substantial middle-class protest as well, including marches of housewives, banging pots and pans, that were reminiscent of the protests against Allende. Protests continued until mid-1986, although open middle-class support for them ebbed much earlier, arguably by the end of 1983.

[3] Barbara Stallings, "Politics and Economic Crisis: A Comparative Study of Chile, Peru, and Columbia," in Joan M. Nelson, ed., *Economic Crisis and Policy Choice: The Politics of Adjustment in the Third World* (Princeton, N.J.: Princeton University Press, 1990), pp. 129–32.

[4] For discussions of this crisis period, see: Arriagada, *Pinochet,* pp. 56–81; Paul W. Drake and Ivan Jaksic, eds., *The Struggle for Democracy in Chile, 1982–1990* (Lincoln and London: University of Nebraska Press, 1991), especially the essays by Maria Elana Valenzuela, "The Evolving Role of Women under Military Rule," (pp. 161–88); Alan Angell, "Unions and Workers in Chile during the 1980s," pp. 188–211), and Manuel Antonio Garreton, "The Political Opposition and the Party System under the Military Regime," pp. 211–51.

Business groups generally stopped short of open calls for democratization, but for the first time since the Allende period, they criticized the government's market-oriented economic policies and demanded a greater voice in the decision-making process.[5] At least a few went further. "We knew this government was repressive," stated one in a *Wall Street Journal* interview. "When the economy was good, it was easy to ignore all that. Now that the good times are over, the veil is off and we want Pinochet out."[6]

Viewed from a long-term perspective, the crisis marked a turning point in Chilean history not unlike those in the crisis-induced transitions. The surge of opposition wounded Pinochet's regime and the situation never completely returned to the status quo ante. One of the most important developments was the reemergence of Chile's political parties; the opposition was led by Christian Democrats and leftist politicians, although beginning in 1983 and 1984, even some politicians on the right began to call for political reform. Until the late 1980s, the government harassed party organizations, which were further weakened by bitter divisions between the center and the left. Nonetheless, the crisis provided an issue around which support could be mobilized.

In contrast to the cases discussed in the previous chapter, however, Pinochet eventually restored political control and was not compelled to withdraw in the face of these challenges. Despite the crisis, the Pinochet government never lost control of fiscal or monetary policy, and by 1985 a new round of privatization and trade reform initiated a period of sustained growth that persisted into the next decade. When Pinochet was at last impelled to step down in 1990, his government had regained the support of important business and middle-class groups and he was able to impose restrictive conditions on the incoming democratic administration.

Sources of Durability: Political Polarization and Military Discipline

Pinochet's extraordinary resilience can be explained in part by the extreme class antagonism and ideological polarization of the Allende period. The perception of a threat from the left deterred more vigorous opposition from middle-class and business groups, who were concerned that a reopening of the political system might lead to a replay of the early 1970s.[7] The legacy of polarization was also reflected in the debilitating conflicts between

[5] Eduardo Silva, "Capitalist Coalitions, the State, and Neoliberal Economic Restructuring: Chile, 1973–1988," *World Politics* 45 (1993): 550.

[6] Quoted in Jeffry A. Frieden, *Debt, Development, and Democracy* (Princeton, N.J.: Princeton University Press, 1991), p. 171.

[7] See ibid., p. 144–46, 169–74. Eduardo Silva has argued further that by acquiescing to the suppression of unions, ISI industrialists were weakened vis-à-vis groups that hoped for

centrist and left opposition groups, conflicts skillfully manipulated by Pinochet. But social and ideological polarization did not fully protect the regime against isolation during the early 1980s. At a time when authoritarian governments in neighboring countries were withdrawing from power, the Pinochet government lost vital support from business elites and the middle class and appeared to be in danger of imminent collapse.

As both Karen Remmer and Genaro Arriagada have argued, the capacity of the regime to withstand such pressures depended heavily on the centralization and discipline of its military base.[8] Political divisions existed within the Chilean armed forces, but these were far more limited than in comparable military establishments. The most important source of cohesion was Pinochet's personal authority over both the armed forces and the state. The general consolidated his power after 1973 through a series of maneuvers that capitalized on the Chilean military's long-standing traditions of internal discipline and obedience to established authority. As commanding general of the army, Pinochet moved quickly to purge potential rivals from the upper ranks and to appoint loyal officers to command positions. Since the army dominated the other service branches, these steps allowed Pinochet to gain the upper hand over his colleagues on the junta. The concentration of power was formalized in subsequent years by decrees that established Pinochet as President of the Republic and as Generalissimo of the Armed Forces. These steps consolidated Pinochet's claim to the obedience that the military had traditionally accorded to civilian heads of state and ratified his control over appointments in both the military and civilian bureaucracies.[9]

The corporate insulation of the military from the political establishment reinforced this discipline. Unlike in Brazil, Uruguay, and Argentina, the institutional role of the military was explicitly separated from that of the government. Individual officers were appointed to government posts, particularly in the early years of the Pinochet government, but they were required to take leaves of absence to accept these appointments and were rotated quickly back into the normal chain of command.[10] Top political positions, such as the finance, economics, and interior ministries, were filled by civilians appointed by Pinochet. Military officers within the normal chain of command had few contacts with political elites or their private-sector counterparts. To raise questions about specific policies was

---

more market-oriented reforms; Silva, "Capitalist Coalitions, the State, and Neoliberal Economic Restructuring," p. 537.

[8] Arriagada, *Pinochet,* pp. 123–69; Karen L. Remmer, *Military Rule in Latin America* (Boulder, Colo.: Westview Press, 1991), pp. 113–45.

[9] See Arturo Valenzuela, "The Military in Power: The Consolidation of One-Man Rule," in Drake and Jaksic, *The Struggle for Democracy in Chile,* pp. 21–72.

[10] Ibid., p. 34.

considered "political" and counter to the professional norms of the military establishment.

The ratification of a new constitution in 1980 also played a role in grounding Pinochet's authority within a formal legal framework. The Constitution was intended to legitimate consecutive eight-year presidential terms for Pinochet, potentially extending his tenure until 1999. At the same time, the provisions for a controlled transition to a "limited democracy" helped to diffuse potential opposition from softliners who feared the political implications of indefinite military rule. As demands for democratization grew during the 1980s, diverse currents within the military establishment could unite around the Constitution as a point of reference for guiding "orderly" change.[11]

The Political Consequences of Military Cohesion

Military discipline contributed to the regime's ability to survive crisis in several ways. In the years prior to the crisis, the military backed radical economic reforms that undermined the social bases of potential labor and business challengers. The government's tough stabilization policies, the only ones in the Southern Cone to reduce public expenditures and fully accept high rates of unemployment, hit labor unions especially hard.[12] Unemployment in Chile averaged over 17 percent between 1975 and 1981; this was about double the rate in Uruguay and over five times that of Argentina, where the military resisted more drastic cutbacks in the public sector.[13]

The radical trade and financial market reforms undertaken during the 1970s also weakened the political influence of the Chilean industrial sector, providing the regime with considerable leverage over business as a whole.[14] Unlike in Argentina and Uruguay, Chilean industrialists could find few points of access among dissident factions within the military establishment.[15]

[11] See Augusto Varas, "The Crisis of Legitimacy of Military Rule in the 1980s," in Drake and Jaksic, *The Struggle for Democracy in Chile*, pp. 73–97. Hector E. Schamis argues that such changes were part of a larger process of state restructuring. See "Re-forming the State: The Politics of Privatization in Chile and Britain," (Ph.D. Diss., Columbia University, 1994).

[12] Joseph Ramos, *Neoconservative Economics in the Southern Cone of Latin America, 1973–1983* (Baltimore: Johns Hopkins University Press, 1986).

[13] Ibid., pp. 14, 26, 36. Military resistence to unemployment is discussed in Frieden, *Debt, Development and Democracy*, p. 211.

[14] Sergio de la Cuadra and Dominique Hachette, "Chile," in Demetris Papageorgiou, Michael Michaely, and Armeane M. Choksi, eds., *Liberalizing Foreign Trade*, vol. 1: *The Experience of Argentina, Chile, and Uruguay* (Cambridge, Mass., and Oxford: Basil Blackwell, 1991), p. 217.

[15] The suppression of unions deprived industrialists of allies in their opposition to liber-

Moreover, although banking and commercial conglomerates did gain influence over policies adopted in the pre-crisis period, their power depended heavily on their alliance with Pinochet.[16] As the economy collapsed during the early 1980s, the influence of these conglomerates evaporated. The government assumed ownership of their assets and arrested several prominent executives for financial irregularities.

At the height of the crisis, from 1982 to about 1984, Pinochet's control over the armed forces left him free to exploit rivalries within the opposition. His first step was to attempt to isolate the left politically by entering into a "dialogue" with opponents from the Christian Democrats and the right. Talks with the non-left opposition began in August 1983 under a newly appointed interior minister, Sergio Onofre Jarpa. Jarpa was the first party politician to occupy that position since 1973, and advocated a Brazilian-style *apertura.* But Pinochet retained firm control over the initiative, and as middle-class support for protest began to ebb in early 1984, he hardened his position on reform and effectively ended serious negotiation.

With centrist groups off balance, Pinochet next deployed his coercive resources against the left. In November 1984, following a series of violent clashes with protesters, the government declared a state of siege and initiated a massive crackdown. In periodic sweeps of shantytown neighborhoods, troops loyal to the regime conducted house-to-house searches, rounded up all men over fifteen years of age, and imprisoned those suspected of political activism. Arrests, which had averaged about 1,500 during 1976–82, increased by more than 300 percent in the next several years.[17] By the end of 1984, the wave of mass protests that had shaken the regime had run its course.

The reestablishment of political control coincided, finally, with the initiation of a new round of economic adjustment, a reconstruction of relations with the private sector, and an impressive economic recovery. Between 1984 and 1990, the economy expanded at an annual rate of over 5 percent, while the rate of inflation remained far lower than in neighboring countries.

The political sources of these adjustment initiatives is a matter of some dispute. In a persuasive criticism of statist explanations that stress the importance of regime change and bureaucratic initiative in the reform process, Eduardo Silva has documented the role of business organizations. While the more radical phase of reform under the Chicago boys was supported by newly emergent financial conglomerates, groups in fishing,

---

alization, leaving them seriously weakened vis-à-vis financial conglomerates and technocrats pressing for market-oriented adjustments. See Silva, "Capitalist Coalitions, the State and Neoliberal Economic Restructuring," p. 537.

[16] For a discussion of this relationship, see ibid., pp. 557.

[17] Arriagada, *Pinochet,* p. 63.

forestry, and agriculture backed the more pragmatic approach to the expansion of exports eventually adopted by the government following the crisis in 1981–82.[18] Yet Silva also suggests that the eventual formulation of a coherent and sustained adjustment strategy depended on the leadership of a highly centralized state authority. During 1983 and 1984, there was considerable policy drift, in part as a consequence of internal conflicts within the private-sector organizations that had gained access to the government. The turning point came in 1985 with the appointment of a new finance minister, Hernán Büchi, a career bureaucrat without direct links to any of the competing business groups. With the backing of Pinochet, Büchi succeeded in implementing a number of key measures contributing to the economic recovery. In the area of macroeconomic policy, these included extensive fiscal adjustment and the maintenance of a competitive exchange rate. Büchi also resisted pressures for the reestablishment of substantial protectionist measures, rolled back temporary tariff increases, and launched a new drive to privatize state-owned enterprises. At the same time, in response to private-sector demands, he also provided credits and tax incentives to export-oriented firms, unlike his neoliberal predecessors.[19]

Whatever the weights one attaches to the social and institutional sources of these initiatives, it is clear that this mix of policies both strengthened export-oriented groups within the private sector and reinforced their links to the Pinochet regime. Privatization policies, competitive exchange rates, and government credits were especially important in expanding the economic base of the export conglomerates.[20] In turn, these groups and their representatives within the producers' associations were incorporated into the policymaking process through appointments to sub-Cabinet positions and representation in a wide network of consultative commissions and sectoral committees.[21]

As broader pressures for democratic reform began to gather steam again in the late 1980s, these close and positive relations with the regime played an important role in shaping the political transition. Business groups did not oppose the transition outright, and some viewed it as an opportunity to

[18] Silva, "Capitalist Coalitions, the State, and Neoliberal Economic Restructuring," pp. 553–55.

[19] Average tariff levels, which had been raised briefly from 10 to 35 percent between 1983 and 1984, were rolled back to 20 percent. De la Cuadra and Hachette, "Chile," pp. 268–71.

[20] Hector E. Schamis, "Re-forming the State: The Politics of Privatization in Chile and Britain" (Ph.D. diss., Columbia University, 1994); Oscar Muñoz, "Crisis and Industrial Reorganization in Chile," *Journal of Interamerican Studies and World Affairs* 31 (1989): 170–92.

[21] The main new groups included Ancleto Angelini in forestry and agribusiness; Luksic and Molineras in food and mining; Matte in forestry; and Yarur, Hirmas, and Comandari in textiles. *Latin American Regional Report: Southern Cone, RS85-08*, 11 October 1985, p. 6.

limit potential threats posed by the concentration of executive power. Unlike their counterparts in Argentina, Brazil, and Uruguay, however, Chilean business elites placed a strong emphasis on the importance of policy continuity and of gradual institutional change. The largest business association, the Confederation of Chilean Producers (CPC), supported Pinochet in the 1988 plebiscite, and most business groups backed Hernán Büchi in the 1989 presidential race.[22]

CRISIS, COLLAPSE, AND THE REASSERTION OF MILITARY RULE: KOREA

Korea's economic crisis in 1979–80 appears milder than those in the Southern Cone or the Philippines, but such cross-national comparisons can be misleading.[23] What constitutes a "crisis" must to some extent be seen in local context, and in Korea during this period economic and social conditions were viewed as having reached crisis proportions. Though inflation did not approach Latin American levels, the annual rise in the consumer price index accelerated to 18.3 percent in 1979 and to nearly 30 percent in 1980, and became a salient political issue (see Table 3.2). GNP declined nearly 5 percent in 1980, before resuming the upward march in 1981 that was typical of Korea's development since the early 1960s. This was the worst annual economic performance since the Korean War. Real wages dropped more than 4 percent in 1980 and another 1.6 percent in 1981, and when real wage growth resumed in 1982, it was at a rate substantially below the robust, if unsustainable, pace of the late 1970s.

The period from 1978 to 1980 also saw a substantial widening of the current-account deficit, which topped 11 percent of GDP in 1980 as a result of slowed export growth and the declining terms of trade associated with the oil crisis. Korea was able to borrow through the crisis (and thus maintain investment), because its stellar export performance made it an attractive risk; this prevented it from falling into the debt-servicing difficulties confronting the Philippines and the Latin American debtors discussed in chapter 2. Nonetheless, financial officials were concerned at the time about the availability of credit, since some banks had begun to cut back on lending or to demand stiffer terms.

---

[22] Guillermo Campero, "Entrepreneurs under the Military Regime," in Drake and Jaksic, *The Struggle for Democracy in Chile, 1982–1990,* pp. 128–61.

[23] The following analysis of the Korean economy draws on Stephan Haggard et al., *Macroeconomic Policy and Performance in Korea, 1970–1990* (Cambridge: Harvard University Press, 1994), chaps. 1–3.

TABLE 3.2
Economic Crisis and Adjustment in Korea, 1979–1983

	1978	1979	1980	1981	1982	1983
GDP Growth	11.0	7.0	−3.3	6.9	7.4	12.1
Inflation	14.5	18.3	28.7	21.3	7.2	3.4
Fiscal Deficit/GDP	−1.2	−1.7	−2.2	−3.3	−3.0	−1.0
Current Account/GDP	−2.2	−6.4	−8.5	−6.7	−3.6	−2.0
Investment/GDP	31.4	35.5	31.7	29.5	28.6	28.8
Real Wage	20.8	10.9	−4.4	−1.6	4.6	5.9

Source: World Bank, *World Tables 1993* (Washington, D.C.: The World Bank, 1994); International Monetary Fund, *International Financial Statistics Yearbook,* various issues.

Note: For definitions of the first five variables, see Table 2.1. Real Wage: growth in earnings per employee.

The economic developments of the late 1970s have their roots in changes in both political institutions and economic strategy in the early 1970s.[24] In 1972, Park restructured the nominally democratic system in an explicitly authoritarian fashion through the imposition of the Yushin Constitution. This political change was followed by a major economic policy initiative: the ambitious Heavy and Chemical Industry Plan. To implement the plan, the government followed the strategy pursued by a number of other developing countries: it borrowed heavily in international capital markets.

A distinctive feature of this period was a marked increase in the extent of government intervention, particularly through the channeling of credit through state-owned banks to favored activities and the use of price controls to curb inflation. Though growth in the early years of the plan was extremely rapid, by early 1978 the economy showed signs of overheating, with strong pressures on the prices of politically sensitive goods: food, housing, and other basic commodities.[25] Since the government remained committed to a fixed exchange rate, increased inflation translated into a real appreciation and declining export competitiveness. The government adopted a strong stabilization plan in 1979, and in early 1980, under a fragile transitional government, undertook a substantial devaluation. These policy measures coincided with the second oil shock and an unusually poor harvest in 1980, resulting in the weak performance of that year.

[24] See Stephan Haggard and Chung-in Moon, "The South Korean State in the International Economy: Liberal, Dependent or Mercantile?" in John Ruggie, ed., *The Antinomies of Interdependence* (New York: Columbia University Press, 1986), pp. 131–90; Jung-en Woo, *Race to the Swift: State and Finance in Korean Industrialization* (New York: Columbia University Press, 1991), pp. 118–47.

[25] This was due in part to unanticipated capital inflows from Middle East construction, but was primarily the result of an investment boom and resulting wage pressures.

The Social and Political Response: The Politics of Adjustment
and the Fall of Park Chung Hee

Economic developments began to have political repercussions for the Park government in the period prior to the general election of December 1978.[26] This election did not appear to pose any threat to Park's rule; under the Yushin system, one third of the 261-seat National Assembly was appointed by the president. The election proved significant, though, since turnout was high, the major opposition party, the National Democratic Party (NDP), polled more votes than the ruling party, and issues of economic management, long the government's strong card, played a role in the opposition's campaign.[27]

Prior to the election, the government faced the typical political dilemma associated with stabilization. Inflation had become a political as well as economic problem for the government by 1978, particularly in the cities where opposition to Park was concentrated. Yet Park's commitment to the heavy industry drive and concerns about the electoral effects of macroeconomic restraint blocked a coherent stabilization effort. Immediately following the elections, Park reshuffled the cabinet. Park was skeptical about the need for fundamental reform, but his new prime minister, backed by forces within the economic bureaucracy, was aligned against the heavy industry plan. Moreover, export performance, a closely watched indicator, continued to weaken. Park relented and on April 17, 1979, the government announced the Comprehensive Measures for Economic Stabilization.[28] The program addressed the problem of stabilization through the traditional means of slowing credit growth and cutting expenditures, but also initiated a wide-ranging set of structural reforms.[29]

This reform effort overlapped with a more assertive stance by the opposition.[30] In May 1979, with backing from the recently freed opposition

[26] For a review of the rise of the opposition, see Hak-kyu Sohn, *Authoritarianism and Opposition in South Korea* (London: Routledge, 1989).

[27] The opposition gained nine seats, increasing its total to 61. The Yushin constitution established two-member districts, in which the top two vote-getters in each district won seats.

[28] See Economic Planning Board, *Economic Survey: Annual Report of the Korean Economy in 1979* (Seoul: EPB, 1980), pp. 119–40.

[29] These included changes in the style of economic management: a shift in the system of monetary management away from direct credit controls toward indirect monetary management; greater independence for the Central Bank; the privatization of the banking sector; liberalization of imports and more general, rather than targeted forms of industrial policy, including realistic exchange-rate policy. The plan also promised to address the problem of increasing industrial concentration by regulating mergers, takeovers, and noncompetitive business practices.

[30] On the background to the crisis of 1979–80, see Donald Clark, "The Kwangju Uprising: An Introduction," in Clark, ed., *The Kwangju Uprising: Shadows over the Regime in South Korea* (Boulder, Colo.: Westview Press, 1988), pp. 1–7.

leader Kim Dae Jung, Kim Young Sam captured the presidency of the NDP by arguing for a full review of the Yushin system. In addition to the call for political liberalization and a return to democracy, the opposition sought to attract support from those sectors that had been disadvantaged under the Yushin system, the heavy industry plan, and the subsequent stabilization effort.[31]

A crucial incident for subsequent political developments occurred on August 9, when 178 female textile workers occupied the headquarters of the NDP, calling on the party to assist them in resolving a labor dispute that had festered since May. The YH Trading Company, for which they worked, was typical of many small and medium-sized firms driven to bankruptcy or temporary closure by rising labor costs and the squeeze on credit, often leaving workers unpaid. After two days, the police launched an assault on NDP headquarters to break up the protest. The "YH Incident" left one woman dead and 30 wounded, including several National Assembly members, and received wide coverage in the press.

Kim Young Sam made a strongly critical statement on the government's handling of the incident, and on October 4, the ruling party ejected Kim from the National Assembly. Kim's ouster sparked violent demonstrations in Pusan and Masan that involved not only increasingly militant students but disaffected workers. At this point, the regime divided over the issue of coercion. Park Chung Hee and Cha Ji Chul, director of the presidential security guard, argued that the Pusan-Masan riots should be put down at all costs. Kim Jae Kyu, head of the Korean Central Intelligence Agency, represented the softline position that some accommodation should be made to the protesters; on October 26, Kim assassinated Park.

The Reassertion of Military Authority

The assassination of Park was followed by conflicts within the army and security apparatus and a dramatic resurgence of civil society.[32] The promise of a democratic opening, the lack of clarity surrounding the precise role of the military in the political system, and deteriorating economic conditions stimulated the mobilization of an array of social forces. Student demon-

---

[31] In an interview in June 1979, Kim noted that "inflation has become worse. The economic position in general has become much more unstable. . . . A handful of entrepreneurs . . . have profited far more than the man in the street from our economic growth. The time has come to stand up and confront the government." *Far Eastern Economic Review,* June 8, 1979, p. 13.

[32] See Clark, *The Kwangju Uprising,* pp. 77–82, and the interpretation of Jang Jip Choi, "Political Cleavages in South Korea," in Hagen Koo, ed., *State and Society in Contemporary Korea* (Ithaca, N.Y.: Cornell University Press, 1993), pp. 29–32.

strations for democratization were widespread and virtually continuous in the spring of 1980. In the first five months of 1980, over 900 strikes occurred, more than had taken place in the entire Yushin period.

In short, Korea appeared to possess all of the elements of a crisis-induced transition. The difference lay in the military.[33] Unlike in Chile, divisions within the military were marked; as in Chile, however, these were quickly resolved in favor of highly centralized and unified control over both government and military. Chun Doo Hwan, the head of military intelligence, was placed in charge of the investigation of Park's assassination. He moved quickly to arrest and prosecute Kim Jae Kyu for the assassination and purged the Central Intelligence Agency, a major contending power center. However, rivalries remained between Chun and army chief of staff and martial law commander Chung Seung Hwa. On December 12, 1979, Chun mounted a mutiny within the army, arrested Chung, and with support from a circle of younger officers who stood to gain professionally, removed a number of older generals. By the end of these internal factional conflicts, Chun controlled the army, military intelligence, and the KCIA.

This centralized control over the coercive apparatus allowed Chun to exercise behind-the-scenes control over the weak interim president, Choi Kyu Ha.[34] Partial martial law had already been in effect since the assassination; the legal distinction between partial and full martial law was important, because under partial martial law, the Cabinet remained nominally in control. In the wake of extensive student demonstrations and strikes in May, Chun instituted full martial law and not only ordered extensive arrests both of opposition politicians, but also of figures who had been close to the Park government. The declaration of martial law triggered an insurrection in the southern city of Kwangju; this was bloodily repressed by Army paratroopers, leaving hundreds dead and demonstrating unambiguously Chun's willingness to use any means necessary to reassert military control over the polity.[35]

Upon seizing office, Chun adopted a strongly moralistic stance, promising a "purification" *(jonghwha)* of society that would eliminate the "three negative attitudes" of corruption, lack of civic-mindedness, and inflation.[36] In pursuit of this goal—and the consolidation of his own personal power— Chun disbanded all political parties, purged their leaders, and banned a

---

[33] See Chung-in Moon and Mun-Gu Kang, "Democratic Opening and Military Intervention in South Korea: Comparative Assessment and Implications," in James Cotton, ed., *Korean Politics in Transition* (New York: St. Martins, forthcoming).

[34] See Lee Chong-sik, "South Korea in 1980: The Emergence of a New Authoritarian Order," *Asian Survey* 21 (1981): 125–43.

[35] See Clark, *The Kwangju Uprising.*

[36] *Far Eastern Economic Review,* May 14, 1982, pp. 46–47.

number of influential politicians and activists; new parties were allowed to form, but only with government approval. The government squashed student protests, rounded up labor leaders and put them in "reeducation camps," and undertook a wide-ranging purge of the press that virtually eliminated published criticism of the government.

In the six months between October 1980 and March 1981, Chun organized a referendum on a new constitution and separate presidential and legislative elections. The referendum was held in October 1980. The Constitution was drafted by the martial law leadership and was not subject to meaningful public debate; as we have seen, major opposition figures and student leaders had been held in detention, and the month before the referendum, Kim Dae Jung, the most prominent opposition leader, was sentenced to death for plotting to overthrow the government in connection with the Kwangju uprising.[37] The Constitution gained overwhelming support at the polls, allowing Chun to stand for election to the presidency in February, which he won against token opposition.[38]

The lifting of martial law prior to the presidential election permitted the formation of new political parties. With severe limitations on campaign activities, a political ban on key opposition leaders, and new controls on the press, Chun's Democratic Justice Party (DJP) received 69.4 percent of the votes cast in the March legislative elections. The DJP won 90 seats out of 92 two-member districts, doing surprisingly well in the cities. Chun's control of the legislature was guaranteed by a system of proportional representation that allocated only two-thirds of the assembly seats on the basis of constituency elections, with the remainder allocated on the basis of total votes. This system, and the conciliatory stance initially taken by a weakened opposition, provided the government with a comfortable margin of legislative support. By early 1981, the authoritarian order had been reconsolidated; as in Chile, the democratic moment had passed.

Interpreting the Failed Transition

Through 1980, the Korean political scene appeared to have many of the elements that were conducive to a democratic transition: a growing economic crisis, widespread social mobilization, and a divided military apparatus. Yet the military and allied institutions that formed the core of the

[37] Under pressure from the United States, his sentence was commuted to life imprisonment.

[38] Unlike in the Yushin system, deputies could campaign for specific candidates. New rules stipulated that the president be elected through an electoral college system; opposition to the system of indirect election later became the rallying cry of the opposition.

authoritarian order not only survived the economic and political crises of 1979–80, but quickly reasserted their control. Why?

One explanation concerns the role of the United States.[39] Given Korea's heavy dependence on the United States for its security, a strong U.S. stance against the declaration of martial law might have paved the way for a democratic transition at that time. Partly by default, partly by conscious policy calculation, the United States acquiesced in the declaration of martial law, in the release of troops to repress the Kwangju uprising, and in Chun's rapid evolution from martial law commander to president. While U.S. acquiescence constitutes a permissive condition for Chun's march to power, however, it doesn't explain why the government was able to effectively pursue this repressive option.

Division within the opposition might also be advanced as a cause of the failed transition. In addition to the programmatic differences that divided the opposition in Chile, a major complicating factor in Korea was the personal rivalry between the "two Kims," Kim Dae Jung and Kim Young Sam, over leadership of the opposition. As in Chile, personal and tactical differences hid deeper political, regional, and even class differences. The intensification of violent student protests, large-scale riots by miners and steelworkers in April 1980, and the Kwangju uprising alienated conservative portions of the middle class; 1980 represents a contrast to 1987 in this regard, when massive participation by the middle class in anti-regime demonstrations played an important role in forcing constitutional changes.[40]

In differentiating Korea from the cases discussed in the previous chapter, however, two factors stand out: the position of the private sector and the concentration of authority and cohesion of the military apparatus. The largest companies, or *chaebol,* had been major beneficiaries of Park's political order under the Yushin Constitution. Though smaller businesses faced a credit squeeze as a result of the channeling of financial resources toward heavy industry, and the major business federation voiced concern over particular policies, such as the credit implications of the 1979 stabilization plan, the private sector did not join the opposition in calling for a change of regime. Indeed, it was the democratic movement that threatened to attack the substantial privileges that big business enjoyed under the Yushin system. As the YH incident and the wave of strikes in 1980 demonstrated, the triumph of democracy would inevitably entail a fundamental restructuring of labor relations. This threat was particularly daunting in a country in which the economic strategy relied heavily on exports and the maintenance of international competitiveness.

---

[39] See for example Woo, *Race to the Swift,* pp. 182–91.
[40] For an elaboration of this interpretation, see Choi, "Political Cleavages," pp. 29–32.

The second component of the story resides in institutional features of the military itself. The power struggles in late 1979, both before and after Park's assassination, suggest severe divisions within the security apparatus. With the internal coup in December 1979, however, these conflicts were resolved. With the declaration of full martial law in May 1980, Chun had powers that resembled Pinochet's, with his monopoly on political authority and domination of the army and the security apparatus.

In consolidating his power, Chun was helped by the loyalty of a cohesive faction of younger officers (Hanahoe) who were graduates of the Korean Military Academy.[41] By purging older generals, he gained the ability to promote these allies through the ranks. A second reason for the quick closing of ranks lies with the external security environment. The Korean military has periodically exaggerated external threats for political ends; this was true at the time of the Yushin Constitution, and was true again in 1980 when the intelligence community argued that domestic instability could tempt the North Koreans to adventurism. Whether threats were exaggerated or not, they remained a unifying factor within the armed forces, just as anti-Communism was a powerful ideological force on the Korean right. A plausible external threat also gave the government much greater political leeway in quelling internal protest.

We have argued that military cohesion in Chile increased the survivability of the regime by allowing the government to undertake economic reforms that undercut the social base that the opposition had enjoyed in the early 1970s, while rebuilding new bases of support. Internal cohesion also allowed the military to exploit divisions within the opposition without risk of defection from its own ranks. To what extent did such factors operate in Korea?

Following a brief period of countercyclical policy in its first six months, the Chun government picked up Park's stabilization and adjustment plan and pushed it vigorously. Chun provided full backing to his economic team, even though the political effects of reform were largely negative for the government.[42] Stabilization measures, and particularly credit policies, placed the government and the private sector at loggerheads throughout the first half of the 1980s. Other reform measures, such as the lifting of subsidies to agriculture and controls on government wages, struck at previous sources of regime support.

---

[41] See Moon and Kang, "Democratic Opening and Military Intervention"; Sung-Joo Han, "South Korea: Politics in Transition," in Larry Diamond, Juan L. Linz, and Seymour Martin Lipset, eds., *Democracy in the Developing Countries,* vol. 3: *Asia* (Boulder, Colo.: Lynne Rienner, 1989), p. 282.

[42] See Stephan Haggard and Chung-in Moon, "Institutions and Economic Policy: Theory and a Korean Case Study," *World Politics* 42 (January 1990): 210–37.

Nonetheless, the combination of favorable external conditions, continued high levels of investment, and the reform measures themselves allowed the government to reestablish the country's strong growth record, and with substantially lower inflation. The government's underlying strategy was to persist in the successful export-oriented policies that Park had initiated in the early 1960s; this in itself constituted a powerful constraint on subsequent democratic politics. As in Chile, the military's economic policies created the social base for a conservative, outward-oriented economic strategy.

Military cohesion allowed Chun to count on the military and police apparatus. With the opposition divided, and with business either acquiescent to or fundamentally supportive of the authoritarian project, Chun consolidated and maintained power over the next seven years the old-fashioned way: through the naked use of force.

WITHDRAWAL IN GOOD TIMES

All of the military regimes in our sample faced pressures for political reform at some point, regardless of whether they encountered economic crises or not. In the four countries in which military governments withdrew in good times—Chile, Korea, Turkey, and Thailand—external pressures played a significant role. American diplomacy toward Chile encouraged democratic reform during the late Pinochet years. The Korean government was constrained by the exposure associated with the 1988 Olympics. The Turkish military had to calculate the European Community's response to its intervention. In Thailand, the private sector expressed concern about the effect of the hardline Thanin government on foreign investors. For all of the incumbent regimes, a repressive response to the opposition carried increasing costs in terms of key international objectives.

The role of domestic opposition forces varied across the four cases. Widespread protests were a critical role in the Korean transition, and the growth and maturation of the Chilean opposition increasingly constrained Pinochet's freedom of maneuver; in both of these cases, the absence of institutionalized linkages to civil society made it difficult for authoritarian governments to contain domestic demands for reform. In Thailand, public mobilization for political reform played little role and in Turkey, the pressure on the military was more foreign and self-imposed than domestic, and the government met its own preannounced schedule for withdrawal. A common feature of all four countries, however, is that the legacy of successful adjustment and good economic performance at the time of the transition enhanced the capacity of incumbent governments to exercise control over the transition process (see Table 3.3).

TABLE 3.3
Economic Crisis and Authoritarian Withdrawal: The Non-Crisis Cases

	Chile						
	1985	*1986*	*1987*	*1988*	*1989*	*1990*	*1991*
GDP Growth	2.4	5.7	5.7	7.3	10.0	2.1	6.0
Inflation	30.7	19.5	19.9	14.7	17.0	26.0	21.8
Fiscal Deficit/GDP	−2.1	−1.7	0.3	3.4	6.1	3.6	2.3
Current Account/GDP	−8.8	−7.1	−4.3	−0.8	−3.0	−2.2	0.5
Investment/GDP	13.7	14.6	16.9	17.0	20.3	20.2	18.8
Real Wage	−3.8	1.7	−0.3	6.6	1.9	1.8	na

	Korea					
	1983	*1984*	*1985*	*1986*	*1987*	*1988*
GDP Growth	12.1	9.2	6.9	12.3	11.8	11.4
Inflation	3.4	2.3	2.5	2.8	3.0	7.1
Fiscal Deficit/GDP	−1.0	−1.2	−1.3	−0.1	0.4	1.6
Currrent Account/GDP	−2.0	−1.5	−1.0	4.4	7.5	8.1
Investment/GDP	28.8	29.8	29.3	28.3	29.5	30.6
Real Wage	5.9	9.1	4.8	2.7	13.6	10.6

	Turkey							
	1977	*1978*	*1979*	*1980*	*1981*	*1982*	*1983*	*1984*
GDP Growth	4.8	3.5	−1.1	−0.7	4.2	4.9	3.8	5.9
Inflation	27.1	45.3	58.7	110.2	36.6	30.8	31.4	48.4
Fiscal Deficit/GDP	−5.7	−3.9	−5.5	−3.5	−1.7	na	−4.2	−10.0
Current Account/GDP	−6.6	−2.4	−2.0	−6.0	−3.4	−1.8	−3.8	−2.8
Investment/GDP	25.2	18.7	18.6	21.9	22.0	20.6	19.6	19.5
Real Wage	18.9	3.9	2.9	−16.4	5.1	−5.0	−0.8	−12.0

	Thailand											
	1972	*1973*	*1974*	*1975*	*1976*	*1977*	*1978*	*1979*	*1980*	*1981*	*1982*	*1983*
GDP Growth	4.2	9.8	4.3	4.8	9.3	9.6	10.6	5.0	4.7	6.3	4.0	7.2
Inflation	4.8	15.5	24.3	5.3	4.1	7.6	7.9	9.9	19.7	12.7	5.3	3.7
Fiscal Deficit/GDP	−4.4	−3.5	1.0	−2.1	−4.1	−3.4	−3.8	−3.8	−5.1	−3.5	−6.7	−4.1
Current Acccount/GDP	−0.6	−0.4	−0.7	−4.3	−2.7	−5.7	−4.8	−7.6	−6.4	−7.4	−2.8	−7.3
Investment/GDP	20.7	25.6	24.3	22.1	21.5	21.5	28.2	27.3	26.4	26.3	23.1	25.9
Real Wage	3.7	−3.8	−8.8	1.8	7.6	1.8	9.6	4.2	−15.1	0.1	2.5	6.5

Sources: The World Bank, *World Tables 1993* (Washington, D.C.: The World Bank, 1994); International Monetary Fund, *International Financial Statistics Yearbook,* various issues; Economic Commission on Latin America, *Economic Survey of Latin America and The Caribbean,* various issues.

Note: For definitions of the first four variables, see Table 2.1. Real wages: for Chile, growth of average nonagricultural wages; for Korea, Turkey, and Thailand, growth of real earnings per employee.

The "Delayed" Transitions: Chile and Korea

A major shift in the strategy of the center and left parties played a decisive role in the transition in Chile. By the mid-1980s, the economic and political crisis described in the preceding section had passed, and it had become increasingly evident that Pinochet could not be dislodged either through "extraconstitutional" negotiations or pressure from below. For the opposition parties, this left few alternatives but to attempt to exploit openings for reform provided by Pinochet's 1980 Constitution. The main opportunity was to defeat Pinochet in a 1988 plebiscite intended by the government to ratify a second eight-year term for the president. According to the terms laid out in the Constitution, a "no" vote was to be followed by an opportunity to compete for the presidency in an open election.[43]

Prospects for the success of this strategy initially appeared very limited. After 1985, however, the opposition received assistance from an unlikely quarter. A new U.S. ambassador, appointed by the Reagan administration, provided strong encouragement for the formation of a united opposition front, and exerted substantial pressure on Pinochet and the Chilean military to respect the rules they themselves had established in the 1980 Constitution.[44] After difficult negotiations, the Christian Democrats and most sectors of the left agreed to form a "Coalition for the No," and defeated Pinochet in the 1988 plebiscite. In 1989, the same coalition defeated Finance Minister Hernán Büchi in a race for the presidency with about 60 percent of the vote. The opposition victory transformed the political scene in Chile, and the transfer of the presidency to Patricio Aylwin inaugurated a new phase in Chilean history.

Though defeated, Pinochet nonetheless was able to impose important constraints on the transition process. First, in contrast to the ousted leaders of the regimes discussed in chapter 2, the government retained considerable political support from business and middle-class groups, some of which had benefited directly from the post-1983 reform program. A powerful set of economic actors were linked to the newly emerging export sector and had strong interests in the continuity of the previous policy thrust.

Preferences for gradual political change were evident at the electoral level as well. Büchi, the architect of the reforms of the early 1980s, was able to secure nearly 30 percent of the popular vote in his bid for the presidency, while a second rightist candidate, Francisco Errázuriz, gained an additional 15 percent. The combined total was over ten points higher

---

[43] Manuel Antonio Garreton, "The Political Opposition and the Party System under the Military Regime," in Drake and Jaksic, *The Struggle for Democracy in Chile*, pp. 211–50.

[44] Carlos Portales, "External Factors and the Authoritarian Regime," ibid., 251–75. Arrigada, *Pinochet*, pp. 67–68.

than the share received by the conservative candidate Jorge Alessandri in the last presidential election held in 1970.[45]

This support had important effects on the programmatic orientation of the opposition. Victory in both the plebiscite and the general elections depended heavily on the ability of the opposition to convince both business groups and the middle class that they would not depart significantly from the previous development model. Patricio Aylwin, a center-right Christian Democrat, relied on technical advisers who recommended only incremental changes in the course charted under Büchi. Most of the political left was constrained to back this formula, despite very high levels of unemployment, and increasing inequality and poverty.

The transition in Korea involved more direct confrontations between the government and opposition, and its political dynamics show greater similarities to the crisis-induced cases of political change.[46] In contrast to Chile, where the opposition felt constrained to operate within the authoritarian constitutional order, the 1980 Constitution was an important target of attack in Korea. That constitution provided for an indirect electoral college system that effectively gave Chun the power to name his successor. Revision of the 1980 Constitution to allow direct election of the president and full guarantees of political liberties became a crucial rallying point.

The opposition also sought to capitalize on economic issues. It appealed to those disadvantaged from stabilization and structural adjustment measures and emphasized the government's continuing and corrupt links with big business. The more radical wing of the opposition emphasized that the entire export-led growth strategy had succeeded only at the expense of workers, farmers, and the less developed regions of the country.[47]

The first round in this struggle came during the legislative election campaign of February 1985; as in Chile and the crisis cases, an electoral

---

[45] A poll of six-hundred Santiago residents in 1986 showed a sizeable percentage predisposed to support the regime. Fourteen percent agreed that under some circumstances nondemocracies would be preferable to democracies. Twenty-eight percent preferred no-parties or one party to a multiparty system, 20 percent preferred a rightist government, and 25 percent a centrist one. *Latin America Regional Report: Southern Cone,* RS86-05, 3 July 1986, pp. 4–5.

[46] For reviews and interpretations of the transition, see Manwoo Lee, *The Odyssey of Korean Democracy: Korean Politics 1987–1990* (New York: Praeger, 1990); James Cotton, ed., *Korea under Roh Tae-woo: Democratization, Northern Policy and Inter-Korean Relations* (St. Leonards, Australia: Allen and Unwin in conjunction with the Australian National University, 1993); Sung-joo Han and Yung Chul Park, "South Korea: Democratization at Last," in James Morley, ed., *Driven by Growth: Political Change in the Asia-Pacific Region* (Armonk, N.Y.: M. E. Sharpe, 1993); Bruce Cumings, "The Abortive Abertura: South Korea in the Light of Latin American Experience," *New Left Review,* no. 173 (January–February 1989), pp. 5–32.

[47] For the role of economic issues in the politics of the transition, see Haggard and Moon, "Institutions and Economic Policy: Theory and a Korean Case Study."

opening provided a crucial opportunity for the opposition. Faced with widespread disaffection, the ruling Democratic Justice Party received only 35.3 percent of the vote, and was able to retain its control of the National Assembly only through the advantages provided by gerrymandering and the biased allocation of at-large seats.[48] This was a stunning upset, particularly since the New Korea Democratic Party, the main opposition force, had been formed only immediately prior to the election campaign.

After the elections, the opposition operated in different arenas. Students had the most staunchly anti-government stance, and played a leading role in organizing anti-government protests; they also sought to forge alliances with worker and farmer groups, in part under the umbrella of the churches. In contrast to the past, radical students received increasing support from opposition politicians and sympathy from the general public.

The government vacillated between an accommodating and repressive stance toward these activities, reflecting growing internal divisions over how to respond to the opposition.[49] Negotiations were initiated with opposition politicians over the issue of constitutional revision, but little progress was made in these talks. On April 13, 1987, President Chun "suspended" the debate on the direct election of the president. This decision, however, sparked a wave of nationwide protests. In June, the DJP officially nominated ex-general Roh Tae-Woo as the ruling party's presidential candidate, all but guaranteeing that he would gain the presidency. This sparked a second wave of national protest. Not only did the protests receive international media attention due to the fact that Seoul was hosting the Olympics the following fall, but this time there was extensive participation by the middle class and professionals in Seoul.

At this point, an increasingly divided authoritarian government capitulated under pressure from highly mobilized social groups. In direct response to the protests, Roh made a declaration of political reform on June 29, 1987, that included direct presidential elections and guarantees of political and civil liberties. This directive set the stage for direct presidential elections in December 1987. Roh Tae Woo won when the two main opposition candidates, Kim Dae Jung and Kim Young Sam, failed to reach agreement on a single candidacy; the two opposition candidates won 28 and 27 percent of the popular vote respectively, allowing Roh Tae Woo to win with a 37 percent plurality.

Despite the dramatic events of 1987, however, the Korean transition

[48] See B. C. Koh, "The 1985 Parliamentary Election in South Korea," *Asian Survey* 25 (1985): 883–97.

[49] For an account of the political events leading up to the presidential elections of December 1987, see James W. West and Edward J. Baker, "The 1987 Constitutional Reforms in South Korea: Electoral Processes and Judicial Independence," *Harvard Human Rights Yearbook* 1 (1988): 135–77.

exhibited important continuities with the past. Notwithstanding tensions with the Chun government, the private sector did not defect as it had in the crisis cases and provided tacit support for the government. Middle-class defection to the opposition in 1987 was misinterpreted by elements on the left as opening the door not only to democracy, but to a social democratic or even more radically redistributive politics.[50] In fact, there was broad support from the middle class for the underlying development strategy that the government had pursued in the past, and skepticism toward the economic and social—as opposed to the political—claims of the opposition. Although the opposition parties captured a majority of the popular vote, and constituted a majority in the National Assembly following the legislative elections in the spring, Roh's relatively strong showing reflected the strength of these conservative bases of support, and a fourth candidate, who was closely associated with the politics of the Park Chung Hee era, Kim Jong Pil, secured another 10 percent of the presidential vote. Thus nearly 50 percent of the electorate supported conservative candidates in the presidential contest, and only slightly less in the National Assembly contests. Moreover, despite tensions with the Chun government, the private sector did not defect as it had in the crisis cases, but provided tacit support for the government.

Compared to oppositions in the other non-crisis cases, that in Korea had considerably greater influence in negotiations over reform of the existing electoral system. A complex and lengthy process of bargaining pitted the ruling DJP against the opposition, and continued to divide opposition leaders. The final outcome contained reforms that, contrary to the ruling DJP's initial expectations, contributed to a sharp reduction in the seats it gained in subsequent Congressional elections. Nevertheless, the ruling elite generally retained the upper hand. DJP leaders believed that given the divisions within the opposition, their proposed electoral rules and redistricting provisions would work in their favor. The final resolution was rammed through the National Assembly in a surprise vote at two o'clock in the morning without reaching a final consensus with the opposition negotiators.[51]

[50] For a useful review of the debate about the political role of the middle class, see Dong Won-mo, "The Democratization of South Korea: What Role Does the Middle Class Play," in Cotton, *Korea under Roh Tae-woo,* pp. 74–91.

[51] There is debate about the determinants of the final outcome, a single-member district system that the ruling party initially opposed. Brady and Mo argue the DJP gradually turned to the single-member district model on the assumption that it would divide the opposition, but they miscalculated its actual electoral effects. Cheng and Tallian believe that Roh was pressured to move toward a fairer system by the same forces that had led him to call for political change in his ground-breaking June 29 speech. We find the Brady-Mo argument more compelling, but in either case it is clear that the government had substantial power to impose its preferences and that the formal properties of the electoral system proved less important for the direction of Korean politics than the realignment of the party system that

As in the other non-crisis cases, finally, the institutional framework provided the executive with extensive powers vis-à-vis the legislature. Authority was particularly broad with respect to the formulation of economic policy; the National Assembly could deliberate on the budget bill, but it did not have the power either to increase any particular budget item or to create any new expenditure lines. At a much broader level, the National Security Law gave the government broad powers to arrest and detain anyone accused of forming or participating in "antistate" organizations, and a restrictive law on assembly and demonstrations was not amended until early 1989.

Turkey: "Corrective" Intervention and Exit

In contrast to the cases examined in the last chapter, and like the early bureaucratic-authoritarian regimes of Latin America, the Turkish military government of 1980–83 did not confront a crisis of its own making.[52] Rather, it sought to "correct"—often brutally—the economic and political failings of a weak democratic regime and an increasingly polarized and violent civil society. A number of factors, including strong international pressures and internal military bargains, kept the period of military rule brief. Nonetheless, with substantial support from the World Bank, the IMF, and Western donors, the military pushed dramatic economic reforms that had been impossible under previous civilian governments, and substantially restructured the political system.

Turkey's debt crisis broke in 1977 rather than in the early 1980s, but the symptoms were much the same as in Latin America: an initial foreign exchange crisis; halfhearted efforts to make needed fiscal and exchange-rate adjustments; and a sharp reduction in investment and growth.[53] GNP

---

occurred in late 1989. See David Brady and Jongryn Mo, "Electoral Systems and Institutional Choice: A Case Study of the 1988 Korean Elections," *Comparative Political Studies* 24 (1992): 405–29, and Tun-jen Cheng and Mihae Lim Tallian, "Bargaining Over Electoral Reform in the Republic of Korea: Evaluating Rational Choice Determinants of Political Decision-Making in Democratic Transition," paper prepared for the American Political Science Association Convention, Chicago, September 1992.

[52] For an introduction to the events of the late 1970s, see C. H. Dodd, *The Crisis of Turkish Democracy* (Walkington: Eothen Press, 1983) and George S. Harris, *Turkey: Coping with Crisis* (Boulder: Westview Press, 1985). For contrasting explanations of the period of military rule see John H. McFaden, "Civil-Military Relations in the Third Turkish Republic," *Middle East Journal* 39 (1985): 69–85; Henri J. Barkey, "Why Military Regimes Fail: The Perils of Transition," *Armed Forces and Society* 16 (1990): 169–92; and Feroz Ahmad, "Military Intervention and Crisis in Turkey," *MERIP Reports,* January 1981, pp. 5–24.

[53] The following discussion of the Turkish crisis and the adjustment program of 1980 draws on Merih Celasun and Dani Rodrik, "Debt, Adjustment and Growth: Turkey," in

growth rates fell steadily after 1976, and turned negative in both 1979 and 1980. Inflation jumped sharply, from over 20 percent in 1977 to over 100 percent in 1980, the year of the military coup. Real wages plummeted.

Electoral politics strongly affected efforts to adjust.[54] Ideological parties gained some ground on the extremes of the political spectrum in the 1970s, particularly the ultra-rightist Nationalist Action party. After 1978, armed groups on both the left and right engaged in various forms of social violence: industrial sabotage, armed assaults and bank robberies, assassinations, and kidnappings. The majority of voters continued to hew to the two major centrist parties, the center-left Republican People's Party (RPP) and the center-right Justice Party (JP); indeed, since 1950, with the exception of Ecevit's election in 1973, Turks have consistently cast more than 50 percent of their votes for parties on the right. But the system became increasingly polarized, as both centrist parties portrayed their opponents as beholden to extremists, while themselves simultaneously courting radical support. On the right in particular, this violence involved collusion with and participation by police and military forces.

In the short-lived governments of the 1970s, no party was capable of forming a government on its own. Key portfolios were therefore in the hands of minority parties, which wielded disproportionate influence on decision-making.[55] Elections were followed by extensive purges of the bureaucracy, not only at the top but in the middle and even the lower ranks of the civil service. Parties effectively "colonized" portions of the bureaucracy, including the police, to their own ends. Until the center-right Demirel government took office in late 1979, successive governments delayed serious adjustment efforts.

Political disaffection with the crisis gave the JP a strong victory at the polls in October 1979, though not an absolute parliamentary majority. By this time, however, civilian politicians were also under pressure from the military, which submitted an ultimatum in late December outlining actions, including economic ones, expected of the new government. On January 24, 1980, the new government announced a sweeping adjustment program that

---

Jeffrey D. Sachs and Susan Collins, eds., *Developing Country Debt and Economic Performance,* vol. 3. (Chicago: University of Chicago Press, 1989), pp. 615–808; and Tosun Arícanlí and Dani Rodrik, eds., *The Political Economy of Turkey: Debt, Adjustment and Sustainability* (London: Macmillan, 1990).

[54] On the political economy of adjustment, see Ziya Öniş and Steven B. Webb, "Turkey: Democratization and Adjustment from Above," in Stephan Haggard and Steven B. Webb, eds., *Voting for Reform: Democracy, Political Liberalization, and Economic Adjustment* (New York: Oxford University Press, 1994), pp. 128–85. On the political deterioration of the late 1970s, see Ergun Özbudun, "Turkey: Crises, Interruptions, and Reequilibrations," in Diamond, Linz, and Lipset, *Democracy in Developing Countries,* vol. 3: *Asia,* pp. 203–7.

[55] This is a theme of Robert Bianchi, *Interest Groups and Political Development in Turkey* (Princeton, N.J.: Princeton University Press, 1984).

included not only typical fiscal and monetary measures, but a maxidevaluation, a liberalization of state-owned enterprise prices, and the freeing of interest rates.

The same economic factors that we have outlined as contributing to the collapse of authoritarian regimes also weakened Turkish democracy. Before 1979, the link between economic crisis and social violence was indirect. Ideological conflicts, intercommunal violence, and the rise in the influence of Islamic fundamentalist forces all predated the crisis. The downturn clearly exacerbated these cleavages, however, and new ones emerged after the announcement of the 1980 adjustment package. The left-wing labor organization (the Confederation of Progressive Trade Unions, or DISK in its Turkish acronym) became more militant, and economic elites were increasingly public in their complaints about the collapse of public order.[56] Moreover, these events unfolded against a backdrop of virtual paralysis within the Demirel government itself, precisely the kind of internal divisions that were to prove deadly for authoritarian governments facing crisis. On September 12, 1980, the military seized power.

As in Chile and Korea, the Turkish military remained relatively cohesive throughout its stay in power. Though the military had in the past been divided between "Nasserist" factions that favored more extensive intervention in the polity and a more moderate wing, the manifest nature of the crisis muted these differences in 1980; as Semih Vaner argues, "in contrast to the situation in 1971 and especially 1960 when various tendencies within the army surfaced openly, it was *the* 'military party' that imposed itself after 1980. . . ."[57] The military, which immediately announced that it did not intend a prolonged stay, united around three central objectives: eliminating "extremist" groups; implementing the economic reforms launched under the Demirel government; and restructuring the political system through a new constitution.

The attack on those of suspicious political loyalties, particularly on the left, was wide-ranging. In the first fifteen days following the coup, all major political leaders were arrested, including many members of parliament, elected municipal administrations were disbanded and taken over by the military, all societal organizations were suspended, and in many cases, their

---

[56] The country witnessed armed clashes between the DISK and the military in February, a general strike in the summer, and explicit efforts by Ecevit to mobilize labor discontent as part of a strategy of ousting the government. Even before 1980, a number of busines leaders had protested union demands and the growing power of the DISK, made calls for the installation of "powerful" governments, and linked economic performance with stricter security meaures, including the establishment of State Security Courts to handle anti-government crimes. For a leftist interpretation of the coup that provides useful chronology see Info-Turk, *Black Book on the Militarist "Democracy" in Turkey* (Brussels: Info-Turk, 1986).

[57] Semih Vaner, "The Army," in Irvin C. Schick and Ertuğrul Ahmet Tonak, *Turkey in Transition: New Perspectives* (New York: Oxford University Press, 1987), p. 242.

leaders arrested, and the press and civil service subjected to an extensive purge. All trade union leaders and about 2,000 union officials were arrested and the DISK effectively closed. In regions where armed resistance posed a challenge, particularly in Kurdish areas, the government initiated wide military sweeps. By one estimate, the military arrested nearly 65,000 people between September 1980 and early 1984.[58]

On the economic front, the military government committed itself to implement the program that the Demirel government had announced in 1980, including aggressive exchange-rate management, the freeing of state-owned enterprise prices, stabilization, and financial market liberalization. There were derogations from the original design, as well as somewhat novel features to the military's economic thinking. Though real wages were dramatically compressed, the government also passed legislation that prohibited layoffs, and in the last eighteen months prior to the elections of 1983, budget deficits increased and the exchange rate once again became overvalued.[59] Nonetheless, it was difficult to argue with the program's success in both generating exports and securing foreign assistance, and the basic thrust of the adjustment program was sustained.

The third component of the military project was the restructuring of the polity. The key to this restructuring was to rewrite the Constitution of 1961, which the military viewed as a major source of the political polarization of the late 1970s. The new Constitution enhanced the power of the presidency, established structures (particularly a National Security Council) that provided for a continued military role in politics, and replaced a bicameral Parliament with a unicameral one.[60] Moreover, the Constitution contained provisions that limited the formation of linkages between interest groups (particularly unions) and political parties.[61] A specific objective of the Constitution, the electoral and political party laws, and other restrictive rules was to purge the system of previous political leaders and to push the country toward a two-party system. This was done both directly and indirectly. In addition to banning a number of politicians from participating in politics, the military exercised a veto over the formation of new parties prior to the elections of November 1983: only three of seventeen proposed parties were allowed to form. Moreover, the new electoral laws contained

---

[58] See Info-Turk, *Black Book,* p. 170, for various estimates of arrests and incarcerations from both the Turkish and foreign press.

[59] Following the "bankers' crisis" of June 1982, when the country's largest money broker and securities house collapsed, Özal was forced to resign, leading to the formation of a new government with a more traditional etatist orientation.

[60] See Özbudun, "Turkey: Crises, Interruptions and Reequilibrations," pp. 207–10.

[61] See Ergun Özbudun, "The Post-1980 Legal Framework for Interest Group Associations," in Metin Heper, ed., *Strong State and Economic Interest Groups: the Post-1980 Turkish Experience* (Berlin: Walter de Gruyter, 1991), pp. 41–54.

very high threshold provisions that disadvantaged small parties, requiring a party to obtain 10 percent of the national vote to seat a single representative.

The escalating social violence of the late 1970s, the support of the private sector, and the infusion of resources from the World Bank and the IMF constituted peculiar features of the Turkish case that gave the military additional degrees of freedom in carrying out its project. Yet we also see important similarities with Korea and Chile. The combination of a relatively unified military, a successful economic adjustment effort, and sharply improved economic conditions, including a rapid resumption of growth, decline in inflation, and dramatic growth in exports, allowed the Turkish military to control the terms of their voluntary exit, which came in 1983 as scheduled.

The 1983 transitional elections resulted in embarrassing defeat for the military-sponsored party.[62] Yet the military had altered the political and social system to a considerable extent, and had garnered support in doing so.[63] Turgut Özal, the winner in the 1983 election, was the market-oriented economic czar who had pieced together the 1980 reform package for the Demirel government and had continued to serve during the first two years of military rule before being replaced in 1982. Özal was not the military's favorite; indeed, he gained from being the one civilian candidate allowed to form a new party. However, Özal was clearly acceptable to the military, and ran on a platform that included strong and unambiguous support for the economic reforms initiated in 1980; he explicitly courted private-sector forces, such as exporters, who had gained under the new order.

As we will show in chapter 7, Özal faced a variety of difficulties in implementing this program and maintaining macroeconomic stability over the 1980s. Nonetheless, new bases of support emerged for sustaining a more outward-oriented development strategy, and the underlying structural change in the party system had its intended effect of moderating political conflict when compared with the 1970s. Not until the late 1980s did populist pressures resurface.

Thailand: Limited Democratization

Thailand's transition to democracy has been a halting and partial one, spread out over nearly two decades and arguably longer.[64] A democratic opening in 1973 lasted three years before the reassertion of harsh military-

[62] Barkey, "Why Military Regimes Fail: The Perils of Transition," pp. 169–92.

[63] The plebiscite on the new Constitution received overwhelming support; 91 percent of voters approved. However, this vote can also be interpreted as support for the military leaving office.

[64] An earlier transition point arguably came in 1932 with the overthrow of the absolute monarchy. We focus here on changes since the coups of 1957–58 that initiated the most

backed government in 1976. A brief period of reactionary rule ended in less than a year when an internal coup brought military liberalizers to the fore. Since the late 1970s, political developments in Thailand have been more gradual, underscoring the crucial distinction that must be drawn between a process of political liberalization and a transition to fully democratic politics. The political opening that began in 1977 had established a relatively liberal regime by 1983, though one in which the military continued to play a prominent role in politics. The military overthrew this limited democracy in 1991. Though the coup marked one of the few authoritarian reversals in the broader trend toward democratization, the military was forced to return power relatively quickly to a new civilian administration. However, it remained unclear as of this writing that the role of the military in Thai politics had been fundamentally reduced.

Why was Thailand's transition so limited? The answers can be found both in the nature of Thailand's political institutions and in economic circumstances. Post-1958 Thai authoritarianism stood on three pillars: the monarchy, the military, and the civil service. These three pivotal groups shared common assumptions about the nature of the political order and have generally been able to resolve their disputes in ways that retain the power and integrity of each. Though the military appears to have been quite factionalized, there were also important points of consensus across factions, including anticommunism and the desirability of continued military dominance.[65] Thus despite factionalism within the military, Thailand bears comparison with the other non-crisis cases in possessing a relatively cohesive political elite.

Good economic performance also has had something to do with Thailand's "semidemocratic" outcome, however.[66] Thailand did borrow heavily in the late 1970s and experienced difficulties around the first and second oil crises; it is not coincidental that political changes coincided with these economic difficulties. In contrast to the crisis cases, however, changes of government did not fundamentally disrupt the economic bureaucracy's control over a number of key policy parameters.[67] Over the long run, the government maintained a realistic exchange rate backed by a high level of

---

recent period of sustained military involvement in politics. For an overview of Thai politics over the longer run, see Chai-Anan Samudavanija, "Thailand: A Stable Semi-Democracy," in Diamond, Linz, and Lipset, *Democracy in Developing Countries,* vol. 3: *Asia,* pp. 305–46.

[65] Chai-Anan Samudavanija and Sukhumbhand Paribatra, "Thailand: Liberalization without Democracy," in Morley, *Driven by Growth,* pp. 126–28.

[66] For excellent reviews of the political economy of Thailand's rapid growth, see Richard F. Doner and Anek Laothamatas, "Thailand: Economic and Political Gradualism," in Haggard and Webb, *Voting for Reform,* pp. 411–53; and Scott R. Christensen, Ammar Siamwalla, and Pakorn Vichyanond, "Institutional and Political Bases of Growth-Inducing Policies in Thailand," paper prepared for the World Bank project on the East Asian Development Experience: Legacies and Lessons, Thailand Development Research Institute, September 1992.

[67] One examination of continuity of institutions is Sylvia Maxfield and Patcharee Siroros,

international reserves, a stabilizing fiscal and monetary stance that has avoided policy-induced inflation, and a trade, foreign investment, and industrial policy that contributed to rapid export growth. During the two oil shocks, price increases were concentrated almost exclusively in traded goods and in both cases monetary authorities responded quickly, inflation fell, and growth resumed. Over the 1970s and 1980s, the country had among the highest growth rates in the developing world, coupled with relatively stable prices.

As a result of this record, the Thai political elite did not face the defection of private-sector elites; to the contrary, as in the other non-crisis cases, authoritarian leaders maintained substantial support from increasingly powerful private-sector allies; during the 1980s there were efforts to institutionalize this support both through corporatist ties with big business and through deeper military involvement in political parties.[68] Nor did the military face the widespread economic disaffection and associated mass movements that contributed to severe internal divisions and regime collapse in the crisis cases. Even when purely political grievances spilled over into substantial urban protest, these were counterbalanced by surprising reservoirs of loyalty, manifest in the support for military-backed political parties throughout the 1980s and into the 1990s.

These institutional, economic, and social constraints on political change can be seen by tracing the process of political liberalization from the early 1970s. The period began with a democratic opening from 1973 to 1976. Unlike the more limited political reforms of subsequent decades, this was a fairly substantial, if temporary, political change, and it occurred in what might be called in the Thai context an economic crisis. Though the worldwide commodity boom of the early 1970s benefited sugar and rice exporters, staple prices in the cities increased and real wage growth slowed. These economic difficulties were mild by international standards, but strikes proliferated and inflation was blamed on the speculative activities of the military-business complex.

Mass political protests were led by a rapidly growing student movement which in 1973 launched a campaign for a new constitution and an elected parliament.[69] In October of that year, following the arrests of a number of student leaders, protests spilled out of the university into the streets and

---

"The Politics of Central Banking in Thailand," paper prepared for the Annual Meeting of the Association of Asian Studies, Washington D.C., April 2–5, 1991.

[68] Kevin Hewison has traced the political rise of the private sector in *Bankers and Bureaucrats: Capital and the Role of the State in Thailand* (New Haven, Conn.: Yale University Southeast Asia Monograph No. 34, 1989) and *Politics and Power in Thailand* (Manila: Journal of Contemporary Asia Press, 1989). Anek Laothamatas focuses on the institutional aspects of business power in *Business Associations and the New Political Economy of Thailand* (Boulder, Colo.: Westview Press, 1992).

[69] On the events of October, see Ruth-Inge Heinze, "Ten Days in October: Students vs. the Military," *Asian Survey* 14 (1974): 491–508.

were joined by a wide cross-section of Bangkok society. On October 14, a massive demonstration of over 400,000 people led to clashes with the police and the deaths of nearly eighty protesters.

The events of October occurred against the backdrop of a growing split within the government and army leadership.[70] A coup led by Narong Kittachorn in November 1971 had resulted in the concentration of power in the hands of a single faction, and aroused disaffection inside the military. After the protests of 1973, concern about the government's ability to maintain stability led the monarchy to take a stand against the violence, requesting that the core members of the dominant Narong clique leave the country. With the military increasingly divided, further repression had become untenable.

From 1973 to 1976, Thai politics was more democratic than in any prior time in the country's history.[71] The lifting of restrictions on political contestation paralleled those in the other crisis transitions, and as we shall see, differed substantially from the far more controlled political reforms instituted in the 1980s and 1990s. The political turbulence of these democratic years, however, also provided the basis for a regrouping of conservative political forces. The prelude to military intervention was similar to that in Turkey and the Latin American cases: increasing social and political mobilization, including demonstrations, strikes, and increasing left-right violence; and a weak, fragmented, and ineffectual parliament. The 1976 election showed a sharp swing away from the distributive politics of 1974–75 back to the right; leftist parties did extremely poorly, and themes of law and order played prominently in the campaign. But the triggering event, as in 1973, involved students. Government police and military forces intervened to quell demonstrations at Thammasat University, and were joined by mobilized right-wing groups who assaulted and killed a number of students. On October 6, the military intervened in the name of order.

The new authoritarian regime was particularly repressive in comparison to other periods of military rule in Thailand. The military declared martial law under a new National Administrative Reform Council, and abolished the democratic Constitution of 1974, Parliament, and all political parties. The appointment of an anticommunist judge, Thanin Kraivichien, as prime minister opened a period of intensely reactionary government: widespread arrest of students and repressive educational "reforms," indoctrination of civil servants, new restrictions on labor activity, censorship, and a rigidly

---

[70] See Samudavanija, "Thailand," pp. 312–13.

[71] For differing views of the collapse of democracy, see Robert F. Zimmerman, *Reflections on the Collapse of Democracy in Thailand* (Singapore: Institute of Southeast Asian Studies, 1978), and Benedict Anderson, "Withdrawal Symptoms: Social and Cultural Aspects of the October 6 Coup," *Bulletin of Concerned Asian Scholars* 9 (1977): 13–30.

anticommunist foreign policy. Moreover, the new government envisioned an extremely long plan for "political development," transferring authority back to civilians only after a twelve- to eighteen-year transition.

Important political forces in both the private sector and the military quickly developed concerns that the Thanin government's hardline tactics were having exactly the opposite effect to that intended: polarizing the country and strengthening the hand of the Communist Party and the lingering rural insurgency. Among these forces was a pivotal group of "Young Turks" at the colonel level within the military which had a broad conception of national security similar to that seen in the bureaucratic-authoritarian governments in Latin America. They had become politically active after 1973, had supported the overthrow of democracy in 1976, and held important political as well as military positions in the new government.[72]

A coup within the military in October 1977 initiated a period of controlled political liberalization. The government adopted a more liberal stance toward the opposition, offering amnesty to students and those who had joined the insurgency. More importantly, military leaders began to forge links with political leaders and the Bangkok-based private sector.[73] The coup leaders replaced the 1977 Constitution with a more liberal one that allowed for a bicameral legislature with an elected lower house. Elections were held in 1979, 1983, 1986, and 1988, an uninterrupted series that was unprecedented in Thai history.

Yet if portions of the military and its private-sector allies showed an interest in liberalizing politics, they had no interest in returning to the freewheeling politics of 1974–76. In the first phase of political liberalization through 1983, transitional provisions of the Constitution guaranteed the military a strong hand.[74] The prime minister (and members of the Cabinet) did not need to come from the elected members of the lower house; Prem held office by virtue of his military, rather than electoral, standing. As in past military regimes, the upper house was appointed by the prime minister and had the right to vote along with the lower house on important issues, guaranteeing the prime minister a winning coalition.

The elections of 1983 marked a further step toward political reform. According to the Constitution, the expiration of the transitional provisions would mean that active-duty military officers and bureaucrats could no longer hold Cabinet posts and the Senate would become an advisory body.[75]

---

[72] See Chai-Anan Samudavanija, *The Thai Young Turks* (Singapore: Institute of Southeast Asian Studies, 1982).

[73] See Laothamatas, *Business Associations,* pp. 80–82.

[74] On the politics and substance of the new Constitution, see Ansil Ramsay, "Thailand 1978: Kriangsak—the Thai Who Binds," *Asian Survey* 19 (1979): 110–12.

[75] A number of steps were also taken to attempt to strengthen the party system. In the

With support from several parties, the military launched a campaign to make the transitional provisions permanent. This was beaten back astutely by Prem, however, who emerged as an honest broker between the parties and the military; he was to continue as Prime Minister until 1988. Unlike previous military leaders, Prem drew on support from the parties and the rapidly growing private sector to expand the political sphere. But he also successfully defended the prerogatives of the military and the economic bureaucracy.

The parliamentary elections of 1988 marked the third stage in the move toward genuine parliamentary rule. Though the new prime minister, Chatichai Choonhavan, was a retired general, he was the first elected leader to head a government since 1976. As we will argue in more detail in chapter 7, economic policymaking and corruption were one stated element in the military's growing disaffection. By far the most important issue, however, was the perceived attacks on the prerogatives of the military. These ranged from an amendment to the Constitution that would have weakened the military-dominated Senate, to the formation of a new foreign policy toward Indochina, to closer scrutiny of the military budget. These political intrusions combined to unleash a power struggle among military factions aligned with and against Chatichai.[76] On February 23, 1991, the military intervened, and with explicit support from important factions of the Bangkok business sector once again closed down the democratic experiment.

As of this writing, it is still too early to fully assess the consequences of the 1991 coup.[77] The new military government clearly overplayed its hand in seeking to impose a more restrictive constitution on the country in 1991. A bloody effort to repress the opposition failed, and the government was forced to make constitutional compromises and call elections in 1992, bringing a coalition government to office that was dominated by the democratic opposition.[78] On the other hand, parties aligned with the military did surprisingly well in those elections and the new political order may represent less of a break with the past than many hoped. Thus it is certainly premature to say that the military has been purged from politics.

1978 Constitution, political parties were required to contest not less than half the seats of the lower house, a provision designed to eliminate individual-based parties. To enhance discipline the Constitution stated that if party members were ejected from their party, they would lose their seats.

A 1981 party law established further regulations for party registration aimed at excluding small parties, including a requirement for five-thousand members with residences in five provinces in each of the four regions of the country.

[76] See Scott Christensen, "Thailand After the Coup," *Journal of Democracy* 2 (1991) 99–100.

[77] A preliminary assessment that puts the issue in a longer historical context is Clark D. Neher, "Political Succession in Thailand," *Asian Survey* 32 (1992): 585–605.

[78] See Daniel E. King, "The Thai Parliamentary Elections of 1992," ibid., pp. 1109–23.

Regardless of future events, we can discern a clear pattern in the two democratic cycles we have reviewed here that are broadly consonant with the non-crisis pattern. Political liberalization and gradual democratization left the independence of the military and bureaucracy intact in many important respects. When political opening threatened social unrest, was at odds with the interests of the increasingly powerful Bangkok-based private sector, or—most importantly—challenged the prerogatives of the military, politics was checked by military intervention. Many traditional and even cultural factors no doubt play into this semidemocratic equilibrium, and it is quite possible that longer-term secular changes such as the growth of the middle class will ultimately destabilize it;[79] the widespread middle-class revulsion against the military's brutal crackdown on anti-regime protest in May 1992 bears some resemblance to the events in Korea in the summer of 1987. But one critical factor has been the ability of successive governments to guarantee relatively robust economic performance, thus maintaining the allegiance of both the military and important segments of the private sector, while forestalling opportunities for wider political mobilization. It is in this crucial regard that the Thai case is comparable to the other non-crisis transitions.

CONCLUSION: AUTHORITARIAN RULE AND THE CREATION OF SOCIAL FACTS

One finding to emerge from the comparison of the crisis and non-crisis cases concerns the effect of economic performance on the power of government and opposition during the transition process. In the crisis cases, the "authoritarian bargain" with the private sector became unglued. Whether the government had attempted a liberalizing project, as in Uruguay and Argentina, or a statist development model based on import substitution, as in Brazil and Peru, economic crisis triggered substantial division and uncertainty within the private sector over the direction of economic policy. As crises deepened, uncertainty over economic policy spilled over into a more general loss of confidence not only in the government's development model, but in the utility of authoritarian rule. The crisis transitions were thus characterized by a disintegration of the core basis of support for the regime.

The transitions that occurred in good times were characterized by altogether different socioeconomic and political alignments. In contrast to the crisis cases, authoritarian governments had launched policy reforms that

---

[79] This expectation is voiced cautiously in Samudavanija and Paribatra, "Thailand: Liberalization without Democracy," p. 141.

had changed the incentives facing the private sector and reoriented its activities, particularly with respect to exports. Important segments of the private sector remained strongly favorable to the underlying economic (and even political) model of the military government, and thus formed a powerful and conservative constituency for continuity. In the following chapter, we explore the implications of these two transition paths for the nature of political institutions.

CHAPTER FOUR

Comparing Authoritarian Withdrawals

IF ECONOMIC conditions affect the balance of power between authoritarian governments and their opponents, they should also influence the conditions under which leaders relinquish office, or what we call the "terms of transition." The terms of transition encompass at least two distinct components. The first is the nature of civil-military relations, including the political, institutional, and budget prerogatives of the military. We pay particular attention to civil-military relations because they are a telling indicator of the capacity of authoritarian governments to constrain the new democratic order. The second component of the terms of transition is the political understandings and constitutional rules that structure political competition and decision-making, including the electoral rules and division of powers within the government.

It is misleading to attribute too much durability to the terms established at the time of the transition. Even in cases where the exit of the authoritarian government is explicitly negotiated, bargains or pacts are subject to renegotiation and modification as the balance of political forces shifts. Moreover, other factors besides the economic and institutional ones that we outline can also influence the ability of authoritarian elites to exercise influence in the new democratic setting. In particular, the presence of armed insurgencies in the Philippines, Thailand, Peru, and Turkey, and of a virulent drug trade in Bolivia, complicate judgments about the effect of the transition on the power of the military.

Nonetheless, we argue that the capacity of outgoing rulers to shape the institutional and political landscape depends on underlying economic conditions and the extent to which authoritarian governments either avoided, or adjusted to, economic crises. We begin with a comparative analysis of military prerogatives and their implications for civil-military relations. In the last two sections, we examine the rules governing political contestation, with particular attention paid to the reconstitution of the party system.

MILITARY PREROGATIVES

A central issue in all democratic transitions is the fate both of the military as an institution and of individual officers. In most transitions, civil-military relations remained fluid well after authoritarian governments had relinquished power. Nevertheless, important cross-national variations appear to be associated with whether the transition occurred in crisis circumstances or not. In the crisis cases, the combination of economic difficulties and loss of support left the military more vulnerable to civilian efforts to reduce their autonomy and influence. In the non-crisis cases, the military was better positioned to defend institutional and political prerogatives and to secure particular guarantees.[1]

The implications of these differences for the stability of democratic rule were complex. In the crisis cases—where civilians appeared to hold the upper hand—we find frequent instances of military backlash against budget reductions, inquiries into past human-rights violations, or other forms of civilian "intrusion" into military affairs. Civil-military tensions over such issues subsequently posed serious threats to the security of democratic governments in Argentina, the Philippines, Bolivia, and Uruguay. In most of the non-crisis cases, by contrast, the capacity of the military to protect its institutional prerogatives reduced the immediate threat of military rebellion, although Thailand is an exception that deserves closer scrutiny.

It is clear, however, that the decisions made about civil-military relations at the time of the transition conditioned subsequent efforts to reassert civilian control. We contrast the crisis and non-crisis cases with respect to two interrelated aspects of military prerogatives: the capacity of the armed forces command to defend their control over decisions related to their internal organization, such as the budget, appointments and personnel, and definition of mission; and the role of the military in the broader political process.

The Non-crisis Cases

Notwithstanding significant cross-national differences, the armed forces in the non-crisis cases generally maintained considerable autonomy vis-à-vis civilian authorities. Ironically, the greater security for the armed forces during the initial years of the transition probably *reduced* the threat to civilian authority in Chile, Turkey, and Korea. In all four non-crisis cases, however, the presence of independent and unreformed military establishments underlined the partial and conditional nature of the transition, and posed potential problems for democratic stability over the long run.

The power of the military was most evident in Thailand, the country in which the transition was most prolonged and in which the final outcome is the most difficult to characterize. The scope of electoral politics in-

---

[1] David Pion-Berlin has advanced a similar argument, "Military Autonomy and Emerging Democracies in Latin America," *Comparative Politics* 25 (1992): 83–103.

creased significantly after 1983 and again between 1988 and the coup of 1991. Yet even in those more democratic years, the military establishment remained an influential actor on the political scene.[2] Prem was a military man, and if he had the support of party politicians, it was because of his capacity to appease the military. Unlike Prem, Chatichai was elected, but partly for that reason he was viewed with greater suspicion by certain military factions.

Institutionally, officers continued to dominate the appointed Senate, even after the revision in 1983 of the controversial "temporary provisions" that gave the Senate effective veto over the decisions of the House of Representatives. Thailand was the only one of the non-crisis cases where political authorities faced coup attempts. The first two, in 1981 and 1985, proved unsuccessful. The third, in 1991, ousted the Chatichai government. Though the military cited increasing corruption as the reason for their intervention, the precipitating events were a series of steps that appeared to encroach on the autonomy of the military.[3] These included an expansion of the powers of the lower house vis-à-vis the military-dominated Senate, the independent formulation of a new foreign policy toward Indochina, and closer ministerial and parliamentary scrutiny of military appointments and budget.

High levels of internal military autonomy reinforced and augmented its broader political role. During the 1980s, newly formed corporate bodies such as the Internal Operation Security Command (ISOC) centralized all counterinsurgency operations in the hands of the army chief of staff and operated beyond the control of political officials. A National Defense Volunteers organization under the ISOC attempted to organize rural areas in a combined political-military effort to counter the Communists in the countryside, with quite obvious political effects. The army also increased its involvement in peacekeeping in Bangkok through the creation of a Capital Security Command that was assigned a wide range of police functions. Even after 1988, when General Chatichai became the first elected prime minister since 1976, he was forced to expand the internal prerogatives of the military with respect to senior appointments in an effort to maintain the loyalty of his chief military rival, General Chaovalit.

[2] The following draws on Chai-Anan Samudavanija, *The Thai Young Turks* (Singapore: Institute of Southeast Asian Studies, 1982); Suchit Bungbankorn, *The Military in Thai Politics, 1981–86* (Singapore: Institute of Southeast Asian Studies, 1987); Chai-Anan Samudavanija and Sukhumbhand Paribatra, "Thailand: Liberalization without Democracy," in James Morley, ed., *Driven by Growth: Political Change in the Asia-Pacific Region* (Armonk, N.Y.: M. E. Sharpe, 1993), pp. 128–34.

[3] See Scott Christensen, "Thailand after the Coup," *Journal of Democracy* 2 (1991): 99–100, and Kevin Hewison, "Of Regimes, State and Pluralities: Thai Politics Enters the 1990s," in Kevin Hewison, Richard Robison, and Garry Rodan, eds., *Southeast Asia in the 1990s* (Sydney: Allen and Unwin, 1993), pp. 164–67.

After the 1991 coup, the military drafted a constitution that greatly expanded their prerogatives, for example, by increasing the powers of the appointed Senate and allowing civil servants and military officers to join the Cabinet without resigning their positions.[4] Though it was forced by public protests to make compromises on these issues and elections, the military simultaneously forged new alliances with the parties; we return to this issue below.

Transitions were more definitive in the other non-crisis cases, but military powers nevertheless remained extensive.[5] In Chile, the military command extracted major concessions with respect to its autonomy and authority. Pinochet himself remained at the helm of the armed forces, and other top officers retained their positions. Under Pinochet's command, the army also maintained extensive control over its own budget; by law, the armed forces were entitled to 10 percent of all revenues from exports of the state copper corporation, CODELCO. A National Commission on Truth and Reconciliation established by the Alwyin government did compile a detailed report on political executions and disappearances under the military, but officers were shielded from reprisals by an encompassing amnesty law accepted by the new government.[6]

The terms of transition also provided the military establishment with leverage over the post-transition constitutional order. As we discuss in more detail below, the design of the electoral system and the judiciary favored Pinochet's political allies. But a number of institutional features of the new democratic order provided avenues for the more direct exercise of military influence. These included representation for Pinochet and his appointees on the National Security Council, and continuing military control over the powerful National Intelligence Command (the CNI). Though Pinochet and other top officers did not overtly threaten the tenure of the Aylwin government, they did continuously test the limits of civilian authority in a series

---

[4] See Clark D. Neher, "Political Succession in Thailand," *Asian Survey* 32 (1992): 598–99.

[5] See Genaro Arriagada Herrera and Carol Graham, "Chile: Sustaining Adjustment during Democratic Transition," in Stephan Haggard and Steven B. Webb, eds., *Voting For Reform: Democracy, Political Liberalization, and Economic Adjustment* (New York: Oxford University Press, 1994), pp. 242–90.

[6] Pinochet's commitment to maintaining military autonomy is well summarized in a speech given on August 23, 1989: "The political powers should refrain from undue intervention in the definition and application of defense policies, particularly in matters that fall under the exclusive professional responsibility of the armed forces such as . . . the command structure and internal organization of each institution . . . , the system for acceptance, promotion and retirement of personnel, the planning of war contingencies, and the elaboration of logistical policies. Furthermore, the armed forces have the right to decide on their needs and budget requirements, and on the jurisdiction of military tribunals as established in the present Constitution." Cited in The Washington Office on Latin America, "Chile's Transition to Democracy," mimeo, November 27, 1989, pp. 15–16.

of smaller and scandalous actions involving financial mismanagement, intrigues within the rightist political parties, and international arms transactions undertaken without civilian authorization.[7]

Arrangements imposed in Turkey paralleled those in Chile.[8] The office of president was initially held by the outgoing military leader, and its formal constitutional powers increased to include the right to dissolve the assembly and to declare a state of emergency. The president controlled appointments to the senior judiciary, the Central Bank, and the state-owned broadcasting organizations. As in Chile, the creation of a National Security Council in the 1982 Constitution, as well as a transitional Presidential Council, provided additional entry points for the military not only on security matters, but on broader political issues as well.

These prerogatives did not go unchallenged after the establishment of a civilian government. In 1987, Özal openly confronted the military by refusing to accept its nomination to the position of chief of staff.[9] The legislative opposition also became increasingly active in calling for investigations of military abuses and corruption. Nonetheless, there were distinct limits on civilian oversight of the military. Martial law remained in place in parts of the southeast where the government became embroiled in an escalating conflict with Kurdish separatists, and to this day, abuses by the military remain a leitmotif of the international human-rights community's scrutiny of the country.[10]

In Korea, the position of the military appears to have been weaker than in Chile and Turkey.[11] Incoming president Roh Tae Woo publicly denounced military intervention in politics, acted in several well-publicized cases to challenge the immunity from prosecution that military officers previously enjoyed, and purged his Cabinet and the upper ranks of the military of a number of hardline officers. On the other hand, Roh Tae Woo was himself a military man and posed no threat to the institutional interests of the armed forces. Through personal connections, appointments, and the Hanahoe officer association initially founded by Chun, Roh maintained the networks that bound the nominally civilian leadership to the army.

[7] See David Pion-Berlin, "Crafting Allegiance: Civilian Control and the Armed Forces in Uruguay, Argentina, and Chile," unpublished ms, pp. 16–21.

[8] For descriptions of the constitutional changes, see John H. McFadden, "Civil-Military Relations in the Third Turkish Republic," *Middle East Journal* 39 (1985): 69–85; Henri J. Barkey, "Why Military Regimes Fail: the Perils of Transition," *Armed Forces and Society* 16 (1990): 169–92.

[9] Barkey, "Why Military Regimes Fail," pp. 180–87.

[10] See for example, "Star of Islam: a Survey of Turkey," *The Economist,* December 14, 1991, p. 9.

[11] See Chung-in Moon and Mun-Gu Kang, "Democratic Opening and Military Intervention in South Korea: Comparative Assessment and Implications," in James Cotton, ed., *Korean Politics in Transition* (New York: St. Martins, forthcoming).

In important ways, Roh also maintained the internal autonomy of the army's political apparatus.[12] The terms of the transition placed no new legal limits on the Agency for National Security Planning (NSP), the successor to the Korean Central Intelligence Agency, which had a long history of domestic surveillance and intervention in politics. The government was also slow in revising the draconian National Security Law, which was used liberally in the offensive against dissidents and labor that began in 1989.[13] Throughout Roh's term, incidents occurred indicating that both the NSP and military intelligence (the Defense Security Command) were engaged in surveillance of prominent civilian opposition figures and other forms of intervention in the political arena. Only with the installation of the Kim Young Sam government in 1993 were moves taken to reduce the power of the NSP, revise the National Security Law, purge the military of corrupt officers, and break up secret political organizations such as the Hanahoe. Despite the drama of these actions, however, it is still not clear that they have created effective civilian and legislative oversight of the military.[14]

The Crisis Cases

Compared to those involved in non-crisis transitions, the armed forces in the crisis cases encountered greater challenges to their institutional autonomy and political influence. A summary indicator of these differences is provided by the data in Table 4.1, which compares average annual military spending as a share of GNP in the pre- and post-transition periods.[15] Seven of the ten new democracies experienced a decline in military spending, but there are predictable differences between the two categories. In Argentina, Bolivia, Brazil, and Uruguay—four of the six crisis cases—expenditures dropped between 22 percent and 33 percent. This contrasts with a slight increase in Thailand, and drops of only 11 percent in Turkey and 9 percent in Chile. The general ability of the Chilean military to maintain its prerogatives is particularly telling; unlike those in the other non-crisis cases, it faced no significant external threats.

[12] The following draws on Peter Beck, "From Transition to Consolidation: Crafting Democracy in South Korea," paper prepared for the Conference on Transformation of the Korean Penninsula, Michigan State University, July 7–11, 1993.

[13] See Asia Watch, *Retreat from Reform: Labor Rights and Freedom of Expression in South Korea* (New York: Asia Watch, November 1990).

[14] See Victor D. Cha, "Politics and Democracy under the Kim Young Sam Government," *Asian Survey* 33 (1993): 849–63; Beck, "From Transition to Consolidation."

[15] The base period is the transition year and the four previous years. The justification for including the transition year itself is the assumption that the budget was determined prior to the transition, and thus should continue to reflect the priorities of the outgoing regime. The post-transition period is defined as the five years following the transition, or where the transition is more recent, all years for which data are available.

Among the non-crisis cases, Korea is somewhat anomalous: military spending as a share of GNP dropped almost 25 percent. However, it should be noted that the decline in military spending as a share of GNP took place in a context of very rapid overall GNP growth, as it did in the other non-crisis cases as well. Among the crisis cases, Peru and the Philippines show substantial increases in expenditures. Though these trends go counter to expectations, they can be explained by the fact that both governments faced rural insurgencies. In Peru, the incoming civilian government initially cut military spending by nearly 50 percent in its first year; increases followed as the Shining Path movement began to pose an escalating threat. In the Philippines, expenditures remained low compared to the other cases. More-over, increases reflected the fact that two key generals—Enrile and Ramos—defected from the Marcos government, sided with Aquino, and subsequently occupied important positions in the Cabinet and as chief of staff respectively.

Other forms of military privilege and influence in the crisis cases also

TABLE 4.1

Military Expenditure before and after Democratic Transitions
(Military Expenditure/GDP)

	Average, Transition and Four Previous Years	Average, Five Years Following Transition[a]	Percentage Increase or Decline
	Crisis Cases		
Argentina	3.2 (1979–83)	2.5 (1984–88)	−22
Bolivia	3.5 (1978–82)	2.6 (1983–87)	−26
Brazil	0.6 (1981–85)	0.4 (1986–89)	−33
Peru	3.9 (1977–80)[b]	6.2 (1981–85)	+59
The Philippines	1.8 (1982–86)	2.3 (1987–89)	+28
Uruguay	3.2 (1981–85)	2.2 (1986–89)	−31
	Non-crisis Cases		
Chile	3.4 (1986–90)	3.1 (1991–92)	−9
Korea	5.3 (1984–88)	4.1 (1989–92)	−23
Thailand	3.6 (1979–83)	3.7 (1984–88)	+2
Turkey[c]	4.7 (1978–80)		
	4.6 (1981–83)	4.1 (1984–88)	−11

Sources: All data are from The International Institute for Strategic Studies, *The Military Balance* (London: Brassey's), various issues, except for Uruguay, which is taken from The Stockholm International Peace Research Institute, *SIPRI Yearbook* (Stockholm: SIPRI), various issues.

[a]Or years for which data are available, as noted in parentheses.

[b]Data for 1976 not available.

[c]The period four years prior to the transition includes both civilian (1978–80) and military (1980–83) governments; the change is measured from the military period.

tended to be more restricted than in the non-crisis cases, though there are interesting variations across the cases that deserve more detailed comment. Overall, the Argentine military emerged from the transition in the weakest political and institutional position, the armed forces in the Philippines and Brazil in the strongest.

The Argentine military, which had been decisively defeated in the Malvinas/Falklands conflict, poses the starkest contrast with the non-crisis cases.[16] The military proved unable to avoid prosecution for human-rights abuses and corruption during its tenure, and was subject to extensive purges. The Alfonsín government also established civilian control over the military budget, challenged the independence of military courts and intelligence units, and eliminated military control over Fabricaciónes Militares, the huge arms and industrial complex. After several years, the purges and attacks on military prerogatives led to a backlash against civilian authority, and a series of military mutinies forced a retreat by Alfonsín and Menem with respect to human-rights cases. Unlike in the past, however, barracks revolts failed to gain civilian backing and all were put down by the civilian government.

In Uruguay, Bolivia, and Peru, the military also emerged in a weakened position, although not to the extent of their Argentine counterpart. In Uruguay, as in Argentina, the president and Congress assumed extensive control over promotions, budget and mission, and reestablished civilian control of the Ministry of Defense.[17] As in Argentina as well, continuing conflicts over the question of amnesty clouded civil-military relations during the Sanguinetti period, leading to open military defiance of the jurisdiction of civilian courts. In Bolivia, command of the badly divided military was taken over by "institutionalist" officers who discharged top-ranking military personnel involved in the cocaine trade. Those most closely identified with the old order were purged, even if subsequent abuses were not vigorously prosecuted.

As in the other crisis cases, the Peruvian military was constrained to accept some reduction in its prerogatives during the negotiations within the Constituent Assembly. A prohibition on "deliberative activities" was widely assumed to bar the armed forces from involvement in broader political contests. Unlike the cases just discussed, however, these provisions were partially undermined during the 1980s by responses to the Shining Path insurgency. Between December 1981 and May 1985, Belaúnde issued twenty-four emergency decrees in various parts of the country, allowing security forces increased discretionary powers of search and seizure and limiting rights to assembly and freedom of movement.

---

[16] The following is drawn from Alfred Stepan, *Rethinking Military Politics: Brazil and the Southern Cone* (Princeton, N.J.: Princeton University Press, 1988), pp. 114–16.

[17] Ibid., p. 90.

The Brazilian and Philippine militaries, finally, were at the opposite end of the spectrum from Argentina and closest to the non-crisis cases in terms of political influence and prerogatives. In the Philippines, the military faction that supported the revolution exercised considerable influence within the heterogeneous political coalition that brought Aquino to power. Defense Minister Juan Ponce Enrile provided an important channel for the representation of military interests. Moreover, the government's "total approach" to countering the insurgency granted considerable operational autonomy to military personnel and allied militia and vigilante forces at the local level, resulting in continuing "disappearances" of opposition figures. Military personnel remained effectively immune from prosecution in connection with such crimes.[18]

Despite this influence, however, important parallels remain between the Philippines military and the other crisis cases. The incoming Aquino government purged high-level Marcos cronies from the military establishment, and new constitutional provisions in 1987 barred active-duty officers from government positions. The military was also constrained by low levels of expenditures. As in Argentina, discontent over low pay and general political disaffection, reinforced in this case by complaints of inadequate management of the rural insurgency, led to a series of coup attempts, the last of which (1989) posed a serious threat to the Aquino government.

The Brazilian military retained the most extensive institutional prerogatives of any of the crisis cases, which may help explain why it posed less of an immediate threat to the security of the new democratic government. Service heads of the army, navy, and air force, and the chief of the general staff all retained ministerial status. All service branches were also represented on the National Security Council. Unlike in Argentina, the control of the huge arms industry remained in military hands. As in most of the non-crisis cases, finally, continuing control over the intelligence apparatus allowed the military to influence the policy process, even in such seemingly unrelated areas as agrarian reform.[19]

Notwithstanding the crisis conditions in which the Brazilian military transferred power to civilians, these prerogatives were comparable to those achieved in Chile, Turkey, and Korea. As in most of the other crisis cases, however, the Brazilian military left office constrained by deep internal divisions and by a substantial decline in support among both politicians

[18] On military involvement in death squad activity, see Amnesty International, *Philippines: The Killing Goes On* (New York: Amnesty International, 1991); Lawyers Committee for Human Rights, *Out of Control: Militia Abuses in the Philippines* (New York, 1990). For a detailed examination of the military's involvement in politics since 1986, see *The Final Report of the Fact-Finding Commission (pursuant to R.A. No. 6832),* (Manila: Bookmark, 1990). Known as the Davide report after the chairman of the commission, the study was initiated following the 1989 coup attempt.

[19] Stepan, *Rethinking Military Politics,* pp. 84–85, 103–14.

and the general population.[20] Unlike in any of the non-crisis cases, neither military men nor their appointees held important political posts in the new government. As we shall see in the following sections, the Brazilian military was generally less successful than its Chilean or Turkish counterparts in restructuring the constitution within which the new government would operate.

STRUCTURING POLITICAL COMPETITION

Though the structuring of civil-military relations is an important component of the terms of transition, the new constitutional order is defined by the informal understandings and specific rules that govern political contestation in the new democratic system. As with the narrower question of military prerogatives, constitutional issues were not definitively settled at the time of the transition in any of the cases we examine here. Nevertheless, the framework established at that time did have some durability, and thus had implications for both economic policy and the consolidation of democracy itself. Differences between the crisis and non-crisis cases are visible both in the *processes* through which new constitutional orders evolved, and in the *substantive arrangements* governing political life, including particularly the degree of centralization of decision-making powers and the rules governing political competition.

Designing the Constitutional Framework

Critical to the constitution-making process was the relative power of the authoritarian government and its allies vis-à-vis the opposition politicians who led the challenge to the old regime. Neither group had exclusive control in any of the cases; all transitions involved explicit or tacit negotiations. But outgoing authoritarian governments had much greater control over the process of constitutional change in the non-crisis cases.

In Chile, Turkey, and Thailand, new democratic governments operated under constitutions written and imposed by the old regime. After its victory in the plebiscite, the opposition coalition in Chile negotiated some important changes in the 1980 Constitution, but many of its most restrictive provisions remained, including very difficult amendment procedures. The Thai Constitution of 1978 and the Turkish Constitution of 1982 were also drafted under authoritarian auspices and granted military elites wide authority during the transition process.

[20] Ibid., pp. 86–88.

The Korean case is somewhat more complex. The Chun government was forced to abandon its original plans for the transition as a result of the mass protests of the spring and summer of 1987. Roh made substantial concessions to opposition demands, and the outgoing military engaged in a greater degree of bargaining over the drafting of the new Constitution than in Chile, Turkey, and Thailand. But the Constitution was nonetheless written prior to the military's exit, and reflected the military government's preferences with reference both to electoral laws and to the contentious issue of the share of seats allocated to Seoul, long a stronghold of the opposition.

Opposition forces wielded much greater influence in the crisis transitions. The relatively swift collapse of authoritarian rule in the Philippines and Argentina allowed opposition politicians to make constitutional decisions with little input from the outgoing government. In the Philippines, a new Constitution was drafted under the Aquino government and ratified by referendum in 1987. In Argentina, military initiatives to negotiate a transitional framework with conservative civilian allies collapsed during the economic crisis of 1981. After the defeat in the Malvinas/Falklands war, Radical and Peronist politicians agreed among themselves to restore the 1853 Constitution. The Bolivian case bears some similarities to Argentina, though with somewhat greater participation on the part of forces linked to the old order. In the chaotic conditions prevailing during the Bolivian transition, most of the contending social and political groups were willing to accept the 1967 Constitution as a focal point for their competition. The Uruguayan transition was characterized by more explicit bargaining, but as we showed in chapter 2, the military was constrained by weak economic conditions and mounting protest to accept the demands of party leaders in the Naval Club negotiations for a restoration of the Constitution of 1967.[21]

Authoritarian leaders and their allies had greater influence over the transitional process in Peru and Brazil, but opposition politicians still played a much larger role than in the non-crisis cases. In Peru, a new Constitution was written while the military remained in power, but the drafting occurred in an elected assembly dominated by the opposition parties. The 1988 Brazilian Constitution was written in a Congress elected one year after the transfer of power to civilians. Its contents reflected the heterogeneous composition of the legislators within the victorious PMDB and its allies within the Liberal Front Party (PFL). A number of provisions, including the overrepresentation of the more traditional-minded northeastern states, reflected the continuing influence of a conservative coalition that cut across party lines. The military itself, moreover, retained substan-

---

[21] Ronald H. McDonald and J. Mark Ruhl, *Party Politics and Elections in Latin America* (Boulder, Colo.: Westview Press, 1989), p. 98.

tial behind-the-scenes influence and played an important role in the decision to maintain a presidential Constitution and the prerogatives of the military itself. Yet the influence of new populist and left forces entering the political arena was also unprecedented, resulting in provisions that drastically eased restrictions on voting, party registration, and union activities, committed the state to land reform and extensive welfare benefits, and provided unprecedented legislative and fiscal authority to the Congress. Commenting on such changes, one noted Brazilian political scientist observed that the new Constitution represented a more important break with the Vargas legacy than the 1964 military coup itself.[22]

Centralization of Decision-Making Structures

The respective weight of authoritarian and opposition forces in the crafting of the rules of the game naturally had important implications for the organization of political competition, the representativeness of the system, and the balance of powers within the government. As Barbara Geddes argues in a penetrating essay, democratic institutions should be viewed as "bargains among self-interested politicians": the substantive provisions of new constitutional orders reflect the calculations of government and opposition about how each will fare under alternative rules.[23]

What, precisely, do oppositions want? Established politicians who were successful under the pre-authoritarian rules are likely to favor a restoration of the status quo ante.[24] This may not necessarily be the case for new political forces, particularly on the left, who stand to benefit from lower barriers to entry. However, all opposition politicians should favor rules that allow them to respond to the pent-up demands of those constituencies that had been systemmatically excluded under the authoritarian order.

Authoritarian elites, by contrast, are typically interested in restraining some, if not all, politicians; this was the reason that they intervened in the political arena in the first place. To the extent that they wield influence over

[22] Maria do Carmo Campello de Souza, "Constitutional Reform in Brazil," presentation at the Brazil Seminar, Columbia University, March 1994. See also Bolivar Lamounier, "Brazil: Toward Parliamentarism?" in Juan J. Linz and Arturo Valenzuela, eds., *The Failure of Presidential Democracy: The Case of Latin America,* vol. 2 (Baltimore and London: Johns Hopkins University Press, 1994), p. 205.

[23] See Barbara Geddes, "Democratic Institutions as Bargains among Self-Interested Politicians," paper prepared for the American Political Science Association, San Francisco, September 1990.

[24] On the politics of such restoration, see Barbara Geddes, "The Leninist Legacy in Eastern Europe," unpublished ms., University of California at Los Angeles, n.d.

the terms of the transition, outgoing military governments can institution-alize such restraint through two mechanisms: by creating insulated decision-making structures that can be counted on to pursue the military's policy agenda; and by placing various limits on the composition and activities of the political opposition.

The effort to create insulated "enclaves" of decision-making that were wholly or partially immune from democratic control and scrutiny was more likely to occur in the non-crisis transitions. Such enclaves were especially important in Thailand and Chile. Thailand's 1978 Constitution provided for an appointed Senate that initially exercised a veto over decisions taken by the elected House of Representatives. Prem's political dominance also guaranteed that Thai technocrats in the economic ministries and the Central Bank maintained their long tradition of independence from legislative scrutiny, which helped offset the effects of a party system that was unusu-ally fragmented.

Pinochet sought to guarantee continuity through appointments of Su-preme Court justices, mayors and regional governors, and even legislators: one-fifth of the new Senate was appointed by Pinochet. The reform of the Central Bank, similarly, provided for a substantial increase in its autonomy from the electoral system. The five-member board of the bank was nomi-nated by Pinochet, and although their terms ranged from two to ten years in order to stagger the turnover of directors, the reform was designed so that Pinochet appointees would dominate the institution throughout the Aylwin presidency.[25]

Although presidents exercised extensive personal discretion in all of the new democratic systems, constitutional arrangements in the non-crisis cases also provided executives and independent agencies with the power to veto policy changes. Executives in Chile, Thailand, and Korea were empowered to establish spending ceilings that could not be raised by the legislature, an authority matched in the crisis cases only by Uruguay.[26] In Turkey, as well as in Chile, an independent Central Bank was established and staffed prior to the transfer of power, and in Thailand the tradition of strong Central Bank independence remained intact. Only in Korea did monetary policy remain under the control of the minister of finance, but by the time of the transition, monetary policy had become much more conservative than during the heyday of aggressive industrial policy in the 1970s. Among the crisis cases, only the Peruvian Central Bank was given

[25] Arriagada Herrera and Graham, "Chile: Sustaining Adjustment during Democratic Transition," pp. 268–69.

[26] Matthew Soberg Shugart and John M. Carey, *Presidents and Assemblies: Constitutional Design and Electoral Dynamics* (New York: Cambridge University Press, 1992), p. 155.

formal authority comparable to that in Chile and Thailand, and that eroded quickly as political conflict escalated in the 1980s.

Regulating Contestation

The second critical aspect of the new democratic framework was the rules and practices governing the actors who could enter the political realm and the scope of their political activity. At the broadest level, a democratic order rests on the guarantee of basic civil liberties. Yet comparison across the cases on this dimension is complicated by the existence of guerilla wars and ethnic conflicts that are only tangentially related to the transition processes we are discussing here. Restrictions on civil liberties related to, or justified by, civil violence are visible in Peru, Thailand, Bolivia, the Philippines, and Turkey—in short, in both crisis and non-crisis transitions.

More directly pertinent to our concerns were the opportunities for political activity open to interest groups that had been excluded under the authoritarian order, particularly unions, and to contending political parties, particularly those on the left. In these areas, there are noticeable and predictable differences between the crisis and non-crisis transitions.

Military leaders in the non-crisis countries succeeded in imposing exclusionary rules on their democratic successors that limited the freedom of both labor and the political opposition. These were most extensive in Turkey. Legal restrictions on Islamic fundamentalism and on support for, or even discussion of, the Kurdish situation were used to intimidate and arrest journalists and politicians. The main labor confederation, the DISK, remained banned after the transition in 1983, and as late as 1986, union activists were indicted for seeking to achieve "the domination of one social class over another." At the end of 1989, there were still an estimated five thousand political prisoners in Turkish jails.

At the broader political level, the military restructured the party system to reduce the influence of the left. In 1983, they did this directly by maintaining a veto over which parties could contest the transitional election. The military also prohibited linkages between parties and interest groups, and banned a number of organizations outright.[27] Indirectly, the military used high electoral thresholds to limit the prospects of minor parties; the influence of these thresholds on Turkish politics was felt long after the military was forced to relent on the bans of old politicians and parties in the mid-1980s.

---

[27] See Ergun Özbudun, "The Post-1980 Legal Framework for Interest Group Associations," in Metin Heper, ed., *Strong State and Economic Interest Groups: the Post-1980 Turkish Experience* (Berlin: Walter de Gruyter, 1991), pp. 41–54.

In several important respects, the political discontinuities in the Korean transition were considerably sharper than in Turkey. The democratic reforms instituted under the new Roh Tae Woo government came in response to overwhelming social pressures for a fundamental political change, and substantially expanded the freedom for public debate. Perhaps because the government expected the establishment of single-member districts to disadvantage the regionally based opposition parties, there were no major restrictions placed on the formation of political parties.[28]

Extensive legal restrictions on labor militancy and political dissidence remained in place, however, and allowed the government to limit contestation over crucial issues such as reunification and workers' rights.[29] These laws were not consistently applied during the wave of labor militancy and strikes that swept the country in 1987 and 1988, but thousands of workers were arrested during this period. Beginning in 1990, following the formation of a grand coalition of the right, the government cracked down on the union movement more systematically: strikes were broken by police, labor activists arrested, and dissident union publications banned. In 1991, over four hundred persons were still being held under the National Security Law, a level of political detainees exceeded only by Turkey.

In Chile, a constitutional ban on left parties was lifted after the 1988 plebiscite, and in 1990, the labor code substantially liberalized restrictions on union activity. Crucial to this political opening, however, was the left's willingness to abandon its historic antipathy to market-oriented policies and its acceptance of the leadership of the centrist Christian Democrats in the anti-Pinochet coalition.

More significant to the restructuring of Chilean politics was the new electoral law promulgated by the military, which established two-member congressional districts under a d'Hondt allocation rule. Under the d'Hondt system of proportional representation and a district magnitude of two, the second seat goes to the second strongest party list only if the first list has less than twice the votes of the second. This has several important effects. On the one hand, it provided an incentive for the left and the center to run together in any district where the combined center-left vote held out the promise of securing two seats; in effect, the rule reinforced the pressure on the left to ally itself with more moderate centrist forces. But the rule

[28] Contrary to initial expectations, the new electoral system contributed to legislative losses for the government party in the 1988 Congressional elections.

[29] These included restrictions on the formation of competing unions, bans on unionization in the public sector, restrictions on "third-party interference" designed to limit the organizing role of leftist groups, bans on workers' participation in rallies and demonstrations, and severe constraints on the right to strike. The National Security Law, passed under the military, authorizes the government to detain anyone accused of participating in "anti-state" organizations. See Asia Watch, *Retreat from Reform,* pp. 7–26.

was also designed explicitly to strengthen the legislative representation of the conservative parties by guaranteeing that they could secure at least one seat in many districts.

In contrast to these other non-crisis cases, Thailand appears on the surface to experience a substantial lowering of the barriers to contestation. In general, interest groups and parties could form freely, with relatively liberal registration laws. But as we have argued, the transition was in fact limited in important ways. Although the government loosened controls over the media, self-censorship still operated during the 1980s, particularly with reference to the military and the monarchy. A system of labor courts established in 1980 failed to protect union activists against dismissal, severely restricting the capacity to organize. Most importantly, the actual powers of the parliament vis-à-vis the prime minister were limited by the looming threat of military intervention. The prime minister was allowed to form Cabinets comprised of nonelected officials who, in a fully open system, would not necessarily have met with electoral approval.

In the crisis cases, despite abuses, the lifting of restrictions on labor and political groups was much more comprehensive. In Bolivia, the Paz Estenssoro government did impose a sharp crackdown on the radicalized labor movement in 1985, but during the preceding four years of the democratic transition, the unions had acquired an unprecedented degree of political power. In several other countries, restrictive labor legislation remained on the books, particularly with respect to public-sector workers. Unlike in Korea and Turkey, however, this was applied only sporadically, if at all, and the unions rapidly regained the right to organize, strike, and press political demands.

Strong opposition pressure also led to more complete openings to political debate and electoral activities than in the non-crisis cases. Virtually all restrictions on the press were lifted in Argentina, Uruguay, Bolivia, and Brazil. In the Philippines and Peru, there was some intimidation of journalists sympathetic to the rural insurgencies, but public debate on most issues remained open.[30] More important, unlike in Turkey and Chile, there were no vetoes or political conditions placed on parties seeking to reenter the political arena. Frequently, there were strong presidential challenges from individuals or parties that had been major targets of the military when it initially seized power: Leonel Brizola in Brazil; Paz Estenssoro in Bolivia; the APRA and Peronist parties in Peru and Argentina; Corazon Aquino, inheriting the mantle of her murdered husband Benigno, in the

---

[30] In addition to the country-specific sources cited, the following draws on various issues of four reviews of human-rights performance: the U.S. Department of State's *Country Reports on Human Rights Practices*; Lawyers Commission for Human Rights, *Critique: Review of the Department of State's Country Reports on Human Rights Practices*; Amnesty International, *Annual Report*; and *Human Rights Watch: World Report.*

Philippines. In Uruguay, the military did succeed in blocking the presidential candidacy of Wilson Ferreira, its most visible opponent, but it opened the door to all of the contending parties, including Ferreira's Blanco list, and the center-left Frente Amplio coalition.

Differences between the two sets of cases were also reflected in the design of registration and electoral rules. Whereas electoral rules in Korea, Chile, and Turkey attempted to restrict the role of smaller parties, constitutional provisions in the crisis cases generally worked in the opposite direction. The voting age and registration requirements were drastically reduced in the new Peruvian constitution, and in legislation passed during the first year of the Sarney government in Brazil. Brazilian legislation also removed existing bans on the Communist Party, eliminated sanctions for breaking party discipline in the legislature, and maintained the open-list ballot system that reduced the power of national party leaders over nominations. Extremely low thresholds for party registration were also maintained in Bolivia, leading during the late 1970s to the appearance of some seventy parties.[31]

In contrast to the single- or two-member districts established in Chile and Korea, finally, most of the crisis cases returned to proprortional representation systems, and in all of these, district magnitudes were relatively high.[32] The principal exception to the proportional representation system was the Philippines, where single-member districts in the lower house had long been a feature of the American-inspired constitutional system.

THE RECONSTITUTION OF PARTIES

We have argued that the rules governing political contestation were conditioned by economic characteristics of the transition path. Explaining the actual nature of the party systems that emerged in the post-transition period through reference to short-term economic conditions is more questionable. Party systems did not emerge de novo in response to economic crisis, nor could they be predicted solely on the basis of the constitutional framework and electoral rules we have discussed briefly in the previous section. In all of the cases examined here, the transition to democracy was really a *re*democratization; as a result, the organization and behavior of political parties was shaped to some extent by historical legacies, and particularly

---

[31] Eduardo A. Gamarra and James M. Malloy, "The Patrimonial Dynamics of Party Politics in Bolivia," in Scott Mainwaring and Timothy Scully, eds., *Building Democratic Institutions: Party Systems in Latin America* (forthcoming), p. 600. Most of these, as the authors note, were labeled "taxi parties" because their national conventions could have been held in a taxicab.

[32] See Shugart and Carey, *Presidents and Assemblies,* p. 176.

by the ideological orientation and political expectations of the party activists.[33] In many instances, these patterns of organization and behavior had been frozen during the long period of dictatorship, but resurfaced once political restraints fell.

It is also important to underline that the party systems that emerged at the time of the transition were by no means fixed, but continued to evolve with subsequent elections. Table 4.2 (summarizing more detailed information contained in Table 4.3, at the end of this chapter) outlines some of the salient structural characteristics of party organization in the crisis and non-crisis cases from their democratization through the early 1990s. One striking feature is the high level of volatility in the party system, measured as the sum of the change in electoral support for each party from election to election.

Despite these caveats, we argue that economic conditions and the institutional rules established at the time of the transition did influence the relative strength of the parties reentering the political arena and thus the extent of fragmentation and polarization. Though these characteristics of the party system did change over time, we will show in Part Two that they had important consequences not only for the economic "governability" of the new democracies, but for the nature of democratic rule as well.

Centrifugal tendencies were greater in the crisis cases, where economic distress and low barriers to entry encouraged both party fragmentation and the polarization that is associated with the reentry of parties with strong anti-market ideological orientations. In the non-crisis cases, there is also evidence of tendencies toward fragmentation and polarization, but these pressures were more likely to be contained, at least initially, by the combination of strong economic performance and the restrictions imposed by outgoing military rulers.

Strength of Continuist Parties

Table 4.2 provides evidence on the distribution of electoral forces in the early transition period in the crisis and non-crisis cases; we generally focus on the first elections for the executive and legislature.[34] One indicator of the balance of political power is the extent of support for parties or movements identified with the outgoing authoritarian regime. Though these

[33] For a treatment that stresses the internal organizational characteristics of parties, see Angelo Panebianco, *Political Parties: Organization and Power* (New York: Cambridge University Press, 1982).

[34] We have also included the Chilean plebiscite, the Peruvian constituent assembly elections, and the Philippine election of 1986, which was certainly not intended to constitute a transitional election.

TABLE 4.2

Party Alignments in New Democracies: Transitional Elections and Post-transition Averages

Country/Election	Continuist Party	Share[a]	Left Party	Share[a]	Continuist/ Left Ratio	Effective Number of Parties
			Crisis Cases			
Argentina						
1983 Presidential	Continuist Total[c]	4.0	Peronists—Italo Luder	39.1	0.1	2.51
1983 Parliamentary	Continuist Total	3.8	Peronists	48.8	0.07	2.53
			Left Parties	2.1		
			Left Total	50.9		
Post-transition Averages					0.085	2.93
Bolivia						
1979 Presidential	ADN—Hugo Banzer	14.9	UDP	36.0	0.36	3.5
			PS-1	4.8		
			VO	1.1		
			Left Total	41.9		
1979 Parliamentary	ADN	14.9	UDP	36.0	.0.36	3.5
			PS-1	4.8		
			VO	1.1		
			Left Total	41.9		
1980 Presidential	ADN—Hugo Banzer	16.8	UDP	38.7	0.34	4.36
			PS-1	8.7		
			VO	0.0		
			FSB	1.6		
			Left Total	49.0		

TABLE 4.2 (continued)

Country/Election	Continuist Party	Share[a]	Left Party	Share[a]	Continuist/ Left Ratio	Effective Number of Parties
1980 Parliamentary	ADN	16.8	UDP	38.7	0.34	4.36
			PS-1	8.7		
			VO	0.0		
			FSB	1.6		
			Left Total	49.0		
Post-transition Averages					0.685	4.36
Brazil						
1986 House[d]	PFL	23.6	PT	3.9	3.14	2.58
	PDS	7.4	PDT	4.9		
			PCB	0.4		
			PC do B	0.4		
			PSB	0.2		
			Left Total	9.9		
	Continuist Total	31.0				
1989 Presidential	PFL	0.9	PT	17.2	0.28	5.69
	PDS— Paulo Salim Maluf	8.9	PDT	16.5		
			PCB	1.1		
	Continuist Total	9.8	Left Total	34.8		
Post-transition Averages					1.58	5.54
Peru						
1978 Constituent[e]	PPC	23.8	APRA	35.3	0.46	4.78
			PSR	6.6		
			PCP	5.9		
			FNTC	3.9		
			Left Total	51.7		

1980 Presidential	PPC—Luis Bedoya	9.6	APRA—Armando Villanueva	27.4	0.31	3.39
			IU— Leonidas Rodríguez	3.7		
			Left Total	31.1		
1980 House	PPC/CODE	9.2	APRA	27.0	0.3	3.93
			IU	3.7		
			Left Total	30.7		
1985 Presidential	PPC—Luis Bedoya	11.9	APRA	53.1	0.15	2.76
			IU	24.7		
			PSP	24.7		
			Left Total	78.0		
1985 House	PPC/CODE	11.2	APRA	50.4	0.15	3
			IU	24.6		
			Left Total	75.0		
Post-transition Averages					0.39	3.8
Philippines						
1986 Presidential	Ferdinand Marcos	40–50	No Left			
1987 House[d]	No Continuist Party		No Left			1.22
1992 Presidential	KBL—Imelda Marcos	10.3	No Left			3.58
1992 House[d]	KBL	1.5	No Left			5.84
Post-transition Averages						3.55

TABLE 4.2 (continued)

Country/Election	Continuist Party	Share[a]	Left Party	Share[a]	Continuist/ Left Ratio	Effective Number of Parties
Uruguay						
1984 Presidential	PC—Pacheco/Piran	9.7	FA	21.3	0.46	2.96
1984 House	No Right		FA	21.3	0	2.96
1989 Presidential	PC—Pacheco/Millor	14.7	FA	21.2	0.69	3.38
1989 House	No Right	FA	FA	21.2	0	3.38
Post-transition Averages					0.29	3.17
			Non-crisis Cases			
Chile						
1988 Plebiscite	Yes Vote[f]	43.0				
1989 Presidential	Independent—Hernan Büchi	29.4	No Left			2.41
	Independent—Francisco Errazuriz	15.5				
	Continuist Total	44.9				
1989 House	RN	18.3	PPD	11.5	2.01	2.52
	UDI	9.8	PSCH	0.2		
	List B Independents	6.1	PAIS	4.4		
	Continuist Total	34.2	List G Independents	0.9		
			Left Total	17.0		
Post-transition Averages					2.01	2.47

Korea						
1987 Presidential	Roh Tae Woo	35.9	Kim Dae Jung	26.5	1.35	3.51
1988 Assembly	DJP	41.8	PDP	23.4	2.29	3.53
	NDRP	11.7				
	Continuist Total	53.5				
Post-transition Averages					1.82	3.45
Thailand						
1992a Parliamentary	Chart Thai	20.6	No Left			6.01
	Samakhitham	21.9				
	Social Action	8.6				
	Continuist Total	51.1				
1992b Parliamentary	Chart Thai	21.4	No Left			6.1
	Prachakorn Thai	0.8				
	Social Action	6.1				
	Rassadorn	0.3				
	Seritham	2.2				
	Chart Pattana	16.7				
	Continuist Total	47.5				
Post-transition Averages						6.62
Turkey						
1983 Parliamentary	NDP	23.0	No Left			2.84
	MP	45.0				
	Continuist Total	68.0				

TABLE 4.2 (continued)

Country/Election	Continuist Party	Share[a]	Left Party	Share[a]	Continuist/ Left Ratio	Effective Number of Parties
1987 Parliamentary	MP	36.0	No Left			4.13
Post-transition Averages					1.12	3.87

Sources: All Latin American cases except Brazilian Chamber of Deputies: *Enciclopedia Electoral Latinoamericana y del Caribe* (San José, Costa Rica: Instituto Interamericano de Derechos Humanos, 1993); Brazil, Chamber of Deputies: *Europa World Year Book 1991* (London: Europa Publications, 1991) and *South America, Central America and the Caribbean, 1993* (London: Europa Publications, 1993); Asian cases: *Europa World Yearbook 1991* (London: Europa Publications, 1991); *Far East and Australasia 1994* (Londo: Europa Publications, 1994); Daniel E. King, "The Thai Parliamentary Elections of 1992," *Electoral Studies* 12 (1993): 268–74; Ziya Oniş and Steven B. Webb, "Turkey: Democratization and Adjustment from Above," in Stephan Haggard and Steven B. Webb, eds., *Voting for Reform* (New York: Oxford University Press for the World Bank, 1994), p 138.

Notes: Party names are as follows: ADN, Nationalist Democratic Action; APRA, Popular Revolutionary Alliance of America; CODE, Democratic Convergence; DJP, Democratic Justice Party; FA, Broad Front; FNTC, National Front of Workers and Peasants; FSB, Bolivian Socialist Falange; IU, United Left; MP, Motherland Party; NDP, National Democratic Party; NDRP, New Democratic Republic Party; PAIS, Broad Party of the Socialist Left; PC, Red Party; PCB, Brazilian Communist Party; PC do B, Communist Pary of Brazil; PCP, Communist Pary of Peru; PDP, Peace and Democracy Party; PDS, Social Democratic Party; PDT, Democratic Labor Party; PFL, Liberal Front Party; PPC, Popular Christian Party; PPD, Party for Democracy; PS-1, Socialist Party One; PSB, Socialist Party; PT, Labor Party; RN, National Renovation; UDI, Independent Democratic Union; UDP, Democratic and Popular Unity; VO, Workers' Vanguard.

[a] All shares are of popular vote except as noted.

[b] The effective number of parties is defined as the inverse of the sum of the squares of the vote or seat share going to each party. See M. Laakso and R. Taagepera, "Effective Number of Parties: A Measure with Application to West Europe," *Comparative Political Studies* 12 (1979): 3–27.

[c] Total includes four small parties associated with the outgoing military regime.

[d] Denotes share of seats.

[e] The Constituent Assembly election of 1978 was the first democratic election after the transition.

[f] Yes votes in the plebiscite indicated support for Pinochet's efforts to extend his rule, and are thus counted as "continuist."

parties did not for the most part support an actual continuation of military rule, we have called them "continuist" since they provided support for the preferences of outgoing rulers with respect to both policies and institutional arrangements. The data suggest strongly that the conservatism associated with the non-crisis transitions was not limited solely to elite beneficiaries of the economic reforms undertaken by the regime; compared to the crisis cases, there was also substantial support for some elements of *continuismo* within broader segments of the electorate.

In Korea, Roh Tae Woo still garnered over a third of the vote in the 1986 presidential elections, and his party fared only slightly worse in the legislative elections. Moreover, the leader of one of the main opposition parties, Kim Jong Pil, was closely identified with Park Chung Hee's authoritarian order. In the 1992 legislative and presidential elections, the ruling party was challenged most vigorously not on the left, but from a new libertarian party organized by a right-wing businessman.

The performance of center-right parties in Chile and Turkey reached comparable levels. In Chile's 1989 presidential race, candidates of the right gathered almost 45 percent of the vote. The combined vote for rightist Congressional candidates in 1989 was even more impressive, over double that obtained in 1973.[35] The Turkish situation is difficult to characterize because the military approved all of the parties and candidates. The candidate supported most directly by the military was defeated by Özal, although he still managed to receive almost a quarter of the vote. Özal's Motherland Party clearly benefited from its status as the one nonmilitary party. However, Özal had been the military's economic czar during the first two years of authoritarian rule, and campaigned on promises to continue and even deepen the economic program the military had intervened to implement; for this reason, we count his party as continuist.

In Thailand, no party on the electoral scene was really in a position to challenge the military's role in politics; Prem's selection as prime minister had to do more with this basic fact than with the electoral outcomes, and in any case most parties maintained links to military factions. In Table 4.2, however, we have defined "military-linked" parties narrowly as those that explicitly campaigned in 1983 to maintain the restrictive transitional provisions of the 1978 Constitution. The most important of these, the Chart Thai and the Prachacorn Thai, received over a third of the popular vote in the 1983 parliamentary elections.

The fate of continuist parties and candidates that campaigned on the achievements of the old regime was far more limited in the crisis cases. In the Philippines, Marcos was able to garner a substantial share of the popular

---

[35] Timothy R. Scully, "Reconstituting Party Politics in Chile," in Scully and Mainwaring, *Building Democratic Institutions*, p. 185.

vote in the 1986 election through a combination of patronage and the maintenance of strong regional loyalties; though his precise share of the vote will never be known due to massive electoral fraud, Marcos's political capabilities were nonetheless surprising. By the time of the 1987 elections for the lower house, however, support for politicians closely associated with Marcos had collapsed. Some Marcos supporters reentered the legislature by switching parties, but there was no organized political force that openly represented continuity with the Marcos era.

In Uruguay's 1984 presidential election, Jorge Pacheco, the candidate identified most closely with the military regime, won less than 10 percent of the vote. In Argentina, right-wing political leaders identified with the military's failed economic project gained only a handful of votes in the 1983 presidential contest. In Peru, the conservative Popular Christian Party (PPC) represented agro-export groups that had strongly opposed the military regime from the late 1960s to the mid 1970s. It is classified as a continuist party, however, because it supported adjustment policies adopted during the last two years of military rule.

Continuist parties were more significant in Bolivia and Brazil, but still fell short of the strength of their counterparts in the non-crisis countries. In Bolivia, the ex-dictator Hugo Banzer eventually emerged as a strong contender for the presidency, in part because his party was not associated with the military factions that ruled so disastrously in the early 1980s. Nonetheless, he gained less than 20 percent of the votes in the 1979 and 1980 elections and finished third behind candidates of the left and center.

The selection of the president in Brazil in 1985 did not come through a popular vote. Surveys indicate that Paulo Maluf, the pro-military candidate, was supported by only 10 percent of the public and received only 26 percent of the electoral college vote.[36] In the 1986 Congressional election, the conservative Liberal Front (the PFL) won a respectable 24 percent of the Congressional seats, and the opposition PMDB itself incorporated many electoral politicians who had formerly supported the military government. But such politicians survived in large part because they had joined the opposition. The loyalist faction (the PDS) won only about 7 percent, and even the combined PFL-PDS total was generally below those obtained in the non-crisis cases, despite the overrepresentation of the poorer states where conservative groups had their greatest strength. (See Table 4.2.)

The comparatively limited electoral support for continuist parties in the

---

[36] For survey results, see: Glaucio Ary Dillon Soares, "Elections and the Redemocratization of Brazil," p. 285; for electoral college results, see David Fleischer, "Brazil at the Crossroads: The Elections of 1982 and 1985," p. 324, both in Paul W. Drake and Eduardo Silva, *Elections and Democratization in Latin America, 1980–85* (La Jolla: Center for Iberian and Latin American Studies, Center for U.S.–Mexican Studies, and Institute of the Americas, University of California, San Diego, 1986).

crisis cases by no means implied a lack of influence for business groups and other elites. Like the military establishment, such groups typically retained substantial capacity to extract particularistic benefits from the system and to defend their core interests. Weakness in the electoral arena did reflect, however, the disorganization and political isolation of the authoritarian coalition as a whole, and the lack of broader support for their political and economic project. The political isolation of the continuist parties also enlarged the spaces for labor unions, social movements, and regionally based interests to press their demands.

Strength of the Left and Party System Fragmentation

Table 4.2 also presents data on the relative strength of left and populist parties, as well as a measure of the extent of fragmentation of the party system. In Bolivia, Peru, Brazil, and Uruguay, left parties, defined as those with socialist or Marxist ideologies, reemerged as important political forces, both when compared to the strength of such parties in the non-crisis cases and when compared to conservative parties within their own political systems. In new Congresses elected in Peru and Uruguay, the share of seats held by the socialist coalition in the legislature ranged from 14 to about 25 percent, well above the totals of their conservative competitors. In Bolivia, the left coalition backing Hernán Siles was the largest political force in the early 1980s. In Brazil, the left's electoral share was smaller, but two leftist politicians, Leonel Brizola and Luís Inácio Lula da Silva, were serious contenders for the presidency.[37]

The strength of anti-market parties in the crisis cases is still more impressive if we include nonsocialist populist or "movement" parties such as the Peronists in Argentina and the Apristas in Peru.[38] The ideological orientation of such parties is notoriously difficult to identify. Over the course of decades, both the Peronists and the Apristas moved toward the right in terms of their relationship to other political forces, but each maintained support through strong statist and distributive appeals that were sharply antithetical to market-oriented reforms. Moreover, although these

---

[37] In their seminal comparative historical study of party systems, Collier and Collier classify pre-1964 Brazil and pre-1973 Chile as "polarized multiparty systems," because of the strong links in each country between the labor movement and radical, anticapitalist electoral forces. Ruth Berins Collier and David Collier, *Shaping the Political Arena* (Princeton, N.J.: Princeton University Press, 1991).

[38] James W. McGuire, "Political Parties and Democracy in Argentina," and Julio Cotler, "Political Parties and the Problems of Democratic Consolidation in Peru," both in Mainwaring and Scully, *Building Democratic Institutions*; Carol Graham, *Peru's APRA: Parties, Politics, and the Elusive Quest for Democracy* (Boulder, Colo.: Lynne Rienner, 1992).

parties (along with most of their socialist counterparts) were increasingly committed to pursuing their objectives through the electoral framework, activists within the parties still favored an exclusivist style that paralleled what Sartori has called "anti-system" parties in the European context.[39] As we discuss in more detail in the following chapter, the relative strength of such parties, together with socialist parties of the left, can be used as a proxy to measure the extent of party system polarization.

At the onset of the democratic period in Peru, Brazil, and Bolivia, there were between three and five effective parties.[40] This is below the five or six that Sartori suggests as a rough empirical threshold for distinguishing the polarized multiparty systems in Europe. The data on the number of effective parties in the new democracies, however, tends to understate the actual degree of fragmentation. The left coalitions in both Bolivia and Peru were deeply divided internally, and a bitter internal power struggle rent the APRA in Peru following the death of its founder Haya de la Torre in 1980.[41] In Brazil, the PMDB had always constituted a wide anti-regime party-movement. The combination of federalism and an open-list proportional representation system reinforced the independence of local bosses and state governors within the PMDB, and the party began to disintegrate quickly after its landslide Congressional victory in 1986.

Finally, although deeply rooted support for the Radicals and Peronists appeared to create a durable two-party structure in Argentina, both parties remained deeply divided internally, and the small provincial parties held the balance of power in the legislature. These patterns implied serious problems for policymakers during the Alfonsín administration, although over time both major parties moved toward the center with reference to economic reform issues.[42]

The party systems reemerging in Uruguay and the Philippines also showed important continuities with the past, but unlike in the other crisis cases, the historical pattern that reemerged reflected the electoral dominance of catch-all parties. The Philippines was the only one of the crisis cases not to have a strong left or populist party. This was partly a function

[39] Giovanni Sartori, *Parties and Party Systems: A Framework for Analysis* (Cambridge, London, New York, and Melbourne: Cambridge University Press, 1976), pp. 132–37.

[40] On the effective number of parties, see Markku Laakso and Rein Taagepera, "The Effective Number of Parties: A Measure with Application to Western Europe," *Comparative Political Studies* 12 (1979): 3–27.

[41] Sandra Way-Hazelton and William A. Hazelton, "Sustaining Democracy in Peru: Dealing with Parliamentary and Revolutionary Challenges," in George A. Lopez and Michael Stohl, eds., *Liberalization and Redemocratization in Latin America* (New York, Westport, Conn., and London: Greenwood Press, 1987), pp. 105–36; Carol Graham, *Peru's APRA: Parties, Politics, and the Elusive Quest for Democracy* (Boulder, Colo.: Lynne Rienner, 1992), pp. 79–83.

[42] McDonald and Ruhl, *Party Politics and Elections in Latin America*, p. 161.

of political sociology, partly a function of the electoral rules. Labor organization was weak compared to Latin America, and the left was marginalized by its failure to strongly back Aquino's bid for the presidency. Despite a presidential system, single-member districts with a plurality voting rule in the House of Representatives, and a single, nationwide constituency for the Senate, there was evidence of increasing party fragmentation over time; however, in comparison to the other crisis cases, there was a distinct absence of ideological polarization.

In Uruguay, the left was a relatively potent political force and had gained an important base not only within the electorate but within the organized labor movement. Throughout the 1980s, however, the influence of the Broad Front (the Frente Amplio, or FA) was limited by the pervasive and stable support for the two traditional parties within the electorate, and by Uruguay's presidential system which reduced the leverage of third parties. As we argue in Part Two, these arrangements worked to counteract the centrifugal tendencies encouraged by the economic crisis and facilitated more effective policymaking during the first democratic administration.

In the non-crisis cases, the left was weaker, the programatic stance of the opposition much more restrained, and the extent of electoral polarization therefore limited. Chile provides the most dramatic evidence of change. During the early 1970s, the historic antagonisms between the Marxist left and other parties had produced one of the most polarized party systems in the world;[43] these divisions resurfaced again in the protests of the early 1980s.[44] By the late 1980s, however, the emergent party system had begun to evolve in a far more consensual direction that muted tendencies to polarization. Compared to its counterparts in most of the crisis cases, the Chilean left was weak relative to the conservative parties, although it remained a significant force. By the time of the transition most components of the left had also moved toward alignment with the centrist Christian Democrats, creating two dominant blocs.

Fragmentation also posed less of a challenge than it had in the past. If individual parties are counted separately, fractionalization within the legislature remained high. But parties had strong incentives to merge their electoral efforts with one of two relatively cohesive blocs, one center-left and the other on the right. This bipolar structure reflected both the narrowing of ideological differences and reduction in the number of effective party competitors.

At the social level, forces on the left were as strong if not stronger in

[43] Arturo Valenzuela, *The Breakdown of Democracy: Chile* (Baltimore and London: Johns Hopkins University Press, 1978), p. 6; Collier and Collier, *Shaping the Political Arena,* pp. 503–4.

[44] Genaro Arriagada, *Pinochet: The Politics of Power* (Boston: Unwin Hyman, 1988), pp. 67–81.

Korea and Turkey than in Chile. As in Chile, however, there were important restraints on electoral polarization. Korea experienced bitter industrial conflicts and extensive mobilization by radical students following the transition. Party forces, however, tended to converge toward the center. The closest thing to a left party in the 1987 and 1988 elections was Kim Dae Jung's Peace and Democracy Party (PDP), which gained about 25 percent of the presidential votes, slightly more than half the share received by "continuists" Roh and Kim Jong Pil; the PDP won a similar number of assembly seats. We count Kim Dae Jung's party as a "leftist" one in order not to bias the results in favor of our hypothesis; however, this characterization is misleading in important respects, in part because the party's base was ultimately regional as much as ideological, in part because its ideology was in fact quite conservative. The formation of the center-right Grand Coalition provided firm evidence that Kim Young Sam's opposition to the government did not have firm ideological roots; this maneuver also reduced the number of effective parties to less than two. The Grand Coalition provided effective legislative support to the Roh government, and further isolated Kim Dae Jung's Peace and Democracy Party. Kim Dae Jung distanced himself from the radicalized positions of the student and labor movement and developed an economic platform that closely resembled the program of his competitors to the right. Efforts to develop a more "genuine" left party after 1990 failed completely.

Distributive conflicts escalated in Turkey during the late 1980s as restraints on political contestation eased. This did not imply a return to the highly volatile and polarized politics of the late 1970s, however. In the early years of the transition, constitutional restrictions and support for Özal constrained tendencies toward fragmentation and polarization. When bans on the left were eased in the mid-1980s, two moderate social democratic parties (Ecevit's vehicle, the Social Democratic Party and the Social Democratic Populist Party) reentered the political fray; again for the sake of comparison, we include these parties in the "leftist" category. But their total vote share was still well below the level of support for the Motherland Party (ANAP) and other conservative parties. Electoral thresholds and the disproportional nature of the modified proportional representation system gave the left only 22 percent of parliamentary seats, less than a third of its conservative rivals' share.

There was only a thin margin of support for relaxing political restrictions in the mid-1980s, a fact that no doubt influenced the electoral strategies of the parties seeking readmittance to the system. The social democratic parties did gain in the municipal elections of 1989 and the general election of 1991, but the biggest winners were the *conservative* opponents of ANAP: the True Path Party and the Republican Party. When ANAP was finally toppled, it was by a coalition that included both the center-left Social

Democratic Populist Party (SHP) and the more conservative, rural-based True Path Party (DYP). While these parties did appeal to the losers from the structural adjustment effort, there was no possibility of an appeal based on a return to the pre-Özal status quo.

Thailand stands out among all of the cases as the most fractionalized of any of the systems in this study. Despite a new electoral law in 1981 aimed at raising the threshold of representation, the number of effective parties in the 1983 legislature was very high: 5.7. But as Doner and Laothomatas argue, the apparently fragmented system can be understood as a single dominant coalition composed of three major parties. Moreover, while many of the Thai parties sought to cater to patronage demands, particularly in the rural areas, none can really be considered leftist, Marxist, or populist.[45] All the parties remained weak relative to the prime minister and technocrats, who continued to wield extensive power over both the political and economic agenda, and more importantly, relative to the military; this was demonstrated dramatically in the coup of 1991.

CONCLUSION

There is substantial variation among both crisis and non-crisis cases with respect to the terms of the democratic transition. Outgoing authorities in the non-crisis cases were not uniformly successful in dictating all of the terms of their transitions, and military elites in some of the crisis cases, particularly Brazil, retained control over important areas of political life. Nonetheless, important differences are visible between the two transition paths. Not even the relatively powerful Brazilian military establishment could exert the kind of direct and indirect influence over the transition characteristic of Chile, Turkey, or Thailand; with respect to the other crisis cases, the contrast is even sharper.

The conditions that defined the terms of the transition, including the factors affecting the polarization and fragmentation of the party system, were not fixed. As the political barriers to entry fell in the non-crisis democracies, they began to exhibit at least some of the strains visible in more acute form in the crisis transitions. Nonetheless, the initial political differences outlined here did have important effects on the ability of incoming democratic governments both to manage the economy and to consolidate democratic institutions; these issues are the subject of the rest of this book.

[45] Richard Doner and Anek Laothamatas, "The Political Economy of Adjustment in Thailand," in Stephan Haggard and Steven B. Webb, eds., *Voting for Reform: The Politics of Adjustment in New Democracies*, pp. 411–63.

TABLE 4.3

Elections and Party Alignments in New Democracies

Country/Election	Continuist Party	Share[a]	Left Party	Share[a]	Continuist/ Left Ratio	Effective Number of Parties	Volatility
Argentina			Crisis Cases				
1983 Presidential	Continuist Total[d]	4.0	Peronists—Italo Luder	39.1	0.10	2.51	
1983 Parliamentary	Continuist Total	3.8	Peronists	39.1	0.09	2.53	
			Left Parties	2.1			
			Left Total	41.2			
1985 Parliamentary	Continuist Total	12.6	Left Parties	3.9	0.44	3.37	50.00
			Peronists	24.7			
			Left Total	28.6			
1987 Parliamentary	UCD	6.0	Left Parties	4.8	0.13	2.94	25.75
			Peronists	42.9			
			Left Total	47.7			
1989 Presidential	AC—Alvaro Alsogaray	6.6	IU—Vicente Zamora	2.5	0.13	2.96	
			Peronists—Carlos Menem	47.4			
			Left Total	49.9			
1989 Parliamentary	UCD	9.9	Left Parties	6.8	0.19	3.30	14.50
			Peronists	44.8			
			Left Total	51.6			
Post-transition Averages						2.93	30.08

Bolivia

Election	Party	%		%			
1979 Presidential	ADN—Hugo Banzer	14.9	UDP	36.0	0.36	3.50	
			PS-1	4.8			
			VO	1.1			
			Left Total	41.9			
1979 Parliamentary	ADN	14.9	UDP	36.0	0.36	3.50	
			PS-1	4.8			
			VO	1.1			
			Left Total	41.9			
1980 Presidential	ADN—Hugo Banzer	16.8	UDP	38.7	0.34	4.36	
			PS-1	8.7			
			VO	0.0			
			FSB	1.6			
			Left Total	49.0			
1980 Parliamentary	ADN	16.8	UDP	38.7	0.34	4.36	20.90
			PS-1	8.7			
			VO	0.0			
			FSB	1.6			
			Left Total	49.0			
1985 Presidential	ADN—Hugo Banzer	32.8	PS-1	2.5	1.27	4.58	
			FSB	1.3			
			MIR	10.2			
			MNRI	5.5			
			MNRV	4.8			
			MNRI-1	0.8			
			IU	0.7			
			Left Total	25.8			

TABLE 4.3 (continued)

Country/Election	Continuist Party	Share[a]	Left Party	Share[a]	Continuist/ Left Ratio	Effective Number of Parties	Volatility
1985 Parliamentary	ADN	32.8	PS-1	2.6	1.27	4.58	59.13
			FSB	1.3			
			MIR	10.2			
			MNRI	5.5			
			MNRV	4.8			
			MNRI-1	0.8			
			IU	0.7			
			Left Total	25.9			
1989 Presidential	ADN	25.4	PS-1	2.8	0.77	4.94	
			MIR	22.0			
			IU	8.1			
			Left Total	32.9			
1989 Parliamentary	ADN	25.2	PS-1	2.8	0.77	5.02	33.50
			MIR	21.8			
			IU	8.0			
			Left Total	32.6			
Post-transition Averages						4.36	37.84
Brazil							
1986 House[e]	PFL	23.6	PT	3.9	3.14	2.58	
	PDS	7.4	PDT	4.9			
			PCB	0.4			
			PC do B	0.4			
			PSB	0.2			
	Continuist Total	31.0	Left Total	9.9			

1989 Presidential	PFL	0.9	PT	17.2	0.28	5.69	77.91
	PDS—Paulo Salim Maluf	8.9	PDT	16.5			
	Continuist Total	9.8	PCB	1.1			
			Left Total	34.8			
1990 House[e]	PFL	18.3	PT	6.8	1.32	8.36	49.36
	PDS	8.0	PDT	9.2			
	Continuist Total	26.2	PCB	0.6			
			PC do B	1.0			
			PSB	2.4			
			Left Total	19.9			
Post-transition Averages						5.54	63.64
Peru							
1978 Constituent[f]	PPC	23.8	APRA	35.3	0.46	4.78	
			PSR	6.6			
			PCP	5.9			
			FNTC	3.9			
			Left Total	51.7			
1980 Presidential	PPC—Luis Bedoya	9.6	APRA—Armando Villanueva	27.4	0.31	3.39	
			IU—Leonidas Rodríguez	3.7			
			Left Total	31.1			
1980 House	PPC/CODE	9.2	APRA	27.0	0.30	3.93	
			IU	3.7			
			Left Total	30.7			
1985 Presidential	PPC—Luis Bedoya	11.9	APRA	53.1	0.15	2.76	49.88
			IU	24.7			
			PSP	0.2			
			Left Total	78.0			

TABLE 4.3 (continued)

Country/Election	Continuist Party	Share[a]	Left Party	Share[a]	Continuist/ Left Ratio	Effective Number of Parties	Volatility
1985 House	PPC/CODE	11.2	APRA	50.4	0.15	3.00	45.71
			IU	24.6			
			Left Total	75.0			
1990 Presidential	No Continuist Party		APRA	22.6		3.98	
			IU	8.2			
			IS	4.8			
			Left Total	35.6			
1990 House	No Continuist Party		APRA	24.8		4.77	67.27
			IU	9.8			
			IS	5.3			
			Left Total	39.9			
Post-transtion Averages						3.80	54.29
Philippines							
1986 Presidential	Ferdinand Marcos	40–50	No Left				
1987 House	No Continuist Party		No Left			1.22	
1992 Presidential	KBL—Imelda Marcos	10.3	No Left			3.58	
1992 House	KBL	1.5	No Left			5.84	100
Post-transition Averages						3.55	100
Uruguay							
1984 Presidential	PC—Pacheco/Piran	9.7	FA	21.3	0.46	2.96	
1984 House	No Right		FA	21.3	0.00	2.96	
1989 Presidential	PC—Pacheco/Millor	14.7	FA	21.2	0.69	3.38	
1989 House	No Right		FA	21.2	0.00	3.38	20.42
Post-transition						3.17	20.42

Non-crisis Cases

Chile							
1988 Plebiscite	Yes vote[g]	43.0					
1989 Presidential	Independent—Hernan Büchi	29.4	No Left			2.41	
	Independent—Francisco Javier Errazuriz	15.5					
	Continuist Total	44.9			2.01	2.52[h]	
1989 House	RN	18.3	PPD	11.5			
	UDI	9.8	PSCH	0.2			
	List B Independents	6.1	PAIS	4.4			
	Continuist Total	34.2	List G Independents	0.9			
			Left Total	17.0			
Post-transition Averages						2.47	
Korea							
1987 Presidential	Roh Tae Woo	35.9	Kim Dae Jung	26.5	1.35	3.51	
1988 Assembly	DJP	41.8	PDP	23.4	2.29	3.53	20.96
	NDRP	11.7					
	Continuist Total	53.5					
1992 Presidential	No Continuist Party		Kim Dae Jung	33.8		3.15	
1992 Assembly	No Continuist Party		DP	29.2		3.60	
Post-transition Averages						3.45	42.97[i]
Thailand							
1983 Parliamentary	Chart Thai	20.7	No Left		5.35		
	Prachakorn Thai	10.1					
	Continuist Total	30.8					

TABLE 4.3 (continued)

Country/Election	Continuist Party	Share[a]	Left Party	Share[a]	Continuist/ Left Ratio	Effective Number of Parties	Volatility
1986 Parliamentary	Chart Thai	18.1	No Left		6.1	43.21	
	Prachakorn Thai	6.9					
	Continuist Total	25.1					
1988 Parliamentary	Chart Thai	24.4	No Left			7.74	29.10
	Prachakorn Thai	8.7					
	Continuist Total	33.1					
1992a Parliamentary	Chart Thai	20.6	No Left			6.01	73.28
	Samakhitham	21.9					
	Social Action	8.6					
	Continuist Total	51.1					
1992b Parliamentary	Prachakorn Thai	0.8					
	Social Action	6.1					
	Rassadorn	0.3					
	Seritham	2.2					
	Chart Pattana	16.7					
	Continuist Total	47.5					
Post-transition Averages						6.27	48.89
Turkey							
1983 Parliamentary	NDP	23.0	No Left			2.84	
	MP	45.0					
	Continuist Total	68.0					
1987 Parliamentary	MP	36.0	No Left			4.13	63.65
			SP	0.4			
1991 Parliamentary	MP	24.0	SDPP	21.0	1.12	4.64	20.30
			Left Total	21.4			
Post-transition						3.87	41.08

Sources: All Latin American cases except Brazilian Chamber of Deputies: *Enciclopedia Electoral Latinoamericana y del Caribe* (San José, Costa Rica: Instituto Interamericano de Derechos Humanos, 1993); Brazil, Chamber of Deputies: *Europa World Year Book 1991* (London: Europa Publications, 1991) and *South America, Central America and the Caribbean, 1993* (London: Europa Publications, 1993); Philippines and Korea: *Europa World Year Book 1991* (London: Europa Publications, 1991), and *Far East and Australasia, 1994* (London: Europa Publications, 1994); Thailand: Daniel E. King, "The Thai Parliamentary Elections of 1992," *Electoral Studies* 12 (1993): 268–74; Turkey: Ziya Önis and Steven B. Webb, "Turkey: Democratization and Adjustment from Above," in Stephan Haggard and Steven Webb, eds., *Voting for Reform* (New York: Oxford University Press for the World Bank, 1994), p 138; *Keesing's Record of World Events* (Cambridge: Longham), various issues.

Notes: Party names are as follows: AC, Alliance of the Center; ADN, Nationalist Democratic Action; APRA, Popular Revolutionary Alliance of America; CODE, Democratic Convergence; DJP, Democratic Justice Party; DP, Democratic Party; FA, Broad Front; FNTC, National Front of Workers and Peasants; FSB, Bolivian Socialist Falange; IS, Socialist Left; IU, United Left; MIR, Movement of the Revolutionary Left; MNRI, National Movement of the Revolutionary Left; MNRI-1, National Movement of the Revolutionary Left/1; MNRV, National Revolutionary Vanguard Movement; MP, Motherland Party; NDP, National Democratic Party; NDRP, New Democratic Republic Party; PAIS, Broad Party of the Socialist Left; PC, Red Party; PCB, Brazilian Communist Party; PC do B, Communist Party of Brazil; PCP, Communist Party of Peru; PDP, Peace and Democracy Party; PDS, Social Democratic Party; PDT, Democratic Labor Party; PFL, Liberal Front Party; PPC, Popular Christian Party; PPD, Party for Democracy; PS-1, Socialist Party One; PSB, Socialist Party of Brazil; PSCH, Chilean Socialist Party; PSR, Revolutionary Socialist Party; PT, Labor Party; SDPP, Social Democratic Popular Party; SP, Socialist Party; RN, National Renovation; UCD, Union of the Democratic Center; UDI, Independent Democratic Union; UDP, Democratic and Popular Unity; VO, Workers' Vanguard.

[a] All shares are of popular vote except as noted.

[b] The effective number of parties is defined as the inverse of the sum of the squares of the vote or seat share going to each party. See M. Laakso and R. Taagepera, "Effective Number of Parties: A Measure with Application to West Europe," *Comparative Political Studies* 12 (1979): 3–27.

[c] Volatility is measured as the sum of the absolute values of the percentage point gains and losses for each party from one election to the next, divided by two.

[d] Total includes four small parties associated with the outgoing military regime.

[e] Denotes share of seats.

[f] The Constituent Assembly election of 1978 was the first democratic election after the transition.

[g] Yes votes in the plebiscite indicated support for Pinochet's efforts to extend his rule, and are thus counted as continuist.

[h] Effective number of parties refers to competing electoral blocs.

[i] In 1990, the Democratic Justice Party, the Reunification Democratic Party, and the New Democratic Republican Party merged to form the Democratic Liberal Party. Volatility is calculated by comparing the vote shares for the DJP, RDP, and NDRP in 1988 with the vote share of the DLP in 1992.

Part Two

THE POLITICAL ECONOMY OF
ADJUSTMENT IN NEW DEMOCRACIES

CHAPTER FIVE

Democratic Transitions and Economic Reform

THE TRANSITIONS discussed in Part One have reopened long-standing debates about the capacity of democratic governments in the developing world to achieve stable economic growth. By the 1980s, fears about the "ungovernability" of advanced industrial democracies had subsided,[1] but quite similar arguments resurfaced in discussions of the new democratic regimes in Latin America, Asia, Eastern Europe, and the republics that emerged from the collapse of the Soviet Union. Could these new democracies make the sacrifices associated with stabilization and market-oriented economic reform? Could such adjustments be sustained over time?

Expectations have been sharply divided.[2] Optimists suggested that democratization advances the cause of economic reform by exposing the inefficiencies of authoritarian rule to competitive politics.[3] The "honeymoon" associated with the transition to democracy provides an opportunity for incoming governments to undertake difficult economic policy reforms that contribute to growth over the longer run; this was the political logic of "shock therapy." New democracies can also draw on a reservoir of consent that authoritarian regimes lacked, and have the potential to forge agreements or "social pacts" that might distribute the costs of adjustment in a more equitable, and thus sustainable, way.

On the other hand, the evident difficulties experienced by some new democracies underlined the fact that political opening can also produce

---

[1] See Michel J. Crozier, Samuel P. Huntington, and Joji Watanuki, *The Crisis of Democracy: Report on the Governability of Democracies to the Trilateral Commission* (New York: New York University Press, 1975). From a different theoretical perspective, see James O'Connor, *The Fiscal Crisis of the State* (New York: St. Martin's Press, 1973).

[2] For a succinct overview of the contending views in these debates, see Peter Gourevitch, "Democracy and Economic Policy: Elective Affinities and Circumstantial Conjunctures," *World Development* 21 (1993): 1271–80.

[3] For a theoretical argument about the positive effects of democracy on growth, see Mancur Olson, "Dictatorship, Democracy and Development," *American Political Science Review* 87 (1993): 567–76. On the efficiency effects of political competition, see Gary S. Becker, "A Theory of Competition among Pressure Groups for Political Influence," *The Quarterly Journal of Economics* 98 (1983): 371–400. Recent policy statements emphasizing the positive relationship between democratization and economic performance include United States Agency for International Development, *Democracy and Governance* (Washington, D.C.: USAID, 1991), and The World Bank, *Managing Development: The Governance Dimension* (Washington, D.C.: World Bank, 1991). A general statement of this relationship is in Milton Friedman, *Capitalism and Freedom* (Chicago: University of Chicago Press, 1962).

new impediments to coherent economic management.[4] New democratic governments face exceptionally strong distributive pressures, both from groups reentering the political arena after long periods of repression and from established interests demanding reassurance. Uncertainties with respect to the stability of the new democratic order, moreover, affect the time horizons of both private and public actors. In some countries, new democratic leaders have pursued policies aimed at managing opposition in the short run while discounting the gains from less popular reform measures.

These contending arguments about the advantages new democratic governments enjoy are all theoretically plausible; individual cases can be deployed to buttress either optimistic or pessimistic conclusions. Yet neither picture has been born out in a general way by the experiences of recent transitions. The growing body of cross-national empirical research on the economic effects of democracy and democratization in developing countries reaches highly ambiguous results. Some studies suggest that democratic governments perform less well, some argue that democracies perform better, but the bulk of the literature finds no significant relationship one way or the other.[5]

The absence of a clear-cut relationship between democratization, policy, and economic performance reflects a fundamental theoretical problem in

[4] For a more detailed summary of these arguments, see Stephan Haggard and Robert R. Kaufman, "Economic Adjustment in New Democracies," in Joan M. Nelson, ed., *Fragile Coalitions: The Politics of Economic Adjustment* (Washington, D.C.: The Overseas Development Council, 1989), pp. 57–59.

[5] The most comprehensive reviews of the cross-national quantitative literature on the relationship between regime type and economic performance are Larry Sirowy and Alex Inkeles, "The Effects of Democracy on Economic Growth and Inequality," *Studies in Comparative International Development* 25 (1990): 126–57; Adam Przeworski and Fernando Limongi, "Political Regimes and Economic Growth," *Journal of Economic Perspectives* 7 (1993): 51–69; John Helliwell, "Empirical Linkages Between Democracy and Economic Growth," *British Journal of Political Science* 24 (1994): 225–48; and Alberto Alesina and Roberto Perotti, "The Politics of Growth: A Survey," unpublished ms., Harvard University, 1993. Sirowy and Inkeles find slightly more evidence of a negative effect of democracy on growth; Helliwell finds no direct effect of democracy on growth, but indirect positive effects through increased investment and education. However, all four reviews emphasize the indeterminacy of the findings.

Fewer studies have tackled the question of the effects of democratic *transitions* on economic policy and performance. Karen Remmer argues that there is no relationship in "Democracy and Economic Crisis: the Latin American Experience," *World Politics* 42 (1990): 315–35. Our other work has found that democratization does lead to short-term economic difficulties in the management of macroeconomic policy and inflation. See Haggard and Kaufman, "Economic Adjustment in New Democracies"; and Haggard, Kaufman, and Steven B. Webb, "Democracy, Dictatorship, and Inflation in Middle-Income Countries," unpublished ms., 1991. Marc Lindenberg and Shantayanan Devarajan reach similar conclusions with a larger sample of countries in "Prescribing Strong Economic Medicine: Revis-

the way the controversy has been framed. The analytic emphasis on regime type glosses over differences both in the nature of the problems new democracies face and in institutional structures that may be important for explaining variations in economic performance. In Part Two, we elaborate the arguments outlined in the introduction concerning differences in policy between the crisis and non-crisis transitions. We emphasize both the nature of economic circumstances, and the way resulting political cleavages and alignments are mediated by institutions, particularly the party system.

New democratic governments that came to power in the wake of crises had incentives to undertake new policy initiatives, but implementation was difficult precisely because economic problems were more acute and demands for short-term economic relief more widespread. Incoming democratic governments in the non-crisis cases faced a political and policy setting shaped by the fact that authoritarian regimes had already undertaken substantial economic reforms and built a coalition of beneficiaries. In these cases, a major question was whether such policies would be sustained under conditions of more open political competition.

Differences in economic conditions at the time of the transition provide an important point of departure for understanding the balance of social forces and the agenda of economic issues faced by new democracies. To understand how these policy issues were resolved, however, it is also necessary to examine the way social conflict was muted or amplified by the political institutions reconstructed during the transition, particularly the powers of the executive and the party system analyzed in chapter 4. In a number of new democratic governments, particularly among the crisis cases, centrifugal forces in the party system increased the opportunities to challenge policy reform, fragmented political support, and made it difficult to sustain stable electoral, legislative, or interest-group coalitions. In other countries, authoritarian rule produced centripetal realignments in the party system that strengthened the center, reduced the power of electoral and partisan forces opposed to reform, and broadened the support for strong executive action.

This chapter provides the analytic framework for the empirical discussion that follows in chapters 6 through 8. We begin with discussions of the policy outcomes we seek to explain, and of the general political challenges posed by those policies. The next two sections provide a framework for analyzing how differences in economic starting point and in the nature of

---

iting the Myths about Structural Adjustment, Democracy, and Economic Performance in Developing Countries," *Comparative Politics* 25 (1993): 169–83. Adam Przeworksi, by contrast, argues that policy reforms can advance quite far under democratic auspices, but that the reforms themselves tend to be politically destabilizing. See *Democracy and the Market* (New York: Cambridge University Press, 1990), pp. 162–87.

representative institutions affect the capacity of new democratic governments to make economic policy. In the last section we preview briefly the empirical arguments of subsequent chapters.

DEFINING THE PROBLEM: ECONOMIC POLICY AND PERFORMANCE

In the broadest terms, our objective is to explain the ability of new political leaderships to define and implement a policy course that contributes to sustainable economic growth with macroeconomic stability. Where existing policies meet these objectives, the task of the government is to sustain those policies. Where policy change is required, we are interested in whether governments initiate and sustain reform efforts, formulate inconsistent policies, or delay reform altogether.

One way of measuring such efforts is to look directly at indicators of economic performance, particularly inflation and growth; this is the approach advocated by Bresser Perreira, Maravall, and Przeworski in their recent study of economic reform in new democracies, and is the typical method in the burgeoning cross-national quantitative literature on the political economy of growth.[6] Yet looking at performance can be misleading, particularly over the relatively short run that is the subject of analysis here. Poor performance may not be an indication of policy failure if it is the best attainable given existing constraints. Similarly, high growth can be purchased through unsustainable policies, but we would not consider such growth to constitute evidence of success. We agree with Bresser Pereira, Maravall, and Przeworski that the success of any adjustment effort must ultimately be measured by its contribution to sustained economic growth. Analytically, we take economic performance into account because it affects the level of support and opposition for a given policy stance. Nevertheless, our primary concern is not to explain economic performance per se; that would require a convincing theory of economic growth that is still lacking. Rather, we examine the determinants of policy choice.

We focus on two broad clusters of policies that recur in virtually all discussions of economic performance in the developing world: macroeconomic policies designed to stabilize the economy, and reforms of the trade and exchange-rate regimes aimed at achieving a sustainable balance-of-payments position. We do not claim that these reforms are sufficient in

---

[6] See Luiz Carlos Bresser Pereira, José María Maravall, and Adam Przeworski, *Economic Reforms in New Democracies: A Social Democratic Approach* (New York: Cambridge University Press, 1993), particularly their critique of our earlier work on pp. 3–4. For a review of the economics literature, see Alesina and Perotti, "The Politics of Growth."

themselves to achieve growth; we return to this issue in chapter 9. For most developing countries, however, some reform in these two policy domains and the maintenance of a relatively stable policy regime constitute necessary conditions for renewed investment and growth.

There is considerable debate about the appropriate policy mix for achieving price stability under different circumstances, and particularly over whether traditional macroeconomic policy instruments are adequate for stabilizing very high inflations. Stabilization may involve wage and price controls as well as the traditional instruments of fiscal, monetary, and exchange-rate policy. Yet there is substantial agreement that high and variable inflation inhibits investment and growth, and that budget deficits have been a major source of inflation. Moreover, there is substantial agreement that stabilization efforts must include a strong and sustained fiscal component, regardless of the sources of inflation or of the nature of the complementary policy measures that may also be required.[7]

There is also debate about how to best achieve a sustainable balance-of-payments position in both the short and long run. There is substantial controversy about the speed and size of required devaluations and the optimal exchange-rate regime, and significant disagreement with regard to the pace or extent of trade liberalization that is desirable, whether there is a role for industrial policy in promoting exports, and how trade reforms should be coordinated with stabilization efforts.[8] Yet there appears to be a significant positive relationship between trade and long-run growth,[9] and a growing consensus that the trade and exchange-rate regimes of most de-

[7] For statements that reflect the convergence on the importance of macroeconomic stability from a variety of analytic and political perspectives, see The World Bank, *Adjustment Lending Policies for Sustainable Growth,* The World Bank Country Economics Department, Policy and Research Series, no. 14, (Washington, D.C.: World Bank, 1990), pp. 44–48; I. M. D. Little et al., *Boom, Crisis and Adjustment: the Macroeconomic Experience of Developing Countries* (New York: Oxford University Press, 1993), pp. 344–59; Jose Maria Fanelli, Roberto Frenkel, and Guillermo Rosenwucel, *Growth and Structural Reform in Latin America: Where We Stand* (Buenos Aires: CEDES, 1991); Luiz Carlos Bresser Pereira, "Efficiency and Politics of Economic Reform in Latin America," Occasional Paper, East-South Systems Transformation, Department of Political Science, University of Chicago, February 1992. For recent empirical evidence on the relationship between fiscal policy, inflation and long-run growth, see William Easterly and Sergio Rebelo, "Fiscal Policy and Economic Growth: an Empirical Investigation," and Stanley Fischer, "The Role of Macroeconomic Factors in Growth," in *Journal of Monetary Economics* 32 (1993): 417–58, 485–512.

[8] See, for example, Dani Rodrik, "The Limits of Trade Policy Reform in LDCs," *Journal of Economic Perspectives* 6 (1992): 87–105; and Robert Wade, *Governing the Market: Economic Theory and the Role of Government in East Asian Industrialization* (Princeton, N.J.: Princeton University Press, 1990), pp. 113–58.

[9] This is one of the few robust findings to emerge from the sensitivity analysis by Ross Levine and David Renelt of a number of cross-national growth studies, "A Sensitivity Analysis of Cross-Country Growth Regressions," *American Economic Review* 82 (1992): 942–63.

veloping countries have been unduly biased against exports, that protection has been excessive, and that exchange rates have been both overvalued and unstable.[10] We are interested in government efforts to address these policy biases and to develop a trade and exchange-rate regime that minimizes the risk of recurrent balance-of-payments crises.

POLITICAL BARRIERS TO ECONOMIC REFORM

If an alternative policy regime is more conducive to overall growth than the existing one, why is it that political leaders may fail to adopt it? The political impediments to reform include collective action dilemmas, distributive conflicts, and the discounts that decision-makers attach to the payoffs from successful reform.

Collective action problems arise to the extent that economic reforms have the properties of a public good, either for the society as a whole or for a large number of potential beneficiaries.[11] In reality, few reforms can be modeled as pure public goods. Nonetheless, the problem of free-riding is visible in a number of policy areas and can be illustrated through reference both to inflation control and to trade liberalization. In most high-inflation settings, a majority would gain from greater price stability. However, the cooperative behavior needed to stabilize might be unobtainable because of the incentives for individuals and groups to defend their incomes. In the case of stabilizing very high inflations, for example, the risks of accepting de-indexation can be substantial if other sectors are not making similar and simultaneous sacrifices. In the case of trade liberalization, a large array of potential beneficiaries lack incentives to organize and lobby, either because they are weakly organized or because they could not be excluded from the gains brought about by a general reduction in trade barriers.

The distributive implications of economic reforms constitute a second political challenge. In the collective action model, all parties would prefer

---

[10] For different angles on this basic point see Jagdish Bhagwati, "Export Promoting Trade Strategy: Issues and Evidence," *World Bank Research Observer* (1988): 27–57; Demetris Papageorgiou, Armeane Choksi, and Michael Michaely, *Liberalizing Foreign Trade: Lessons of Experience in the Developing World* (Cambridge: Basil Blackwell, 1990); Albert Fishlow, "The State of Latin American Economics," in Interamerican Development Bank, *Economic and Social Progress in Latin America: External Debt, Crisis and Adjustment)* (Washington, D.C.: IDB, 1985), pp. 123–48; Colin Bradford and William Branson, "Patterns of Trade and Structural Change," in *Trade and Structural Change in Pacific Asia* (Chicago: University of Chicago Press, 1987), pp. 3–26.

[11] Barbara Geddes has placed particular emphasis on the role of collective action problems in economic reform. See *Politician's Dilemma: Building State Capacity in Latin America* (Berkeley: University of California Press, 1994).

a cooperative outcome but are blocked from it by incentives to defect. In a distributive model, policy reform is supported by winners and opposed by losers, and the outcome is given by the balance of political power between the respective coalitions. Trade reforms and devaluations again provide a useful example. Though such measures might increase both aggregate social wealth and the income of specific groups, they also typically encounter opposition from import-competing interests and the non-traded goods sector respectively.

There are several reasons why the losers from reform may prevail, even if the policy reform is optimal for society as a whole. One classic problem with many reforms is that the costs of reform tend to be concentrated, while benefits are diffuse, producing perverse organizational incentives; losers are well organized, while prospective winners face daunting collective action problems and are not. In principal, a reform that generates a net social gain should be politically viable if a portion of the gains are used to compensate the groups experiencing losses. Yet such compensatory mechanisms may not exist. Moreover, as Fernández and Rodrik have pointed out, additional difficulties are introduced if we assume uncertainty about the outcome of the reform, as we certainly must.[12] Not only are prospective winners likely to be poorly organized, they may not even know who they are. Finally, as we will discuss in more detail below, institutional arrangements may amplify the veto power of losers by effectively granting them a disproportionate weight in policy considerations.

Both the collective action and distributive approaches to policy reform assume that policy is ultimately the result of conflicts among contending social groups. A third set of problems arise if we examine the incentives faced by government decision-makers. Again, politicians should be willing to undertake reforms that provide net social gains; our cases do provide several examples of leaders who were punished not for undertaking reform, but for the failure to act aggressively enough. Yet institutional and political factors can lead the politician to discount future gains steeply, for example, because of impending elections or the fear of sparking demonstrations or riots.[13] This does not mean that politicians are irrational; it simply means

[12] Raquel Fernández and Dani Rodrik, "Resistance to Reform: Status Quo Bias in the Presence of Individual-Specific Uncertainty," *American Economic Review* 81 (1991): 1146–55.

[13] There has been a substantial theoretical debate about the utility of political business-cycle models. The traditional model postulated that parties in power manipulate macroeconomic policy in the short run in order to maximize electoral chances, stimulating the economy as elections approach, and stabilizing immediately after them. Empirical evidence supporting the model proved weak for the advanced industrial states. Proponents of the alternative partisan business-cycle model argued that if voters had rational expectations about the future effects of expansionary policies, efforts to manipulate macroeconomic policy in the short run should have no political or economic effect. Rather, incumbent governments and oppositions appealed to segments of the electorate with different policy preferences. We

that given some institutional and political constraints, the time horizons over which they assess the political costs and benefits of reform may be too short for reform to constitute a viable policy equilibrium.

These three problems—of collective action, distributive conflicts, and time horizons—suggest that the political and institutional prerequisites of successful reform can be daunting, particularly where economic problems are severe. Solving collective action problems requires either leadership or institutional mechanisms that coordinate the actions of different parties and provide credible assurances.[14] Managing distributive conflicts requires either the resources to effectively compensate losers—resources that are typically in short supply during economic crises—or the political capacity to override their objections. Finally, some degree of security of tenure would appear to be a minimal requirement of successful reform, since a high degree of insecurity shortens time horizons and increases the discount assigned to future payoffs.

Simply listing these conditions suggests why newly established democratic governments may have difficulty undertaking economic reform. First, new democratic governments conduct economic policy in an institutional environment undergoing profound change. The security of the new order cannot necessarily be taken for granted, and even where it can, electoral pressures are likely to be intense during the early phases of democratic rule. To consolidate the transition in the short run, and their own political positions, new leaders may be tempted to pursue economic policies that cannot be sustained.

The ability to coordinate may also be substantially weakened in the early period following a democratic transition. Conceivably, such transitions can increase the incentive to resolve collective action problems through the negotiation of social pacts. Yet as we argue in more detail in chapter 10, contending economic interests typically lack the organization and trust

---

argue below for a partisan political-cycle model, but it is worth noting that developing countries lack many of the characteristics that mute opportunism in the advanced industrial states, including an informed public, consultative mechanisms that provide socioeconomic groups with information about government policies and their likely effects, and insulated government institutions such as an independent central bank or budget bureau. Lower levels of income, extensive poverty, and the absence of welfare systems to cushion the costs of economic crisis also shorten the time horizons of voters; under such conditions, electoral support might plausibly be linked to government delivery of short-term material benefits. For an overview of the theoretical debate on the political business-cycle literature, see Alberto Alesina, "Macroeconomics and Politics," *Macroeconomics Annual* (Cambridge: MIT Press, 1988), pp. 13–52. For an empirical effort to test for political business cycles in Latin America, see Barry Ames, *Political Survival: Politicians and Public Policy in Latin America* (Berkeley: University of California Press, 1987).

[14] William T. Bianco and Robert Bates, "Cooperation by Design: Leadership, Structure, and Collective Dilemmas," *American Political Science Review* 84 (1990): 133–48.

required to form such encompassing bargains, while the government itself typically lacks institutionalized mechanisms for consultation. The organizational weakness of both political parties and economic interest groups has led to alternation between periods of immobilism and efforts to solve coordination problems through the exercise of executive power without adequate bases of organized political support.

Finally, it is clear that transitional democracies typically face intense distributive pressures. These do not come exclusively, or even mainly, from low-income groups; equally important are demands from business, military, and other elite veto groups seeking to maintain their privileges under the new order. Though all constitutional governments face the problem of assuring the powerful that democratic processes will not undermine their status, the uncertainties associated with regime change intensify the demand for such assurances.

Previously excluded sectors of the population, of course, can also be expected to increase efforts to press distributive claims within the new political order. This problem is particularly severe where economic performance is poor and governments confront the need for major economic reform. Yet even where performance is good, the uneven distribution of income and the perception of unfairness regarding the policies of the authoritarian order provide incentives for groups reentering the system to challenge the status quo.

Over the long run, the consolidation of reform within a democratic context ultimately rests on the construction of broad bases of support, drawing on the beneficiaries of the policy measures in question. As we will argue in Part Three, this may involve the construction of various forms of social insurance against the risks associated with market-oriented policy. However it may take some time both for new winners to emerge and to organize politically. In the interim, policy remains vulnerable to distributive challenges.

THE POLITICAL IMPLICATIONS OF ECONOMIC INHERITANCE

A central argument of Part Two is that the severity of the political problems just outlined depends on the initial economic conditions facing new democratic governments. New democratic governments that assume office amid crisis face both opportunities for reform and serious political dilemmas. The opportunities derive from broad public demands that "something must be done." Under crisis conditions, publics are willing to grant executives wide leeway in formulating and initiating reform programs, though the extent of public tolerance will depend on the depth of the crisis and the extent to which it is attributed to particular policy failures of the previous government. The political dilemmas arise from the fact that crises also escalate the demands on the government from specific groups and economic interests, demands that are likely to cut against the thrust of the reform effort. The tension between the broad demand for change and the claims of particular interests is likely to be especially acute during the initiation phase of reform, when the benefits of policy change remain uncertain and organized bases of support for the new policy course have not yet emerged.

The resolution of this tension will depend in the first instance on the strength of "popular mandates" and the relative power of organized interests. In the former socialist countries, the economic failures of the late 1980s were widely attributed to "socialism," granting new governments incredible leeway to act. Moreover, organized interests were initially weak. This opened large windows of political opportunity to initiate sweeping market-oriented reform programs. Difficulties set in, however, as the costs of adjustment became apparent, as political honeymoons came to an end, and as broad popular movements fragmented into a diversity of conflicting and organized interests.

In the mixed economies of Latin America and Asia, the crises that led to the displacement of authoritarian rule had different effects. The perception that the preceding economic model was to blame for economic distress was less widespread, and affected interests were generally better organized. As a result, reform was either delayed or partial in its scope. As we show in chapter 6, more comprehensive reform efforts came only when the profound economic failure of these early reform efforts strengthened broad public support for drastic action and weakened organized opposition.

One component of these early failures was an acceleration of inflation, which created additional political difficulties.[15] The stabilization of high, and particularly hyperinflations, arguably holds out the promise of substantial political gain, since the disruption they entail is so immense. But stabilizing high, inertial inflations poses particularly difficult coordination and distributional problems.[16] In such settings, the formal or informal indexing of prices, wages, and interest payments is widespread and makes the price level extremely vulnerable to exogenous shocks, as temporary

---

[15] The single exception was the Philippines, where Marcos had stabilized prices under intense pressure from external creditors.

[16] There are also difficulties in conducting fiscal policy in high-inflation settings. Since financial instruments are typically indexed, interest payments on government debt can cause spending to spiral out of control even when fiscal authorities are undertaking substantial cuts in non-interest expenditures. Under conditions of high inflation, lags in tax collection and in the adjustment of tax brackets contribute to an erosion in the real value of government revenues. In all of the crisis cases, fiscal stress was compounded by reduced access to foreign borrowing and large external debt burdens.

price changes are quickly transmitted throughout the economy and become permanent. As inflation accelerates, contract periods shorten, and the appropriate inflation adjustment for current contracts becomes the source of severe distributional conflict. While each sector might be better off from a general de-indexing the staggering of contracts makes this difficult; the sector that is de-indexed first risks substantial losses in real income. These problems constitute virtually a textbook example of a collective action dilemma and explain why heterodox measures involving incomes policy are not only politically attractive for breaking inertial expectations, but economically necessary as well.

The gains from such heterodox measures, however, will not be sustainable without other adjustments that also pose acute distributive dilemmas. Changes in fiscal and monetary policy are almost always necessary, not only for their direct effect on prices but because of the crucial role of expectations in perpetuating high inflations. Adjustment programs that lack credibility because they are inconsistent will be undermined quickly by forward-looking economic agents.[17] Credible macroeconomic policy adjustments are particularly difficult in settings already characterized by economic stagnation, and where the ability of the government to extract taxes is limited by the political power of high-income groups and their ability to shift assets and income abroad. Finally, problems of stabilization typically overlap with pressures to correct severe balance-of-payments disequilibria. In addition to the fiscal, monetary, and incomes policies just outlined, correcting such imbalances involves politically charged adjustments in the exchange rate.

The non-crisis cases did not face the severe policy dilemmas characteristic of the crisis cases. Where aggregate economic performance is strong, there are fewer incentives for governments to change course, and fewer demands from social actors that they do so. The principal challenge for these governments was how to sustain what had gone before, and this was an easier task both economically and politically. As we argued in chapter 4, the combination of a coherent policy project and good performance served to consolidate a bloc of interests, rooted in the private sector, that was committed to defending the policy status quo.

Notwithstanding such advantages, however, non-crisis governments did face important political difficulties in maintaining coherent macroeconomic policy. Despite the general success of the authoritarian governments with

---

[17] An important example of the government's vulnerability in this regard centers on the exchange rate. Expectations of future inflation are reflected in flight into foreign exchange, which will result in widening black-market premia (where there are exchange controls), deteriorating balance of payments and strong pressure to devalue (under a fixed rate), and an increase in the price of foreign exchange (under a floating-rate regime). These exchange-rate dynamics themselves constitute a major source of instability.

respect to macroeconomic policy, controversial adjustment issues remained on the agenda in all of the non-crisis cases. The incoming governments in Turkey and Chile faced risks of resurgent inflation, and all of the non-crisis cases faced politically controversial trade and financial policy reforms.

The most serious political challenges in the non-crisis cases, however, related to questions of equity and distribution. The reforms undertaken by the military in Chile and Turkey cut against the interests of a large non-traded goods sector, which included workers in informal urban services, unionized labor, public employees, and small businesses. Approximately 40 percent of the Chilean population lived below the poverty line in 1990, the year the government changed hands.[18] In Korea and Thailand, sustained high growth had been accompanied by rapidly rising real wages. But increasing income disparities began to appear under the big push policies of the 1970s in Korea, and were exacerbated by the boom of the mid-1980s. These distributional issues were an important motivation for labor protest against the old regime, and continued under the Roh administration. In Thailand, the concentration of the benefits of growth in the urban areas, and particularly in Bangkok, raised the question of whether the rural population had been left out of the boom. In all four cases, the transition to democracy increased the opportunity for politicians appealing to marginalized groups to protest the government's policy commitments and to argue for greater attention to social welfare considerations; indeed, good economic performance made such demands appear both reasonable and just.

The business elites that had supported the policy project of the authoritarian government constituted an important counterweight to these appeals, but it is important not to exaggerate the extent of their political capabilities within a democratic context. Even with electoral rules stacked in their favor, the transition to democracy had, as Przeworski suggests, increased uncertainty with respect to policy outcomes.[19] In no case did those groups with a strong interest in policy continuity constitute an outright electoral majority, even if they were capable of mobilizing significant electoral support.

In sum, economic conditions themselves constitute an important determinant of the severity of the political problems surrounding economic adjustment. The reforms required by new governments in the non-crisis cases were generally less severe than in the crisis cases, and governments enjoyed a degree of fiscal leeway that allowed them to make side-payments

[18] Nathaniel C. Nash, "Chile Advances in a War on Poverty, and One Million Mouths Say Amen," *New York Times,* April 4, 1993, p. 14.

[19] Adam Przeworski, "Some Problems in the Study of the Transition to Democracy," in Guillermo O'Donnell, Philippe C. Schmitter, and Laurence Whitehead, eds., *Transitions from Authoritarian Rule: Prospects for Democracy,* (Baltimore and London: The Johns Hopkins Press, 1986), pt. 3, *Comparative Perspectives,* pp. 58–61.

to negatively affected groups. Nevertheless, it is important not to underestimate the political difficulties facing governments in the non-crisis cases; as we will show in more detail, these were quite substantial and did influence the course of policy in important ways.

POLITICAL STARTING POINTS: EXECUTIVE POWER AND PARTY SYSTEMS

The capacity to manage the political pressures associated with the initiation and consolidation of economic reform was not simply a function of economic circumstance; it also depended on the way new democratic institutions aggregated the preferences of contending social groups and empowered executives to act. In chapter 4, these institutions were treated as the dependent variable; the analytical focus was on the way economic conditions and the balance of power among competing socio-political interests shaped the reconstruction of constitutional and party systems at the time of the transition. Yet the institutional arrangements emerging at the time of the transition can also be treated as the independent variable, since they had an impact on stabilization and adjustment policies that was quite distinct from the effects either of regime change or economic conditions.

In most instances, the "new" institutional arrangements were built on political foundations that predated authoritarian rule. Yet even where new constitutions lacked such a history, or even widespread legitimacy, political actors quickly developed stakes in the new rules. Following our discussion in chapter 4, we focus on two institutional variables that affected policy and performance in new democracies: the authority of the executive, and the structure of the party system—particularly the extent of its fragmentation and polarization.

Executive Authority

For reasons already discussed, centralized executive authority plays a pivotal role in overcoming the collective action problems and distributive conflicts associated with the initiation of comprehensive economic reforms. Key decisions about the design of policy and political and legislative strategy are typically taken by the president or prime minister on the basis of counsel from a handpicked team of advisers. The effective promulgation and initial pursuit of the reform strategy will depend, however, on the powers of the executive.

There are several contextual factors that may expand the freedom of executive maneuver. As we show in chapter 6, political honeymoons provide new democratic leaders with opportunities to change policy and crisis conditions provide incentives for legislators and other political groups to defer to the executive. However, the ability of the executive to act—even during honeymoons and crises—is also a function of more permanent institutional arrangements and constitutional powers; in most new democracies, recognition of this fact played into the design of new institutions.

As will be discussed in more detail in chapter 10, it is a subject of substantial controversy as to whether presidential or parliamentary systems grant executives greater authority. Critics argue that presidential systems are vulnerable to executive isolation, divided government, and the problem of the lame duck; we find some evidence for all of these difficulties in the experiences of the crisis cases.[20] In parliamentary systems, by contrast, executive and legislative powers are fused, divided government is therefore impossible, and weak governments can be removed through votes of no confidence. In theory, these formal features of parliamentary systems buttress executive authority. In practice, however, executive power may have less to do with the difference between presidentialism and parliamentarism than with other features of the political system, such as the number of political parties and the degree of polarization among them.

In Latin America, the Philippines, and Korea, the choice of presidentialism over parliamentarism reflected deeply rooted historical traditions, rather than calculations about the ability of executives to initiate or sustain economic reform. Nonetheless, it is important to underline that in a number of the crisis cases—all of which are presidential systems—attempts were made to further buttress executive power over economic decision-making through constitutional provisions that granted presidents expansive legislative powers or decree authority, or that permitted legislatures to delegate such powers. These expanded presidential powers played a significant role in the initiation of reform.[21]

The politics of executive power are different in the non-crisis cases. As

---

[20] The most comprehensive statement of this critical perspective is Juan J. Linz, "Presidential or Parliamentary Democracy: Does it Make a Difference?" in Juan J. Linz and Arturo Valenzuela, eds., *The Failure of Presidential Democracy,* 2 vols. (Baltimore: Johns Hopkins University Press, 1994), vol. 1, *Comparative Perspectives,* pp. 3–87. For an outstanding review of the debate that emphasizes some of the advantages of presidentialism, see Scott Mainwaring and Matthew Soberg Shugart, "Presidentialism and Democracy in Latin America: the Debate," unpublished ms., University of California, San Diego, 1994. In countries such as Chile, Uruguay, and Brazil, earlier shifts to presidentialism as well as the strengthening of presidential powers were motivated by the objective of overcoming parliamentary immobilism. Arturo Valenzuela, "Party Politics and the Crisis of Presidentialism in Chile: A Proposal for a Parliamentary Form of Government," in Linz and Arturo Valenzuela, *The Failure of Presidential Democracy,* vol. 2, *The Case of Latin America,* p. 138.

[21] For a comprehensive analysis of the nature of presidential powers, see Matthew Soberg Shugart and John M. Carey, *Presidents and Assemblies* (New York: Cambridge University Press, 1992), pp. 148–205.

is true in all transitions, parties and social groups excluded under the old order sought constitutional changes that would check the potential for executive abuse. But there were also strong economic and political forces with an interest in sustaining the policies initiated under the old regime, and as we argued in chapter 4, these typically exercised some influence over the design of the democratic constitution. Those favoring policy continuity naturally sought to insulate technocratic centers of decision-making within the executive from the "interference" of elected politicians, not only in the legislature but in the executive as well. The mechanisms for doing this included the establishment of independent central banks or other agencies, granting the executive veto powers, and more broadly, placing institutional restrictions on the range of groups and parties that could enter politics or gain legislative representation in the first place.

Though constitutional arrangements can strengthen the hand of the executive by expanding the discretionary power to initiate policy or by insulating decision-making from short-term political pressures, such mechanisms cannot provide an effective basis for policy coordination and the management of distributive conflict over the long run. To the contrary, strong executive discretion can weaken the incentives for party, legislative, and interest group leaders to provide political support for policy initiatives.[22] Legislators with limited influence over policy are likely to distance themselves from the chief executive, particularly during times of economic distress. This is especially true in presidential systems, where legislators enjoy independent mandates.

Efforts to insulate decision-making can also backfire. The purpose of such institutional arrangements is to offset the dangers to policy continuity caused by the resurgence of opposition, particularly in countries with long histories of polarization and social conflict over economic issues. However, as both Turkey and Thailand demonstrate, an insulated executive is not sufficient to prevent opposition to reform as barriers to political contestation fall, and may itself become the focus of the opposition.

In sum, the constitutional powers of the executive are an important factor for understanding both the initiation of reform and the ability of governments to sustain policies once launched. However, a strong executive is not a reliable substitute for organized party support that can provide cohesive legislative and electoral backing for the government's policy course. The building of such coalitions can even be undermined if strong or insulated executives lack the incentive to negotiate broader acceptance of their policy agenda. Particularly where parties are weak and legislative majorities unstable, executives risk increasing isolation and difficulty in sustaining reforms.

---

[22] For a discussion of the correlation between strong presidents and weak parties, see Shugart and Carey, *Presidents and Assemblies,* pp. 174–93.

The Structure of the Party System: Fragmentation and Polarization

To understand the effects that party systems have on the initiation and consolidation of reform, it is important to examine the incentives facing individual politicians. Ultimately, politicians seek election and reelection and are therefore responsive to the interests of voters. Politicians' views of reform should thus reflect trends in public opinion among their constituents: they are likely to acquiesce to adjustment initiatives during honeymoons, oppose those elements of reform that cut against the interests of core constituents, and adopt more favorable views when—and if—the reforms yield results and gain broader acceptance within the electorate.

However, party politicians, and particularly party leaders, must also respond to political pressures emanating from the competitive context and organizational structures in which they find themselves, and the party system itself constitutes a critical component of that context. Politicians are engaged in a strategic interaction with adversaries; their positions with respect to reform and their willingness to compromise are in part a function of the strategy and tactics of their opponents.[23] Party leaders must also respond to competing factions, backbenchers, and organizational activists within their own ranks. The extent of centralized control exercised by party leaders and the internal politics of party organizations can thus have a profound influence on the way politicians define issues and mobilize support or opposition to reform.[24]

There are a number of features of party systems and party organization that are salient for understanding political behavior and resulting policy outcomes, but two that have received sustained attention are fragmentation and polarization.[25] Adapting these concepts to new democratic regimes is difficult, because both the party system and individual parties are typically in flux. By extending and elaborating these concepts it is possible to suggest answers to the question of why some countries achieve relatively stable political compromises on economic policy reform while others experience serious social conflict, failed adjustment strategies, and destabilizing policy cycles.

Fragmentation is defined in terms of number: fragmented systems are

---

[23] The clearest statement of this perspective with respect to issues of economic reform is Geddes, *Politician's Dilemma.*

[24] For an analysis of economic reform focusing on internal party characteristics, see Matthew Soberg Shugart and Daniel Nielson, "A Liberal Dose: Electoral Reform and Economic Adjustment in the Wake of the Debt Crisis," paper prepared for the American Political Science Association, New York, September 1994. See also Angelo Panebianco, *Political Parties: Organization and Power* (Cambridge: Cambridge University Press, 1988).

[25] See Scott Mainwaring and Timothy R. Scully, "Party Systems in Latin America," in Mainwaring and Scully, eds., *Building Democratic Institutions: Party Systems in Latin America* (forthcoming).

characterized by many competing parties.[26] The number of parties is influenced by both institutional and broader sociopolitical factors. Proportional representation with high district magnitudes and low thresholds for representation, for example, encourages the proliferation of parties. Fragmentation will also be influenced by the stability of the social and organizational roots that parties have managed to establish in the electorate. Weakly institutionalized party systems are characterized by unstable voter loyalties and large swings in party support from election to election. This, in turn, is likely to contribute to fragmentation, as parties disappear and new ones form. Cohesive party systems have the opposite characteristics: a small number of larger, more encompassing parties, typically with more stable organizational structures and bases of electoral support.

Polarization is defined by the ideological distance among parties.[27] It is notoriously difficult to measure this distance, particularly where there are multiple issue cleavages. In developing countries, parties that occupy the extremes of the political system often cannot be placed on the same left-right dimension that has been the core of the analysis of party systems in the advanced industrial states.

One way to solve this problem is to focus on the presence or absence of parties of a particular type. In the European context, for example, polarization has been indicated both by the distribution of parties across the left-right continuum and by the presence of anti-system parties characterized by weak commitment to constitutional government and aspirations to dominant-party status.[28] We adopt a broadly similar strategy in distinguishing polarized and nonpolarized systems among our cases. One indicator of polarization is the presence of left and populist parties that have historically mobilized followers around anticapitalist or anti-oligarchic protests. However, we also consider the presence and strength of "movement parties" as an indicator of polarization. These parties are characterized by strong sectarian loyalties and aspirations to political hegemony, even where their policy positions are not sharply different from those of other parties. In a number of our cases, including Peru and Argentina, such

[26] More precisely, fragmentation is usually measured by the number of effective parties or the Rae fractionalization index. For a review of these concepts and their measure, see Rein Taagepera and Mathhew Soberg Shugart, *Seats and Votes: The Effects and Determinants of Electoral Systems* (New Haven, Conn.: Yale University Press, 1989), pp. 77–91; Giovanni Sartori, *Parties and Party Systems* (New York: Cambridge University Press, 1976), pp. 185ff.; G. Bingham Powell, *Contemporary Democracies: Participation, Stability, Violence* (Cambridge, Mass.: Harvard University Press, 1982), pp. 80–84.

[27] Sartori, *Parties and Party Systems*, pp. 132–37; Gary W. Cox, "Centripetal and Centrifugal Incentives in Electoral Systems," *American Journal of Political Science* 34 (1990): 903–35.

[28] The importance of extremist parties has been noted by Sartori, *Parties and Party Systems*, chap. 6; Powell, *Contemporary Democracies*, pp. 92–96.

parties contributed to profound partisan antagonisms. The strength of these two types of parties is indicated in Tables 4.2 and 4.3

In nonpolarized party systems, by contrast, left and populist parties are weak or nonexistent. Nonpolarized systems rest on "pragmatic" parties in which ties between leaders and followers are largely instrumental and in which members are motivated primarily by shared interests in obtaining political office rather than strong ideological commitments or aspirations of hegemonic domination.

The sources of party polarization are even more complicated than those of fragmentation, and far exceed the bounds of this study. They include social structural factors, such as the level of income inequality, the nature of sectoral conflicts, and differences in regional endowments, as well as electoral rules. However, one of the most important determinants of party polarization is patterns of exclusion and incorporation of disadvantaged groups. As Collier and Collier argue, for example, attempts to exclude unions from party politics eventually opened the way to the formation of left parties and radical movements.[29] Even when exclusionary periods end and countries return to democratic rule, the ideological orientations of such parties constitute a legacy that colors the parties' programmatic focus, their political style, and the attitudes of other parties toward them.

If we plot fragmentation on one axis, measured by the average number of effective parties in all legislative contests since the transition, and polarization on the other, measured by the average vote share for left and movement parties in all legislative elections, it allows us to distinguish several ideal-typical combinations, as shown in Figure 5.1. Our cutoff points for distinguishing categories—3.5 effective parties and 15 percent vote for leftist and populist parties—are necessarily arbitrary. However, they are useful for comparing our cases and for exploring the consequences of fragmentation and polarization for the patterns of compromise and conflict surrounding economic reform.

Though the primary focus of our analysis is on the effects of fragmentation and polarization of the party system on political competition and policymaking, it is important to underline that there are important internal characteristics of parties that are also salient, including the extent of internal party fragmentation. The extent of factionalism at the top of the party and the degree of cohesion between leaders, legislators, and activists are also important determinants of economic policy. We return to this issue in the analysis of our cases, but we suggest that it is likely to be more salient for the policy issues we are addressing when seen in the context of the broader characteristics of the party system.

---

[29] Ruth Berins Collier and David Collier, *Shaping the Political Arena* (Princeton, N.J.: Princeton University Press, 1991), pp. 9–10, and subsequent discussions of Brazil, Chile, Argentina, and Peru.

FIGURE 5.1

Effective Number of Parties and Average Share of Votes for Left and Populist Parties in
Post-transition Parliamentary Elections

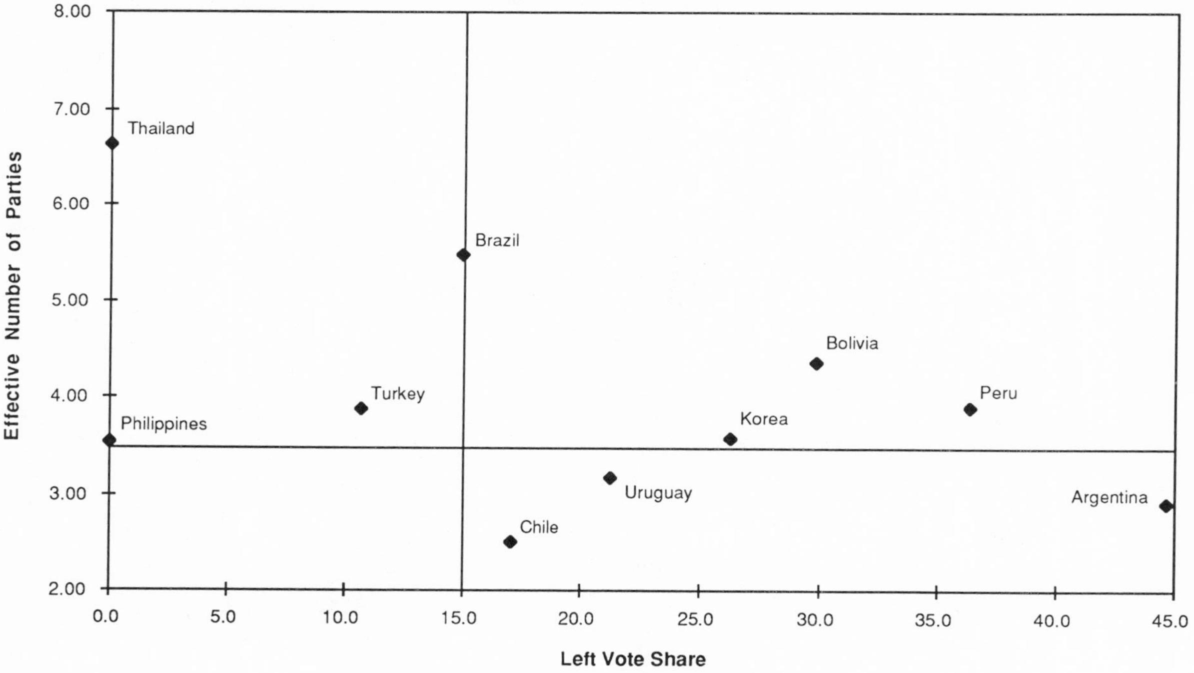

THE POLICY CONSEQUENCES OF PARTY SYSTEMS

Our basic hypothesis is that characteristics of the party system have predictable policy consequences. Fragmentation creates impediments to the
coordination required to both initiate and sustain policy changes; more
cohesive systems, by contrast, are more likely to generate the stable electoral and legislative support that are prerequisites for consolidating economic reform. However, fragmentation alone says nothing about the underlying preferences of the contending political forces in the system nor
about the extent of cleavage among them; polarization captures these
characteristics of the system. We expect that reform will be more difficult
in polarized systems in which strong left, populist and movement parties
are competing, both because of their effects on partisan conflict and because of their influence on the stance of interest groups, particularly the
labor movement and the popular sector.

Fragmentation can affect coordination within the ruling coalition, between executive and legislative branches, and among different levels of
government. How these effects operate will depend in part on whether the
system is presidential or parliamentary. In parliamentary systems based on
proportional representation with high proportionality, a multiplicity of
unstable parties increases the difficulty of forming and sustaining coalition
governments. The division of cabinet posts among contending parties that
is required to form such coalitions can undermine the capacity of central
authorities to undertake the coordinated implementation of reform programs. When such governments are formed, small coalition partners can
hold veto power over policy decisions.[30]

Analogous problems can exist in presidential systems. As Scott Mainwaring has argued, party fragmentation in presidential systems compounds
the chances that executives will become politically isolated and powerless
to pursue their agenda.[31] The incentives for small parties to cooperate with
the government are weaker than in a parliamentary system, since there is
no ability to threaten early elections, and the temptations to legislative
blackmail are correspondingly greater.

The effects of fragmentation on policymaking will depend to a significant extent on whether the system is also polarized. Among our cases,
Thailand and Brazil show the greatest extent of fragmentation at the time
of the transition, followed by Bolivia and Peru. However, Thailand showed

---

[30] This is the central argument of Jeffrey D. Sachs and Nouriel Roubini, "Political and
Economic Determinants of Budget Deficits in Advanced Industrial Democracies," National
Bureau of Economic Research Working Paper no. 2682, 1988.

[31] Scott Mainwaring, "Presidentialism, Multipartism, and Democracy: The Difficult Combination," *Comparative Political Studies* 26 (1993): 198, 228.

no signs of polarization; left or populist movements were significant competitors only in the three Latin American countries. In the absence of strong left or populist parties, the principal coordination problems center on the struggle for pork: with multiple contenders and weak internal party organizations, there are few constraints on intense competition for patronage and pork-barrel expenditures, and limited incentives to cooperate around reforms that provide public goods.

Coordination becomes even more difficult when the centrifugal pressures in fragmented systems are compounded by polarization. Parties in such systems are more likely to engage in bidding wars in order both to differentiate themselves from opponents and to maintain the allegiance of relatively narrow constituencies. For very similar reasons, fragmented and polarized systems amplify the distributional demands coming from anti-adjustment interest groups. These two consequences are likely to be particularly marked when there are splits among populist or left parties which then compete among themselves for the support of labor unions and other popular-sector groups.

A third way in which the combination of polarization and fragmentation affects economic management is through its exacerbation of political business cycles.[32] Not only do elections in such systems invite opportunistic behavior and encourage the delay of adjustment efforts, but the combination of an unstable and volatile party landscape with deep programmatic or partisan antagonisms among contenders increases uncertainty and destabilizes expectations about the future course of policy due to the potential for large policy swings between successive governments.

In cohesive party systems, competition is organized between a smaller number of larger parties. Chile showed low levels of fragmentation, as parties moved toward the formation of broad-based political blocs, and in Argentina, the Peronists and Radicals predominated within the electoral arena. The Uruguayan system was also relatively cohesive, but that case is complicated by institutionalized factional competition within each of the major parties. At the time of the transition, the Philippines had formally the most cohesive party system; the transitional election was fought between two blocs consisting of the pro- and anti-Marcos forces. In subsequent elections, the weakness of party organizations and the tendency to personalism and fragmentation were revealed more clearly, but these tendencies were constrained at least to some extent by the centripetal incentives associated with single-member electoral districts for the lower house.

Averages for Korea exaggerate both the fragmentation and the polarization within that political system. Though the number for effective parties

---

[32] This is a theme of Albert Alesina, "Macroeconomic Policy in a Two-Party System as a Repeated Game," *Quarterly Journal of Economics* 101 (1987): 651–78.

is 3.5, this does not reflect the formation of the "Grand Coalition" in 1990; during 1990–92, Korea even evolved "past" a two-party system toward a dominant-party model along Japanese lines. As discussed in chapter 4, moreover, the "left" vote reflects support for Kim Dae Jung, whose electoral appeal was actually quite moderate. Turkey also constitutes an ambiguous case; at the time of the transitional election in 1983, the country had less than three effective parties, but this was the result of a military ban on full party participation. By the late 1980s, the Turkish party system had become both more fragmented and more polarized, which helps explain the growing incoherence of economic policy in the country.

In the limiting case of a two party system, both inter- and intraparty structures are conducive to moderation.[33] First, we would expect parties to compete for the support of swing voters in the middle of the political spectrum. Second, the small number of large parties has a moderating influence on the way interests are aggregated. Interest groups are forced to operate in the context of an encompassing coalition in which diverse interests are represented and among which compromises must be struck.

Given these incentives, it could be argued that the combination of a cohesive yet polarized system is unlikely.[34] There are fewer opportunities for strongly ideological or movement parties to operate in a system with a small number of parties; most of the cohesive systems in our sample are not polarized. As we would also expect, the left and movement parties that did resurface in cohesive systems had strong incentives to move toward the political center. The exception that proves the rule is Turkey, which did become more polarized over time. However, this was partly the result of lowering the barriers to political entry and allowing more parties to compete; the system became more polarized as it became more fragmented.

Nevertheless, two countries, Chile and Argentina, did combine tendencies toward bipolar competition with the presence of parties with strong populist and socialist legacies. Though these parties had moderated their views in some, though by no means all respects, this history had an important effect on the expectations and preferences of other actors in the system.

What are the effects of a cohesive party system with a low degree of polarization on the conduct of economic policy? First, we would expect politicians to crowd the center and to avoid strong programmatic appeals that would differentiate them sharply from their competitors. Where the median voter opposes reform, or where there are powerful interests that would stand to lose from policy change, such competition can delay needed adjustments and even lead to stalemates. Perhaps even more than politi-

---

[33] For an overview, see Cox, "Centripetal and Centrifugal Incentives in Electoral Systems."

[34] For arguments that fragmentation and polarization are likely to be correlated see Sartori, *Parties and Party Systems,* pp. 132–37; Powell, *Contemporary Democracies,* p. 99.

cians in sectarian parties, activists in pragmatic parties often rely heavily on patronage resources dispensed through the public sector; this is particularly true where electoral rules encourage personalistic voting. Like politicians in more fragmented systems, party leaders in cohesive, nonpolarized settings can also be expected to resist reforms when these threaten patronage opportunities or remove protection from core constituents. If we assume that there are strong interest-group and electoral forces arrayed against reform in most countries, then a cohesive, nonpolarized system would militate against radical market-oriented reforms.

But broad-based catchall parties also have advantages with respect to initiating and sustaining reform. Given the tendency for such parties to move toward the center, we would expect cohesive, nonpolarized systems to generate strong organized support for the initiation of reform in crisis situations where voters are disaffected with the policy status quo. Such party systems can also facilitate the organization of support for economic policies when and if they have begun to produce favorable results. In opposition, catchall parties will naturally seek to discredit the policies of the government. But when things are going well, they are less likely to press for the wholesale reversal of government initiatives; when things are going badly, they are less likely than leftist or movement parties to gravitate toward radical, polarizing solutions or to back strikes, demonstrations, and protests that complicate the ability of governments to act.

We have already noted that when compared to movement parties in more fragmented systems, those in cohesive systems have a strong incentive to broaden their appeal and deemphasize traditional solidarities. By around 1990, parties like the Chilean Socialists and the Peronists, once highly sectarian, had taken on many properties of pragmatic catchall parties. But the actual behavior of left and movement parties operating in a cohesive party system will depend on whether these parties are in or out of power.

Incentives for left and populist parties to resist reform are strongest when they are in the political opposition and adjustments are initiated by their rivals. As in more fragmented systems, left or movement parties in opposition in non-fragmented systems are much more likely than catchall parties to launch a "principled" opposition to adjustment initiatives. They are also more inclined to back these appeals with support for labor activism and other forms of social protest. As the case of Argentina demonstrates, this behavior has an important effect on the position of more moderate groups within both the government and opposition. Militant opposition increased the electoral risks of initiating reforms or of continuing their implementation, even when these seemed important for averting more severe economic difficulties. In short, cohesive but polarized party systems can come to resemble fragmented and polarized systems under some circumstances.

The policy orientation of left or populist parties can change substantially, however, if they are incorporated into the government. This outcome is much more likely to occur in consolidated than in fragmented systems. In the latter, the movement of some left or populist groups toward the center is likely to be resisted by other factions that can gain through militant appeals to narrow core constituencies; left parties moving toward the center are likely to face electoral rivals further to their left. Consolidated systems, by contrast, provide opportunities for left or populist parties to gain office by extending their appeal beyond their core constituency and demonstrating their capacity for moderation; there is space to move toward the center. Left parties in power have an additional advantage in cohesive systems: their links with organized labor and other groups disadvantaged by reform may actually make it easier for them to gain trust and negotiate compensatory agreements that permit reform to move forward. Our analysis of Chile in chapter 6 makes this point clear; we return to the issue in more detail in chapter 10.

POLITICAL INSTITUTIONS AND ECONOMIC POLICY IN THE CRISIS AND NON-CRISIS CASES: A PREVIEW

The performance of new democratic governments in the crisis and non-crisis cases provides some initial support for the hypothesis that there are systematic differences between them in terms of the ability to initiate and/or sustain policy reforms. Table 5.1 shows averages for growth, inflation, fiscal deficits, and investment during the five-year period preceding the democratic transition, the transition year itself, and the first and second democratic administrations. With the exception of the fiscal deficit, these indicators do not directly measure the policy stance of the new government; nonetheless, they offer a useful summary comparison and point of reference for arguments elaborated in more detail in the next two chapters.

Even taking differences in initial conditions into account, new democratic governments in the crisis cases experienced considerably greater difficulties than those in the non-crisis transitions. Under the first democratic administrations in the crisis cases, average fiscal deficits were almost twice the level of the pre-transition period, whereas in the non-crisis cases, deficits remained at comparatively low levels. Not coincidentally, four of the crisis cases—Argentina, Bolivia, Brazil, and Peru—experienced hyperinflations; as a result, averages for the category as a whole increased from just under 70 percent in the pre-transition period to almost 900 percent during the first new democratic governments. In contrast to the non-crisis cases, finally, investment dropped and growth remained at an extremely low level. Although new democratic governments inherited conditions that

TABLE 5.1
Economic Performance in New Democracies

	Five Years prior to Transition (Annual Average)	Transition Year	First Democratic Government (Annual Average)	Second Democratic Government (Annual Average)
		Crisis Cases		
Argentina	*1978–82*	*1983*	*1984–89*	*1990–92*
GDP Growth	−1.5	3.1	−2.2	5.9
Inflation	141.0	343.8	823.0	1,243.0
Fiscal Deficit/GDP	−5.2	−3.8	−4.4	−0.8
Investment/GDP Growth	20.9	17.3	12.8	15.1
Bolivia	*1977–81*	*1982*	*1983–85*	*1986–89*
GDP Growth	2.1	−6.6	−3.0	1.2
Inflation	23.7	296.5	3,558.3	28.7
Fiscal Deficit/GDP	−3.8	−19.0	−19.2	−0.3
Investment/GDP Growth	19.0	12.5	13.2	12.4
Brazil	*1980–84*	*1985*	*1986–89*	*1990–92*
GDP Growth	2.0	8.4	2.5	−0.9
Inflation	132.8	228.0	805.6	1,462.5
Fiscal Deficit/GDP	−3.3	−11.2	−14.2	−3.3[a]
Investment/GDP Growth	19.4	16.9	22.2	19.3
Peru	*1975–79*	*1980*	*1986–89*	*1986–90*
GDP Growth	1.9	3.8	−2.8	−2.3
Inflation	48.3	59.7	108.1	2,465.0
Fiscal Deficit/GDP	−3.3	−2.4	−4.3	−3.4
Investment/GDP Growth	17.7	28.9	26.2	20.9
Uruguay	*1980–84*	*1985*	*1986–89*	*1990–92*
GDP Growth	−1.8	0.3	3.9	2.5
Inflation	44.2	72.2	70.7	94.3
Fiscal Deficit/GDP	−3.9	−2.2	−1.5	1.7[a]
Investment/GDP Growth	14.7	11.4	12.5	12.2
Philippines	*1981–85*	*1986*	*1987–91*	
GDP Growth	0.8	−7.8	4.8[b]	
Inflation	23.4	0.8	11.5	
Fiscal Deficit/GDP	−2.6	−5.0	−2.7[b]	
Investment/GDP	24.7	16.3	20.2	

TABLE 5.1 *(continued)*

	Five Years prior to Transition (Annual Average)	*Transition Year*	*First Democratic Government (Annual Average)*	*Second Democratic Government (Annual Average)*
	Non-crisis Cases			
Chile	*1985–89*	*1990*	*1991–92*	
GDP Growth	6.2	2.1	7.3	
Inflation	20.4	26.0	18.6	
Fiscal Deficit/GDP	−0.7	3.6	2.3	
Investment/GDP	16.5	20.2	20.1	
Korea	*1982–86*	*1987*	*1988–92*	
GDP Growth	9.6	11.8	8.3	
Inflation	3.6	3.0	7.5	
Fiscal Deficit/GDP	−1.3	0.4	−0.1[b]	
Investment/GDP	28.9	29.5	35.0	
Thailand	*1980–82*	*1983*	*1984–87*	*1988–91*
GDP Growth	5.0	7.2	6.3	10.9
Inflation	12.6	3.7	1.9	5.2
Fiscal Deficit/GDP	−5.0	−4.1	−4.0	3.0
Investment/GDP	25.3	25.9	23.7	31.8
Turkey	*1981–82[c]*	*1983*	*1984–89*	*1990–92*
GDP Growth	4.6	3.8	6.4	4.9
Inflation	33.7	31.4	61.1	65.5
Fiscal Deficit/GDP	−1.7 (1981)	−4.2	−6.5	−4.2[a]
Investment/GDP	21.3	19.6	27.4	20.3
Average for Crisis Cases[d]				
GDP Growth	0.6	0.2	0.5	1.5
Inflation	68.9	166.8	896.2	1,062.3
Fiscal Deficit/GDP	−3.7	−7.3	−7.7	−1.8
Investment/GDP	19.4	17.9	17.8	16.0

TABLE 5.1 (*continued*)

	Five Years prior to Transition (Annual Average)	Transition Year	First Democratic Government (Annual Average)	Second Democratic Government (Annual Average)
Average for Non-crisis Cases[e]				
GDP Growth	6.3	6.2	7.1	7.9
Inflation	17.5	16.0	22.3	35.4
Fiscal Deficit/GDP	−2.2	−1.1	−2.1	−0.6
Investment/GDP	23.0	23.8	26.6	26.1

Source: International Monetary Fund, *International Financial Statistics Yearbook,* various issues.
Note: For definitions of the variables, see Table 2.1.
[a]Data not available for 1992.
[b]Data not available for 1991.
[c]The democratically elected Demirel government was overthrown in September 1980; we include only the two full years of military rule for comparison.
[d]Data for second administration does not include Philippines.
[e]Data for second administration includes only Thailand and Turkey.

were already extremely bad, policy actions taken after the transition typically contributed to further economic deterioration.

The non-crisis cases were far more successful in maintaining macroeconomic stability and actually experienced higher levels of growth and investment following the transition. To an important extent, this record reflected the ability of incoming governments to maintain existing policy commitments. Most new democratic administrations proved able to make short-term corrections as economic conditions changed, and in all four cases the reform thrust initiated by the military was deepened in some important aspects.

Despite these broad differences based on economic inheritance, however, other variations in policy behavior *within categories* and *over time* require attention; these are summarized in Figure 5.2. These differences are attributable in part to the evolution of political institutions, including particularly the party system. In chapter 6, we show how the relatively polarized and/or fragmented party systems in Argentina, Brazil, Bolivia, and Peru had an important influence on the difficulties experienced by new democratic governments in their efforts to gain control over fiscal and monetary policy and to coordinate negotiated stabilization efforts. Polarization and fragmentation had virtually all of the effects we have noted,

FIGURE 5.2

The Political Economy of Adjustment in New Democracies

	Economic Crisis	No Economic Crisis
I. ECONOMIC INHERITANCE	Severe balance of payments difficulties; high inflation; low growth; longer-term distributional issues	Strong growth, low inflation; distributional problems vary
II. POLICY PROBLEMS	Balance-of-payments adjustment; stabilization; structural adjustments for reigniting growth	To sustain basic policies and make incremental adjustments in the model as required
III. POLICY OUTCOMES Fragmented systems	Stabilization and reform initially blocked; economic deterioration; radical reforms undertaken under subsequent governments (Bolivia, Brazil, Peru)	Coherence of policy deteriorates as barriers to political entry fall (Thailand, Turkey 1983–87)
Cohesive party systems, large left populist or movement parties present	1. Polarizing parties in opposition: distributive conflicts are amplified; reform is delayed (Argentina, 1983–89) 2. Polarizing parties in power: government initiates and sustains reform. (Argentina, 1989–94)	1. Polarizing parties in opposition: distributive conflicts are amplified, reform is delayed (Turkey 1988–91) 2. Polarizing parties in power: government sustains policy reform. (Chile)
Cohesive party systems, pragmatic parties dominant	Avoid macroeconomic deterioration; moderate policy reform; incrementalism (Philippines, Uruguay)	Avoid macroeconomic deterioration; moderate policy reform (Korea)
Dominant party systems	Sustained stabilization; radical reforms (Mexico)	Avoid macroeconomic deterioration; moderate policy reform; incrementalism (Taiwan)

though to differing degrees across cases: a strengthening of anti-reform interest groups, executive-legislative stalemates, and virulent political business cycles.

Post-transition political institutions and alignments continued to evolve in these four countries as social and economic conditions changed, however. In response to the devastating effects of hyperinflation, governments elected during the second half of the 1980s initiated comprehensive reform packages that included trade liberalization and privatization as well as stabilization. With the exception of Brazil, this produced a sharp drop in rates of inflation, although this outcome is not fully reflected in the incomplete data provided in Table 5.1.

In part, the capacity to undertake such steps reflected the debilitating impact that the sharp deterioration in economic conditions had on both labor and business groups. Nonetheless, realignments within the party system and their effects on the centralization of executive power help to explain variations in the capacity to follow through on these programs and to correct course over time. The greatest difficulties were experienced in Brazil and Peru, where continuing polarization and fragmentation led to the election of political outsiders who attempted to govern without adequate legislative support. In contrast, implementation was more effective in Argentina and Bolivia. In Argentina, the polarizing effects of a populist opposition were reduced by the transfer of governing responsibility to the Peronists themselves. In Bolivia, the left coalition that had backed the Siles government was defeated electorally, and isolated by the formation of a new center-right coalition formed under the leadership of Victor Paz Estenssoro.

The post-transition political economy in the Philippines and Uruguay was not characterized either by the dramatic deterioration nor by the subsequent radical reformism of the four hyperinflation cases. The moderate structural adjustments initiated in the Philippines case owed much to the fact that, unlike in the other crisis cases, the Aquino government inherited a stabilized economy and a windfall of external financial backing. Yet these initial advantages were reinforced by the extraordinary executive powers exercised by Aquino during her first eighteen months in office and, despite the existence of strong policy differences in her cabinet, the absence of broader polarization within the political system. Neither the left nor the unions constituted an important force in toppling the Marcos government, and Aquino initially enjoyed presidential powers that rivaled those of her predecessor. The reemergence of party politics resulted in increasing fragmentation and placed new pressures on economic policy, but the centrist tendencies of the Philippine electoral system muted the types of distributive conflicts visible in the four hyperinflation cases.

Uruguay is a critical case for our analysis, because unlike the Philippines it did face a highly unfavorable set of initial economic conditions. The ability of the first democratic government to bring fiscal deficits under control and to avoid an acceleration of inflation rested in significant measure on the continuing importance of the broadly based Colorado and Blanco parties within the electoral system, and on constitutional provisions that provided greater leverage for the executive to sustain macroeconomic control.

Developments within the non-crisis cases are discussed in chapter 7. The restraints on the full play of partisan politics that characterized all of these countries during the early years of democratic rule clearly had an influence in guaranteeing the continuity of economic policy in those countries, but with important differences among them. Chile stands in contrast to the other non-crisis cases because "reformed" left parties participated in a new, broadly based governing coalition on terms acceptable to the right. This in turn provided the new democratic government with an important channel to unions and other popular-sector groups that might otherwise have been disruptive to economic policy.

In the other non-crisis transitions, new governments on the right initially benefited from restraints on political competition, but these were bound to come under challenge over time from those groups that were excluded under the authoritarian regime and failed to gain from the democratic transition. In these cases, success in sustaining policy reforms over time depended directly on the extent to which political barriers to entry were allowed to fall. In Thailand, the "challenge from below" proved relatively weak and the economic policymaking machinery exceptionally powerful. Nonetheless, during the Chatichai government the importance of parties increased with important implications for the conduct of economic policy. In Korea, the executive was also relatively strong, but the government faced more serious challenges, not only from labor and students, but from the opposition in the legislature. The formation of a "grand coalition" of the center-right constituted an important effort to resolve these problems.

In Turkey, finally, the political challenges were most severe. Over the course of the 1980s, the government had to contend with the reemergence of interest-group politics and the reentry of opposition parties into the political arena. The political challenges to the Özal strategy, as well as the expanding patronage and compromises required to meet them, undermined the autonomy of the economic bureaucracy and the coherence of economic policy. As a result, Turkey had the weakest record of the non-crisis cases in maintaining macroeconomic stability, and experienced a partial reversal of its trade liberalization policies during the late 1980s.

Taiwan and Mexico constitute a third category of cases that will be analyzed in chapter 8 as an extension of the comparative arguments made in the preceding chapters. These countries differed from both the crisis and non-crisis cases in that authoritarian rule was organized under the aegis of a dominant party. Even more than in the non-crisis cases, authoritarian elites were able to retain control over the pace of political reform. Though both governments undertook some political liberalization, and Taiwan arguably had achieved a democratic transition by the early 1990s, dominant parties held sway.

The economic circumstances facing the two governments in the 1980s differed, with consequences that are analogous to the cases we have already discussed. Taiwan, though facing some adjustment difficulties, engaged in political reform against a backdrop of continued high growth and price stability that had been established in earlier decades. As in the non-crisis cases, the relative success of the government's policies created a base of support that included not only business, but a wide swath of the middle class as well. This support had distinct political advantages, contributing to the dominant Kuomintang Party's ability to pursue political reform in a gradual way while maintaining electoral support.

Mexico, by contrast, experienced the difficulties of high indebtedness, inflation, and recession as in other Latin American countries; as in those countries, it also faced loss of support on both the left and right for the apparent failure of its economic policies. In contrast to the crisis cases, however, the government was not only able to maintain political power but to initiate a sustained and comprehensive strategy of economic reform. By the early 1990s, as the economy began to recover, the regime initiated a series of significant, though partial steps toward further political liberalization.

Though these two regimes differed from one another in many respects, they are distinctive in terms of the capacity of state elites to manage social conflict over economic policy and political reform itself. In this respect, they are at the opposite end of the spectrum from the crisis cases, and provide important points of contrast with the non-crisis transitions as well. In contrast to the crisis transitions, any tendencies toward polarization that existed in these systems were managed by the existence of a dominant party. Even more than in the non-crisis cases, this party configuration and the broader political rules provided the state elites with distinct advantages in managing the economy. In addition to controlling and reducing the political conflicts that characterize more open polities, the party apparatus provided a mechanism for exercising strong control over the state and for integrating potentially disaffected groups through patronage and electoral mobilization. Thus while these two cases differ in important ways from the democratic transitions that constitute the major focus of this book, they provide an important point of comparative reference.

CONCLUSION: POLITICAL CONSEQUENCES OF
ECONOMIC POLICY

The central focus of Part Two is on the effects of political organization on economic policy and performance. Yet as this introduction already suggests, there are profound political consequences for the patterns of economic policymaking and adjustment we have outlined. Just as these different transition paths were characterized by different policy problems and patterns of policymaking, so they exhibited characteristic political challenges as well.

In the crisis transitions, the second or third democratic administration eventually exploited crisis conditions and the weakness of the political opposition to initiate sweeping economic reform efforts. Yet this "politics of packages" posed severe dilemmas for further democratic development, as the Fujimori *autogolpe* demonstrated most clearly. The effort to centralize political power raised the specter of plebiscitarian politics, while not necessarily solving the underlying problem of political polarization and institutional fragmentation.

In the non-crisis transitions, the political challenges have been different. The outgoing authoritarian leadership succeeded in structuring the political space in the new democracies to a greater extent, yet this was achieved only through the continuing exclusion of certain groups, an exclusion that inexorably ran up against the logic of democratization itself. In these societies, the main political problem has been how to reintegrate the left into the political system without reverting to the patterns of political polarization that had made democracy unstable in the past.

In the dominant-party cases, the control exercised by authoritarian elites was even greater. As a result, the central political issue was whether trends toward political liberalization would stop short of a fully competitive electoral and constitutional system, or whether incumbent rulers would be pressed by international trends and their own economic reforms to break fully with the control mechanisms provided by a dominant party. These themes of political consolidation are the subject of Part Three.

New Democracies and Economic Crisis

IN FOUR crisis-induced transitions—Argentina, Brazil, Bolivia, and Peru—the first new democratic governments experienced substantial problems of economic management. In Peru, there was further deterioration during the administration of the second elected president, Alan García, who launched a disastrous populist program. These governments were not responsible for the daunting economic challenges they inherited from their predecessors; even so, none was able to initiate coherent stabilization programs or broader structural reforms.

Why were these governments unable to capitalize more effectively on the political goodwill generated by the transition? Subsequent policy initiatives in these four countries and more successful performance in the other crisis cases suggest that such extreme policy failures were neither irreversible nor typical of democratic transitions generally. Nevertheless, an analysis of the difficulties encountered by new democratic governments in Argentina, Brazil, Bolivia, and Peru provides a baseline both for understanding their subsequent efforts at adjustment and for comparisons with more successful transitions.

We begin with an analysis of the political and institutional factors that contributed to policy failure. The ambitious reform initiatives launched in each of these countries during the late 1980s and early 1990s are then examined, and the way in which differences in the constitution of executive authority and party structure affected the coherence and sustainability of these efforts is explored. Finally, we review the experiences of the Philippines and Uruguay, crisis-induced transitions in which incoming governments managed the transition with fewer macroeconomic disruptions.

POLICY FAILURES: ARGENTINA, BOLIVIA, BRAZIL, AND PERU

In the four cases of policy failure, high and accelerating inflation constituted a major policy and political challenge for incoming democratic governments. In all cases, the difficulty of adjusting was compounded by the debt crisis of 1982–83. The loss of access to external financing hit Peru about halfway through Belaúnde's term. In all of the other cases, new democratic governments were severely constrained from their inception by their limited capacity to borrow. Nevertheless, institutional features of the party system played an important role in the failure to resolve internal policy inconsistences or to sustain fundamental fiscal and monetary adjustments. Each system was characterized by strong partisan divisions over economic issues, substantial factionalism and decentralization within party organizations, and volatile and unstable bases of party and electoral support. Even taking into account the economic constraints associated with external debt and high inflation, these patterns of instability and polarization within the reemerging party systems made effective responses more difficult.

Bolivia

The emergence of the left-oriented Siles government in Bolivia was a result of the economic and political stalemate that prevailed at the end of the authoritarian period. The Nationalist Democratic Action party (ADN) and the National Revolutionary Movement (MNR)—the heirs of the Banzer coalition and the pre-military dominant party respectively—shared a majority of the seats won in the 1980 Congressional elections. However, Siles's coalition of Marxist and populist parties (the UDP, or Democratic Popular Union) also had broad support. It had been closely allied with the Confederation of Bolivian Workers (the COB) in the mobilization of popular protest against the military regime, and with backing from the union movement, the coalition gained a solid plurality of the electoral vote (38.7 percent) and an approximately equal proportion of Congressional seats.[1]

According to Article 90 of the 1967 Constitution, the Congress selects the president in the event that no candidate gains an outright majority, a circumstance likely to occur given the fragmentation of the party system. In later elections, this "quasi-parliamentary" aspect of the Bolivian Constitution provided an incentive for the negotiation of alliances between the parties in Congress and the executive.[2] In the polarized context of the early 1980s, however, the standoff among competing party and social forces was resolved through a behind-the-scenes bargain struck among the military, unions, business groups, and parties: Siles would assume the presidency, but the opposition parties would control the legislature.[3]

[1] René Antonio Mayorga, "La Democracia en Bolivia: El Rol de las Elecciones en las fases de transición y consolidación," in Rodolfo Cerdas-Cruz, Juan Rial, and Daniel Zovatto, eds., *Una tarea inconclusa: Elecciones y democracia en América Latina: 1988–1991* (San José, Costa Rica: IIDH-Capel, 1992), p. 283.

[2] Eduardo A. Gamarra, "Market-Oriented Reforms and Democratization in Bolivia," prepared for project on Market-Oriented Reforms and Democratization, Overseas Development Council, Washington D.C., March 1993.

[3] Ibid., p. 6; Matthew Soberg Shugart and John M. Carey, *Presidents and Assemblies: Constitutional Design and Electoral Dynamics,* (New York: Cambridge University Press, 1992), p. 82.

The ensuing record of economic mismanagement constitutes the most extreme case of policy immobilism of any of the transitions discussed in this chapter. The principal problem facing the new democratic government was managing the debt crisis, which hit in 1983.[4] The technocratic team attempted to respond to the sharp decline in revenues and external financing with relatively standard stabilization measures: devaluation, price adjustments for the state-owned enterprises, wage restraint, and tax reform. The government proposed six such packages between 1982 and 1985. Implementation of each was blocked almost immediately by the Cabinet and affected interest groups. As a consequence, the steep decline in revenues and finance was unmatched by adjustments in expenditures; fiscal deficits, shown in Table 6.1, averaged an incredible 23 percent of GDP between 1982 and 1984, financed almost wholly by monetary emissions.

A crushing-debt service burden was the primary cause of these deficits, but the inability of the parties to restrain interest-group pressures undermined efforts at both fiscal adjustment and negotiations with external creditors. The most immediate difficulties lay within Siles's own coalition and its allies in the Bolivian labor movement. As in the other crisis countries, union militancy was a response both to years of severe material hardship and to inflation itself. As inflation accelerated, the unions pressed continuously for a shortening of contract periods, vetoed efforts to reduce subsidies and social expenditures, and organized occupations of plants in the state-owned mining sector to protest scheduled closings. At the same time, the COB refused repeated invitations to join the Siles cabinet and share governing responsibilities. The intransigence of the unions was exacerbated by deep internal rivalries among the left and populist parties for control of the COB. "The logic of [the left's] internal politics," write Malloy and Gammara, "only served to heighten its differences with the government and push it along a more adversarial path."[5]

Labor militancy was not the only factor contributing to a breakdown of control. With the central government stalemated, regional "civic committees" enlarged their de facto control of public policy in many key provinces. Military groups protested cutbacks in wages and perquisites.[6] The Congressional opposition, backed by the private sector, blocked tax reform and challenged executive attempts to exercise decree powers with threats of

---

[4] Jeffrey D. Sachs, "The Bolivian Hyperinflation and Stabilization," NBER Discussion Paper No. 2073, as cited in Miguel A. Kiguel and Nissan Liviatan, "Stopping Three Big Inflations: Argentina, Brazil, and Peru," *Working Paper,* WPS999, World Bank, Transition and Macro-Adjustment Division, Country Economics Department, October 1992, p. 8. See also Manuel Pastor, Jr., "Bolivia: Hyperinflation, Stabilization and Beyond," *Journal of Development Studies* 27 (1991): 211–37.

[5] James M. Malloy and Eduardo Gamarra, *Revolution and Reaction: Bolivia, 1964–1985* (New Brunswick, N.J.: Transaction Books, 1988), pp. 160–61.

[6] Ibid., pp. 157–88.

impeachment. By 1985, the Bolivian economy was collapsing. Siles yielded to Congressional pressures to advance the calendar for new presidential elections and resigned from office eighteen months ahead of the scheduled end of his term.

Peru under Belaúnde and García

The Peruvian transition began under more auspicious political and economic circumstances. Belaúnde's Popular Action party (AP) won a decisive victory over the Popular Revolutionary Alliance of America (APRA) and United Left in the 1980 elections; and the economy—buoyed by rising commodity prices—had also begun a tentative recovery from the deep recession of the mid-1970s. The economic team assembled under Belaúnde sought to build on these advantages. The team was headed by Finance Minister Manuel Ulloa, a liberal technocrat with strong links to Peru's traditional agro-export oligarchy. Ulloa's program emphasized structural reforms: a deepening of the trade liberalization begun during the last years of the military government, new measures to attract foreign investment in

TABLE 6.1
Post-transition Economic Developments in Bolivia

	1977–81	1982	1983	1984	1985	1986
GDP Growth	1.5	−4.4	−4.5	1.0	−0.7	−3.2
Inflation	23.5	123.5	275.6	1,281.4	11,749.6	276.3
Fiscal Deficit/GDP	−3.8	−19.0	−8.8	−29.7	na	−0.1
Current Account/GDP	−5.8	−2.8	−2.3	−2.6	−4.3	−8.3
Investment/GDP	20.0	12.5	12.2	10.6	10.2	7.9
Real Wage	−3.8[a]	−27.0	2.9	−16.4	−46.0	−30.2

	1987	1988	1989	1990	1991	1992
GDP Growth	2.6	3.8	2.9	2.4	4.2	3.4
Inflation	14.6	16.0	15.2	17.1	1.4	na
Fiscal Deficit/GDP	0.7	−0.6	−1.2	−1.5	−0.1	na
Current Account/GDP	−8.6	−5.8	−4.8	−3.6	−4.3	na
Investment/GDP	11.1	12.1	12.0	12.7	13.8	15.8
Real Wage	16.0	14.5	−10.5	−7.5	53.8	na

Sources: World Bank, *Trends in Developing Economies,* various issues; World Bank, *World Tables 1993*
International Monetary Fund, *International Financial Statistics Yearbook,* various issues; International Monetary
Fund, *Government Financial Statistics Yearbook,* 1993; Economic Commission on Latin America, *Economic
Survey of Latin America and The Caribbean,* various issues.

Note: For definitions of the first five variables, see Table 2.1. Real Wage: Annual increase in minimum wage
[a] Average for 1978–81.

mining and agriculture, and privatization of firms nationalized during the Velasco period.[7]

As in Bolivia, the failure of these efforts to produce positive results resided in part with forces beyond the government's control. The abrupt termination of external credit in 1983, combined with severe natural disasters, worsened fiscal deficits. Inflation accelerated and forced painful stabilization efforts throughout the remaining portion of Belaúnde's term. The economy's vulnerability to these shocks was increased substantially, however, by the failure during the preceding years to back up trade liberalization with fiscal adjustment. IMF data reported in Table 6.2 show that central government deficits jumped from 2.4 percent of GDP to 1980 to 4.0 percent the following year; other sources report even steeper increases.[8] Higher inflation and an appreciating exchange rate in turn undermined the competitiveness of the export sector. In 1982, with the economy virtually stagnant, Ulloa came under increasing attack from opposition legislators and members of the AP itself, and was abruptly dismissed as finance minister at the end of the year.

Characteristics of the party and electoral system help explain Belaúnde's failure to manage macroeconomic policy. Notwithstanding his strong showing in 1980, Belaúnde faced substantial challenges from both the APRA, historically Peru's largest party, and the newly formed United Left (IU) opposition, with its strong base in the union movement; the APRA and the IU had won about 32 percent of votes in the 1980 presidential contest, only slightly less than Belaúnde's 35 percent. In the legislature, a coalition between Belaúnde's AP and the rightist PPC provided the government with a solid majority, but APRA and IU legislators retained some capacity to delay or block aspects of the president's program by aligning with dissident members of his own party.[9] Much more important was the electoral threat posed by the left and populist opposition in municipal and Congressional elections, elections certain to be interpreted as referenda on the govern-

---

[7] Barbara Stallings, "The Politics of Adjustment in Chile, Peru, and Colombia," in Joan Nelson, ed., *Economic Crisis and Policy Choice: The Politics of Adjustment in the Third World* (Princeton, N.J.: Princeton University Press, 1990), pp. 132–35.

[8] Pastor and Wise cite data from *Cuánto: Perú en Números 1990*, edited by Richard Webb and Graciela Fernández Baca de Valdez, showing a jump in the deficit from 3.9 percent in 1980 to 7.3 percent in 1982. "The Peruvian Economy in the 1980s: From Orthodoxy to Heterodoxy and Back," *Latin American Research Review* 27 (1992): 102.

[9] Harsh and extended Congressional interpellations of Ulloa contributed to his dismissal. Sandra Way-Hazelton and William A. Hazelton, "Sustaining Democracy in Peru: Dealing with Parliamentary and Revolutionary Challenges," in George A. Lopez and Michael Stoll, eds., *Liberalization and Redemocratization in Latin America* (New York, Westport, Conn., and London: Greenwood Press, 1987), p. 115. The fact that the APRA's legislative obstructionism during the first Belaúnde administration had contributed to his ouster in 1968 no doubt heightened executive concerns.

TABLE 6.2

Post-transition Economic Developments in Peru

	1975–79	1980	1981	1982	1983	1984	1985
GDP Growth	2.3	3.1	7.4	−1.6	−12.2	6.7	2.0
Inflation	43.9	59.1	75.4	64.4	111.2	110.2	163.4
Fiscal Deficit/GDP	−3.3	−2.4	−4.0	−3.2	−7.5	−4.4	−2.2
Current Account/GDP	−4.9	−0.5	−6.9	−6.5	−4.6	−1.2	0.5
Investment/GDP	21.4	29.0	33.9	32.4	23.3	19.6	18.4
Real Wage	−7.0	9.9	−1.8	2.2	−16.7	−15.3	−11.0

	1986	1987	1988	1989	1990	1991	1992
GDP Growth	7.7	9.8	−8.3	−11.9	−4.5	2.8	−3.0
Inflation	77.9	85.8	595.0	3,764.9	7,481.7	409.5	73.5
Fiscal Deficit/GDP	−3.7	−6.0	−2.8	−4.7	−2.1	−0.5	na
Current Account/GDP	−4.5	−3.8	−3.7	0.2	−3.1	−3.6	−4.6
Investment/GDP	21.4	22.0	25.5	17.2	14.6	16.0	15.2
Real Wage	25.6	3.9	−26.3	−45.5	−12.1	7.9	na

Sources: Economic Commission on Latin America, *Economic Survey of Latin America and The Caribbean,* various issues; United Nations Economic Commission for Latin America, *Statistical Yearbook 1992;* International Monetary Fund, *International Financial Statistics Yearbook,* various issues; International Bank for Reconstruction and Development, *Trends in Developing Economies,* 1993; World Bank, *World Tables,* 1993.

Note: For definitions of the first five variables, see Table 2.1. Real Wage: Real growth of private-sector wages in metropolitan Lima.

ment's performance.[10] The Finance Ministry urged the new government to capitalize on its honeymoon to push through painful adjustments in state-owned enterprise prices, but the president delayed action until after the November 1980 municipal elections. By this time, writes Richard Webb (then the governor of the Central Bank), "the initially calculated and politically approved price adjustments had become too small. . . ."[11] As declining commodity prices eroded government revenues, efforts to adjust expenditures met with similar difficulties; Cabinet ministers linked to AP patronage networks resisted recommendations from the Ministry of Finance. In early 1982, alarmed officials at the Central Bank refused the government additional financing and there were sharp exchanges between Webb and the government in the national press. But the government circumvented Central Bank restrictions through massive external borrowing, which increased its vulnerability to the collapse of lending in 1983.[12]

[10] Fernando Rospigliosi, "Las Elecciones Peruanas de 1990," in Cerdas-Cruz, Rial, and Zovatto, *Una tarea inconclusa,* p. 387. Data include null and blank ballots. If these are excluded, the figures are 45.4 percent for AP and 41.3 percent for the APRA and the IU.

[11] Richard Webb, "Peru," in John Williamson, ed. *The Political Economy of Policy Reform* (Washington D.C.: Institute for International Economics, 1993), p. 360.

[12] Ibid., p. 361.

In contrast to Bolivia, direct interest-group opposition did not play a significant role in undermining government policy between 1980 and 1982. In the aftermath of the debt crisis, however, the inability of the AP to secure the confidence of union and business groups increased the government's political vulnerability and weakened its capacity to manage the ensuing economic crisis. Opposition from industrialists contributed to the rapid reversal of Ulloa's trade liberalization measures after 1983, and general strikes and demonstrations by the opposition-led unions added to the political pressures on macroeconomic policy through much of 1984. Stabilization measures initiated from late 1984 to mid-1985, the last months of Belaúnde's term, did eventually help to improve the balance-of-payments situation and to slow inflation, but they were also perceived by most opposition groups to have compounded the recession. Thus, the combination of inconsistent policy, external shocks, and declining performance served not only to discredit the incumbent administration, but also to reinforce the perception that economic orthodoxy was to blame. Support for the AP and its program evaporated during the presidential election of 1985, and the political pendulum swung toward the left.

Belaúnde's successor, Alan García, sought to revive growth through a vigorous government stimulus package and a unilateral reduction in external debt service. This sharp reversal of policy was partly a reaction to the perceived failures of the Belaúnde government, but the inattention to macroeconomic constraints was also shaped by factors specific to APRA and its position in the political system. The emphasis on distribution reflected the inexperience of a long-repressed opposition movement that had never controlled the presidency. A populist stance had helped García both to consolidate his victory in a bitter internal succession struggle within the APRA and to strengthen the party's electoral position vis-à-vis the IU on the left.[13]

The macroeconomics of the García government have been analyzed extensively elsewhere, and need not be treated in detail here.[14] Ironically, the accumulation of foreign exchange reserves during the last months of the Belaúnde period provided the basis for the demand-led boom—and political euphoria—of the early García years. This was followed in 1987, however, by a predictable fiscal and balance-of-payments crisis. The government proved unable to formulate a coherent adjustment strategy and a

---

[13] Adversarial relations between the IU-dominated unions and the government continued during the García period, despite the latter's populism. The APRA government excluded the unions from early efforts to negotiate investment commitments from industrialists; the IU opposed most aspects of the García program.

[14] For an orthodox critique, see Ricardo Lago, "The Illusion of Pursuing Redistribution through Macropolicy: Peru's Heterodox Experience, 1985–1990," in Rudiger Dornbusch and Sebastian Edwards, *The Macroeconomics of Populism in Latin America* (Chicago and London: University of Chicago Press, 1991), pp. 263–331.

precipitate nationalization of the banking system thoroughly alienated the private sector. As the economy deteriorated in 1988, the more conservative wing of the APRA reasserted itself and sought to reverse policy, but it was too late; by the end of the decade, hyperinflation had devastated state revenues and real wages, and a severe depression had deepened the cycle of guerilla violence and state terrorism.

Argentina under Alfonsín

Alfonsín's first eighteen months in office were marked by neo-Keynesian policies that resulted in an escalation of inflation and serious balance-of-payments difficulties. In February 1985, however, a new team of economists led by Finance Minister Juan Sourouille. For the next four years (1985–89), the Sourouille team launched a series of stabilization packages which attempted to combine standard macroeconomic adjustments with wage and price controls beginning with the Austral Plan. By 1987, it included gradual trade liberalization and privatization.[15]

These reform packages introduced under Sourouille reflected a determination to attack inertial inflation through a combination of orthodox and heterodox means; they were generally well conceived and viewed favorably by international creditors. However, the Tanzi effect and rising interest payments on the public debt repeatedly undermined efforts to control public finances. These difficulties reinforced long-standing skepticism about the government's ability to implement fiscal adjustment, undermined confidence in the exchange rate, and increased pressure on prices. Each successive package did stabilize prices, but only temporarily, and was quickly followed by the resurgence of ever higher levels of inflation.

Several aspects of the party system compounded the government's credibility problem. First, deep partisan rivalries impeded cooperation between the Radical government and the Peronist-oriented labor movement. One of the first major conflicts of the Alfonsín period was over how to reorganize the unions, which had been barred from operating for most of the preceding seven years. A government proposal for new internal union election procedures got things off to a bad start in 1983 and 1984. Virtually all segments of the Peronist movement saw the bill as a Radical effort to undermine their support within the unions, and they successfully blocked its passage in the Congress.

Union leaders, on the other hand, had only limited incentives to coop-

---

[15] For a description of the politics of this period, see William C. Smith, *Authoritarianism and the Crisis of the Argentine Political Economy* (Stanford, Calif.: Stanford University Press, 1989); Robert R. Kaufman, "Stabilization and Adjustment in Argentina, Brazil, and Mexico," in Nelson, *Economic Crisis and Policy Choice*, pp. 63–112.

TABLE 6.3
Post-transition Economic Developments in Argentina

	1978–82	1983	1984	1985	1986	1987
GDP Growth	−0.7	3.7	1.8	−6.6	7.3	2.6
Inflation	141.0	343.8	626.7	672.1	90.1	131.3
Fiscal Deficit/GDP	−5.2	−12.7	−5.1	−7.4	−2.6	−3.8
Current Account/GDP	−1.7	−3.8	−3.2	−1.4	−2.7	−3.9
Investment/GDP	20.8	17.3	11.3	17.5	8.8	16.4
Real Wage	0.8	25.5	26.4	−15.2	1.6	−5.9

	1988	1989	1990	1991	1992
GDP Growth	−1.9	−6.2	0.1	5.3	8.7
Inflation	343.0	3,079.8	2,314.0	171.7	24.9
Fiscal Deficit/GDP	−2.7	−0.5	−2.5	−0.6	0.6
Current Account/GDP	−1.2	−1.7	1.3	−1.5	−3.7
Investment/GDP	16.4	12.0	14.0	14.6	16.7
Real Wage	−5.5	−14.4	−5.5	4.0	na

Sources: Economic Commission on Latin America, *Economic Survey of Latin America and The Caribbean,* various issues; International Monetary Fund, *International Financial Statistics,* various issues; World Bank, *World Tables,* 1993; International Bank for Reconstruction and Development, *Trends in Developing Economies,* various issues.

Note: For definitions of the first five variables, see Table 2.1. Real wages: Manufacturing industry wages.

erate with Alfonsín in restraining wages. The costs of failing to halt inflation, though substantial, were partially mitigated by the expectation that union influence would increase substantially if the Peronists were to recapture control of the presidency. Moreover, although moderate union factions affiliated with Lorenzo Miguel's Group of 62 were inclined to avoid confrontational tactics, rival factions within the movement continually pulled them toward more militant stances. In any event, union leaders had been virtually shut off from access to economic decision-making, except for a few brief months in 1987.[16]

Throughout Sourouille's tenure as finance minister, ongoing confrontations between the government and the unions undermined efforts to estab-

[16] James W. McGuire, "Union Political Tactics and Democratic Consolidation in Alfonsín's Argentina, 1983–1989," *Latin American Research Review* 27 (1992): 37–74; Ian Roxborough, "Organized Labor: A Major Victim of the Debt Crisis," in Barbara Stallings and Robert Kaufman, eds., *Debt and Democracy in Latin America* (Boulder, Colo.: Westview Press, 1989), pp. 91–108. In January 1985, the unions did negotiate an accord with the major business associations, the "Pact of Olivos," but this was based on demands for expansionist policies that could not be sustained in the context of Argentina's deteriorating balance-of-payments position. See Smith, *Authoritarianism and the Crisis of the Argentine Political Economy,* p. 287.

lish a credible incomes policy. The one short lull alluded to above also proved disastrous. Prior to the 1987 Congressional elections, Alfonsín sought to diffuse union protests by naming the head of the powerful electrical workers' union as minister of labor, but resulting wage agreements reached over the objections of the Finance Ministry contributed both to a resurgence of inflation and to Radical Party losses in the September elections.

Local electoral cleavages and Argentina's federal system compounded the effects of the Peronist-Radical rivalry. Patronage networks linking leaders of both parties to local political bosses undermined the capacity of the Finance Ministry to control spending. From 1983 to 1987, the central government reduced its deficits substantially, but provincial government deficits climbed to 4.6 percent of GDP from an average of 1.0 percent during the military period.[17]

Argentine federalism also provided opportunities for small regionally based parties to exercise disproportionate influence. Argentina's closed-list electoral system provided Alfonsín with substantial leverage over Radical party legislators, but Peronists and conservative regional party bosses controlled enough seats to block or dilute reform initiatives. During the last three years of Alfonsín's term, the government failed to secure support for tax reform, or to follow through on commitments to privatization and trade liberalization. As the presidential election campaign drew closer, concern about the prospects of a Peronist victory compounded underlying uncertainties.

These difficulties came to a head in the failure of Alfonsín's last major stabilization effort, negotiated with industrialists in August 1988.[18] The Spring Plan, as it was called, fixed the exchange rate and established price controls to halt the inflationary spiral, and it provided for emergency increases in the tax on agricultural exports in order to hold down federal deficits. But although these measures did produce a temporary decline in inflation, the government remained unable to implement the broader tax reforms that were also part of the package. In January 1989, the effort began to unravel. The World Bank concluded that the government had not made sufficient progress toward its reform goals and suspended disbursements on a structural adjustment loan.[19] Intense speculation against the exchange rate followed, growing stronger as the presidential election approached.

---

[17] Osvaldo H. Scenone, "Public Sector Behavior in Argentina," in Filipe Larraín and Marcelo Selowsky, *The Public Sector and the Latin American Crisis* (San Francisco: International Center for Economic Growth Publication and ICS Press, 1991), p. 19. In contrast, SOE deficits were "only" 3.0 percent of GDP during this period. Significantly, provincial deficits also increased notably between 1973 and 1976, the only other democratic period since 1966.

[18] The politics of this period are discussed in Juan Carlos Torre, "Transicíon democrática y emergencia económica: El gobierno de la economía bajo la presidencia de Alfonsín," unpublished ms., Princeton University, Princeton, N.J., n.d.

[19] Some Radical party leaders accuse Cavallo of deliberately encouraging that decision in order to weaken the Radicals in the coming presidential campaign.

In the months immediately preceding the May elections, sharp depreciation of the Argentine currency against the dollar triggered a hyperinflation and insured the defeat of the Radical candidate in the May elections. The loss to the Peronist Carlos Saúl Menem in turn eliminated any hope that the incumbent government could regain control of the economy; the hyperinflation did not abate until Menem assumed office in July, six months ahead of schedule.[20]

Brazil under Sarney

As in Argentina, Sarney's government attempted to use incomes policy to halt inertial inflation, beginning with the Cruzado Plan in February 1986. However, the executive faced a political system characterized by an almost uniquely unfavorable combination of institutional arrangements.[21] The party system was both fragmented and riven by ideological divisions.[22] Unable to govern on its own, Sarney's Liberal Front Party (PFL) formed a loose coalition with the Party of the Brazilian Democratic Movement (PMDB). The PMDB, however, was itself internally divided, encompassing a wide range of political forces from a powerful populist wing to conservative local bosses. The effects of these divisions were exacerbated by the emergence of new populist political forces. Leonel Brizola, the most prominent populist politician in the early 1960s, became a national political force after capturing the governorship of the state of Rio de Janeiro in 1982. The socialist-oriented Labor Party (PT) emerged out of the radicalized union movement of the late 1970s, maintained a strong base of working-class support in São Paulo, and became a significant electoral force.

Problems of governance were further complicated by the revival of a federal Constitution and an open-list proportional representation system. With the reinstitution of direct gubernatorial elections in 1982, regional political elites became pivotal figures in negotiating the 1985 transition to a civilian president.[23] This structure also provided opportunities for gover-

---

[20] Juan Carlos Torre, "Transición democrática y emergencia económica," p. 101.

[21] Maria do Carmo Campello de Souza, "Evolucão e crise do sistema partidario," in David V. Fleischer, ed., *Os partidos políticos no Brasil* (Brasília: Editora Universidade de Brasília, 1981), pp. 63–90; and "The Brazilian 'New Republic': Under the Sword of Damocles," in Alfred Stepan, ed., *Democratizing Brazil* (Oxford: Oxford University Press, 1989), pp. 351–94.

[22] Collier and Collier classify the pre-1964 Brazil and pre-1973 Chile as "polarizing multiparty systems" because of the strong links in each country between the labor movement and radical, anticapitalist electoral forces. Ruth Berins Collier and David Collier, *Shaping the Political Arena* (Princeton, N.J.: Princeton University Press, 1991), pp. 512–26.

[23] Frances Hagopian documents how the turn to electoral politics as source of legitimation pushed the military authorities to rely on regional bosses for support. "The Politics of Oligarchy: The Persistence of Traditional Elites in Contemporary Brazil," (Ph.D. diss., Massachusetts Institute of Technology, 1986).

nors and local officials to gain influence over electoral politics, and thus over policy, at the national level. As was the case in Argentina's federal system, state and municipal expenditures grew rapidly, especially after the 1982 gubernatorial elections and the 1985 transition. Central Bank bailouts of state banks, which had become an important source of discretionary finance for state governments, also constituted a growing problem for the central government.

José Sarney was very much a product of this system. His core base of support lay with conservative political bosses from the poorer northern states, whom he cultivated by allocating control of the "spending ministries" to allies within both the PFL and the PMDB. Officials in charge of the country's monetary authorities and various state banks were generally presidential appointees who found it difficult to refuse requests for financing coming from Congressional politicians or governors allied to the president.

These features of the party and governmental system strongly affected economic policy. Unlike Argentina's Austral initiative, Brazil's Cruzado Plan was characterized by relatively limited concern for orthodox macroeconomic measures, and represented a calculated attempt to outflank or coopt opponents on the left. Large wage increases granted prior to the price freeze, a fixed exchange rate, and limited adjustments in public-sector prices combined to produce sharp increases in real incomes and a brief surge of consumption and growth. A comparatively strong balance-of-payments position at the outset of the plan made these initiatives possible, but it quickly became apparent that the economy was becoming dangerously overheated. However, neither Sarney nor his Congressional allies within the PMDB were willing to risk adjustments prior to legislative elections scheduled for November 1986. These elections were viewed as especially important, because the Congress was also given the mandate to draft a new Constitution for the country.[24]

The PMDB won an overwhelming victory in the election, but the economic dam burst in the following months. Long-delayed attempts to ease the price freeze triggered bitter conflicts with the union movement over indexation, and in early 1987, a new wage-price spiral ensued. As the current account deteriorated, the government declared a moratorium on the service of its medium- and long-term external debt, but this failed either to recoup government's declining political support or to enhance the credibility of the stabilization effort. Subsequent initiatives followed under new finance ministers Luiz Bresser Pereira in 1987 and Mailson da Nobrega in 1988–89. Each placed a higher priority on controlling the macroeconomic fundamentals, but the centrifugal pressures within the political system made it difficult to follow through and, as in Argentina, prices

[24] Kaufman, "Stabilization and Adjustment in Argentina, Brazil and Mexico."

TABLE 6.4

Post-transition Economic Developments in Brazil

	1980–84	1985	1986	1987	1988
GDP Growth	1.5	7.9	8.0	3.3	−0.2
Inflation	125.1	226.9	145.2	229.7	682.3
Fiscal Deficit/GDP	−3.3	−11.2	−13.3	−12.1	−15.3
Current Account/GDP	−4.8[a]	−0.1	−2.0	−0.5	1.3
Investment/GDP	20.0	19.2	19.1	22.3	22.8
Real Wage	0.8	24.4	25.2	−5.0	6.2

	1989	1990	1991	1992
GDP Growth	3.3	−4.2	1.2	−0.2
Inflation	1,287.0	2,937.8	440.9	1,008.7
Fiscal Deficit/GDP	−16.1	−5.6	−0.9	na
Current Account/GDP	0.2	−0.6	−0.3	1.0
Investment/GDP	24.9	21.5	18.9	17.5
Real Wage	8.6	−14.0	−11.8	na

Sources: Economic Commission on Latin America, *Economic Survey of Latin America and The Caribbean,* various issues; International Monetary Fund, *International Financial Statistics Yearbook,* various issues; International Monetary Fund, *Government Financial Statistics Yearbook,* various issues; World Bank, *Trends in Developing Economies,* various issues; World Bank, *World Tables,* various issues.

Notes: For definitions of the first five variables, see Table 2.1. Real Wages: Manufacturing wages in São Paulo.

[a]1980–83.

escalated out of control during the last months of the Sarney administration (see Table 6.4).

Brazil's fragmented and decentralized political structure provided numerous opportunities for both business and labor to pressure the government. In 1987, the Federation of Industries of São Paulo (FIESP), Brazil's most powerful industrial association, led a fierce campaign against Bresser Pereira's proposed tax reform. Sarney yielded, effectively forcing Bresser from office. Both Bresser and his successors also faced withering attacks from public-employee unions over efforts to contain wage demands. As in several other of the crisis cases, links to opposition parties and internal divisions within the labor movement made it difficult to manage such confrontations. Efforts to initiate talks between the government and the General Confederation of Labor (CGT) were undercut by opposition from more radical unions in both 1985 and 1987.[25]

Problems of controlling fiscal policy were compounded by the 1988

[25] Ian Roxboro, "Organized Labor." pp. 93–98.

Constitution, drafted by the Congressional politicians elected two years earlier. The new document provided for a large increase in the transfer of federal tax revenues to states and municipalities and granted them substantial discretion over spending; the federal government, on the other hand, retained the responsibility for politically important expenditures in areas such as health, agriculture, culture, and police. Among other things, these arrangements reduced the incentive for state and municipal officials to rationalize local administration, and increased the duplication of services and intragovernmental turf battles.[26]

Why Did Things Get Worse?

What accounts for the persistent policy failures among these new democratic governments? An important part of the explanation is that they faced a combination of extraordinarily adverse economic circumstances coupled with widespread yet highly unrealistic public expectations about the economic benefits that would flow from democratization. Expansionist policies pursued during the first year of the Alfonsín government, during the Cruzado Plan in Brazil, and in Peru under Alan García were in part a response to these broad public expectations. It is also clear that part of the problem lay with the hopes pinned on technically flawed heterodox adjustment strategies, which were attractive to both politicians and publics precisely because they promised to stabilize the economy without imposing serious hardships on anyone.

In virtually all cases, however, policy incoherence and drift persisted well after it had become clear that failure to act would not only be expensive in economic terms but politically costly as well. In Bolivia, the devastating impact of high inflation was evident almost as soon as the new Siles government came to power; the inability to stabilize ultimately contributed directly to Siles's exit from office, eighteen months ahead of the scheduled end of his term. In Argentina and Brazil, the failure of the Austral and Cruzado plans left little room for doubt that heterodox programs could not halt the acceleration of inflation without fundamental fiscal corrections. Yet incumbent presidents in both countries failed to support these more orthodox measures, even though they might have arrested the drastic decline in the economy and their political fortunes. In Peru, Belaúnde's market-oriented policies had been widely discredited, but it is far from

[26] Francisco Dornelles, "Reforma do Estado e reforma fiscal," in João Paulo Dos Reis Velloso, ed., *Combate a Inflacão e Reforma Fiscal* (Rio de Janeiro: José Olympio, Editora, 1992), pp. 17–23; Eliza J. Willis, "The Decentralization of Economic Policy under the 1988 Constitution," paper delivered at the Annual Meeting of the American Political Science Association, Washington, D.C., August 29–September 1, 1991.

clear that Alan García's reckless program was the only politically acceptable antidote, and the correction of obvious policy mistakes lagged well behind the growing evidence of macroeconomic deterioration and declining presidential popularity.

Although many factors contributed to these policy and political failures, we emphasize how institutional characteristics of the party systems aggravated partisan conflict and underlying social divisions. Though party systems differed in the extent of fragmentation, and Argentina appears to possess a relatively cohesive party structure, each system contained centrifugal tendencies that presented serious impediments to policy coordination.

The central challenge faced by these new democratic governments lay in the combination of fragmentation with the polarizing effects of populist and left oppositions. This party structure produced such effects through a number of mechanisms, the most important of which was the nature of partisan conflict itself. In all four countries, incumbent leaders confronted opposition parties that were willing and able to mobilize legislative and nonlegislative challenges to their adjustment programs. The stronger the opposition, the greater the political risks of sponsoring unpopular policies, and the more severe the internal strains within the governing party or coalition itself. Partisan pressures were particularly important for understanding policy slippage prior to elections. Municipal election campaigns in Peru (1981) and Congressional contests in Argentina (1987) and Brazil (1986) provided strong incentives for officials to delay adjustment. In all four cases, the final descent into hyperinflation overlapped with the onset of presidential campaigns, fundamental uncertainty about the policies of the successor administration, and a virtually complete deflation of the power and credibility of the incumbent government.

Fragmentation and polarization also posed serious challenges to the coordination of policy within the ruling coalition and among the branches and levels of the government itself. In Bolivia and Brazil, Siles and Sarney presided over highly unstable coalition governments characterized by fierce competition for patronage and serious internal divisions over economic strategy. In the legislature, Siles faced a center-right majority bloc strongly opposed to his government, while Sarney depended on a PMDB majority that began to splinter immediately after the collapse of the Cruzado Plan. In Brazil's federal system, control of state-level sources of patronage granted provincial party leaders substantial independence from the center, while in Bolivia weak party organizations left regional governments exposed to informal colonization by business elites, local notables, and drug lords.

In Argentina and Peru, the party configuration seemed somewhat more propitious. In Argentina, two large, relatively stable parties dominated the system. In Peru, substantial victories for the AP and the APRA in 1980 and 1985 provided both Belaúnde and García with large legislative majorities. However both countries suffered problems analogous to those in Bolivia and Brazil. In Argentina, small regional parties held the balance of power in the Congress, and joined with the Peronists to block tax and trade reforms. In Peru, unstable party organizations and uncertain electoral support intensified the struggle for patronage within the governing parties and increased the difficulty of maintaining centralized control over regional political bosses.

Finally, party competition in these polarized and/or fragmented systems also impeded efforts to negotiate agreements on policy among contending interest groups. We have focused particular attention on the confrontational nature of state-labor relations because an incomes policy is a crucial component of heterodox stabilization plans, and one that uniformly ended in failure in all four countries. Such failures were in large part the consequence of the profound hardships already endured by many low-income groups and the extraordinary fiscal constraints that reduced the ability of governments to cushion the costs of adjustment through compensatory measures. But as we will discuss in more detail in chapter 10, the failure of "concertación" can also be traced to the ties between the unions and populist electoral oppositions and deep partisan and factional competition for control of the union movement. The latter was particularly important in Bolivia, Brazil, and Peru.

Notwithstanding our emphasis on labor, the absence of business support for the government's adjustment efforts was also a hallmark of these crisis cases. The private sector strongly resisted measures that might have alleviated the fiscal crisis, including particularly tax reform, and continued to press particularistic claims on the government. As with the left, the political behavior of business might have been different if the party system had provided institutionalized channels for representation through programmatic center-right parties.

TURNAROUND: THE NEOLIBERAL INITIATIVES
OF THE LATE 1980s

Despite the immobilism and inconsistency that characterized the first democratic administrations in the crisis cases, democratic governments did launch comprehensive stabilization and structural adjustment initiatives during the second half of the 1980s. These occurred under the administrations of Paz Estensorro in Bolivia (1985–89), Carlos Saúl Menem in Argentina (1989–94); and Fernando Collor de Mello and Alberto Fujimori, both elected in 1990, in Brazil and Peru respectively. How did democratic systems that appeared immobilized suddenly begin such wide-ranging policy initiatives? What accounts for cross-national differences in the way these policies were implemented?

It is important to begin with the observation that these reforms were not simply imposed by outside actors; all four initiatives were either home-grown products or developed in collaboration with economists who operated outside, and at times in opposition to, the usual IMF and World Bank networks.[27] Although international pressure and encouragement from creditors and the multilateral financial institutions contributed to the new policy stance, this cannot fully account for why they were adopted or how they were implemented. Our explanation focuses, rather, on domestic economic and political factors.

The initiation of these packages can be attributed to changes not only in the incentives facing new executives, but in their political capabilities and institutional powers as well. The economic and social consequences of earlier policy failures, and particularly the emergence of devastating hyperinflations, allowed incoming presidents to concentrate executive authority while at the same time substantially weakening the political hand of those social forces that had previously opposed reform.

First, escalating inflation contributed to a profound fiscal crisis of the state. The dramatic erosion of the ability of national governments to extract resources and to provide services provided politicians a crucial incentive to act. During the hyperinflations of the late 1980s tax revenues dropped by more than two-thirds in Bolivia, and by more than 50 percent in Argentina and Peru (see Table 6.5). Revenues fell much less in Brazil, which may help to explain that country's less aggressive approach to fiscal adjustment. By the onset of the new stabilization efforts, however, all four governments had witnessed a severe deterioration in their capacity to administer justice, maintain basic transport and communications systems, or deliver basic health and welfare services.

One effect of these government failures was to increase broad public tolerance for executive initiative. Even in Brazil, where indexation was most extensive, accelerating inflation made it increasingly difficult to conduct business, make contracts, or simply manage day-to-day household finances. Fears of a social breakdown not only drove presidents to stabilize, but also bolstered their capacity to push through previously unpopular measures such as trade liberalization and privatization.[28]

[27] Catherine M. Conaghan, "Reconsidering Jeffrey Sachs and the Bolivian Economic Experiment," in Paul W. Drake, ed., *Money Doctors: Foreign Debts and Economic Reforms in Latin America from the Foreign Debts and Economic Reforms in Latin America from the 1890s to the Present* (Wilmington, Del.: Scholarly Resources, 1994), pp. 236–66.

[28] Dani Rodrik, "The Rush to Free Trade in the Developing World: Why So Late? Why Now? Will It Last?" in Stephan Haggard and Steven B. Webb, eds., *Voting for Reform: Democracy, Political Liberalization, and Economic Adjustment* (New York: Oxford University Press, 1994), pp. 61–89. See also Albert Hirschman for a seminal discussion of the way support for controversial measures can be increased by linking them to perceived solutions of highly salient problems, *Journeys toward Progress* (New York: Twentieth Century Fund, 1963), pp. 231–35.

TABLE 6.5

Hyperinflation and Government Finances in Argentina, Bolivia, Brazil, and Peru

	Total Revenue (% of GDP)		Tax Revenue (% of GDP)		Revenue/ Expenditure		Inflation (%)
	1980	1985	1980	1985	1980	1985	1985
Bolivia	40.5	13.9	9.7	2.9	.83	.58	11,750
	1985	1989	1985	1989	1985	1989	1989
Argentina	38.8	26.7	22.0	11.5	.91	.69	12,459
Peru	14.8	6.0	14.3	6.5	.62	.45	33,398
Brazil	27.1[a]	26.2	20.0[a]	18.4	.93[a]	.75	1,287

Source: Miguel A. Kiguel and Nissan Liviatan, "Stopping Three Big Inflations: Argentina, Brazil, and Peru," Policy Research Working Paper, Country Economics Department, The World Bank, October 1992, pp. 15 and 18.

Note: Data for Argentina for 1989 are for the second quarter, the period of the first hyperinflation episode.

[a] 1986.

Deepening macroeconomic crises also had longer-term sociological effects, weakening some of the very groups that had exercised a veto over previous adjustment efforts. The combination of prolonged recession and escalating inflation eroded the social base of both unions and employer groups, particularly in the industrial sector. The data in Table 6.6 show that the size of the manufacturing sector declined sharply in Argentina, and that during the early 1980s, unemployment and the size of the informal sector increased substantially in Argentina, Bolivia, and Peru. The industrial sector fared better in Brazil, but that was partly a function of an unsustainable expansion that was exhausted by early 1987. It is interesting to note, moreover, that during the recession of 1981–83, the informal sector grew more rapidly in Brazil than in any other country.

In such settings, the political costs of further delay outweigh the costs of "shock" programs. Despite populist rhetoric during the electoral campaign, each incoming president faced an emergency situation and was forced to cope with the fiscal aspects of the crisis through whatever means were at hand. In Peru and Bolivia, this included steep increases in the prices and rates charged by state-owned enterprises, emergency tax levies, and the establishment of cash management committees that placed public finances entirely on a pay-as-you-go basis. Bolivia sought extra breathing room by suspending its external debt service.[29] The Brazilian and Argentine govern-

[29] In all of the other countries, debt service had been suspended prior to the onset of the hyperinflation crisis.

TABLE 6.6
Changes in Class and Industrial Structure in Latin America

	Labor Force in Manufacturing (%)		Urban Minimum Wage (1980=100)		Urban Informal Sector (1981=100)	Urban Unemployment (%)		
	1970	1984	1976	1985	1983	1976	1980	1985
Argentina	32.1	24.6	104	127	125.3	4.9	2.6	6.3
Bolivia	na	na	na	na	112.1	7.9	7.5	12.6
Brazil	18.3	18.9	98	88	132.1	6.8	7.2	5.3
Chile	21.0	17.5	68	76	98.2	16.3	11.7	17.0
Mexico	22.9	23.6	114	72	114.8	6.8	4.5	5.0
Peru	18.4	15.6	107	53	123.0	8.4	10.9	16.4
Uruguay	na	na	172	94	98.7	12.7	7.4	13.1

Source: Alejandro Portes, "Latin American Urbanization during the Years of the Crisis," Latin American Research Review 29 (1989): 26.

ments drastically reduced access to private savings, thereby reducing liquidity and in effect postponing payments on the public debt financed through such savings.

The need to control high inflation also produced a new rationale for ambitious structural reform. The Menem government took especially dramatic steps toward privatization, which promised both a short-term infusion of revenue and a reduction of fiscal transfers to loss-making companies. Extensive trade liberalization in Argentina, Bolivia, and Peru was rationalized partly on the grounds that it would dampen prices. Though Brazil moved more slowly, it also began to phase in tariff reductions and to prepare a sizeable number of state enterprises for privatization. Apart from their direct effect on prices, such programs were intended to bolster the overall credibility of the program by demonstrating the government's commitment to stay the course.

These combined stabilization–structural adjustment efforts did contribute to a rapid decline of inflation within a period of months, and generally garnered governments political support. However, the key question was whether such reforms could be sustained and consolidated. How would governments react once the initial surge of popularity subsided, or in the face of a political backlash against the real and perceived costs of reform?

Success in meeting these challenges was highly problematic in all four countries throughout the early 1990s. The wisdom of the neoliberal programs was disputed, in terms both of their social costs and of their potential for reigniting growth. Implementation faced many of the same institutional weaknesses discussed in the preceding sections. However, we see an important contrast between both the economic performance and the political circumstances that surrounded the reform effort in Argentina and Bolivia on the one hand, and in Brazil and Peru on the other. In the first two countries, governments sustained adjustment policies; in the second pair, one government slowed reform and the other suspended the constitutional framework itself.

As we argued in the last chapter, a crucial variable distinguishing the initiation and consolidation phases of reform is the ability to build viable bases of party and interest-group support. In Argentina and Bolivia, incoming presidents led opposition parties that had long been major political forces within their respective systems. The base of party support provided them with a firm political foundation for the concentration of executive authority; presidents were able to construct legislative majorities and either to coopt or neutralize populist or left opponents.

In Peru and Brazil, candidates of established opposition parties were either linked to earlier policy failures or represented politically isolated working-class parties. As a consequence, party systems fragmented further. New presidents were elected as "anti-party" outsiders. Though they were able to capitalize on initial honeymoons to initiate reforms, their lack of a firm party base ultimately proved a profound disadvantage and left them isolated from legislators and organized economic interests.

Bolivia and Argentina

The 1989 elections in Argentina resulted in a sweeping victory for the Peronists; in Bolivia, conversely, the presidential elections marked a crushing defeat for Siles's National Democratic Union coalition (UDN) and a resurgence of two more conservative parties, Paz Estenssoro's National Revolutionary Movement (MNR) and the Nationalist Democratic Action (ADN), headed by Banzer.[30] Though populist parties were apparently victorious in one country and losers in the other, however, these outcomes had surprisingly similar consequences for economic management. First, both the Peronist victory and the disintegration of Bolivia's UDN had the effect of eliminating electoral threats on the left of the incoming government. In the second place, both presidents headed large parties, which facilitated control of the legislature. In Argentina, Menem's Peronists had a majority in both branches of the Argentine Congress. In Bolivia, the MNR fell short of a majority, but provided a major building bloc in the governing alliance

---

[30] The combined support of the parties backing the Siles government dropped from about 38 percent of the electorate in 1980 to just above 13 percent in 1985, with Siles's own MNRI receiving less than 5 percent. René Antonio Mayorga, "La democracia en Bolivia: El rol de las elecciones en las fases de transición y consolidación," in Cerdas-Cruz, Rial, and Zovatto, *Una tarea inconclusa,* pp. 282–83.

forged between Paz Estensorro and Banzer, the so-called "Pact for Democracy." Although weakly institutionalized party organizations remained a serious problem, these realignments reduced the extent of polarization and fragmentation within each system.

BOLIVIA

The "Pact for Democracy" between the MNR and the ADN laid the political foundation for economic reform in Bolivia by enhancing executive power. In part, the pact reflected personalist ambitions that had long characterized Bolivian politics, resting in no small measure on Banzer's expectation (later disappointed) that he would receive the MNR's backing in the 1989 presidential contest. Yet the agreement did allow Paz Estensorro to avoid the democratic stalemate suffered by his predecessor. In 1985, the coalition backed a Congressional declaration of a state of siege, which gave wide decision-making latitude to Paz and his technocratic team. Congressional politicians were rarely consulted on policy issues, but they accepted the overall policy course charted under Paz and provided the necessary votes for implementing legislation.

The most immediate and controversial challenge to the program continued to come from the radicalized union movement. To halt the hyperinflation, the government program relied heavily on two key elements: fiscal retrenchment, including a reduction of extensive, but politically sensitive, consumer subsidies; and devaluation followed by the fixing of the exchange rate, which was to serve as the nominal anchor for other prices.[31] As in the past, the unions demanded compensatory wage increases which would have nullified the effects of the program, and they began to mobilize for a general strike and a blockade of La Paz. Unlike under Siles, however, Paz Estensorro responded with harsh measures. Using the authority granted by the state of siege, the government closed union headquarters and arrested hundreds of union leaders; it followed this crackdown with mine closings and massive layoffs. From 1985 to 1987, the work force in the state-owned companies fell from 32,000 to about 7,000, effectively destroying the base of the miners' unions.[32]

These coercive actions had tragic consequences for the workers involved; but radicalization of the union movement made it difficult to avoid confrontation, and the crackdown played a pivotal role in establishing the credibility of the stabilization effort. In terms of the preservation of Bolivia's fragile democratic system, it is significant that the authorization to

---

[31] Kiguel and Liviatan, "Stopping Three Big Inflations: Argentina, Brazil, and Peru," pp. 12–16.

[32] *Latin American Weekly Report,* January 15, 1987, no. 2; p. 4.

take such actions had come from Congress. Unlike the situation that later faced Fujimori in Peru, Paz's broad legislative majority meant that he did not face a choice between immobilism and constitutional legality in dealing with anti-system oppositions.

The backing provided by the MNR-ADN coalition also had implications for the government's relations with business elites. The latter had little access to the technocrats in charge of economic policy, and complained bitterly about the lack of consultation.[33] Nevertheless, business opposition was constrained by the fact that the ADN and the MNR were their closest political allies, and they generally backed the overall direction of the adjustment program.

Within the Congress itself, finally, the coalition provided the backing for legislative initiatives essential to the adjustment effort. One of the most important examples was the package passed in May 1986, which simplified the tax structure, imposed a broadly based value-added tax (VAT), and strengthened collection agencies.[34] While formally less progressive than the older tax structure, the new system was easier to administer and contributed significantly to sustaining the fiscal adjustment. Domestic tax receipts rose from 1.3 percent of GNP in 1985 to 7.7 percent in 1989—over half of total revenues.[35]

These measures put an abrupt end to the hyperinflation. The resumption of growth was disappointingly slow, but by the late 1980s, per capita growth rates turned positive, and a moderate recovery continued into the 1990s. Success in curbing inflation also affected the policy stance of the major parties. The new policy direction was endorsed by all of the major contenders in the 1989 presidential contest, including Jaime Paz Zamorra from the Left Revolutionary Movement (MIR), who was eventually selected president in the Congressional bargaining that followed. Although analysis of the Paz Zamorra period is beyond the scope of our analysis, the initial continuity of policy across administrations was an important indication that key elements of the reform had been consolidated.

ARGENTINA

As Kiguel and Leviatan argue, hyperinflation in Argentina was more difficult to bring under control than in Bolivia. In Bolivia, as in Europe after World War II, there had been no prolonged history of high inflation prior

[33] Catherine M. Conaghan, "Capitalists, Technocrats, and Politicians: Economic Policy-Making and Democracy in the Central Andes," The Helen Kellogg Institute for International Studies, Working Paper no. 109, May 1988, pp. 43–44.

[34] Richard M. Bird, "Tax Reform in Latin America: A Review of Some Recent Experience," *Latin American Research Review* 27 (1992): 7–37.

[35] Ibid., p. 10.

to the outburst of hyperinflation itself. In these "classical cases," hyperinflation resulted from sudden fiscal shocks and ended abruptly once governments had reduced deficits and established credible exchange-rate anchors. In Argentina, as well as in Brazil and Peru, long periods of high inflation and failed stabilizations preceded the hyperinflations of the late 1980s. This history made it far more difficult for the government to establish its credibility.[36]

During the first eighteen months of Menem's term, a succession of three finance ministers struggled with this problem through emergency taxes, adjustments in the exchange rate, and incomes policies negotiated with the private sector. Speculation against the exchange rate triggered a new flareup of hyperinflation between December 1989 and March 1990, followed by new emergency taxes, suspension of payments to suppliers, and deep cuts in public service expenditures. Stabilization efforts did begin to take hold after that point, however. A positive assessment of economic policy under Menem is clouded by high levels of corruption and erratic behavior on the part of the President and his family; nonetheless, the economy grew substantially during the early 1990s.

As in Bolivia, Menem's strong party and electoral base facilitated his government's continuing adjustment efforts. With the Peronists now the government party, Menem faced no serious electoral challenges from a populist electoral opposition. This allowed him to move quickly during the early honeymoon period to assuage the fears of international creditors and the domestic industrial elite. His first finance ministers had been executives in Bunge e Borne, a leading Argentine multinational, and initial policy steps were undertaken in close consultation with the major industrial groups. The influence of the industrial groups precluded adjustments in costly subsidies and tax shelters; it diminished under later finance ministers, leading on occasion to serious conflicts. But the initial rapprochement between the Peronist government and the private sector was a significant fact; it sent welcome signals to the international financial community and established a framework of mutual assurances that persisted beyond the end of the so-called "Bunge e Borne period" in November 1989.

Predictably, there were major strains within the Peronist movement as a consequence of the government's policy course, but dissidents lacked compelling political or economic alternatives. Some unions pressed for confrontational strategies, but most were unwilling to abandon the advantages of remaining within the movement, including direct representation of a labor bloc in the Chamber of Deputies. The important federations, particularly those in the private sector, either remained loyal to the official-

---

[36] Kiguel and Liviatan, "Stopping Three Big Inflations: Argentina, Brazil, and Peru," pp. 16–24.

ist CGT, or maintained a position of cautious neutrality with respect to government policy. Thus, unlike Alfonsín, Menem encountered no general strikes or other broad forms of union protest.[37]

These political circumstances allowed the government to undertake changes that would otherwise have been politically risky. On the one hand, the government reduced subsidies to industry and expanded the coverage and effectiveness of tax collection, measures indicating a growing independence on the part of the government from the particularistic claims of allies in the business sector. On the other hand, the government initiated a wide-ranging privatization program and other reforms typically viewed as antagonistic toward labor.

To push through such measures, Menem resorted frequently to decree powers, a practice that posed disturbing threats to the prestige and effectiveness of representative institutions. Ferreira Rubio and Goretti calculate that between 1989 and 1994, Menem issued 308 decrees without prior Congressional authorization ("need and urgency decrees," or NUDs), as contrasted with only about 25 under all preceding constitutional regimes. Some, such as the Bonex Plan in January 1991, dealt with serious emergencies like the resurgence of hyperinflation and followed broad legal precedents. Many other decrees, however, had much more particular, often political, objectives, and appeared to overstep constitutional boundaries.[38]

As was the case in Bolivia, however, the president's legislative majority did provide a legal foundation for action on many key issues. Most of the decrees issued during the initial phases of Menem's program were, unlike the NUDs, explicitly authorized by the Administrative Emergency and Economic Emergency laws that Congress passed during the hyperinflation crisis of 1989. Among the measures covered by these laws were the first big steps toward privatization, the sale of the state airlines and public utilities. Although these sales were marked by extensive corruption, they helped to establish the credibility of the government's intentions at a critical point in its struggle to gain control of a collapsing economy.

Menem's Congressional majority played an even more direct role in the passage of the Law of Convertibility, sponsored in April 1991 by Menem's fourth finance minister, Domingo Cavallo. The legislation was a critical turning point in the stabilization effort. It provided for a fully convertible currency pegged to the dollar and prohibited currency emissions not backed by hard currency reserves. The effect was similar to that of placing Argentina on a gold standard. The law eliminated government discretion over

[37] Adolfo Canitrot and Silvia Sigal, "Economic Reform, Democratization, and the Crisis of the State in Argentina," prepared for the project on Economic Reform and Democratization, Overseas Development Council, Washington D.C., March 1993.

[38] Delia M. Ferreira Rubio and Matteo Goretti, "Government by Decree in Argentina," paper delivered at the 18th International Congress of the Latin American Studies Association, Altanta, Ga., March 10–12, 1994, pp. 21–31.

monetary and exchange-rate policy, and could not be legally reversed without new legislation that could trigger dangerous new rounds of financial speculation.

Economically, the strategy faced important risks. The most serious cause for concern was the appreciation of the exchange rate. Because of residual domestic inflation, the real value of the currency drifted upward throughout the early 1990s, producing a lag in export growth and unprecedented trade deficits. On the other hand, inflation rates remained much lower than in the past, financial capital began to flow into the country, and there was a substantial economic expansion. Most important, although new episodes of macroeconomic crisis remained possible, the deep changes in the structure of the economy and the scope of state intervention were not easily subject to reversal.

Executive Isolation: Peru and Brazil

In Peru and Brazil, the 1990 presidential elections were marked not by the transfer of power to major opposition parties, but by a virtual collapse of all major parties. In Peru, the failed administrations of Belaúnde and García sorely wounded both the AP and the APRA, and each suffered a sharp deterioration in its support in the 1990 election. In Brazil, the backlash against Sarney hit the PMDB as well, and the party's candidate came in a distant fifth in the first round of presidential voting.

In both countries the tendency toward political fragmentation was reinforced by the constitutional provision requiring a second-round runoff among the top two contenders in the event that none won an outright majority. The possibility of gaining enough votes to get into a second round encouraged a large number of candidates to enter the race, including outsiders such as Fujimori and Collor who had little organized party support. Both candidates managed to win by direct mass media appeals to voters.

The absence of party support did not prevent either Collor or Fujimori from launching wide-ranging initiatives during their first months in office. In contrast to their counterparts in Argentina and Bolivia, however, the new presidents controlled only a small fraction of their respective legislatures. As programs initiated by decree began to encounter opposition from affected interest groups, each president became increasingly isolated.

PERU

The Fujimori government in Peru persisted in its shock program, but at extremely high social and political cost. Inflation during 1991 and 1992 fell from its astronomical highs, but stability remained fragile and a deep recession continued until 1993 when the economy began to improve rapidly. There were also signs that the government might have erred by rushing into radical trade reform before the stabilization was fully consolidated. Tariffs had traditionally been an important source of government revenues, and the exchange-rate appreciation discouraged exports and created new incentives for import-competing business to protest.[39]

In April 1992, Fujimori abruptly closed Congress, suspended party activities, and assumed dictatorial power. Although terrorism and drug trafficking had as much to do with this sudden decision as controversy over his economic program, the latter was also a major factor. Conflicts over fiscal policy with the APRA-dominated Congress had been raging since January, and although the legislature had no effective control over the cash-based budgeting process still in effect, the stalemate provided part of the rationalization for Fujimori's action. Economic circumstances mattered in a more fundamental sense as well: Peru's deep recession had contributed to the spread of the Shining Path movement into urban areas, which was the central justification for the coup.

Fujimori's *autogolpe* was widely popular, and it was followed in 1993 and 1994 both by substantial victories against the Shining Path and by a marked upturn in economic activity. Nevertheless, in a number of ways, the action threatened not only democratization but the process of economic adjustment. In the short term, the most immediate cost was a disruption of the government's effort to rebuild ties to international creditors.[40] A consortium of donor governments led by the United States slowed or suspended over $1 billion in bridge loans that had been part of a larger package of lending from international financial institutions. Disbursements from the World Bank and IDB eventually resumed, but at lower levels and with the main purpose of financing arrears. Though Fujimori himself attached a low priority to antipoverty programs, it should also be noted that nongovernmental organizations also suspended some $700 million in funds intended to support such programs. This was a particularly devastating blow given that the Fujimori stabilization package had included no welfare cushions to protect the poor.

Much more worrying were the prospects for the long-run sustainability of the reform. Economic conditions did begin to improve substantially in 1993 and 1994, and fiscal surpluses provided some opportunity for public spending to reactivate the economy and alleviate unemployment. The capacity to implement such policies was seriously weakened, however, by the "bunker mentality" of an economic team that made decisions without

---

[39] See Pastor and Wise, "The Peruvian Economy in the 1980s," pp. 110–13.

[40] Carol Wise, "The Politics of Peruvian Economic Reform: Overcoming the Legacies of State-Led Development," *Journal of Interamerican Studies and World Affairs* 36 (1994): 75–125.

input from other parts of the bureaucracy. The suspension of the Constitution had reinforced this isolation. Outside the government, it might have been possible to tap the talent available in Lima's private think tanks. As Carol Wise writes, however, "the new authoritarian persona and near paranoid secrecy now enshrouding the regime has rendered the Fujimori team a club to which most well-qualified technocrats would prefer not to belong."[41]

The largest question mark was whether the adjustment program could be sustained after 1995, the scheduled end of Fujimori's term. As of the early 1990s, Fujimori had succeeded in maintaining his personal popularity, but as we have argued, the consolidation of reform requires both an economic payoff and the conversion of that payoff into dependable social and institutional foundations of support. Efforts to institutionalize the program in 1992 and 1993 included the election of a Constituent Assembly, the holding of municipal elections, and the organization of a pro-Fujimori party, which gained broad support in both contests.[42]

On the other hand, opportunities for a sustained recovery were severely constrained by limits on fiscal resources, a weakened state apparatus, inflation that was still well above targeted levels, and an appreciated currency. If recovery is not sustained, Fujimori's high personal popularity could evaporate rapidly and his economic program could falter. Because it is now associated with the "autogolpe," the legality as well as the economic wisdom of the program is subject to challenge by the traditional parties. All of these parties, it should be noted, boycotted the elections for the Constituent Assembly, and although they were weakened by the events of the 1980s, they remained potential sources of opposition.

BRAZIL

The Collor administration did not formally usurp power as Fujimori had done, but the momentum of its reform efforts slowed over time and in 1993, scandal and impeachment cut short the tenure of the government. Significant signs of an economic recovery did begin to appear under Collor's successor, Itamar Franco, spurred in part by the trade liberalization program initiated under Collor. Nevertheless, the first half of the 1990s was marked by a continuation of the severe political and economic instability that had characterized Brazil since the early 1980s, and as of the mid-1990s, the future of the reform process remained uncertain.

The centerpiece of the Collor government's initial anti-inflation strategy was a sharp monetary contraction, achieved through the suspension of

---

[41] Ibid., p. 113.

[42] All of the major opposition parties boycotted the constituent elections, however.

access to private savings accounts. In Brazil's decentralized monetary system, however, it was impossible to prevent money from "leaking" back into the system. As these leakages became increasingly evident, the government's credibility declined rapidly. The young technocrats appointed by the new president tried frantically to manage the repercussions of their initial policy steps. As pressures on prices mounted, the government issued a barrage of decrees and new plans, but they were erratic and often internally contradictory, and failed to restore stability. Relations with the business elite deteriorated quickly as the government began to complain bitterly about the "oligarchies" and "cartels" that dominated the Brazilian economy.

A second, less stormy policy phase unfolded between late 1991 and October 1992 under the leadership of a new finance minister, Marcilio Marques Moreira. The appointment of Moreira, a career diplomat with extensive contacts within the Brazilian elite, had a calming effect on industrial groups and other political forces, and contributed to the maintenance of a gradual program of tariff reductions initiated during the preceding year. Moreira failed, however, in his effort to contain monthly inflation at 20 percent through the implementation of a moderately orthodox stabilization program, and by early 1994, Brazil again faced the threat of hyperinflation. Mounting economic problems overlapped with massive corruption scandals that led to Collor's impeachment in 1993; scandal subsequently engulfed many prominent members of Congress as well, including some who had played a leading role in the investigation of Collor.

A third, more positive phase, finally, unfolded during the last twelve months of the presidential term under Collor's successor, Itamar Franco. Among the most significant developments of this period was the launching of a dramatic new stabilization program under Fernando Henrique Cardoso, Franco's finance minister and the victorious candidate in the 1994 presidential election. As was the case in earlier stabilization programs, Cardoso's initiative was based in part on an effort to brake the inertial components of inflation through the introduction of a new currency, the real, which provided the name for the new program. Just as important, however, was Cardoso's success in gaining Congressional acceptance of a tight fiscal adjustment, including a one-year suspension of constitutional provisions for disbursing federal revenues to state governments. By the middle of 1994, the Real Plan had brought a temporary halt to inflation and was pivotal in Cardoso's overwhelming electoral victory, in which he drew on support of parties on both the center-left and the traditional right. The longer-term question, still open at the time of this writing, is whether the incoming president will be able to build on his preliminary successes to consolidate the reforms.

As finance minister, Cardoso displayed formidable skills as a negotiator and coalition builder in steering his program through a divided Congress, but he was also able to capitalize on exceptional circumstances, including corruption scandals, fear of hyperinflation, and elite fears that the presidency could be captured by the Labor Party's charismatic leader, Luís Inácio Lula da Silva (Lula). Within Franco's caretaker administration, Cardoso quickly became an indispensable and dominant figure—a world-famous academic and a respected political actor who could be fired only at great political cost to the president himself. With presidential backing secured, Cardoso was also in a position to use decree powers to press a highly discredited legislature to accept the temporary spending restraint vital to the credibility of his program.

Sustaining this credibility will depend in part on whether such adjustments can be deepened through more permanent institutional reforms, including both a restructuring of the tax system and a rationalization of the federal revenue-sharing procedures mandated by the 1988 Constitution. As finance minister, Cardoso was unable to secure legislative support for these and other constitutional reforms, despite his political leverage. The hope as he entered presidential office was that a political honeymoon would provide a new and better opportunity to gain this backing, and the chances of at least partial successes seemed reasonable. As in the previous administrations, however, the fragmentation and heterogeneity of Cardoso's legislative coalition posed a formidable challenge to coherent macroeconomic policymaking; failure to control inflation would place the gains from commercial liberalization and privatization at risk.

THE PHILIPPINES AND URUGUAY

Two crisis-induced transitions—the Philippines and Uruguay—avoided the policy incoherence and hyperinflation that plagued Argentina, Bolivia, Brazil, and Peru. Though there are important differences between these cases, they offer a comparative perspective on the patterns described in the preceding sections. In the Philippines, the ability of the new government to avoid further economic deterioration can largely be attributed to the fact that the Marcos government stabilized the economy before leaving office and the international community responded to Aquino's election with substantial financial support. In Uruguay, however, the economic and political challenges inherited by the new democratic administration were more typical of the other crisis cases.[43] Inflation, which had briefly dropped

---

[43] Martin Gargiulo provided valuable assistance on this section. Data in this paragraph are from Economic Commission on Latin America, *Economic Survey of Latin America 1985*, pp. 600–601.

below 30 percent in 1981 and 1982, surged to over 66 percent in 1984, the general government deficit stood at about 10 percent of GDP, and the country was one of the most heavily indebted in Latin America.[44] It should also be noted that, unlike in Argentina and Brazil, where wages had begun to recover during the last years of military rule, Uruguayan wages had dropped especially sharply in the years immediately preceding the democratic transition.

We argue that the capacity of these governments to adjust must be attributed in part to institutional differences that set them off from the other crisis cases. The Philippines benefited not only from less adverse economic circumstances, but also from a strong executive and the absence of a polarized party system. Similarly, Uruguay differs from its Latin American counterparts precisely in the reemergence of a centrist party system that bolstered executive initiative.

Uruguay

The Sanguinetti government sought to deal with the economic problems it had inherited by combining a moderate recovery of real wages with an emphasis on reducing the fiscal deficit and normalizing relations with external creditors. Wage increases, it was hoped, would contribute to a reactivation of the economy and the high priority on bringing public finances under control would avoid inflationary pressures.[45] Although the incoming government thus avoided a shock stabilization program or rapid structural reforms, it quickly concluded an IMF agreement and unlike Argentina, Brazil, and Bolivia, it implemented fiscal adjustments during its first years in office.

THE INSTITUTIONAL FRAMEWORK

The institutional framework within which these policies were implemented was in most respects the same as that which preceded the military takeover in 1972–73, and has been the subject of intense political and academic debate.[46] Three highly controversial aspects of the political system are

[44] According to one estimate, the general deficit in March was an astonishing 40 percent of GDP, as a result of the general collapse in revenue collections. Ibid., p. 599.

[45] Ibid.

[46] For an excellent review of these issues, see Charles Guy Gillespie, "Presidential-Parliamentary Relations and the Problems of Democratic Stability: The Case of Uruguay," in Matthew Shugart and Scott Mainwaring, eds., *Presidentialism and Democracy in Latin America,* unpublished ms., University of California, San Diego, 1994.

especially relevant to understanding policymaking during the Sanguinetti period.

The first is a constitutional provision allowing for direct popular referenda on legislation. A referendum calling for the prosecution of human-rights abuses by the armed forces came close to passing during the first years of Sanguinetti's term, and seriously strained civil-military relations during that period. As we shall see below, plebiscites also began to figure prominently in the politics of adjustment during the late 1980s and early 1990s.

A second controversial feature of the system concerned the powers granted to the president by the constitutional reforms of 1967. The issue of presidential authority has been contested in Uruguay since the establishment of a collegial executive in 1918.[47] Throughout the twentieth century, the legislature has generally been granted extensive power, including the right of qualified majorities to censure Cabinet ministers. Growing economic difficulties after World War II led to increasing pressure to establish a strong presidency, however. The 1967 constitutional reform replaced the collegial executive with a single president and endowed the office with extensive authority.

The legal powers most relevant to the present analysis included: extensive decree powers, the right to set limits on legislative spending proposals, and the right to call new legislative elections once during the presidential term.[48] An additional clause, also included in earlier Constitutions, authorized the president to "take prompt security measures" in cases of "internal disorder"; these powers were used extensively in the period prior to the military takeover.[49]

The final feature of the Constitution was the double-simultaneous voting system which had provided the framework for party politics since 1910. In this system, voters elected both the president and legislators by choosing simultaneously among parties and among competing lists *within* parties. Under this system, the winning lists are those that receive the most votes *within the party* that receives the most votes. This system biased incentives strongly against the formation of independent third-party movements that might challenge the long-standing electoral hegemony of the traditional Colorados and Blancos; political groups could compete with intraparty

---

[47] The collegial executive was repealed during the Depression, then reestablished in 1951.

[48] Presidential power was bolstered in several other ways that increased leverage over policy during the Sanguinetti period. The restored Uruguayan Constitution provided for concurrent elections for all major offices once every five years; unlike in most of the other crisis cases, the Sanguinetti government faced no midterm electoral tests. Congressional seats, moreover, were allocated among lists headed by presidential candidates; voters were not allowed to split their tickets. This encouraged considerable discipline within the president's legislative faction, although he still had to attract support from other lists in order to form a Congressional majority.

[49] Gillespie, "Presidential-Parliamentary Relations," pp. 15–16.

rivals while still capitalizing on strong voter attachments to the party label. On the other hand, the system also undermined the programmatic coherence and discipline of the major parties and arguably reduced their capacity to back decisive executive action.[50]

This complex institutional structure was an enduring characteristic of Uruguay's stable democratic system throughout the twentieth century, including the twenty-year period of increasing economic difficulties that preceded the 1973 coup. Nevertheless, the combination of undisciplined governing parties and a strong president who could not be removed by Congressional vote created legislative deadlocks that arguably contributed to the breakdown of democracy. The conservative Colorado presidents of the late 1960s had only fragile legislative majorities, and relied increasingly on special powers to cope with mounting inflation, labor unrest, and the urban guerilla challenge posed by the Tupamaros. The situation deteriorated still further after the 1971 elections, when the left-oriented Broad Front finally established itself as a significant third force, and the governing Colorados lost their majority. Both radical protest and government repression escalated under the right-wing president Juan María Bordaberry, opening the way to an incremental seizure of power by the military itself.[51]

During the post-1985 period, the balance of power among the contending parties was virtually identical to the one that had prevailed prior to the onset of the dictatorship in the early 1970s. As the new president, Sanguinetti not only lacked a legislative majority, but could not count completely on the legislative support of rival lists within his own party. As in the pre-authoritarian period, therefore, avoiding deadlocks on economic policy required the negotiation of legislative coalitions and/or the use of executive powers available within the restored constitution.

These political and institutional parallels with the pre-authoritarian period had disturbing implications both for the capacity of the government to manage the complex economic problems it faced and for the long-term stability of Uruguayan democracy itself. Yet although the challenges faced by the restored constitutional system were severe, they differed in significant ways from those of the early 1970s. At the broadest level, the differences included an intensely negative reaction against the failed military dictatorship and the demise of the Tupamaros as an anti-system threat.

---

[50] See Luis González, "Political Parties and Redemocratization in Uruguay," Wilson Center Working Paper no. 163, 1984; Gillespie, "Presidential-Parliamentary Relations," pp. 31–37.

[51] Ibid. For other analyses of the breakdown, see Martin Weinstein, *Uruguay: The Politics of Failure* (Westport, Conn: Greenwood Press, 1975), pp. 113–41; Edy Kaufman, *Uruguay in Transition: From Civilian to Military Rule* (New Brunswick, N.J.: Transaction Books, 1979) pp. 21–73; Collier and Collier, *Shaping the Political Arena,* pp. 640–66; and Charles Guy Gillespie, *Negotiating Democracy: Politicians and Generals in Uruguay* (New York: Cambridge University Press, 1991), pp. 17–79.

The party system, in turn, both reflected and reinforced these broader tendencies toward moderation and compromise.

The most important change within the parties was the resounding defeat of the pro-military lists within the Colorados and Blancos, first in the 1984 "primaries" and then in the 1985 general elections.[52] These results were particularly significant for the Colorados, the party most closely identified with the military takeover. The moderate factions led by Sanguinetti regained the predominance within the party that they had lost in the years prior to the coup, while the legislative share of more conservative lists dropped from 28 percent in 1971 to only 6 percent in 1985.

These outcomes were facilitated by the catchall character of the traditional parties and by the incentives for inclusiveness inherent in the double simultaneous vote. More disciplined and programatic parties might well have been slower to register the strong centrist preferences held by a majority of the Uruguayan population in the aftermath of the dictatorship. At the same time, the factional diversity within each of the traditional parties helped to prevent strong ideological or partisan antagonisms between them. Blancos criticized the Colorados for complicity in the 1973 coup and for their willingness to accept a ban on Wilson Ferreira's presidential candidacy in 1985. But efforts at reconciliation did not require party leaders to transcend divisions as deep as those among rival parties in Argentina, Peru, Bolivia, or Chile.

The options available to the Uruguayan left were also affected by the centrist trends within the party system. The Broad Front was able to maintain the 20 percent share of the electorate it had established in the early 1970s, but it also faced important incentives to move toward the center. Opportunities for legislative blackmail were limited, since Congressional majorities could also be forged by alliances among lists from the traditional parties. Given continuing voter attachments to the traditional parties, moreover, the Front also had relatively little immediate hope of capturing the presidency. Under these circumstances, the possibilities for influencing the policy process depended on establishing cooperative ties with the ruling Colorados.

POLICY CHALLENGES AND POLITICAL RESPONSES DURING THE SANGUINETTI PERIOD

Throughout Sanguinetti's term, these centripetal tendencies generally encouraged the maintenance of the moderate policy course described briefly above. These institutional factors were particularly important during the

[52] Juan Rial, "The Uruguayan Elections of 1984: Triumph of the Center," in Paul W. Drake and Eduardo Silva, eds., *Elections and Democratization in Latin America, 1980–1985* (La Jolla: Center for Iberian and Latin American Studies, Center for U.S.–Mexican Studies, and Institute of the Americas, University of California, San Diego, 1986), pp. 245–72.

initial years of the transition, when the government faced important challenges from the military and labor unions that might otherwise have led to a deepening of the economic crisis.

As in the other crisis cases, union militancy was driven by efforts to recoup severe losses suffered under authoritarian rule.[53] During the months preceding Sanguinetti's inauguration, leaders of the major parties and economic interest groups attempted to head off major industrial conflicts through the negotiation of social pacts, but these agreements broke down almost as soon as Sanguinetti took office. Like their counterparts elsewhere in South America, the unions strongly criticized the IMF agreements and called for a moratorium on external debt payments. Notwithstanding the government's moderate wage policies, the first three years of Sanguinetti's presidency were marked by especially bitter strikes in the textile industry, the ports, and the railways.[54]

Moderate sectors of the Broad Front played an important role in steering the labor movement away from such confrontations.[55] Within a few years, relatively cautious Communist leaders had gained the upper hand over more militant rivals within the labor confederation, and relations with the government began to stabilize. Though labor conflicts continued, they were settled more quickly, notwithstanding the tendency for real wage growth to slow during the latter part of the decade.

Challenges from the military arose over the referendum on prosecutions for human-rights abuses committed under the dictatorship. The threat of a military backlash was very real, and for the Sanguinetti government, it substantially increased the risks of unpopular reform initiatives. Cooperation with the Blancos, however, played an important role in reducing these dangers. Although the heads of the main Blanco list refused Sanguinetti's invitation to enter a coalition cabinet, they provided assurances of support with respect to civil-military relations and pledged to avoid forms of

---

[53] This was considerably sharper drop, it should be noted, than in Argentina and Chile, where real wages had dropped only 9 percent and 13 percent during comparable periods. Charles Guy Gillespie, "Democratic Consolidation in Uruguay," in John Higley and Richard Gunther, editors, *Elites and Democratic Consolidation in Latin America and Southern Europe* (Cambridge, New York, Port Chester, Melbourne, and Sydney: Cambridge University Press, 1992), p. 201; Joseph Ramos, *Neoconservative Economics in the Southern Cone of Latin America, 1973–1983* (Baltimore: Johns Hopkins University Press, 1986), p. 60; *Economic Survey of Latin America 1985,* p. 604.

[54] For a useful discussion of state-labor relations in Uruguay, see Martin Gargiulo, "The Uruguayan Labor Movement in the Post-Authoritarian Period," in Edward Epstein, ed., *Labor Autonomy and the State in Latin America,* (Boston: Unwin-Hyman, 1989), pp. 219–46. The following paragraphs are also indebted to a number of conversations with Gargiulo during the fall of 1991.

[55] Jennifer L. McCoy, "The Collective Dilemma of Economic Reform: Uruguay in Comparative Perspective," presented to the Instituto de Ciencia Política, Universidad de la Republica, Montevideo, Uruguay, September 1992, p. 28.

opposition that would jeopardize the "governability" of the system.[56] Such assurances did not preclude criticism of the government's economic policy, but they made it easier for the president to back the cautious macroeconomic approach of the finance minister at a time when concerns about military dissatisfaction and labor unrest might have increased the temptation to relax fiscal controls.

In a more general way, the government's room for maneuver on economic policy was strengthened by the fact that important segments of the Blanco opposition shared its basic economic views. In most of the other crisis cases, incumbent party politicians initially faced substantial electoral challenges from opposition electoral movements making strong antireformist appeals. In Uruguay, the major opposition candidate and eventual winner in the 1989 election was Luis Alberto Lacalle, a moderate Blanco politician advocating fiscal caution, trade liberalization, and privatization.

Within the context of strong centrist tendencies in the party system, finally, the constitutional powers available to the president helped to sustain the basic direction of macroeconomic policy. The authority to limit public expenditures was especially important during the first years of the transition. In 1985 and 1986, the president blocked large-scale social spending increases demanded by opposition legislators; though subsequent compromises restored some of these cuts, they helped to bring the looming fiscal crisis under control. The government's authority to set public-sector salaries and the minimum wage also played a role in labor relations. Within the private sector, wage accords were generally negotiated in tripartite councils reestablished after the transition. Because of continuing difficulties in negotiating agreements with public sector unions, however, Sanguinetti relied increasingly on decree powers to limit wage increases, which lagged behind those in the private sector.

In contrast to his predecessors in the late 1960s and early 1970s, Sanguinetti deployed these powers sparingly, and relied on a broader process of negotiation with party and interest group leaders. In pre-coup Uruguay, as well as in Brazil and Peru during the 1990s, special presidential powers were deployed as a substitute for support derived from the party system and were thus more likely to lead to the political isolation of the president. As a supplement to a process of compromise among contending parties and interests, on the other hand, presidential authority provided a means to avoid policy immobilism when negotiations could not resolve economic disputes.

Over the longer run, the most important institutional constraint on economic policy proved to be the opportunities for popular referenda,

[56] Ibid.; Martin Weinstein, *Uruguay: Democracy at the Crossroads* (Boulder, Colo., and London: Westview Press, 1988), pp. 83–104.

rather than characteristics of the presidential or party system. In 1989, a plebiscite mandating substantial increases in pension benefits received the support of over 80 percent of Uruguay's aging population. The strains placed on the overextended social security system resulted in substantial widening of fiscal deficits, and contributed to inflation surging back over 80 percent.[57] A new round of fiscal adjustments under Sanguinetti's successor did help to bring inflation under control, although the underlying financial problems of the social security system remained unchanged.

The implications to be drawn from the political compromises and limited adjustments under Sanguinetti are ambiguous. Dramatic economic policy innovations were predictably limited by the numerous institutional and political checks built into the Uruguayan system, and perhaps as a consequence, performance was mixed (see Table 6.7). The economy did experience a moderate recovery in 1986 and 1987; and real wages increased, particularly in the private sector. But serious structural problems were not addressed, and the economy began to slow again in the late 1980s.

However, if Sanguinetti's cautious policies had failed to generate a turnaround in the economy, they also avoided the sharp deterioration that initially characterized the more polarized political systems in Argentina, Brazil, Bolivia, and Peru. This was no small accomplishment. Despite the problems appearing at the end of Sanguinetti's term, there was no uncontrollable escalation of inflation.

These incremental patterns of policymaking continued during the presidency of Lacalle. Despite an ambitious agenda of structural reform, Lacalle was forced to go slowly by legislative opposition and by defeat in a referendum on privatization. Compared to the turnaround programs of the early 1990s in Argentina and Peru, Lacalle's appeared to move ahead in fits and starts, with a good deal of backtracking in the face of political and interest-group opposition. On the other hand, with differences among the parties still relatively narrow, Lacalle was able to push through a tough stabilization program and to move forward on the formation of Mercosur, the regional trading bloc with Argentina, Brazil, and Paraguay that implied further trade liberalization.

The Philippines

Despite the unfavorable economic conditions that preceded the fall of the Marcos regime, the Philippines occupies an ambiguous position between the crisis and non-crisis cases. The deterioration of the economy clearly

---

[57] The macroeconomic instability was at least partially attributable to the Argentine hyperinflation, which stimulated a large inflow of hard currency deposits into Uruguay and made it difficult for the government to control the domestic money supply.

TABLE 6.7
Post-transition Economic Developments in Uruguay

	1980–84	1985	1986	1987	1988
GDP Growth	−1.9	1.6	8.5	8.0	0.0
Inflation	44.2	72.2	76.4	63.6	62.2
Fiscal Deficit/GDP	−4.1	−2.4	−0.7	−0.9	−1.7
Current Account/GDP	−3.5	−2.2	0.6	−1.8	0.2
Investment/GDP	18.4	11.7	11.2	14.3	13.2
Real Wage	−6.0	−4.2	6.8	4.6	1.5

	1989	1990	1991	1992
GDP Growth	1.2	0.8	1.7	5.0
Inflation	80.4	112.5	102.0	68.5
Fiscal Deficit/GDP	−3.3	−0.4	na	na
Current Account/GDP	2.0	2.7	0.7	−1.4
Investment/GDP	11.3	11.0	12.8	12.8
Real Wage	−0.3	−7.2	3.7	na

Sources: World Bank, *Trends in Developing Economies,* various issues; International Monetary Fund, *International Financial Statistics Yearbook,* various issues; United Nations Commission for Latin America, *Economic Survey of Latin America and The Caribbean,* various issues; World Bank, *World Tables 1993.*

Note: For definitions of the first five variables, see Table 2.1. Real Wage: Real average wage growth.

played a role in spawning both business and mass protest in 1983–85, which in turn ultimately contributed to the fall of the Marcoses. As in the other crisis cases, the actors most directly associated with the old regime were politically discredited, and the transition opened the way to a resurgence of civil society and a wide array of new political forces and demands on the government.

However the Philippines also exhibits a number of economic and political characteristics that parallel the non-crisis cases. First, the economic constraints facing the new government were not as daunting as those confronting the Latin American countries discussed in this chapter. As discussed in chapter 2, the Marcos administration brought down inflation prior to its exit from office. Aquino, moreover, received substantial foreign financial support from the United States, other bilateral donors, the IMF, and the World Bank.[58] Under these circumstances, the incoming govern-

---

[58] Although negotiations over the external commercial debt hit some initial impasses, the government eventually arrived at a rescheduling agreement roughly comparable to the "extraordinary" terms previously granted only to Mexico, and even accumulated adequate reserves that by 1991 it could enter into a Brady Plan program that involved substantial debt buybacks. See Robert S. Dohner and Ponciano Intal, Jr., "The Marcos Legacy: Economic

ment could focus directly on reigniting growth, rather than on the more contentious task of stabilizing prices and the balance of payments.

The alignment of political forces also distinguished the Philippines from the other crisis cases. Though the Aquino coalition was highly unwieldy and fragmented, the extent of effective polarization was much less than it appeared. Aquino faced a long-standing leftist insurgency and a secessionist movement in Mindanao, but populist and leftist political groups were relatively weak. This weakness resulted from a combination of sociological and political factors. Slow employment growth in industry and internal political divisions weakened the Philippine union movement. More importantly, the decision to withhold full backing for Aquino during the transition and the continuing commitment of important factions of the left to armed struggle proved political liabilities following the transition to democracy.

The strength of the right and traditional political forces had ambiguous consequences for both economic reform and political stability. The right was highly heterogeneous, including disaffected officers, Marcos loyalists, and other regionally based clientelistic networks. The "oligarchy" of the most wealthy landed families was resistant not only to land reform, but to other market-oriented measures that threatened their diversified business and financial holdings and access to state largesse.[59] But as in the non-crisis cases, the government also had an anchor of support in the reformist wing of the private sector and in the urban middle class. This link was epitomized by Aquino's choices for the two key economics portfolios. Finance Minister Jaime Ongpin was chairman of a large mining concern, an outspoken critic of cronyism, and advocate of liberalization. Central Bank Governor José Fernandez, who was responsible for the extremely tough stabilization program of 1984–85, was the sole holdover from the previous government. The relative independence of the Central Bank under Fernandez and the tight monetary policies he pursued provided a stabilizing element in the system, albeit a highly controversial one.

It is also important to underline that the constitution of executive authority in the Philippines also differentiated it from the other crisis cases. Aquino ruled by decree during her first eighteen months in office, enjoying extensive emergency powers not much different from those wielded by Marcos. Party politics and representative government were only restored after the legislative elections and constitutional convention of 1987, and it was in that later period that Aquino faced the most serious challenge to

Policy and Foreign Debt in the Philippines," in Jeffrey D. Sachs and Susan M. Collins, eds., *Developing Country Debt and Economic Performance*, vol. 3: *Country Studies: Indonesia, Korea, Philippines, Turkey* (Chicago: University of Chicago Press, 1989), pp. 371–614.

[59] See Paul D. Hutchcroft, "Booty Capitalism: Government-Business Relations in the Philippines," in Andrew MacIntyre, ed., *Business and Governing in Industrializing East and Southeast Asia* (Ithaca, N.Y.: Cornell University Press, 1994), pp. 216–43.

democratic rule: the failed coup attempt of December 1989. The economic policy and performance of the new government is most usefully examined within the context of these two distinct phases of the Aquino presidency.

THE DECREE PERIOD: THE AQUINO ADMINISTRATION THROUGH THE RECONVENING OF CONGRESS (FEBRUARY 1986–JUNE 1987)

In devising its economic program, the administration drew on a group of University of the Philippines academics who had been involved in critical analysis of the Philippine economy under Marcos.[60] The economic policies advocated by this group included renewed efforts to alleviate poverty and land reform, but also a number of market-oriented reforms that had long been advocated by the multilateral institutions: reduced government intervention in agricultural markets; moderate trade liberalization; the establishment of a competitive exchange rate; tax reform; and privatization. This combination of policies gained support both from the center-left opponents of the Marcos regime and from some segments of the private sector.

The performance of the Aquino government during its early days has been the subject of considerable debate.[61] The slow progress on land reform was particularly disappointing. Bureaucratic infighting and the continued power of both large and small landholders stalled initial efforts, and the government's proposals were watered down to the point where even the World Bank voiced its objections. Critics argue that with her extraordinary legal powers and personal popularity, the president could have accomplished much more in this area than she did. But the focus on land reform holds the Aquino government to a standard that few governments, authoritarian or democratic, have met.

When the Philippines is compared with the other crisis cases, on the other hand, the early accomplishments of the new government appear more

[60] Their 1984 report was circulated as Emmanuel S. De Dios, *An Analysis of the Philippine Economic Crisis* (Manila: University of the Philippines Department of Economics, 1984), and was strikingly critical of government economic policies. On the influence of University of the Philippines economists in the new government, see Rigoberto Tiglao, "UP Economists Gain Influence," *Business Day* (Manila), May 19, 1986.

In general, this section draws on Stephan Haggard, "The Political Economy of the Philippine Debt Crisis," in Nelson *Economic Crisis and Policy Choice.*

[61] For an example of a skeptical assessment, see Walden Bello and John Gershman, "Democratization and Stabilization in the Philippines," *Critical Sociology* 17 (1990): 35–56. For other reviews of the debate, see Rigoberto Tiglao, "The Dilemmas of Economic Policy-making in a 'People Power' State," in David G. Timberman, ed., *The Politics of Economic Reform in Southeast Asia* (Manila: Asian Institute of Management, 1992), pp. 77–89; Emmanuel S. De Dios, "A Political Economy of Philippine Policy-Making," in John W. Langford and K. Lorne Brownsey, eds., *Economic Policy-Making in the Asia-Pacific Region* (Halifax, N.S.: The Institute for Research on Public Policy, 1990), pp. 109–47.

substantial.[62] Though the government did not face a major stabilization effort, it did have to reverse a sharp monetary expansion associated with the snap election; with tacit backing from the administration, a strong Central Bank undertook this crucial action with alacrity.[63] Exchange-rate policy became more flexible than it had been under Marcos, though there was resistance to rapid devaluation, and exports increased as a share of GNP.

External financing provided the government greater leeway with reference to fiscal policy, and permitted the initiation of an ambitious rural public works program and an expansion of classic patronage. Although budget deficits widened, their inflationary effect was dampened by surplus capacity in the manufacturing sector and an extremely tight monetary policy, as well as the continued approval and support of foreign donors. The new government initiated an extensive tax reform program that raised revenues, lowered the taxation of poor families, and strengthened tax administration. Though revenues did not keep up with growing expenditures after 1987, the tax reform and improvement in the balance sheets of the state-owned enterprises contributed to keeping budget deficits and inflationary pressures under control (see Table 6.8). The government also resumed the trade liberalization program that had been interrupted by the crisis, though further progress was ultimately limited by solid business resistance.[64]

The new government also moved quickly to dismantle the system of agricultural trade monopolies in sugar and coconut that had been at the core of rural cronyism, and resumed a gradual trade reform that had been initiated but dropped by Marcos. Not surprisingly, privatization moved much more slowly.[65] Though the government committed itself to a large-scale privatization scheme, technical as well as political constraints limited the number of transactions.

In sum, economic conditions, including foreign support, strong backing from the "progressive" wing of the domestic private sector, and the relative weakness of the left help explain the relative continuity in macroeconomic

[62] For a comprehensive review, see Manuel F. Montes, "The Philippine Economy in 1990: Recovery and Restoration," in F. Desmond McCarthy, ed., *Problems of Developing Countries in the 1990s*, vol. 2: *Country Studies* (Washington D.C.: World Bank, 1991), pp. 151–82.

[63] See, however, Paul Hutchcroft, "Selective Squander: The Politics of Preferential Credit Allocation in the Philippines," in Stephan Haggard, Chung H. Lee, and Sylvia Maxfield, eds., *The Politics of Finance in Developing Countries* (Ithaca, N.Y.: Cornell University Press, 1993), pp. 192–96.

[64] An excellent case study of the Philippine policymaking system is Manuel F. Montes, "The Politics of Liberalization: the Aquino Government's 1990 Tariff Reform Initiative," in Timberman, *The Politics of Economic Reform*, pp. 91–116.

[65] For an early assessment of the privatization program, see Stephan Haggard, "The Philippines: Picking Up after Marcos," in Ray Vernon, ed., *The Promise of Privatization* (New York: Council on Foreign Relations, 1988), pp. 91–121.

TABLE 6.8

Post-transition Economic Developments in the Philippines

	1981–85	1986	1987	1988
GDP Growth	1.2	3.4	4.8	6.3
Inflation	21.3	0.8	3.8	8.8
Fiscal Deficit/GDP	−2.9	−5.0	−2.4	−2.9
Current Account/GDP	−5.6	−3.2	−1.3	−1.0
Investment/GDP	24.4	16.0	18.0	18.4
Real Wage	na	−2.0	1.5	1.5
	1989	1990	1991	1992
GDP Growth	6.0	2.4	−1.0	0.5
Inflation	12.2	14.1	18.7	8.9
Fiscal Deficit/GDP	−2.1	−3.5	−2.1	−1.2
Current Account/GDP	−3.4	−6.1	−2.3	−1.9
Investment/GDP	21.8	22.5	20.0	20.4
Real Wage	13.0	1.3	na	na

Sources: World Bank, *Trends in Developing Economies,* various issues; International Monetary Fund, *International Financial Statistics Yearbook,* various issues; World Bank, *World Tables 1993;* World Bank, *The Philippines: An Opening for Sustained Growth,* (April 1, 1993, Report no. 11061-PH), vol. 3, Table E.2, p. 47.

Note: For definitions of the first five variables, see Table 2.1. Real Wages: Average monthly real wages of unskilled labor in Metro Manila.

policy, the initiation of some important reforms, and economic recovery. Aquino's authority, stemming both from her personal popularity and formal powers, contributed to this outcome.

THE REOPENING OF THE DEMOCRATIC POLITICAL ORDER

Though the fractious nature of the Aquino coalition continued to be a major constraint on policy, institutional features of the Philippine political system began to have a more pronounced effect on the conduct of economic policy after the reconvening of Congress in 1987.[66] Plurality voting in single-member districts for both president and the lower house in concurrent elections had historically given the Philippines (along with the United States) one of the purest two-party systems in the world. As one would expect, Philippine political parties had historically been ideologically in-

[66] For a review of changes in the party system under Aquino, see Carl Lande and Allan Cigler, "Philippine Elections and the Transformation of the Political Party System After Martial Law: the Role of Social Cleavages," paper prepared for the Association for Asian Studies, Washington D.C., April 2–5 1992.

distinguishable, internally diverse, weakly disciplined, and focused primarily on pork-barrel politics. This system provided numerous opportunities for the wealthy political families to dominate legislative politics and to use the state as a source of patronage.[67]

During the controlled elections of the martial law period, the effective reservation of the presidency for Marcos and his effort to construct his own ruling party machine reduced the incentive for parties to coalesce at the national level and contributed to more fragmented patterns of party competition. Personal and regional parties joined forces in the anti-Marcos election of 1986 and during the constitutional plebiscite; but without the concentrating effect of a concurrent presidential election, the 1987 Congressional contest provided the space for a wider variety of parties to enter the fray. Pro-Aquino politicians almost completely dominated the Senate, which is elected at large, but in the House, the Aquino forces failed to secure a majority. Some of the local leaders from the Marcos era remained popular, and a number of other regional and personalist parties gained representation, giving the legislature a highly fragmented structure. Centrifugal forces remained strong even during the presidential contest of 1992, when—in the absence of clear front-runners—seven candidates entered the race in the hope of winning a plurality.

The fragmented and decentralized character of party competition reinforced the tendency to pork-barrel politics, and placed important constraints on policy. Indeed, these institutional features had been associated with profound policy failures in Argentina, Bolivia, Brazil, and Peru. In the Philippines, they contributed to the failure to push through a comprehensive land reform, a failed trade liberalization, and ongoing conflicts over the costly subsidization of oil.

But the Philippine party system had two characteristics that distinguished it from most of the other crisis cases. First, it was not polarized. A variety of political as well as institutional factors limited the possibility for an organized leftist party to gain effective entry into the system. We have already noted the left's tactical blunder of failing to support Aquino more aggressively at the time of the revolution. But single-member districts also disadvantaged smaller parties, as did the continuing power and intimidating activities of local elite machines and the left's own failure aggressively to play the electoral game. Left candidates fared extremely poorly in both the 1987 and 1992 elections, despite a much improved electoral organization in the latter contest.[68]

---

[67] For a review of the patrimonial features of the Philippine political system, see Paul Hutchcroft, "Oligarchs and Cronies in the Philippine State: the Politics of Patrimonial Plunder," *World Politics* 43 (1991): 145–60; Alfred W. McCoy, ed., *An Anarchy of Families: State and Family in the Philippines* (Madison: University of Wisconsin Center for Southeast Asian Studies, 1993).

[68] See Cristina Jayme Montiel, "Organizational Dynamics in a Left-of-Center National

Second, during the final years of the Aquino period, the apparent fragmentation of the party system was offset by the tendency of legislators to bandwagon around a popular president who still controlled significant channels of state patronage. In September 1988, an important faction of Aquino backers organized a new party, the Philippine Democratic Party (LDP), designed to provide her a legislative vehicle. Aquino remained independent and even aloof from the LDP, but the formation of the party set off a wave of party switching, thinned the ranks of the other parties, and gave Aquino an overwhelming majority in the lower chamber. The LDP was in important respects a typical Philippine machine, and as such it constituted a constraint on a number of policy measures, including an important trade reform. Nonetheless, the party provided the president a network of support that could be mobilized on some critical issues, such as the country's conservative debt strategy.

The effects of the party system were evident in both the failures and the accomplishments that characterized the government's response to growing economic difficulties in the late 1980s and early 1990s. The recovery that began in 1986 was sustained for several years, but by 1989, widening fiscal and current-account deficits had again become problems.[69] Particularly serious conflicts emerged over domestic oil prices, which were managed by the government through an Oil Price Stabilization Fund. A price increase in December 1989 triggered widespread urban protests that served as the pretext for the most serious military rebellion of the Aquino presidency. The coup was put down only after the United States showed its willingness to back the regime militarily with air power.

In 1990, still another round of shocks hammered the country, including a string of natural disasters and the spike in oil prices that accompanied the Iraqi invasion of Kuwait. In response to these developments, the cabinet committed itself to a new round of reforms in June 1990, but implementation was only partial. By the end of the year, the country was thus threatened once again by a balance-of-payments crisis, a resurgence of inflation, and confrontation with its creditors.[70]

Unlike in most of the other crisis cases, however, the government's vacillation never led to a loss of control over macroeconomic policy. The real exchange-rate appreciation that had occurred in 1989 was reversed through a gradual depreciation over the course of 1990, and an effective 8 percent devaluation in October. Monetary policy was also tightened sig-

---

Coalition: the Salonga-Pimentel Campaign," paper presented at the Fourth International Philippine Studies Conference, Canberra, July 1, 1992.

[69] For overviews of policy in the late Aquino years, see World Bank, *Trends in Developing Economies 1991* (Washington, D.C.: World Bank, 1991), pp. 449–51; and *Trends in Developing Economies 1992* (Washington, D.C.: World Bank, 1992), pp. 447–49.

[70] The remainder of this section draws on Economist Intelligence Unit, *Philippines Country Report*, no. 4, 1990 (London: Business International, 1991), and subsequent issues.

nificantly. albeit at great cost. In December 1990, the government imposed a new round of oil price increases, despite threats by a broad coalition of urban groups to organize a national strike. This controversial step, similar to that which had triggered the coup attempt of the preceding year, was undertaken under intense pressure from external creditors. But the absence of any polarizing leftist party force, either inside or outside the Congress, strengthened the government's hand. The combination of the October devaluation and December oil price increases was enough to convince the IMF to sign a new eighteen-month standby in February on the basis of the promise of substantial fiscal tightening in 1991 and 1992.

Bargaining between the government and legislative leadership over fiscal policy went through a series of ups and downs, but also moved toward important adjustments during the last two years of the Aquino period. The key issue was taxes. An emergency "budget summit" in October 1990 between top members of the Aquino team and Congressional leaders resulted in an agreement to reduce expenditures for 1991 in real terms, but the finance minister's proposal for increased taxes on wealth was rejected by the Congressional representatives in favor of an import surcharge that ran directly counter to the government's intention to liberalize. Both fiscal and monetary targets held through the first half of 1991, but as the import surcharge was phased out, the government once again ran afoul of the IMF and drawings were suspended in the second half of the year.

As in the other crisis cases, pressure from creditors was not in itself sufficient to overcome domestic opponents. Indeed, during the crisis of 1991, legislators persisted for some time in opposition to a series of tax increases pressed by the government and the IMF to get the program back on track. The eventual resolution of these conflicts in early 1992 owes something to the fact that Aquino was not running for the presidency, and could thus take difficult measures without incurring any political cost. However, this in itself would have been insufficient without the capacity to muster the necessary support in the recalcitrant Congress.

As suggested above, an important factor in overcoming the apparent fragmentation in the system was the weight in the Congress of the LDP machine, composed of legislators who supported Aquino and senior leaders who had consolidated their power bases through their connections with the president. This network was mobilized in December 1991 to remove the left-of-center Jovito Salonga as Senate leader. Salonga had been an influential opponent of the adjustment program, and his replacement by an ally of the administration permitted an extremely stringent budget and new taxes to pass through Congress in January 1992 despite impending elections that brought Fidel Ramos to office.[71]

---

[71] On the elections, see David Timberman, "The Philippines at the Polls," *Journal of Democracy* 3 (1992): 110–24.

CONCLUSION

The economic and political pressures associated with economic crisis, and particularly with very high inflation, posed daunting problems for new democratic governments in Argentina, Bolivia, Brazil, Peru, and Uruguay. The government of Uruguay staved off hyperinflation, and the others eventually formulated wide-ranging adjustment initiatives. In all cases except Peru these were carried out under democratic auspices. Democratization per se cannot, therefore, be considered the culprit for policy failures. As the Philippines and the non-crisis cases discussed in the next chapter demonstrate, regime change may have only a slight effect on policy, or even provide opportunities for new reform initiatives.

Rather, one must look to institutional arrangements, and particularly the interaction between the party system and the power of the executive. In Argentina, Bolivia, Brazil, and Peru, the coherence of government policy was undermined not simply by the existence of strong social demands but by centrifugal pressures within the party system that enhanced the veto power of interest groups and made strong executive action difficult if not impossible.

Given these institutional weaknesses, it should not be surprising that stabilization packages and broader reform initiatives came from small, closed circles of technocrats rather than emerging from a broader process of legislative or interest-group consultation or pact-making. Nor is it surprising that executives would be tempted to overcome legislative and interest-group stalemates through presidential decrees and plebiscitarian appeals. Though this tendency toward "decretismo" has been widely criticized as undemocratic, the findings of this chapter suggest that such exercises of executive power are as much a reflection of the weaknesses of democratic institutions as their cause. We argue in Part Three that the absence of coherent party structures has implications not only for economic adjustment, but for the prospects for stable democratic rule as well; we turn first, however, to a comparative analysis of the non-crisis transitions and the distinctive problems of one-party governments.

Economic Management in Non-crisis Democracies

VIEWED COMPARATIVELY, the most striking feature of the non-crisis transitions is the continuity in economic policy between authoritarian governments and their democratic successors. Political change did not initially undermine the relatively stable macroeconomic policy achieved by the outgoing regime or the structural reforms that had resulted in effective, outward-oriented development strategies. Nor did the transition strongly affect the ability of democratic governments to make further policy adjustments: in all four countries, new democratic governments undertook reforms that deepened the policy course inaugurated by their predecessors.

It is important to emphasize at the outset that though new democratic governments in all four countries enjoyed the benefits of relatively favorable economic circumstances, they nonetheless faced significant political pressures on economic policy. In Turkey, the vehicle for militant labor protest, the Confederation of Revolutionary Labor Unions (DISK) was banned, but unionized workers and lower- and middle-level public employees provided the base of support for the reconstruction of opposition parties on the center-left. In Korea, the transition to democracy was associated with a wave of strikes that seemed to point toward the development of an ideologically based opposition, and in the late 1980s, labor in Thailand also began to flex its political muscles. In all three countries, there were long histories of student militancy as well.

There was also considerable ambivalence about further economic reform among business groups and in the rural sector. In Turkey, the Turkish Industrialists' and Businessmen's Association (TÜSAD), the main business association, was divided between outward-oriented conglomerates that supported the policy course initiated in 1980, and large firms rooted in the domestic market. Peasants, who suffered substantial income losses as a result of the reform, and small businesses provided the base for a right opposition in the True Path Party (DYP). In Korea, big business had profited immensely from its close relationship with the government. Though it stood to gain from certain liberalizing reforms, it stood to lose the financial subsidies and protection that had been hallmarks of the Korean model since the early 1960s. Korean farmers vehemently protested the reduction of price supports and the liberalization of agricultural trade. Business groups in Thailand resisted trade reform and clamored successfully for new subsidies. As politics became more open in the second half of the 1980s, the favoritism toward Bangkok and the relative neglect of rural areas became increasingly salient political issues in Thai politics and generated new pressures on the government.

Evidence from Chile is particularly interesting because, despite broad acceptance of market-oriented policies among party leaders, opinion surveys conducted between 1986 and 1991 indicated substantial opposition to the economic model pursued by the Pinochet government.[1] A survey of Santiago residents found that over 70 percent favored protection of domestic industry, "even if this means that the cost of imported goods will rise." Substantial majorities also favored controls on foreign investment, full or partial control of prices, and continued public ownership of the largest domestic corporations.

Two sets of factors explain the comparative continuity in economic policy and performance in the face of these political pressures. The first centers on how economic reform over the long run and good economic performance in the short run affected the sociopolitical landscape. In contrast to the crisis cases, economic conditions created a strong bloc of beneficiaries as well as diffuse public support that favored maintaining the broad outlines of the prevailing economic model. The parties that led the opposition to the authoritarian regime were relatively weaker and had less incentive to differentiate themselves sharply from the policy status quo with respect to economic issues. As a result, antireform interest groups had narrower scope for maneuver than they did in the crisis cases.[2]

The second set of factors affecting policy were the institutional arrangements established during the course of the transition. As we saw in chapter 4, the constitutions and other institutional structures adopted in the non-crisis cases contained provisions deliberately aimed at locking in the policy reforms initiated under the old order. In general, there was greater insulation for the centers of technocratic decision-making committed to policy continuity, and more extensive restrictions on the political parties and social forces that might challenge existing approaches.

Although these coalitional and institutional configurations provided an important basis for policy stability during the process of political transition, they left open the question of what would happen as restrictions on contestation were challenged and reduced. Did a more open politics necessarily

---

[1] Data are from surveys of residents of greater Santiago, conducted by FLACSO (1988), and CIEPLAN, October 1990, February 1991, and May 1991. Cited in Genaro Arriagada Herrera and Carol Graham, "Chile: the Meaning for Stability," in Stephan Haggard and Steven B. Webb, eds., *Voting for Reform: Democracy, Political Liberalization, and Economic Adjustment* (New York: Oxford University Press, 1994), pp. 242–90.

[2] This political configuration also had the effect of reducing the destabilizing effects of electoral cycles visible in the crisis cases.

mean challenges to the existing development strategy over time? Under what conditions would labor, the left, and populist parties mobilize against the status quo?

The answers to these questions depended in part on the distributional consequences of economic policy under authoritarian rule, and in part on the way the evolution of the party system mediated emerging distributional struggles. Where low-income groups had benefited from expanding employment opportunities and income growth—as was true to an important extent in Korea and Thailand—it was less likely that an opening of the political space would result in fundamental, organized challenges to existing policy. Where incomes were more concentrated and the distribution of benefits was unequal—a pattern more characteristic of Turkey and Chile—there was greater potential for mobilized political opposition. In all four countries, however, the extent of fragmentation and polarization within the party system shaped the way policy choices were made.

Korea and Thailand provide the clearest illustrations of how strong growth and favorable patterns of income distribution can affect the government's ability to formulate policy. Despite a widening of income and regional disparities in the 1970s in Korea, inequality remained low by developing country standards. By the time of the transition, a wide array of social groups had acquired a vested interest in the successful export-oriented strategy, including not only middle-class groups but segments of the working class as well. Democratization was accompanied by an upsurge of labor protest and strikes, and distributional issues played into the politics of the first democratic administration, but these did not translate into a sustained, labor-based opposition on the left. Notwithstanding important disparities in regional income, Thailand also experienced robust growth in employment and income; in addition, it lacked the urban social base for strong leftist movements.

While these underlying structural conditions provided a favorable context for policy continuity, the party system had important effects as well. In Korea, the formation of a "grand coalition" in the new Democratic Liberal Party (DLP) marked a turning point in the efforts of the post-transition political elites to construct a stable basis for their policy initiatives. The founding of the new party reflected, and sought to capitalize on, the underlying conservativism of the Korean electorate; it was partially a response to a highly militant student and working-class movement that emerged in the late Chun years. Yet the formation of the "grand coalition" also marked a step toward greater cohesion within the party system as a whole. It brought an end to the difficulties posed by divided government and even further weakened the ideologically based opposition.

Thailand's much more incremental political transition presents a more complex picture. For most of the 1980s, the military continued to play a role in politics, key bureaucratic centers of decision-making retained greater independence than in the other cases, and blue-collar unions and left-oriented opposition movements were extremely weak. Within this comparatively restricted political context, however, the fragmentation of the Thai party system did have a distinct effect, particularly after 1988 when the parliament became a more important locus of decision-making power. As politics became more open, so did the struggle for patronage, undermining to some extent the authority of the technocrats.

In Turkey and Chile, unlike Korea and Thailand, the social consequences of authoritarian rule included high levels of inequality and long periods of high unemployment and stagnating wages, conditions one would associate with destabilizing distributional conflicts. Other things equal, therefore, the lifting of institutional restrictions on the full play of politics should have been associated with political mobilization against the policies of the authoritarian regime.

Differences in the party system produced different policy outcomes in the two cases. In Turkey, restraints imposed by the military severely limited the activities of left politicians and union leaders. In combination with the social support generated by successful reforms, these restrictions guaranteed the election of a center-right government in 1983 and provided it with some insulation from partisan and distributive challenges. By 1987, however, the restraints on the free play of politics came under fire and the government had to contend with a broadening of partisan conflict and the reemergence of labor militancy. Politicians seeking to mobilize support from such conflicts could draw on long-standing networks of party and union activists; thus, as the party system opened up, it became both more fragmented and more polarized. Though the achievements of the Özal government are substantial when compared to the first democratic administrations in the crisis cases, Turkey has the weakest record of the non-crisis cases in maintaining macroeconomic stability and has seen some structural adjustment efforts either slow down or go into reverse.

In Chile, the Pinochet Constitution also sought to guarantee against a recurrence of the political polarization that characterized the pre-authoritarian period. Structural changes in the economy and society and ideological changes among the major party contenders contributed to a fundamental realignment in the party system that had the effect of muting partisan and social conflict. Pinochet did not succeed, however, in preventing an alliance of center and left forces in the plebiscite and ultimately in the new government itself. The opportunity to occupy a "seat at the table" guaranteed that the government would address social welfare concerns to a greater extent than in Turkey, Korea, and Thailand. At the same time, participation in the government also strengthened the incentive for the left leadership to moderate its demands.

KOREA

We begin our analysis with Korea because the transition process bears a number of interesting similarities to the crisis cases. Prior to the transition, the opposition augmented its political demands with populist appeals that pointed up the government's links with big business and the costs of the Chun government's stabilization and adjustment efforts for workers, farmers, and the less-developed regions of the country. The authoritarian government was forced to make important political concessions to the opposition as a result of massive street demonstrations, and was not able to impose all of the institutional conditions on the transition that it would have liked. Immediate post-transition politics also resembled the crisis cases in some important aspects. In its first two years, the Roh government attempted to cloak itself in a more progressive mantle than its predecessor, but remained at loggerheads with the opposition over the legacy of the Fifth Republic. Opposition dominance of the legislature stymied action on a host of pressing issues. The country was also torn by continual strikes and student demonstrations.

Yet these apparent similarities with the crisis cases are ultimately misleading. Even before the formation of a new conservative ruling coalition in January 1990 there were important signs of continuity in Korean politics, and economic strategy did not fundamentally deviate from the broad direction of the Chun government. Macroeconomic policy exhibited a mildly countercyclical pattern, but remained cautious and conservative. The new government took some actions aimed at the *chaebol* and continued the incremental process of economic liberalization initiated under Chun, but continued the pro-business, state-supported export-oriented strategy that had characterized Korea's development since the early 1960s.

Some of this continuity can be attributed to features of the executive branch, including a strong president, highly competent economic teams, and a meritocratic bureaucracy. However, the latitude that the new center-right government enjoyed must be seen in the context of broader political forces and how they were organized. Though the urban middle class joined students and workers in calling for the overthrow of the Chun regime, the more conservative middle-class opponents of the authoritarian regime quickly separated their demands for political reform from the more far-reaching social agenda of their erstwhile allies.[3] Roh appealed to these conservative bases of support in forming the Grand Conservative Coalition in January 1990.[4] The initiative capitalized on disaffection with legislative stalemates

[3] See Hagen Koo, "Middle Classes, Democratization and Class Formation: The Case of South Korea," *Theory and Society* 20 (1991): 485–509.

[4] The new coalition merged Roh Tae Woo's DJP with the parties of Kim Young Sam and the conservative opposition leader Kim Jong Pil, who was closely identified with Park Chung Hee.

and continuing labor and student protests and revealed starkly the continuing power of conservative political forces in the government, the private sector, and the electorate at large.

Institutions and Alignments

One interesting difference between Korea and the other non-crisis transitions was that there was some negotiation between the outgoing authoritarian government and the opposition over the shape of the new electoral system. Direct election of the president had been a prime demand of the opposition; Roh capitulated on this central point, though divisions within the opposition enabled him to win the election. Following the presidential election, attention turned to the issue of the electoral system. The electoral system under Chun Doo Hwan was a direct descendent of the authoritarian Yushin system, based on a combination of two member districts and a national list that heavily favored the ruling party. Moreover, district boundaries were drawn to favor conservative rural voters.

Opposition forces did not succeed in eliminating the proportional representation component or gerrymandered districts, but they did win some concessions. The share of the total number of seats allocated to the national list was reduced from one-third to one-quarter, and their distribution was less biased. The two-member district system, through which the Chun government had captured two seats in conservative rural districts and the second seat in urban districts where the opposition was divided, was replaced by a single-member district system. The Democratic Justice Party (DJP) accepted these reforms under the assumption that single-member districts would favor them because of the divisions in the opposition.[5] In fact, they miscalculated; all the opposition parties had strong regional bases, and were able to make substantial gains. The DJP's share of the total vote in the legislative elections dropped by only 2.6 percent, to 34 percent,

---

[5] There is debate about the determinants of the final outcome, a single-member district system that the ruling party initially opposed. Brady and Mo argue the DJP gradually turned to the single-member district model on the assumption that it would divide the opposition, but they miscalculated its actual electoral effects. Cheng and Tallian believe that Roh was pressured to move toward a fairer system by the same forces that had led him to call for political change in his ground-breaking June 29 speech. In either case it is clear that the government had substantial power to impose its preferences and that the formal properties of the electoral system proved less important for the direction of Korean politics than the realignment of the party system that occurred in late 1989. See David Brady and Jongryn Mo, "Electoral Systems and Institutional Choice: A Case Study of the 1988 Korean Elections," *Comparative Political Studies* 24 (1992): 405–29, and Tun-jen Cheng and Mihae Lim Tallian, "Bargaining Over Electoral Reform in the Republic of Korea: Evaluating Rational Choice Determinants of Political Decision-Making in Democratic Transition," paper prepared for the American Political Science Association Convention, Chicago, September 1992.

but this now translated into "only" 38.8 percent of the seats. As a result, Roh Tae Woo had to contend with the problems of divided government.

Nonetheless, Roh retained important political resources. His position was rooted not only in the formal institutional powers outlined in chapter 3, or in the continuing power of conservative forces in the state itself; he also drew on substantial electoral and social backing. His June 29 speech promising political liberalization was extremely popular, and during the presidential campaign he drew effectively on regional bases of support, and played on concerns about national security and fears of domestic instability were the opposition to win.

The economy was an additional plus, buoyed by the strong currency and massive investments associated with the Olympics. In contrast to the crisis cases, Roh had the fiscal latitude to distance himself from his predecessor by outlining a more progressive social agenda. One of Roh's most ambitious, and economically controversial, proposals was a pledge to construct two million new housing units to respond to the rapid inflation of housing costs. The DJP itself introduced amendments into the labor law that guaranteed collective bargaining, collective action, and the freedom to form new unions, and moved quickly to institute a minimum wage and a national worker pension program. Roh's campaign platform also converged with the opposition's in calling for the elimination of policy loans, progressive taxation of large landholders, the implementation of a "real name" financial transaction system that would provide a means for more effective taxation, and a reduction of preferential treatment for big business.

Roh also acted aggressively on the foreign policy front. He sought to preempt the upsurge of public support for reunification by announcing on July 7, 1988 a "Nordpolitik" aimed at reopening dialogue with the North and actively courting contacts with the Soviet Union, China, and Eastern Europe. His administration received a substantial boost from these policies following the historic summit on June 4, 1990, between Roh and Gorbachev in San Francisco, and the rapid move toward normalization that followed.

Roh's surprising political strength vis-à-vis both left and right was demonstrated in early 1989. He had made an election pledge to subject himself to a referendum within a year of taking office. In March, he canceled the referendum on the grounds that it would threaten social stability. Though Kim Young Sam initially tried to exploit the issue to bring the government down, he was unable to do so, in part because Kim Dae Jung had already agreed that the referendum would be consultative only, carrying no obligation on Roh's part to step down. With his position bolstered by the resolution of the referendum question, Roh quickly moved to replace some of the hardline holdovers from the Chun era within his cabinet.

There were already signs that Roh had begun to move in a more conservative political direction as early as the end of 1988. During 1988, the wave of strikes that had followed Roh's June 27, 1987, speech continued unabated. Student demonstrations were muted in the first half of 1988 by a tacit truce surrounding the Olympics, but after September anti-government demonstrations began again in earnest and became a persistent, and often violent, feature of Korean political life. The combination of labor strife and student unrest clearly alienated portions of the middle class that initially supported the political transition. With a Cabinet reshuffle in December 1988, the government moved toward a tougher position with respect to social protest. Arrests of students, activists, and labor leaders increased, and the government sided openly with management in breaking several important strikes.[6]

The confrontation on the streets was matched by deadlock in the legislature that contributed to perceptions of government weakness. The opposition was preoccupied with addressing the legacy of the Fifth Republic,[7] leaving a number of important issues in legislative limbo. The perception of drift was heightened when growth slowed in the second half of 1989, inflation increased, and the stock market began a long and politically contentious slide. By the spring of 1990, Roh himself was referring to the political situation—somewhat hyperbolically—as one of "total crisis."[8]

In mid-December 1989, Roh reached an eleven-point agreement with the opposition on the major Fifth Republic issues, an agreement eased by a costly and ultimately misguided scheme to support stock prices. This agreement paved the way for a surprising merger of the DJP not only with conservative Kim Jong Pil's party, but also with Kim Young Sam's RDP. The result was the creation of a new Democratic Liberal Party (DLP) which despite some defections effectively controlled more than two-thirds of the seats in the legislature. This democratic coup not only froze out Kim Dae Jung and his Peace and Democracy Party (PDP)—the closest to a center-left party Korea had—but it provided the political backing for a more extensive crackdown on both labor and the left and for a complete turnaround in the pattern of legislative politics. In July 1990, the new party flexed its muscles by ramming through a cluster of bills that had been stalemated by divided government; similarly, the DLP majority was used in 1991 to limit the extent of reform in legislation governing the police and in the revision of the much-reviled National Security Law.[9]

The power of the new ruling party was tested twice in 1991 in separate

---

[6] For details of this shift to the right, see Asia Watch, *Retreat from Reform: Labor Rights and Freedom of Expression in South Korea* (New York: Asia Watch, 1990); Manwoo Lee, *Odyssey of Korean Democracy: Korean Politics, 1987–1990* (New York: Praeger, 1990), pp. 118–20.

[7] The agenda of Fifth Republic issues included assigning responsibility for the 1980 coup and subsequent political persecution, and allegations of corruption on the part of Chun and members of his family.

[8] Kyong Eun Lee and June Hyoung Rhie, "An Anatomy of South Korea's 'Total Crisis' in the Spring of 1990," *Pacific Focus* 5 (1990): 155–83.

[9] See *Far Eastern Economic Review*, July 26, 1991, p. 13.

local elections in March and June. Despite low turnout, the DLP won large majorities of the contested seats in both, even in Seoul where the opposition traditionally did well.[10] In the March 1992 legislative elections, however, it was revealed clearly that support for the DLP was not equal to the support for its constituent parts. The DLP captured only 38.5 percent of the popular vote, and was thus once again denied a clear majority in the National Assembly. Yet the conservative nature of Korean politics was underlined by the fact that the most surprising gainer was not Kim Dae Jung's new Democratic Party—which had already moved sharply toward the center—but a quickly formed party on the right led by business leader Chung Ju Yung. An attempt to form a "genuine" leftist party in 1990 failed miserably, proving unable to capture a single seat. Despite substantial internal conflict within the DLP, culminating in Roh Tae Woo adopting a neutral stance in the election, Kim Young Sam won both the party's nomination and the presidency with a strong showing: 41.4 percent of the popular vote against 33.4 percent for Kim Dae Jung and 16.1 percent for Chung Ju Yung.

The Course of Economic Policy

Korean macroeconomic and trade policy in the immediate post-transition period was characterized by dilemmas that were altogether different than those in both the crisis and other non-crisis cases (Table 7.1). The governments in the crisis countries typically faced severe balance-of-payments constraints and the difficult task of establishing control over fiscal and monetary policy. Even in the other non-crisis cases, the maintenance of such stabilizing policies remained an important policy goal. In Korea, by contrast, the "three blessings" or "three lows"—low interest rates, low oil prices, and a depreciated won-dollar exchange rate—coupled with massive public investments associated with the Olympics and Roh's housing pledge, contributed to boom conditions. These conditions created their own economic problems, but they were problems that politicians in the crisis countries would have envied.

Fiscal policy did not constitute a constraint. Despite the Olympics, the Roh government had maintained his predecessor's generally cautious approach to spending, and the overall fiscal position was buoyed by a boom in revenues that held for much of Roh's term in office. The main policy challenges centered, rather, on how to manage mounting current-account surpluses. As the government intervened in the market to slow the appreciation of the won by buying dollars, it increased the money supply, adding

[10] The second local election in June came on the heels of weeks of violent student protests. Strong support for the DLP was interpreted broadly as representing a backlash against the Left.

TABLE 7.1

Post-transition Economic Developments in Korea

	1983–87	1988	1989	1990	1991	1992
GDP Growth	1.5	11.4	6.1	9.0	8.4	6.5
Inflation	2.8	7.1	5.7	8.6	9.7	6.2
Fiscal Deficit/GDP	−0.6	1.6	0.2	−0.6	−1.7	na
Current Account/GDP	−0.3	8.1	2.4	−0.9	−3.1	−1.5
Investment/GDP	29.2	30.6	33.4	36.9	39.1	na
Real Wage	7.2	10.6	18.8	−1.1	na	na

Sources: International Monetary Fund, *International Financial Statistics Yearbook,* various issues; Asian Development Bank, *Asian Development Outlook,* 1992; UN, *Economic and Social Survey of Asia and the Pacific,* various issues; World Bank, *World Tables 1993.*

Note: For definitions of the first five variables, see Table 2.1. Real Wage: Real earnings per employee.

to inflationary pressures generated by the construction boom, the government effort to lift stock prices, and the ongoing pressures from the highly leveraged private sector to expand credit. Despite massive issues of stabilization bonds, inflationary pressures increased, creating a "bubble economy" similar to Japan's. The rapid inflation of land prices was probably the single most contentious economic issue of the Roh years, and gave rise to some of the sharpest confrontations with the private sector as the government attempted to control land speculation.

The surpluses also created difficult structural adjustments. If there was no intervention in the foreign exchange market, then the exchange rate would naturally appreciate. This policy option, pressed on Korea by the United States, would squeeze the powerful export sector. On the other hand, large surpluses increased pressure for trade liberalization. However the logical sectors for liberalization, such as agriculture, were both heavily protected and politically overrepresented.[11]

The boom and changes in the system of industrial relations also contributed to rapid growth in wages. This development was initially viewed with equanimity; the argument was even advanced that rapidly rising wages had positive advantages. Higher unit labor costs would force adjustment in sectors dependent on low wages and higher labor income would increase imports and reorient the economy toward domestic-led growth.

Though these policy dilemmas should by no means be minimized, they constituted a politically manageable set of trade-offs. The first economic team under Ra Woong Bae had a somewhat more expansionary tilt than the outgoing Chun team, and placed greater emphasis on social spending,

[11] The surpluses strengthened the case for liberalizing capital flows, but as other experiences with capital-account liberalization had demonstrated, there are complex problems associated with this policy course as well.

but in December 1988 a more conservative team was installed under Cho Soon. During its early tenure, the Roh government pursued a conservative fiscal and monetary policy, allowed some controlled appreciation, moved ahead with its gradual trade liberalization program, and distanced itself from management in labor disputes.

Booms do not last forever, though, and by the second half of 1989 the question arose of how the government would respond to conflicting political pressures on its economic program in the context of slower growth. The answer came very soon after the formation of the Grand Coalition. In March 1990, Roh reshuffled his cabinet, removing the three most important economic ministers, men who had been identified with a policy of stable growth, rapid liberalization of the economy, greater distance between business and government, and a concentration on issues of social justice and equity. Their successors did initiate a series of measures aimed at the *chaebol,* including efforts to limit corporate speculation in land and to force greater specialization on the sprawling corporate conglomerates. At the same time, however, the new team also went out of its way to emphasize its growth-oriented credentials by announcing a new set of stimulus measures on April 4 that included devaluation, an easing of credit and interest rates, and a corresponding breach in monetary targets. The government abandoned previous efforts to move toward a "real name" financial system and greater taxation on property holdings. New financial supports were extended to exporters over the next year as part of a revitalization of industrial policy. Fiscal policy also changed in a more expansionist and pork-barrel direction amid charges that the government was seeking to influence the outcome of the 1991 and 1992 elections.

Yet what is striking about the Korean case is that the government moved quickly to contain inflationary pressures, despite the facts that these pressures were modest and that elections loomed. Some factions within the government argued that the level of inflation was tolerable given the structural adjustments Korea required. But by 1990 the stabilizers gained ground, particularly as critics of the administration began to charge that Roh was using macroeconomic policy to influence the presidential elections.[12] In February 1991, the Cabinet was once again reshuffled and a more conservative economic team shifted monetary and credit policy in a stabilizing direction. As always, the liberalization of trade and the financial markets followed a slow and circuitous route, but the general direction of policy was clearly toward a deepening of the market-oriented reforms initiated by Chun Doo Hwan.

---

[12] Roh's hand was strengthened in taking difficult policy measures by his surprising adoption of a neutral posture toward both the DLP nomination process and the election itself.

In characterizing economic policy under Roh Tae Woo, it is important to be clear about the baseline of comparison. In a number of important ways, democratization altered the course of economic policymaking in Korea. The government's vast housing program, increased social spending, the stock-market fiasco, credit policy, and the ouster of pro-stabilization technocrats in 1990 all reflected a decline in the insulation of the economic team. Business-government relations became decidedly more strained as the government came under pressure to distance itself from the *chaebol*.[13] Political sensitivity to farmers slowed import liberalization, and the government was decidedly more sensitive to workers than it had been in the past.

Yet when we view Korea from the perspective of the crisis democracies, the striking feature is the strong continuity in the most central features of economic policy, a continuity that can be traced to the conservative base of support the government enjoyed and the dominance of the ruling party in the legislature. The government maintained and deepened the country's outward orientation, in part through selective liberalization, in part through a revival of industrial policy. A countercyclical macroeconomic policy and the aggressive use of the exchange rate were certainly not new, but these were counterbalanced by strong executive control over fiscal policy and a willingness to undertake difficult stabilization measures when required. Despite tensions with the private sector, the overall stance of the government was clearly pro-business, reflected particularly in credit policy and an increasingly pro-management stance with respect to labor disputes.

The extent of this conservative consensus can be seen clearly in the role that economic issues played in the presidential election of 1992.[14] Kim Young Sam's platform called for a gradual reform of the financial markets, including freeing of interest rates, slightly looser money, and tight fiscal policy. Deregulation would proceed gradually, with controls on big business and more support for small enterprises. Yet the proposals of Kim Dae Jung—presumably the candidate on the left—contained even more conservative policy proposals. Harping on the threat of inflation, Kim Dae Jung argued for a strengthening of the Central Bank, a tight money policy based on an immediate freeing of interest rates, conservative fiscal policy, and rapid deregulation, though with strong controls on the activities of the *chaebol*. There is perhaps no clearer evidence of the strong underlying consensus surrounding economic policy in the country, despite apparently deep and contentious policy debates and political divisions.

---

[13] Chung-in Moon, "Bringing Politics Back In: State-Business Relations in South Korea since 1980," in Andrew MacIntyre, ed., *Government-Business Relations in Industrializing East Asia* (Ithaca, N.Y.: Cornell University Press, 1994), pp. 192–96.

[14] See *Far Eastern Economic Review,* December 10, 1992, pp. 20–22.

THAILAND

As we argued in chapter 3, the Thai transition was extremely gradual; the military and bureaucracy continued to exercise quite substantial control over both economic policy and the play of politics more generally. Despite the semi-democratic nature of Thai politics in the 1980s, the country remains analytically significant precisely because it demonstrates the effects of institutional factors on the politics of adjustment. With increasingly organized business support, the government was able to undertake quite profound policy reforms in the first half of the 1980s. As the barriers to political entry fell rapidly after 1988, policy became less coherent, and in 1991 the military once again intervened.

Institutions and Alignments

The gradual process of political liberalization that followed the authoritarian crackdown on democratic politics in 1976 can be divided into three phases. The first phase, from 1977 to 1983, was one of military-dominated liberalization.[15] From 1983 to 1988, the military remained a central political force but parties gained in influence.[16] A further stage of political opening occurred under the Chatichai government after 1988, during which the influence of the military on politics continued, but elected party politicians did finally capture the position of prime minister and the majority of Cabinet slots.

Transitional provisions of the 1978 Constitution facilitated the military's continuing domination of politics during the first period. The upper house was appointed by the king on the prime minister's advice and could vote along with the lower house on important issues; this guaranteed the government a winning coalition. More importantly, the prime minister and Cabinet were not required to come from the elected lower house. Military and bureaucratic officials were thereby shielded from electoral scrutiny.

In 1983, factions of the military and some political parties attempted to block the scheduled expiration of these provisions, but the parliament defeated the measure under the leadership of Prime Minister Prem. Prem subsequently consolidated two important bases of support outside the military: an increasingly organized Bangkok-based business elite and the political parties. The growing influence of the parties was directly related

---

[15] This period included the second and third Kriangsak governments (May 1979–February 1980; February–March 1980) and the first three Prem governments (March 1980–January 1981; January–December 1981; and December 1981–May 1983).

[16] This period included the fourth and fifth Prem governments (May 1983–August 1986; August 1986–July 1988).

to the expiration of the transitional provisions, which relegated the Senate to an advisory role and shifted power toward the House of Representatives and the parties.[17]

The party system that emerged appears highly fragmented. Many small parties contested elections, and none had the organization, support or policy expertise to actually govern. In contrast to other fragmented party systems, however, there were no strong, ideological parties on either the right or the left, and three parties (Social Action Party [SAP], Chart Thai, and the Democrats) effectively dominated the electoral landscape. Moreover, the significance of these parties to the formulation of policy was limited by the fact that the transition was by no means complete at the outset of Prem's administration, and the parties remained heavily dependent on him to guarantee that liberalization would proceed.

The continuing power of the executive was reflected in a variety of institutional arrangements, including a highly independent military machinery. The internal politics of the military constitutes a Byzantine story of infighting, intrigue, and corruption that is far beyond the scope of our story here.[18] It is important to note, moreover that portions of the military launched unsuccessful coup efforts in 1981 and 1985, and that over the 1980s the military increased its role in village defense and development issues. Through the Internal Security Operations Command, the military maintained a parallel organizational structure that arrogated to itself some important powers of government and served as a stepping-stone for top military officers seeking to enter politics.

For purposes of understanding economic policy, however, the formal powers of the prime minister constitute the most important feature of the political system. Prem maintained the prerogative to promote or transfer senior civil servants as he wished without legislative approval, and to appoint nonelected officials to his cabinet. This had the effect of shielding economic decision-making from direct party political influences to a substantial degree. The National Economic and Social Development Board (NESDB), an important agency in developing the policy agenda and monitoring implementation, was entirely technocratic in make-up. Party-based

[17] A number of steps were also to attempt to strengthen the party system. In the 1978 Constitution, political parties were required to contest not less than half the seats of the House, a provision designed to eliminate individual-based parties. To enhance discipline the Constitution stated that if party members were ejected from their party, they would lose their seat. A 1981 party law established further requirements for party registration aimed at excluding small parties, including the demand for five thousand members with residences in five provinces in each of the four regions of the country.

[18] For an introduction, see Suchit Bunbongkarn, *The Military in Thai Politics 1981–86* (Singapore: Institute of Southeast Asian Studies, 1987); and Kevin Hewison, "Of Regimes, State and Pluralities: Thai Politics Enters the 1990s," in Kevin Hewison, Richard Robison, and Garry Rodan, eds., *Southeast Asia in the 1990s* (Sydney: Allen and Unwin, 1993).

Cabinet officials were represented on a second important decision-making body, the Council of Economic Ministers, but they were outnumbered by bureaucrats, advisers, and nonparty politicians appointed by Prem.

Party and interest-group access to decision-making varied by functional area. With reference to the formulation and implementation of macroeconomic policy, the executive and bureaucracy were extremely strong. Party politicians in the cabinet had the right to review budgets prepared in the bureaucracy, but the proposals submitted by the Budget Bureau were rarely changed significantly. Parliamentary accountability was even more limited. The Senate and the House were not permitted to initiate spending bills or increase expenditures. They could set ceilings on the level of taxation, but adjustments under those ceilings remained in the hands of the economic bureaucracy.

In effect, politicians were limited to seeking pork-barrel projects for their districts within parameters strictly controlled by the bureaucracy. The bureaucracy's discretion, in turn, was circumscribed by a number of rules that limited the government's capacity to spend.[19] A further check on policy was provided by the Central Bank, which despite its formal subordination to the Ministry of Finance had long enjoyed a history of independence.[20]

In sum, institutional arrangements guaranteed that Prem's support from the parties did not significantly interfere with his ability to defend the prerogatives of the military and the economic bureaucracy. His position was further strengthened by the development of corporatist ties with Thai big business.[21] Business organizations had become more coherent during the authoritarian interlude of 1976–79, and responded to the government's call for a consultative committee to review economic policy in 1978. The relationship with the major business associations was further consolidated in 1981 through the creation of a Joint Public and Private Sector Consultative Committee (JPPCC). Chaired by Prem himself, the JPPCC linked

[19] Three regulations governing central government expenditure are of particular interest. First, the total budget deficit may not exceed 25 percent of expected revenues. Second, direct foreign borrowing by the Ministry of Finance must be under 10 percent of expenditures. Finally, foreign loans for state enterprises cannot exceed 10 percent of total expenditures. Peter Warr and Bandid Nijathaworn, "Macroeconomic Policies and Long Term Growth: Thailand Part I," unpublished ms., The World Bank, February 1988.

[20] The institutions for trade policymaking provided access for party and business interests. Yet even in this somewhat more porous policy area, features of both the economic model and political institutions served to constrain the extent of rent-seeking. At the outset of Prem's tenure, business interests were not organized for trade policy lobbying, though they became more adept at it; were not in any case strongly protectionist; and were overshadowed by the interests of the Ministry of Finance, which relied heavily on tariffs for revenue.

[21] On the rise of business, see Anek Laothamatas, *Business Associations and the New Political Economy of Thailand* (Boulder, Colo.: Westview Press, 1992); Kevin Hewison, *Bankers and Bureaucrats: Capital and the Role of the State in Thailand,* Yale University Southeast Asian Monograph no. 34 (New Haven, Conn.: Yale University Press, 1989).

the economic bureaucracies with representatives of the largest business associations.

Laothamatas argues that the JPPCC served as a channel for business demands on government and reflected the rise of business power.[22] Yet he also notes that the JPPCC provided a base of support for the government both "to create an alliance with leading business groups to make up for the temporary loss of stable military support" at the outset of the political liberalization exercise. Though business-government relations were not routinely harmonious, private-sector organizations generally offered support for difficult adjustment measures during the 1981–84 period.

The parliamentary elections of 1988 marked yet another step toward genuine parliamentary rule, further lowering the barriers to entry by political groups. Despite excellent economic performance, Prem was increasingly criticized on political grounds for his failure to stand for office. A split within one coalition party, the Democrats, resulted in a motion to censure the government. Prem preempted by dissolving the parliament and calling for elections, but also announced unexpectedly that he would not run for office.

A new government was formed by General Chatichai that included the three large parties—Chart Thai, the SAP, and the Democrats—and two smaller ones. Though a retired military man with close links to the army, Chatichai was the first elected leader to head a government since 1976. In contrast to Prem, whose cabinets were dominated by nonelected members, usually technocrats, Chatichai appointed politicians or wealthy party backers to virtually all Cabinet posts. He also weakened or intervened in the bureaucracy in various ways: he interfered more extensively in appointments, downgraded the previously powerful NESDB to an advisory role, thereby allowing ministers to bypass it, and staffed the boards of state-owned enterprises with political clients.[23] The government also relied much less on business support through the JPPCC system. Business influence was now channeled to an increasing extent through the parties, in part precisely to circumvent the technocratic influence that had characterized the JPPCC system under Prem.[24]

In sum, the electoral connection became increasingly important in Thai politics, with some predictable effects.[25] The limits on the ability of political parties to raise funds, coupled with the traditional practice of vote

[22] Laothamatas, *Business Associations,* pp. 76–78.

[23] On the Chatichai government, see Larry Niksch, "Thailand in 1988: the Economic Surge," *Asian Survey* 29 (1989): 166; Scott Christensen, "Thailand After the Coup," *Journal of Democracy* 2 (1991): 99.

[24] Laothamatas, *Business Associations,* p. 74–75.

[25] On the corruption of the Chatichai period, see Hewison, "Of Regimes, State and Pluralities," pp. 177–80.

buying, gave rise to closer relations between politicians and the private sector. Party bosses also cultivated relations with local officials who provided an important base of support and linkage with constituencies, particularly in the rural areas. To solidify, and pay for, these bases of support, politicians naturally became more aggressive in seeking government favors.

In 1989, the new government advanced an amendment to the Constitution that would allow for the president of the elected House of Representatives to act as president of the National Assembly, a position previously held by the president of the appointed Senate which the military continued to dominate. The proposed constitutional amendment would shift power even further toward the parties. This move, increasing charges of corruption, and other attacks on military privilege, unleashed a power struggle among military factions aligned with and against Chatichai.[26] On February 23, 1991, the military deposed Chatichai in a bloodless coup that had explicit support from important factions of the Bangkok business sector,[27] and initially at least, broad public acquiescence as well.

Policy Consequences

Though Thailand's economic performance throughout the 1980s was exemplary by any standard, the economy did undergo difficult adjustments. As we saw in chapter 3, fiscal and current-account deficits increased following the military intervention in 1976, as did foreign indebtedness (see Table 3.6). In contrast to the first oil shock, when Thailand benefited from a concurrent boom in the prices of its agricultural exports, the terms of trade in 1979–80 were highly adverse. External borrowing, much of it short-term, grew sharply. In 1979 the growth rate halved, from 10.4 to 5.3 percent. Though modest by comparison with the crisis cases, inflation accelerated in 1979, and again in 1981 and 1982.

What is distinctive about Thailand is the preemptive nature of the government's response to these problems and the relatively swift and comprehensive nature of the policy response. Even before the signing of a Structural Adjustment Loan (SAL) agreement with the World Bank in 1982, the government undertook a number of reform measures, including reductions of export taxes, a devaluation in 1981, price liberalization, and a lifting of some subsidies. In conjunction with the SAL, the government undertook major changes in fiscal policy, another painful and highly controversial devaluation, and effective desubsidization of energy prices. Trade liberalization measures were halting, but the combination of devaluation,

---

[26] For an excellent overview of the intramilitary conflicts, see ibid., pp. 164–67.

[27] The president of the Federation of Thai Industries was named prime minister.

subsidies to exporters, and an open posture toward foreign investment positioned Thailand for a dramatic export boom in the second half of the decade (see Table 7.2).

The political puzzle surrounding these policy reforms has been stated succinctly by Doner and Laothamatas: "First, the reforms generated opposition: parties opposed sectoral liberalization, sectors of business and the military came out against the 1984 devaluation; the military was frustrated by general fiscal constraints; and sections of business suffered under the crackdown on the formal financial markets. Second, the Prem period was marked by political instability; coups were attempted in 1981 and 1985, and unplanned elections occurred in 1983, 1986 and 1988."[28] Given these apparent political constraints, what explains the effectiveness of the government's adjustment strategy?

One component of the story lies with the generally good economic conditions themselves. The deceleration of growth in 1979 should not be underestimated; in the Thai context, this arguably constituted a crisis. Yet it is clear that the government was under less binding economic constraints than in the crisis cases, and had the room to undertake reforms gradually and to postpone some politically difficult measures.

Political institutions also played a critical role in deflecting opposition and guaranteeing support; this can be seen by contrasting the politics of several key reform measures during the Prem and Chatichai periods. The budget deficit did widen somewhat during the early Prem governments, going from an average of 3.1 percent of GNP per year in 1979–81 to 3.7 percent a year in 1982–84. This minor deterioration took place against a backdrop of substantial decline in export earnings and government revenues, however. An even worse deterioration was prevented by an aggressive reduction of government spending through limits on government wages, cuts in capital expenditure, and an important ceiling on public-sector foreign borrowing by both ministries and state-owned enterprises; fiscal control exercised by the government stands in sharp contrast to the crisis cases. Revenue measures were introduced more gradually, but prices were raised on controversial public goods and services, including water, bus fares, and energy. By 1987, the government had met the World Bank's target for expenditure as a share of GNP, and the economic boom had ushered in a period of large budget surpluses.

The conduct of monetary policy shows evidence of the unusual powers of the monetary authorities. Warr and Nidiprabha have found a discernible countercyclical pattern in Thai monetary policy: the inflationary shocks of the 1978–81 period were countered by a contractionary monetary policy

[28] Richard F. Doner and Anek Laothamatas, "Thailand: Economic and Political Gradualism," in Haggard and Webb, *Voting for Reform*, p. 429.

TABLE 7.2
Economic Developments in Thailand, 1983–1992

	1978–82	1983	1984	1985	1986	198:
GDP Growth	6.1	7.2	7.2	3.4	5.1	9.(
Inflation	11.1	3.7	0.9	2.4	1.8	2.:
Fiscal Deficit/GDP	−4.6	−4.1	−3.5	−5.5	−4.5	−2.(
Current Account/GDP	−5.8	−7.3	−5.1	−4.1	0.6	−0.'
Investment/GDP	26.3	25.9	24.9	24.0	21.8	23.(
Real Wage	−0.2	6.5	8.0	5.8	8.2	10.:

	1988	1989	1990	1991	1992
GDP Growth	13.4	12.2	10.3	8.0	7.5
Inflation	3.9	5.4	5.9	5.7	4.1
Fiscal Deficit/GDP	0.7	3.2	5.0	na	na
Current Account/GDP	−2.8	−3.6	−9.2	−8.6	−8.2
Investment/GDP	28.8	31.5	27.9	38.9	37.9
Real Wage	6.9	0.5	−1.3	na	na

Sources: Asian Development Bank, *Asian Development Outlook 1992* (Manila: Asian Development Bank, 1992); International Monetary Fund, *International Financial Statistics Yearbook,* various issues; World Bank, *World Tables 1993;* United Nations, *Economic and Social Survey of Asia and the Pacific,* various issues; World Bank, *Trends in Developing Economies,* various issues.

Note: For definitions of the first five variables, see Table 2.1. Real Wages: Real earnings per employee.

stance, contributing to the slowdown in growth, followed by an easing in 1982–83, a second contractionary phase in 1984 and a second round of easing in 1985–86.[29] The 1984 contraction is particularly interesting, since it should reflect most clearly the conflict between the dictates of stability and political opening. Responding to a deterioration in the balance of payments in 1983, the government instituted a squeeze on credit in 1984. The policy was met with substantial protest, particulary from small- and medium-sized businesses. Nonetheless, the government held the policy line for seven months—long enough to correct the trade imbalance—and lifted the credit ceilings only to undertake an even more controversial devaluation.

Another challenge to austerity surfaced in 1986, when portions of the military made an alliance with dissidents within the Social Action Party in opposition to austerity measures and the unwillingness of the government to support the SAP's rice price intervention scheme. Partly in response to this challenge, Prem called elections in 1986, unleashing a spirited public debate on the goverment's macroeconomic policy. Nonetheless, the parties

[29] Peter G. Warr and Bhanupongse Nidiprabha, "Macroeconomic Policies, Crises, and Long-Term Growth in Thailand," unpublished ms., The World Bank, 1991.

once again turned to Prem to form a government, and though he replaced his controversial finance minister, it was with a close associate who maintained the basic thrust of previous policies.

The devaluation of 1984 provides further evidence of the power of the government, even vis-à-vis the military. A small 1981 devaluation had been highly contentious in the parliament. Following the announcement of the currency realignment in November 1984, the attack was led by a more powerful foe; the supreme commander of the armed forces made a public attack on the policy, which substantially reduced the ability of the military to import weaponry, and argued that the finance minister should be removed. Nonetheless, Prem timed the move to exploit the fact that the parliament was in recess, drew on tacit support from an increasingly export-oriented private sector, and made active appeals to rice farmers to maintain the policy. The army was ultimately compensated through increased expenditures, but these did not fully match the losses from the devaluation. The army commander ultimately backed down and Prem was able to ride out the controversy as exports responded quickly to the new measure.

In sum, there were periodic conflicts over macroeconomic policy within the government, between the government and the military, and in the broader political arena, particularly in 1986. Doner and Laothamatas, as well as Christensen, also argue that the ability of the government to insulate macroeconomic policymaking was not matched by a similar control over trade policy, and politicians were given some access to policy favors through particular pork-barrel projects and concessions on tax policy. Yet all analyses of policymaking under Prem emphasize the government's capacity to control the overall agenda, to maintain the coherence and stability of policy, and to initiate difficult reforms when required.[30]

Economic conditions muted protests, and the organizational power of potential social opponents, such as labor, was limited; less than 10 percent of the labor force was in manufacturing, and less than 2 percent was unionized. Yet the government could also count on a base of support among big Thai business, and on certain issues, from agricultural exporters and the financial community as well. More importantly, and in striking contrast to the crisis cases, the power of both parties and interest groups was limited by institutional structures imposed by the military.

After 1987, fiscal surpluses and strong growth, fueled in part by a huge infusion of Japanese capital, prevented the increasing politicization of economic policy from having the negative economic consequences that it had in the crisis cases. Good economic performance muted the difficult

---

[30] See also Sylvia Maxfield and Patcharee Siroros, "The Politics of Central Banking in Thailand," paper prepared for the Association for Asian Studies meeting, Washington D.C., April 2–5, 1992.

trade-offs faced by other countries, and granted the government the leeway to formulate more expansionist budgets. Nonetheless, the course of policy after 1988 did reflect the increasing salience of the electoral connection, or as one analyst characterized Chatichai's victory, "the elected MPs' frontal assault on the state."[31]

Perhaps the main instrument for rewarding party and business followers was an expansion of pork-barrel infrastructure projects and a new emphasis on "regional development." In fiscal 1988–89 (September to September), the bureaucracy delayed a number of infrastructure projects on the grounds that they were too costly; the 1989–90 budget, by contrast, was revised under pressure from the House Finance Committee to include large environmental programs for the south and northeast. The prime minister himself underlined the new political importance of these constituencies by convening a series of meetings of the Council of Ministers in different regional capitals.

These projects were also important for rewarding business patrons. The privatization of the provision of infrastructure was initially seen as a way to avoid patronage, but the opportunity for collusion and corruption between ministers and particular state-owned enterprises on the one hand, and bidders on the other, increased. Large contracts were won by investors with little experience; a special committee established by the military in 1991 to investigate corruption under Chatichai found evidence of it in telecommunications, road and elevated commuter railway ventures, cable television contracts, and oil refineries.[32] Though the military itself was by no means immune from corruption, it seized on the issue to justify the coup of February 1991.

Epilogue: The Coup of 1991 and the Return to Democracy

A full discussion of the coup of 1991 and the tortuous path back to democratic rule in Thailand is beyond the scope of this chapter,[33] but several observations about the interim military government underline the crucial role of institutions in the conduct of economic policy. Having acted against the money politics and corruption of the Chatichai era, the military-appointed Anand government and his technocratic team took as one of its first tasks to revamp political institutions so as to decrease the role of party politicians. Though the military was finally forced to back down

[31] Christensen, "Thailand after the Coup," p. 99.

[32] Ibid., p. 101; Clark D. Neher, "Political Succession in Thailand," in *Asian Survey* 32 (1992): 596.

[33] See Hewison, "Of Regimes, State and Pluralities," and Daniel E. King, "The Thai Parliamentary Elections of 1992: Return to Democracy in an Atypical Year," *Asian Survey* 32 (1992): 1109–23.

from its original plans, which bore a close resemblance to the transitional provisions of the 1980 Constitution, the Anand government did enjoy an unprecedented degree of independence. In 1991 alone it passed more legislation than in the entire Chatichai period, and pushed through extensive trade liberalization, deregulation, the introduction of a value-added tax, and the abolition of state-owned enterprise unions. Despite such controversial policy changes and the closure of the political system, a coalition of parties aligned with the military still managed a narrow victory in the elections of March 1992. Those same parties were only narrowly defeated in the second legislative elections in September 1992, despite the violent repression of anti-regime protestors during "Black May." Although we would anticipate that the reopening of the political system would move politics in the direction of the Chatichai years, the continuing power of both the military and of pro-military parties is testimony both to the limits on Thai democracy and the capacity of conservative forces to garner electoral support.

TURKEY

The democratic transition in Turkey was more sharply delineated than in Thailand, but less dramatic than Korea's. Nonetheless, the Turkish experience reveals several broad similarities among the three cases. First, the improved economic performance asssociated with the reforms contributed to Özal's electoral success: he was able to become prime minister against two military opponents while promising not only to maintain but to deepen the structural adjustment measures initiated in 1980. A second similarity to the other non-crisis cases is that Özal's economic strategy found an important base of support in powerful segments of the Turkish private sector. Business-government relations were not institutionalized to the extent they were in Thailand or Korea, and the fragmentation of formal business organizations was more pronounced.[34] But if the business associations did not support every measure Özal advanced, the new policy course did create a substantial base of business support in the financial sector and among the larger conglomerates that reoriented their activities toward construction, booming Middle East markets, and foreign trade more generally.[35]

---

[34] In particular, the division between the larger groups and the smaller entrepreneurs grouped in the National Union of Chambers of Commerce and Industry was marked. See Ziya Öniş and Steven B. Webb, "Political Economy of Policy Reform in Turkey in the 1980s," in Haggard and Webb, *Voting for Reform*, pp. 143–45.

[35] Selim Ilkin, "Exporters: Favored Dependency," in Metin Heper, ed., *Strong State and Economic Interest Groups: the Post-1980 Turkish Experience* (Berlin: Walter de Gruyter, 1991), pp. 89–98.

A third similarity with the other non-crisis cases centers on the nature of political institutions. During the first phase of democratic rule from November 1983 through the elections of 1987, Özal benefited from a variety of restrictions on party and union activity and constitutional rules that favored executive discretion and limited the extent of fragmentation and polarization. These institutional arrangements helped Özal sustain and even deepen the economic adjustments that had been initiated under the Demirel and military governments.

By 1987, despite good aggregate performance, opposition forces began to challenge both the restrictions on their freedom of maneuver and the substance of government policy. Political grievances were paramount among the opposition, but the regressive distributional consequences of the government's adjustment program also came in for attack. As the restrictions on both union and party activities fell, policy became less coherent, macroeconomic instability increased, and a number of structural adjustment measures either stalled or reversed.

Institutions and Alignments

The military's rewriting of the 1961 Constitution affected virtually all aspects of Turkish political life, from the relative powers of the executive and legislature, to the organizational possibilities for the opposition. In 1982 the military submitted the Constitution to a referendum, which was combined with presidential elections. A vote for the Constitution also meant a vote for General Evren—the sole candidate—to continue for seven years as president. Despite a virtual ban on debate, electoral support for the new order was surprisingly high; with a turnout of 91 percent, 91 percent voted in favor of the new Constitution.[36]

As in Thailand, some features of the new constitutional system were explicitly transitional. The National Security Council, which had been the chief executive body under military rule, was transformed into a Presidential Council that would continue to meet for six years following the transitional election. The powers of the council were supposedly advisory, but the president retained the power to veto any constitutional amendments (and could only be overridden by a three-quarters majority of the legislature), to submit new amendments to referenda, and to bring a suit of unconstitutionality against any law passed by the parliament. The opposition successfully tested these powers over time, but in the early years of the new democratic regime they served as a visible reminder of the con-

---

[36] The high turnout is explained by the fact that citizens not voting forfeited the right to vote in the upcoming parliamentary elections.

tinuing power of the military. Other presidential powers had a more direct impact on politics, particularly the ability to appoint judges and top officials in the state-owned media.

Despite these presidential powers, the new government was essentially a parliamentary one, though of a restricted sort. To prevent the return of the Cabinet instability that plagued Turkey in the late 1970s, electoral rules guaranteed the dominance of the larger parties and severely curtailed the prospects for small ones. The new Constitution adopted the d'Hondt system of proportional representation, which limits the reallocation of additional seats to increase proportionality, and introduced several key thresholds to limit the opportunities for small parties. A national threshold stipulated that parties could not win seats in the legislature unless they received at least 10 percent of the total valid votes cast. A further constituency threshold established barriers that were particularly onerous in the many rural constituencies with only two seats. In 46 districts, only one member was elected on the basis of simple majority, further hindering the chances of small parties.

The military was not content to trust such rules to guarantee stable, conservative majorities. Initially, the government's plan was simply to create a two party system consisting of a center-right and center-left party; all other parties were to be proscribed.[37] Yet Özal was deemed acceptable, and the military allowed him to lead a third party. As a result, he benefited from restrictions placed on the activities of both interest groups and politicians that were designed to assist the military's chosen parties.

One important component of those controls was to forbid any organizational links between political parties and interest groups. In principle, this applied to business as well as labor, but its main effect was to proscribe the formation of a social democratic party with institutionalized ties to unions; this restriction buttressed the effect of the other restraints on labor we have already outlined in chapter 4. Restrictions on the activities of politicians prohibited the leaders of former political parties from establishing or becoming members of new political parties or to stand for any elected office for a period of ten years. A five-year ban was placed on previous parliamentarians. The scope of political debate was further limited by provisions of the penal code that prohibited political activities on the basis of class, ethnic, or racial appeals, or which threatened the secular basis of the state.

In addition to the advantages inherent in the electoral and party system, reforms of the executive branch further enhanced the power of the prime minister vis-à-vis the legislature. In 1983, Özal created a new Under

---

[37] Henri Barkey, "Why Military Regimes Fail: The Perils of Transition," *Armed Forces and Society* 16 (1990): 179–80.

Secretary for the Treasury and Foreign Trade, and put it under a new minister of state for economic affairs who was concurrently the deputy prime minister. The reform changed the relative standing of the ministries, and increased the coherence of the economic team. The powerful and etatist State Planning Organization lost functions and influence. The Central Bank was moved out of the Ministry of Finance and placed under the new minister of state for economy, gaining some greater degree of independence in the process. The concentration of decision-making also gave the prime minister himself greater control over economic decision-making, which he was not averse to using for political purposes.

These institutional advantages did not last forever. As early as the 1984 municipal elections, it was clear that the artificial parties created by the military would not survive, and new parties began to crystallize around old political leaders or their surrogates. By early 1986, the opposition parties were tacitly cooperating as a "rejection front" for the revision of the ban on politicians. In 1987, General Evren was forced to retreat on the ban, and Özal put the issue to a referendum in September. The margin was extremely narrow, reflecting the electorate's conservatism and voter concern that politics not return to the status quo of the late 1970s. Nonetheless, the banned politicians did win reinstatement. 1987 also marked a partial turning point in the system of industrial relations, as the ban on strikes and the requirement for binding arbitration were finally lifted.

Following the repeal of the ban on politicians, the d'Hondt system initially continued to favor the Motherland Party (ANAP). In the 1987 elections, four minor parties received 19 percent of the vote, yet did not elect a single deputy; ANAP, by contrast, claimed two-thirds of the seats in the parliament with only 36 percent of the popular vote. Yet the strong showing of the newly formed Social Democratic Populist Party, based on a campaign critical of the adjustment strategy of the government, was striking. In the municipal elections of 1989, ANAP's popularity plummeted further and it was outpolled by both Demirel's True Path Party and the Social Democratic Populists. In the general elections of October 1991, when we end our account, ANAP finally went down to defeat at the hands of a coalition of these two major opposition parties.

The new constitutional order designed by the military initially provided the Özal government with substantial freedom of maneuver in pursuing its reform agenda, even though this independence was not to last. One particular constitutional characteristic did reduce the government's freedom of maneuver from the outset, however: the staggering of elections. The government faced general elections in 1983, 1987, and 1991, but also municipal elections in 1984, 1987 (nonconcurrent with the general election), and 1989, as well as bye-elections in 1986. The interim elections became virtual referenda on the government's performance. This grueling election schedule provided opportunities for the new parties to gel and to air grievances with the government's economic strategy. The effect of electoral pressures and growing partisan conflict can be seen by turning to the course of policy during the nearly ten years of ANAP dominance from 1983 to 1991.

The Policy Record

We have already noted that the Özal government sought not simply to maintain past policy but to push the reform process further. In doing so, the government faced a dilemma similar to that confronting Roh Tae Woo in Korea: good aggregate economic performance may not generate adequate social support to maintain power and the effort to undertake further structural reforms threatened to alienate significant social groups. Even with the advantages imparted by the Constitution, Özal faced growing electoral and interest-group challenges to the dominance of his center-right coalition. The result was a dualistic policy regime. In some areas, such as support for the export drive, the central thrust of policy was sustained, albeit through somewhat heterodox means. With regard to fiscal policy, reforms were delayed, modified or implementation simply slipped, with consequences for inflation (Table 7.3).[38] This can be seen by focusing on the three central policy areas of stabilization, trade policy, and privatization.

Almost immediately on taking office, the government abandoned its commitment to orthodox macroeconomic stabilization to some extent by opting for a stimulus program that included tax cuts, expanded public investment in infrastructure, export subsidies, and an accelerated depreciation of the currency. As the budget deficit increased and inflation rose, the government acted quickly to devise a stabilization program. Drawing on assistance from the IMF, World Bank, and OECD, the program included a substantial fiscal adjustment and important structural reforms such as a value-added tax and a reduction of subsidies to both exporters and to the state-owned enterprises. This effort succeeded in reducing the budget deficit in 1985. The VAT made an important contribution to this outcome and to the government's longer-term fiscal position. More flexible price adjustments trimmed state-owned enterprise losses, thereby reducing a major drain on the budget.

Wage policy implicitly played an important role throughout the decade, contributing to both stabilization efforts and the export drive. The restrictive regime governing industrial relations had the effect of moderating, if

---

[38] This argument is made by John Waterbury, "Export-Led Growth and the Center-Right Coalition in Turkey," *Comparative Politics* 24 (1992): 127–28.

TABLE 7.3
Post-transition Economic Developments in Turkey

	1978–82	1983	1984	1985	1986	1987
GDP Growth	2.2	3.8	5.9	5.0	8.3	7.:
Inflation	56.3	31.4	48.4	45.0	34.6	38.(
Fiscal Deficit/GDP	−3.7[a]	−4.2	−10.0	−7.4	−3.2	−4.(
Current Account/GDP	−3.1	−3.8	−2.8	−1.9	−2.5	−1.:
Investment/GDP	20.4	19.6	19.5	21.0	24.4	25.4
Real Wage	−1.9	−0.8	−12.0	−3.5	−4.3	6.4

	1988	1989	1990	1991	1992
GDP Growth	3.7	1.6	8.7	1.0	5.1
Inflation	75.4	63.3	60.3	66.0	70.1
Fiscal Deficit/GDP	−3.8	−4.5	−4.2	na	na
Current Account/GDP	2.3	1.2	−2.4	na	na
Investment/GDP	24.0	22.7	23.1	19.0	18.8
Real Wage	−6.9	25.9	−2.4	na	na

Sources: International Monetary Fund, *International Financial Statistics Yearbook,* various issues; World Bank *Trends in Developing Economies,* various issues; World Bank, *World Tables 1993.*

Notes: For definitions of the first five variables, see Table 2.1. Real Wage: Growth of real earnings pe employee.

[a] 1978–81.

not repressing, wages and thus helped check inflation and maintain a competitive real exchange rate.[39] The result, however, was a decline in real wages over the decade and a significant worsening in the distribution of income that provided opportunities for the opposition.[40]

The stabilization effort of 1985 did not hold, and for the remainder of the decade fiscal deficits constituted a central barrier both to macroeconomic stability and to the consolidation of other economic reforms.[41] The slippage occurred through a number of channels. Export subsidies that had been reduced early in Özal's term reemerged when export growth slowed in 1985–86. Transfers to the state-owned enterprises grew as the government sought to limit price increases or to use certain state-owned

[39] Öniş and Webb, "Political Economy of Policy Reform," pp. 160–65.

[40] See Korkut Boratov, "Inter-Class and Intra-Class Relations of Distribution under 'Structural Adjustment': Turkey during the 1980s," in Tosun Arícanlí and Dani Rodrik, eds., *The Political Economy of Turkey: Debt, Adjustment and Sustainability* (London: Macmillan Press, 1990), pp. 199–229.

[41] See Dani Rodrik, "Some Dilemmas in Turkish Macroeconomic Management," ibid., pp. 183–96.

enterprises as a channel for subsidies to politically significant constituencies. The most politically innovative channel for increased government spending came through the proliferation of extrabudgetary funds. Parliamentary approval was required to set up the funds, but they subsequently operated outside parliamentary scrutiny by drawing on earmarked revenues and by borrowing; this borrowing increased substantially in the 1988–91 period. As Waterbury summarizes, funds were disbursed "nominally, with specific targets in mind such as public housing, but because their budgets are not subject to prior approval by the Grand National Assembly, and few of them are scrutinized by the High Auditing Council, disbursements can be guided by political as well as economic motives."[42]

Macroeconomic policy after 1986 shows clearly the influence of electoral considerations, as the opposition challenged restrictions on party activity and partisan differences became more marked. In 1986 and 1987, in anticipation of the general elections, public-sector borrowing increased sharply, driven partly by a stimulus package directed at the rural sector. The government held prices of state-owned enterprises in check despite rapidly rising prices in other sectors of the economy. The result was another surge in inflation immediately following the election when price controls were lifted. In conjunction with the lingering fiscal problem, this precipitated a second stabilization package in February 1988.

As the effects of the program were felt in sharply lower growth, the fiscal component of this package ran into difficulty with party politicians; both the anticipation of the municipal elections of 1989 and ANAP's poor performance in them are the prime culprit. A comprehensive tax reform faced resistance from the private sector and the government's continuing demand for credit undermined the effort of the Central Bank to develop an annual monetary program.[43] The reemergence of the labor movement compounded problems of macroeconomic management. In 1988, union leaders reached an agreement with the government on a framework pay deal in support of the stabilization effort, and threats of strikes were shelved. But in 1989, the rank and file proved less willing to accept such a package; a campaign of passive protest was launched, and large strikes shut down two state-owned steel mills.

The government's efforts with reference to trade policy were somewhat more successful, though a similar pattern of policy oscillation is also evident. Trade and exchange-rate reforms were the hallmark of the Turkish adjustment experience, and a number of the more important reforms were undertaken by the new democratic government. Exploiting his early days

[42] Waterbury, "Export-Led Growth," p. 134.
[43] Öniş and Webb, "Political Economy of Policy Reform," pp. 169–75.

in office, Özal reduced quantitative restrictions and tariffs, and substantially liberalized foreign-exchange regulations. These reforms were pushed further in 1988–89.

From the beginning, the government designed the reforms to reduce their distributive effects. For example, liberalization was targeted so that the most heavily protected sectors would not be exposed immediately to foreign competition, and so that those firms hurt by liberalization might also gain from new export opportunities provided by subsidies, the exchange rate, and access to inputs. Nonetheless, additional protection crept in through the extrabudgetary funds, which relied on import taxes for funding. The heavily protected consumer goods industry and the agricultural sector were the most important beneficiaries of these levies. Turkish firms also proved successful in securing increased export subsidies, particularly during periods when export growth and overall performance lagged.

Efforts at privatization reveal a strikingly similar pattern. Despite the high priority given to privatization in Özal's campaign, a full privatization plan was not prepared by foreign advisers until 1986, and it almost immediately came under political attack.[44] Though a privatization law was passed in 1986, it was not until 1988 that the first firm was actually privatized. When the government moved to prepare two further privatizations, the True Path and Social Democratic parties went to court to block the deal. In late 1989, the courts suspended the sales on the grounds that they violated the promise to offer shares to the workers, small savers, and the public, and the privatization process ground to a halt.

Epilogue: The End of ANAP Rule

The 1989 municipal elections signaled decisively that ANAPs' center-right coalition was coming unglued, and economic performance was clearly one of the reasons. Growth in the late 1980s proved highly erratic, dropping below 2 percent in 1989, shooting up in 1990, and falling again in the election year of 1991 due to the impact of the Gulf War (see Table 7.3). In the local elections in March 1989, the Social Democratic Populist Party was the clear victor, and it had campaigned explicitly on a program of opposition to ANAP's economic strategy. Özal chose this moment to abandon the position of prime minister to a relatively weak successor, and to accept the position of president. Though this may have contributed to ANAP's problems, and certainly constituted a setback for reform efforts, the underlying difficulties were more profound. In the October 1991 gen-

---

[44] Roger Leeds, "Turkey: Rhetoric and Reality," in Raymond Vernon, ed., *The Promise of Privatization* (New York: Council on Foreign Relations, 1988), pp. 149–78.

eral elections, the vote was fragmented among five contending parties, with Demirel's rural-based True Path Party the largest gainer.

The economic changes of the 1980s have undoubtedly transformed both the sociopolitical landscape and the character of economic discourse in Turkey; for example, of the five main parties, only the pro-Islamic Welfare Party is in principle opposed to Turkey moving in the direction of a market-oriented economy, and concomitantly, toward entry into the European Community. But the Welfare Party was the largest gainer in both the 1991 general elections and the municipal elections of 1994, when they won elections for mayor in both Istanbul and Ankara. The opening of Turkish politics to a wider spectrum of social and political forces and the increasing fragmentation of the party system and the coalition politics that it implies have severely complicated economic decision-making. The Kurdish war remains a quagmire with potentially dire implications for democracy itself. Though the Çiller government did respond aggressively to the balance-of-payments crisis of early 1994, the role of fiscal policy in that crisis was a reminder of the fact that macroeconomic policy remains volatile and that a number of reforms of the state sector are far from fully consolidated.

CHILE

As in the other non-crisis cases, the outgoing military government in Chile played an important role in shaping both the social and the institutional parameters of the new democratic order. By the late 1980s, structural changes in the economy and improved economic performance gave rise to a coalition of business elites and middle-class groups that strongly supported continuity in the policy course launched by the dictatorship. Opposition political forces were further constrained by constitutional provisions imposed by the outgoing regime that granted veto powers to Pinochet appointees in the judiciary, the newly independent central bank, and even in the legislature itself.

The case is distinctive, however, in one important respect. The presidency was captured not by a conservative party, but by a center-left coalition (the Concertación for Democracy or simply Concertación), led by the centrist Christian Democrats (PDC) and joined by most elements of Chile's large Socialist movement.

In the context of the social and institutional legacy bequeathed by the Pinochet regime, such a victory was possible only because the leaders of the new coalition committed themselves to an economic program that was acceptable to conservative political forces. Yet the change of government did bring parties to office that had historic links to groups hurt by the Pinochet reforms. Inclusion of the left led to an emphasis on social policies that was largely absent in the other non-crisis cases, an emphasis that may have contributed to the consolidation of market-oriented reforms.

Institutions and Alignments

The smooth transfer of power to a center-left coalition in Chile was made possible by a remarkable convergence among party elites on economic policy. As late as the mid-1980s, however, it was far from clear that the process of reconciliation that had become evident by 1990 would succeed in bridging the deep divisions within the Chilean party system. To form a coherent center-left coalition capable of winning office and governing effectively, Christian Democratic and Socialist leaders had to overcome decades of bitter ideological and political rivalry. More than fifteen years of dictatorship, moreover, had left the parties and the party system highly fragmented and disorganized: the formation of the Concertación required negotiations with over seventeen parties, most of them uncertain of their electoral strength.

There were also significant impediments to any rapprochement between the Concertación and its adversaries on the political right. The survey results cited in the introduction to this chapter indicate that significant segments of the general public had serious reservations about the economic policies of the military regime.[45] In one survey, over 70 percent of the opponents to Pinochet cited dissatisfaction with the economy as a reason for voting "no" in the plebiscite.[46]

To understand how these impediments to reconciliation were overcome we look both at organizational features of the parties that resurfaced over the 1980s and at how their policy positions were reshaped by political incentives in the party system.

One of the most important historical features of the Chilean party system that distinguished it from other non-crisis cases was the extent to which one party, the PDC, occupied the center of the political spectrum. With a base of support comprising about one-third of the electorate, the PDC was the largest party in Chile's otherwise fragmented system and was well positioned to assume the leadership of the democratic opposition to Pinochet.

Efforts to forge a coalition with the left initially placed significant

---

[45] The Concertación's program during the 1988 plebiscite campaign did in fact contain themes that have figured prominently in more populist appeals, including an end to privatization, more control on foreign investment, and increased public spending for the poor. Economist Intelligence Unit, *Chile Country Report,* no. 3, 1988, p. 6.

[46] Augusto Varas, "The Crisis of Legitimacy of Military Rule in the 1980s," in Paul W. Drake and Ivan Jaksic, *The Struggle for Democracy in Chile, 1982–1990* (Lincoln and London: University of Nebraska Press, 1991), p. 76.

internal strain on the party, which in the past had harbored ambitions to govern the system without permanent alliances; so called "third roaders" within the party remained strong, as did factions deeply opposed to an alliance with the left.[47] By the mid-1980s, however, street confrontations with the regime had failed, while the breakdown of negotiations with conservative politicians within the regime appeared to foreclose the possibility of a center-right alliance.[48] An alliance with the left thus increasingly appeared to be the best option for the party to oust Pinochet and regain power.

The importance of building such a coalition under moderate Christian Democratic leadership was enhanced by the expectation that victory in the plebiscite would not lead automatically to the ouster of Pinochet, but to negotiations over further political reforms that might permit truly competitive elections within a reasonable period of time.[49] This implied that opponents of the regime would not only have to cooperate in the registration and mobilization of "no" voters, but in the development of a common bargaining position vis-à-vis the regime in the post-plebiscite period.

Within the Chilean left, the prospects of an alliance with the Christian Democrats posed even greater dilemmas. The Communists had historically advocated a more cautious political line than the Socialists, but had begun during the late 1970s to advocate a strategy of mass insurrection. They were excluded from the coalition by the PDC leadership. Meanwhile, however, the Socialists had begun an evolution in the opposite direction. The most moderate factions, grouped under the umbrella of the Party for Democracy (PPD), had begun to work closely with the PDC as early as 1986.[50] A more orthodox wing (the Almeyda Socialists) was more reluctant to break definitively with the Communists, but in February 1988 most of this faction also joined the multiparty "Command for the No," headed by Patricio Aylwin.[51]

The Socialists' movement toward a strategic alliance with the PDC was

---

[47] See Manuel Antonio Garretón, "The Political Opposition and the Party System under the Military Regime," ibid., pp. 211–50. The sectarianism of the PDC during earlier decades limited opportunities for power-sharing alliances with the Left and the Right, and had thus contributed to the polarization of the system. Arturo Valenzuela, *The Breakdown of Democracy: Chile* (Baltimore and London: Johns Hopkins University Press, 1978) pp. 34–39; Giovanni Sartori, *Parties and Party Systems: A Framework for Analysis* (Cambridge, London, New York, Melbourne: Cambridge University Press, 1976), pp. 132–37.

[48] See above, chapter 3.

[49] Garretón, "The Political Opposition and the Party System," p. 228.

[50] This decision followed an incident in August and September, in which the discovery of an opposition arms cache and an assasination attempt against Pinochet—both linked to the Communist-backed Manuel Rodriguez Patriotic Front—brought a state of siege and a demobilization of the opposition.

[51] Over one-third of party activists supported opposition slate in vote for Central Committee in 1990. Economist Intelligence Unit, *Chile Country Report,* 1991, no. 1, p. 10.

motivated by a number of factors. The most fundamental was a perception by many leaders of the left that their own maximalism had contributed to the tragedy of the Allende government in 1973. Such lessons were reinforced, however, by circumstances already discussed above: the failure to overthrow Pinochet in the early 1980s, the continuing veto power of the authoritarian elites, and in 1989, electoral rules that encouraged the formation of large electoral blocs.

Despite the Socialists' internal divisions, its leaders were members of long-standing networks of activists formed during decades of participation in the electoral system. As with the Christian Democrats, therefore, relatively large groups of loyalists were inclined to support agreements reached in the electoral arena and the legislature. In the years following the formation of the Concertación, the influence of the moderate Socialists was consolidated by the victory in the plebiscite and then by a strong showing for the PPD in the 1989 Congressional elections (see Table 4.2).

A third, and arguably the most distinctive, feature of the Chilean party system was the resurgence of large, powerful rightist parties that had been eclipsed by the military and technocratic rule of the Pinochet era. Prior to 1973, the stability of Chile's constitutional order owed much to the unusual capacity of these parties to defend conservative interests within the electoral system.[52] On the other hand, rightist politicians also had an incentive to package their positions in ways that would appeal to broader sectors of the electorate.

Similar incentives operated as electoral competition increased after 1988. Within the legal framework imposed by the old regime, the rightist bloc as a whole did enjoy advantages that did not depend directly on popular votes; for example, senators appointed by Pinochet provided the right with the means to block legislation in the upper chamber. Nevertheless, rightist politicians were not immune from pressures to move toward the electoral center. Although one rightist party, the Independent Democratic Union (UDI), remained closely identified with the hardline positions of the old regime, a larger faction, the National Renovation (RN), was headed by more traditional and flexible conservative politicians. These politicians defended the achievements of the Pinochet era, but were inclined to disassociate themselves from its repressiveness and inequality. As we shall see below, the cooperation of this more moderate sector of the right was essential for the passage of several key initiatives launched by the Aylwin government.

---

[52] See Robert R. Kaufman, *The Politics of Land Reform in Chile, 1950–1970* (Cambridge, Mass.: Harvard University Press, 1972), pp. 45–73, 147–86. For more general discussion, see Douglas Chalmers, Atilio Borón, and Maria do Carmo Campello de Souza, eds., *The Right and Democracy in Latin America* (New York: Praeger, 1992).

Mention should be made, finally, of the long-standing role that intellectuals played in the leadership of the Chilean party system.[53] In the late 1980s, professional economists with political ties to the opposition parties contributed significantly to narrowing ideological differences among the contending electoral forces. During the Pinochet years, American and European foundations provided funding for the formation of a number of independent research centers, which allowed many of these economists to work outside the government-controlled universities and to maintain informal ties with party networks.

Economists based in CIEPLAN, a research center linked closely to the Christian Democrats, were highly influential in encouraging the party's policy reorientation during the transition years.[54] During the 1970s and early 1980s, CIEPLAN economists were deeply critical of the social costs of Pinochet's reforms. At the end of the decade, they still emphasized the importance of addressing the "social debt" and equity goals, but also pressed the opposition leadership to endorse the objectives of maintaining macroeconomic stability and an open economy.

The most comprehensive statement of their general approach came two months before the plebiscite in an open letter signed by twelve of CIEPLAN's senior economists.[55] The letter called for an expansion of public health and education, renegotiation of the external debt, and greater freedom for unions. But it also emphasized the gains achieved during the authoritarian period in reducing the fiscal deficit and inflation and establishing a modern, export-oriented economy. These achievements, the economists argued, "will permit the democratic government to initiate a new stage without the sharp macroeconomic disequilibria inherited by other countries that have recently experienced democratic transitions."[56]

In the period following the plebiscite, many leading members of CIEPLAN were appointed to official leadership positions within the Concertación, along with a number of Socialist party economists with similar views. The most prominent was CIEPLAN's director, Alejandro Foxley, who served as Aylwin's principal economic advisor during the post-plebiscite

---

[53] In the pre-Pinochet era, the integration of intellectuals and academics into competing party networks generally began as early as secondary school or the university, and continued throughout their professional careers.

[54] The role of CIEPLAN was paralleled by a number of Socialist think tanks and by returning Socialist exiles such Carlos Ominami and Sergio Bitar, as well as by Centro de Estudios Económicos (CED), also linked to the PDC. Genero Arriagada Herrera and Carol Graham, "Chile: Sustaining Adjustment during Democratic Transition," in Haggard and Webb, *Voting for Reform,* p. 258.

[55] "El consenso económico-social democrático es posible," *La Época,* August 28, 1988. The twelve signatories included Ph.D.s in economics from Harvard, Cambridge, Columbia, Chicago, Wisconsin, and Berkeley, and two each from Yale, MIT, and Pennsylvania.

[56] Ibid., p. 3.

negotiations and in the 1989 presidential campaign. His presence in the leadership provided important reassurances to business elites and the Right and facilitated agreements over crucial constitutional reforms. When the new Aylwin government took power, Foxley was appointed minister of finance and quickly became the leading figure in the conduct of economic policy.

Economic and Political Reform under Aylwin

The Chilean transition is the most recent of the ones discussed in this volume and the record of economic policy is thus least complete. The Aylwin period from 1990 to 1994, however, was one in which the government managed both to sustain the extraordinary dynamism of the Chilean economy while at the same time making some progress in tackling inherited social problems. The policies that contributed to this distinctive success story owed much to the centripetal political tendencies discussed above.

The incoming government attached the highest priority to containing inflationary pressures that had built up during the election campaigns of 1988 and 1989. By 1990, the consumer price index had risen over 27 percent, the highest increase in five years. Interestingly, candidates of the right had attempted to distance themselves from the Pinochet government by emphasizing new government spending programs during the 1989 campaign. Aylwin and Foxley, on the other hand, sought to dampen expectations by warning against a relaxation of economic discipline, and they followed through during their first year in office with a very tight monetary and fiscal policy.[57] The Central Bank, reorganized under Pinochet, played an important role in bolstering the government's hand on this issue, but there was very little dissent from Concertación parties in the legislature, despite a substantial drop in the growth rate during Aylwin's first year. The government actually ran fiscal surpluses in its first three years, and inflation dropped to single digits by 1993.

Meanwhile, the government pressed forward with additional tariff reductions and privatization initiatives. As with stabilization policies, these steps met with virtually no dissent from the major parties. Spurred by exports and a massive inflow of external finance, the economy rebounded. In 1991 and 1992, GDP growth averaged 7.3 percent. Real wages rose by 12 percent during this period, and the minimum wage by 36 percent (see Table 7.4).[58]

Within the parameters of its stance toward fiscal discipline, the long-standing commitments of both Christian Democrats and Socialists resulted in a social agenda that was much more ambitious than in the other non-

---

[57] Arriagada and Graham, "Chile: Sustaining Adjustment," pp. 264–65, 272.
[58] See *Financial Times*, May 19, 1993, p. 31.

TABLE 7.4

Post-transition Economic Developments in Chile

	1985–89	1990	1991	1992
GDP Growth	6.2	2.1	6.0	8.6
Inflation	20.4	26.0	21.8	15.4
Fiscal Deficit/GDP	1.2	3.6	2.3	2.3
Current Account/GDP	−4.8	−2.2	0.5	−1.5
Investment/GDP	16.5	20.2	18.8	21.3
Real Wage	1.2	2.5	na	na

Sources: International Monetary Fund, *International Financial Statistics Yearbook,* various issues; Economic Commission for Latin America, *Economic Survey of Latin America and The Caribbean,* various issues; World Bank, *Trends in Developing Economies,* various issues; World Bank, *World Tables 1993.*

Note: For definitions of the first five variables, see Table 2.1. Real Wage: Nonagricultural workers.

crisis cases. Social welfare expenditures increased by an estimated 10 percent during Aylwin's first year,[59] targeted primarily to expanding health and educational services and poverty relief.

The most striking feature of this effort—one that highlighted another aspect of convergence within the Chilean party system—was the decision of the rightist National Renovation to back tax increases necessary to finance these measures. Legislation negotiated with the RN in April 1990 raised corporate tax rates from 10 to 15 percent and increased the value-added tax by 2 percent for a four-year period. The UDI opposed this increase, as did much of the business elite. However RN leaders hoped to position themselves more effectively to contest for moderate voters in coming elections, and since the Concertación lacked a majority in the Senate, the RN's legislative support was crucial. Given the political constraints on cutting military expenditures, it was probably the only way to finance social policies without exceeding the fiscal limits established by the Concertación.

The tax measures provided between $600 million and $1 billion in new revenues annually.[60] These were used exclusively for social expenditures, which included increases in pensions and family benefits, low-cost housing and increased pay for teachers and health workers.[61] Some of these initiatives were modeled along the lines of the targeted antipoverty programs initiated under Pinochet.[62] The emphasis and funding attached to them was

[59] Arriagada and Graham, "Chile: Sustaining Adjustment," p. 277.

[60] Ibid., p. 277; *Financial Times,* May 19, 1993, p. 34.

[61] Ibid.

[62] See Carol Graham, *Safety Nets, Politics, and the Poor: Transitions to Market Economies* (Washington, D.C.: The Brookings Institution, 1994).

new, however, and some components of the program were characterized by greater attempts to respond to initiatives coming directly from local communities and low-income social groups.[63] In any event, although social problems remained serious during the Aylwin period, these efforts appeared to have had some impact; estimates of the proportion of the population living in poverty fell from 40 percent in 1990 to about one-third in 1993.[64]

One motivation for these programs was to address the declining fortunes of the working class. Though Chile's once-powerful union movement had been severely weakened during the Pinochet era, it continued to provide a major social base for both the Socialists and the Christian Democrats. Thus, the reintegration of the union movement into the political system constituted a major concern of the Aylwin government. The most salient question in the initial year of the transition was the reform of the restrictive labor code that had been imposed under Pinochet. In the direct negotiations that followed the plebiscite, peak associations of business and labor failed to reach agreement on this issue. In 1990, however, compromise with RN again facilitated the passage of a new code. Though not fully satisfactory from the perspective of the unions, the code restored the rights to organize and engage in collective bargaining and thus helped the Concertación parties to meet important commitments to a key constituency group.

In contrast to most of the other transitions we have discussed, both crisis and non-crisis, the challenges posed by a resurgent union movement were moderate, and had little impact on the conduct of economic policy. Labor representatives were at times critical of the relative caution showed by government policymakers, and in 1991 strikes broke out in parts of the low-paid public sector and in several of the major copper mines. Unlike in earlier decades, however, leaders of the Concertación did not press the managers of the mines to accept a favorable settlement, and the risks of excessive militancy were well understood by most union leaders themselves.

Epilogue

After only four years of the Aylwin government, the end of the Chilean transition is yet to be told. First, it remained unclear whether the stunning economic performance of the early 1990s could be sustained. As Aylwin approached the end of his term, there were growing concerns that the economy was overheating, that the exchange rate was overvalued, and that

---

[63] An important example is the Social Investment and Solidarity Fund (FOSIS). This paralleled closely the organization and rationale of the Solidarity Program initiated in Mexico around the same time.

[64] Nathaniel C. Nash, "Chile Advances in a War on Poverty, and One Million Mouths Say Amen," *New York Times,* April 4, 1993, p. 14.

Chilean exports were overly dependent on sluggish North American and European markets. The expiration of the four-year tax reform agreement again raised questions about how to continue the financing of the Concertación's social agenda. Weakening economic performance would also call into question the durability of the strategic realignments within the party system. Though these realignments seemed solid in the early 1990s, they could come under increasing strain if and when economic growth slowed.

Yet however these issues are resolved, the accomplishments of the Aylwin period remain impressive. Performance with respect to macroeconomic and adjustment policies contrasted not only with the crisis cases, but also with Thailand, Turkey, and Korea, where new governments had to deal with considerable economic instability and political turmoil. These achievements were not unrelated to the integration of the left into the governing coalition and the narrowing of ideological differences with the right. These arrangements facilitated greater emphasis on equity and labor issues, which in turn strengthened the legitimacy of the market-oriented model.

CONCLUSION: THE POLITICS OF REFORM IN THE NON-CRISIS CASES

We began this chapter with two complementary hypotheses about the path of economic policy in the non-crisis cases. The first explained continuity by the fact that good economic circumstances created important social bases of support for the project of the old regime and weakened the position of groups that had been disadvantaged by the reforms. Our second hypothesis put greater weight on the constraining role of institutional factors; insulated economic decision-making structures and restrictions on political contestation played a more important role.

Though we have seen evidence of both factors in each case, the implications of the two hypotheses for the consolidation of economic reform are somewhat different. Where opposition is held in check primarily by institutional constraints, the consolidation of reform is likely to be tenuous. As restrictions on contestation are eased and decision-makers become more vulnerable to electoral pressures, there is greater likelihood that polarization will increase, with unsettling consequences for public policy.

The capacity to avoid such an outcome depends most fundamentally on the distributive effects of reforms: these are more likely to be sustained where elite supporters within the policy and business communities could mobilize broader bases of electoral and interest-group support. In all four cases we examined, however, important segments of the population had lost ground in relative, if not absolute terms, and thus the potential for the mobilization of antireform sentiment was common across them.

For this reason, as in the last chapter, we have placed special emphasis on the way party systems aggregated the preferences of competing economic interests. Variations in party system fragmentation and consolidation were important even in Korea and Thailand, where opposition challenges were mitigated by relatively favorable distributions of income. They were especially important, however, in Turkey and Chile, where large popular sectors were among the most important losers in previous reforms. In Turkey, outgoing elites had relied primarily on exclusionary means to encourage consolidation and depolarization of the party system. This contributed to policy stability in the short term, but excluded groups had limited incentive to cooperate with the center-right government and the country eventually experienced a renewal of distributive conflicts and a deterioration of macroeconomic performance. In Chile, the incorporation of the left into the incoming political coalition encouraged tendencies toward the formation of large political blocs and contributed significantly to the depolarization of the system. Through the early 1990s, this appeared to enhance the chances that the system could sustain its high-growth trajectory while also paying greater attention to social policy and moving toward a more equitable distribution of income.

CHAPTER EIGHT

Economic and Political Reform in Dominant-Party Systems: Mexico and Taiwan

IN CONTRAST to the other authoritarian systems we have examined, Mexico and Taiwan have had dominant-party regimes. In such regimes, authoritarian elites govern through a political party and opposition parties face legal and institutional barriers that eliminate any significant probability that they could take office. Such barriers can include: a breakdown of the boundary between state and party that favors the dominant party; de jure or de facto restrictions on the freedom of new parties to organize; and outright bans on the entry of new parties, and on political association more generally.

It is important to distinguish dominant-party regimes from democratic regimes with dominant parties. Democracies in Scandinavia, Japan, and India have experienced long periods when single parties either governed alone or predominated within ruling coalitions.[1] Unlike in dominant-party regimes, however, opposition parties faced no serious official constraints or harassment, and though ruling parties exploited the powers of office to maintain political support, the legal separation of party and state was generally respected. Put differently, barriers to entry were high, but not prohibitively so; subsequently we have seen a number of once-dominant parties voted out of office, most recently in Japan in 1993.

In Mexico and Taiwan, dominant parties were pillars of authoritarian rule. Compared to military rulers—even those in the non-crisis cases—political elites in Taiwan and Mexico were able to broaden the base of their regimes without losing control over the political system; political change in both countries was tightly managed from the top. The existence of dominant parties also helps explain certain features of economic policy in the two countries. In Taiwan, as in the non-crisis cases, the dominance of the Kuomintang (KMT) guaranteed that the political opening would not produce significant change in the country's export-oriented development strategy. In Mexico, reforming political elites could draw on the organizational resources available through the Institutional Revolutionary Party (PRI) to initiate wide-ranging economic adjustments.

This chapter explores the dynamics of economic and political reform in

---

[1] For a discussion of the dominant-party democracies, see T. J. Pempel, ed., *Uncommon Democracies: The One-Party Dominant Regimes* (Ithaca, N.Y.: Cornell University Press, 1990).

these two dominant-party systems. We begin with a discussion of economic management in authoritarian regimes, and particularly the tension between the fact that centralized authority may be necessary for effective policy innovation and the risk that dominant parties will become either predatory or sclerotic. We then review the institutional foundations of Taiwan's export-led growth strategy and the role of the dominant-party system both in the origins of the economic crisis of the early 1980s in Mexico and in the profound policy adjustments that ensued over the next decade.

The remainder of the chapter turns to the question of political reform. The dominant-party systems present a contrast to the other countries analyzed in this volume. As of 1994, neither had made an unambiguous transition to democracy; the PRI and KMT still dominated their respective political landscapes. However, both governments had launched reforms that broadened opportunities for effective political participation.

Both economic circumstances and political institutions help explain the controlled nature of the political transformation in the two countries. In Taiwan, successful economic performance and centralized control of the state allowed the KMT to maintain its hold on political power while undertaking a gradual electoral opening. In Mexico, the economic recovery of the 1990s provided the opportunity for a new round of political reforms aimed at modernizing the PRI and providing additional space for opposition groups. However, Mexico differs from Taiwan in the greater uncertainty surrounding its recovery. Unsure of whether they could prevail in more open contests with opposition parties, ruling elites in Mexico proved less willing than those in Taiwan to relinquish the institutional controls that were the basis both of economic adjustment and their party's continued political dominance.

THE POLITICAL ECONOMY OF DOMINANT-PARTY RULE

Throughout this book, we have emphasized how party systems structure the political environment in which economic policy is made. If fragmented and polarized party systems create incentives that undermine stable policy, then decision-making in dominant-party regimes should be more coherent. A centralized, dominant party gives political elites the independence to initiate unpopular measures, but also provides them the organizational means for building the bases of organized support that are crucial for sustaining reforms over the long run.

If fragmented and polarized party systems have characteristic defects, however, so do dominant-party regimes. As with military governments, the presumed advantages of concentrated authority rest on the questionable assumption that rulers will use their power to enhance social welfare. Yet the preferences of authoritarian leaders may coincide only weakly with the public good; indeed, the very monopoly position rulers enjoy provides a powerful temptation to extract resources for themselves or a narrow group of allies within the party, the military, or the state apparatus.

Predation is a threat wherever power is concentrated. However, dominant party organizations have an additional, and distinctive, liability. Militaries that intervene in politics can return to the barracks; the raison d'être of political parties is to rule. There is thus likely to be particularly strong resistance to some economic reforms and particularly to political change in dominant-party regimes, as interests within the party organization seek to preserve their privileged position.

The theoretical indeterminacy concerning the expected economic performance of dominant-party rule parallels that for authoritarian governments more generally, and is reflected in the wide variation in economic achievement among them. Some dominant-party governments, including Taiwan, Singapore, and Indonesia, have experienced exceptionally high growth rates for very long periods. But there are also examples of spectacular economic failure; these include a number of African dominant-party states, such as Zambia,[2] and the erratic and economically self-destructive governments of Saddam Hussein in Iraq and Nicolas Ceauşescu in Romania.

Most communist systems and Mexico have more mixed economic records. Mexico experienced very high growth during the period of "stabilizing development" in the 1950s and 1960s, mounting difficulties in the next two decades, and then dramatic reform efforts and some recovery by the late 1980s. Communist governments in Eastern Europe, Cuba, and North Korea enjoyed high growth in the 1950s and 1960s, but most began to encounter structural problems in the 1970s and 1980s. In the last two decades, only China and Vietnam managed to combine sustained high growth with the maintenance of Communist Party rule, and they did so largely as a result of successful economic reform programs.

The range of possible explanations for these variations is quite long, but we focus on two factors that are related to the political organization of the dominant party. The first is the centralization of decision-making authority within the party organization. As with the military regimes discussed in Part One, parties are more cohesive when they are dominated by individual rulers rather than collegial executives. A second set of factors is equally if not more important over the long run: the checks on executive authority

---

[2] Robert H. Bates and Paul Collier, "The Politics and Economics of Policy Reform in Zambia," in Bates and Anne Krueger, eds., *Political and Economic Interactions in Economic Policy Reform* (Cambridge: Basil Blackwell, 1993), pp. 387–443.

that prevent abuse of office. We emphasize the existence of an independent private sector and the delegation of policymaking authority to insulated technocratic teams.

Party Centralization

The model of the effective party machine assumes that lower echelons do the bidding of the executive. Yet dominant parties can also anchor authoritarian systems immobilized by vested interests. One way this can occur is through the "limited pluralism" that Juan Linz identifies as a defining feature of all authoritarian—as opposed to totalitarian—regimes.[3] Mexico constitutes an example. The PRI always operated in a context in which preexisting social forces retained a significant measure of independence from central government authority. After the incorporation of labor and agrarian organizations during the 1930s, the party evolved into a powerful instrument of social control. Nevertheless, the system allowed the continued existence of the private sector, small opposition parties, and some independent labor organizations, as well as substantial factional contestation within the party itself.

A different, but comparable set of problems arises in post-totalitarian regimes, where independent centers of social power have been weakened or destroyed by revolutionary party organizations.[4] Dominant parties in such systems continue to claim a monopoly of legitimate authority, but their very inclusiveness actually undermines the capacity to impose control from the center of the political system. Communist regimes in the former Soviet Union and Eastern Europe demonstrate this problem clearly. In the post-Stalinist era, these governments clung to "vanguardist" claims to a complete monopoly of political power, the nationalization of all economic activity, and the control and penetration of organized social life. Yet the very success of such efforts was associated with increased difficulties in coordinating and monitoring the diverse factions within the party and government itself. Despite a formally hierarchical structure, both the demands of efficiency and the nature of political competition within the party necessarily made leaders sensitive to a variety of interests: ministries, re-

---

[3] Juan Linz, "Totalitarian and Authoritarian Regimes," in Fred Greenstein and Nelson Polsby, eds., *Handbook of Political Science,* vol. 3 (Reading, Mass.: Addison-Wesley, 1975), pp. 174–411. See also Susan Shirk's innovative analysis of Chinese Communist politics, *The Political Logic of Economic Reform in China* (Berkeley: University of California Press, 1993) pp. 53–146.

[4] The term is from Juan J. Linz and Alfred Stepan, *Problems of Democratic Transition and Consolidation: Southern Europe, South America, and Eastern Europe* (Johns Hopkins University Press, forthcoming).

gional authorities, the military, and lower echelons within the party hierarchy itself.[5]

Under what conditions do dominant-party regimes avoid bureaucratic ossification? One key factor is the way authority is organized at the top of the system. Party organizations are more likely to be responsive to central directives when final decision-making authority, particularly control over recruitment and appointments, is in the hands of a single ruler. It is undeniable that single rulers may themselves constitute a major impediment to political and economic reform. The development of extensive networks of personal loyalty, the exploitation of charismatic status by founding leaders, and the emergence of cults of personality can provide the basis for surprisingly stable, yet highly inefficient and myopic forms of rule; North Korea provides a clear example.[6] Yet our concern here is with the *capacity* of governments to initiate reforms in the face of economic and political crisis. If a dominant leader is committed to a reform program, then centralized discretionary authority enhances the likelihood that it will go forward.

There are several reasons why this might be the case. As we argued with respect to military organization in chapter 1, collegial executives are more likely to either reflect or create factional conflicts in the state and party apparatus. These divisions send mixed signals when policy decisions are taken and provide the opportunity for lower echelons to appeal or even challenge distasteful commands. Such divisions often rest on more or less organized factions within the party and state apparatus, and can lead to wider politicization as contending groups seek allies outside the government. Single rulers need bases of support as well, but their control over appointments and systems of monitoring and coercion allows them to create networks of followers with strong career incentives to obey and the capacity to purge opponents. As we have argued with respect to the initiation of reform more generally, leadership helps solve collective action problems and reduces ambiguity with respect to any decisions taken.

Taiwan provides a particularly clear example of such a "leaderist" system.[7] The traumatic experience of defeat in civil war provided Chiang Kai-shek with the opportunity to increase his personal power, purge rival factional leaders, and streamline party organization. The concentration of

---

[5] Similar problems exist in noncommunist one-party states in Africa and the Middle East, where the internal political dynamics of the party machine have result in extensive patronage and rent-seeking that are wholly inimical to either economic or political reform.

[6] See, for example, Bruce Cumings's discussion of "The Corporate State in North Korea," in Hagen Koo, ed., *State and Society in Contemporary Korea* (Ithaca, N.Y.: Cornell University Press, 1993), pp. 197–230.

[7] For an interesting discussion of "leaderism" in the context of other Leninist systems, see Constance Squires Meaney, "Liberalization, Democratization, and the Role of the KMT," in Tun-jen Cheng and Stephan Haggard, eds., *Political Change in Taiwan* (Boulder, Colo.: Lynne Riener, 1992), p. 96.

power in a single leader increased the cohesion of state and party, limited the possibility that organized interest groups in society would constitute sources of political pressure on the government, and provided unambiguous political backing for reform initiatives.

The more bureaucratized parties of the Soviet Union and Central Europe did not experience similar crises in the postwar period, and evolved in the direction of more collegial leaderships concerned primarily with creating collective constraints that would eliminate the terror and insecurity experienced under Stalin. The result was the creation of a power structure in which strong status quo interests were represented in the highest decision-making bodies: industrial enterprise managers, the military, and the *nomenklatura* itself. As early as the 1960s, reformist factions also emerged, but reformers faced a difficult predicament. The need to accommodate conservatives within the party placed important limits on the scope of reforms, but appeal to groups outside the party framework risked unraveling the authoritarian system itself. These dilemmas became especially apparent during the Gorbachev era, when economic reformers confronted strongly entrenched opposition within the party apparatus and the planning bureaucracy.[8] The political liberalization (perestroika) essential for weakening the hand of conservatives also opened the door to a political process that undermined the hold of the Communist Party and unleashed divisive political conflicts.

The Mexican system occupies an intermediate position between "leaderist" and more collegial forms of dominant-party rule. On the one hand, presidential authority is limited by a fixed six-year term. The no-reelection principle was established explicitly to prevent the long-term dominance of a single individual and to offer rival power contenders a periodic opportunity to advance. Peter Smith's landmark study of elite recruitment from the 1940s to the 1970s shows that approximately one-third of all middle- and top-level officials were replaced with each presidential turnover, and that over two-thirds failed to hold onto office over a twelve-year period.[9]

The corollary, though, is that presidents exercise enormous personal power for most of their term in office, particularly through control over appointments. Mexico's Constitution provides for a division of executive and legislative powers and for a federal system; but the president, in his role as head of state and of the ruling party, names all major government and party officials, and controls the nomination of federal legislators and elected governors. Presidential power tends to deflate during the last year

---

[8] This is a consistent theme of the literature on the Soviet reforms. See, for example, Ed Hewett, *Reforming the Soviet Economy: Equality versus Efficiency* (Washington, D.C.: Brookings Institution, 1988).

[9] Peter Smith, *Labyrinths of Power* (Princeton, N.J.: Princeton University Press, 1979). Such rates of turnover, notes Smith, were far higher than in the Soviet Union (pp. 180–81).

of the term, as lame-duck effects set in. Even so, as Ann L. Craig and Wayne A. Cornelius suggest, "metaconstitutional power to seat and remove officials throughout the system has the effect of enforcing discipline within the PRI and loyalty to the incumbent president."[10] This concentration of power was crucial, as we shall see, in the initiation of economic reforms during the 1980s and 1990s.

Checking Predation

The very capabilities that make it possible for centralized parties to initiate reform also raise the question of whether reforms are credible; what authoritarian leaders do, they can also undo. The effective institutionalization of policy reform thus hinges on an apparent contradiction: the evolution of some checks on the discretion of the ruler.[11]

One such check is in a strong and independent private sector. Communist governments expropriated most of the private sector on coming to office, whether through revolution or conquest. A number of African and Middle Eastern one-party regimes have also severely circumscribed private economic opportunities through large state-owned enterprise sectors, legal restrictions and controls, or the creation of strong dependencies between private actors and the state. In other settings, however, highly centralized dominant parties have coexisted with dynamic private sectors, either because of the party's political preferences and strategies or because of the effective power of the private sector to resist state incursion. We do not argue that the existence of an independent private sector is a precondition for rapid growth; the Communist regimes of Eastern Europe had a long run of growth prior to the difficulties that began to emerge in the 1970s. Nonetheless, the strength of the private sector—both economic and political—does effect the politics of economic policy in authoritarian settings in a number of important ways.

First, a strong and independent private sector can constitute a check on the predatory tendencies of the state. Coercion may be effective in controlling social demands on the government, but it is less effective in inducing private actors with independent resources to invest. Thus while most analyses emphasize that the protection of property rights is necessary for the

---

[10] Ann L. Craig and Wayne A. Cornelius, "Houses Divided: Parties and Political Reform in Mexico," in Scott Mainwaring and Timothy R. Scully, eds., *Building Democratic Institutions in Latin America* (forthcoming), p. 369.

[11] For arguments along this line, see Douglass C. North and Barry R. Weingast, "Constitutions and Commitment: The Evolution of Institutions Governing Public Choice in Seventeenth-Century England," *Journal of Economic History* 49 (1989): 803–32; Mancur Olson, "Dictatorship, Democracy, and Development," *American Political Science Review* 87 (1993): 567–76.

private sector to thrive,[12] the logic can also be inverted. Strong private sectors constitute an inducement for leaders to stabilize property rights and provide incentives for economic activity, and provide the political leadership with an alternative to interests embedded in the party and state-owned enterprise sector. As we will see, the political option of aligning with the private sector against some segments of the party and state apparatus played a rule in crucial adjustment decisions in both Taiwan and Mexico.

Finally, the strength of the private sector will affect the response of the economy to the changes in incentives associated with economic reform. The supply response to market-oriented reforms is likely to be more swift and robust where the private sector is well-developed than where it is weak or nonexistent. In Taiwan, for example, companies in textiles and other labor-intensive sectors that developed during the 1950s responded relatively quickly to price and export-promotion incentives introduced after 1958. Similarly, the Mexican leadership enjoyed the advantage of a sophisticated and increasingly internationalized domestic private-sector when it initiated its reform efforts in the mid-1980s. Neither the Eastern European nor low-income African countries enjoyed these advantages when launching their reform efforts. The rapidity of the supply response affects not only the economics of reform, but its politics as well, since it will determine the extent to which new private sector constituencies for reform can be built.

An independent private sector is closely related to a second check on the abuse of leadership and dominant-party power: delegation of decision-making authority to technocrats or technocratic agencies that are at least somewhat insulated from leaders' and interest groups' short-term demands. In the face of an independent private sector, dominant-party governments face a problem of assuring economic agents that their property rights will not be altered or attenuated at the whim of the ruler.[13] By explicitly delegating authority over economic decision-making, rulers provide this assurance to private actors and enhance their credibility, in part because such an action raises the cost of opportunistic reversal.

The delegation of decision-making authority was clearly more extensive in Taiwan than it was in Mexico. As Robert Wade's account makes clear, economic decision-making was dominated by a few key "pilot agencies" including particularly the Central Bank, and the Council on Economic Planning and Development or its predecessors.[14] Chalmers Johnson argues

[12] The classic statement of this perspective is Douglass C. North, *Structure and Change in Economic History* (New York: W. W. Norton, 1981). See also Yoram Barzel, *Economic Analysis of Property Rights* (New York: Cambridge University Press, 1989), pp. 8–10.

[13] For a discussion of the role of different political institutions in solving commitment problems, see Barry Weingast, "The Economic Role of Political Institutions," unpublished ms., Stanford University, January 1993.

[14] Robert Wade, *Governing the Market: Economic Theory and the Role of Government in East Asian Industrialization* (Princeton: Princeton, N.J.: University Press, 1990), pp. 195–227.

that a sharp distinction between the social control functions of the dominant party and the governing functions delegated to the economic bureaucracy was a key feature of the developmental state model, of which Taiwan represents perhaps the clearest example.[15]

Delegation in Mexico was less complete, but ran along parallel lines. The Central Bank and Finance Ministry constituted especially powerful centers of technocratic decision-making throughout the post–World War II period. Constraints on these agencies were greater than in Taiwan; they sometimes faced significant challenges from other factions of the party and the bureaucracy, and were by no means immune to political interference from the president himself. Nevertheless, the "financial bureaucracy" in Mexico maintained high standards of recruitment and technical competence and was allowed to exercise extensive control over macroeconomic policy for long periods of time.[16] The high points of technocratic influence came during the long period of "stabilizing development" in the 1950s and 1960s, and again during the period of economic adjustment in the 1980s and 1990s.

In contrast to both Taiwan and Mexico, the insulation of technocratic agencies was far less extensive in either Communist or African one-party states. The extent of meaningful delegation in the African cases was limited in part by the extreme scarcity of technocratic talent. Yet it is also a consistent leitmotif in the literature on one-party African systems that the absence of delegation was driven by political rather than technical or administrative constraints.[17] Political leaders consistently used the party framework as a vehicle for maintaining support through the dispensation of patronage, a pattern of political control that clearly affected the coherence of economic management.

Delegation and insulation of technocratic agencies in the Communist countries faced different limitations related to the fundamental nature of these countries as command economies. In principle, central planning agencies had considerable authority. But actual leverage over the state apparatus was diluted not only by the political constraints we have noted above, but also by technical features of command economies that drew central planners into complex bargains with their subordinates. Because economic policymakers lacked arms-length policy instruments, macroe-

---

[15] Chalmers Johnson, "Political Institutions and Economic Performance: the Government-Business Relationship in Japan, South Korea and Taiwan," in Fred Deyo, ed., *The Political Economy of the New Asian Industrialism* (Ithaca, N.Y.: Cornell University Press, 1987), pp. 136–64.

[16] Sylvia Maxfield, *Governing Capital* (Ithaca: Cornell University Press, 1990), pp. 45–94.

[17] See, in particular, the work of Thomas Callaghy, "Lost Between State and Market: the Politics of Economic Adjustment in Ghana, Zambia, and Nigeria," in Joan Nelson, ed., *Economic Crisis and Policy Choice* (Princeton, N.J.: Princeton University Press, 1990), pp. 257–320.

conomic policy entailed extensive negotiations on the direct allocation of spending and credit. Regulatory policy that operated by controlling incentives to private actors was also altogether absent. Negotiations were therefore also a component of the microeconomics of socialism: the design and implementation of the plan. Thus despite their apparent authority, central planners in Communist systems necessarily became enmeshed in a web of principal-agent relationships in which the potential for agency slack, shirking, inefficiency, and corruption has been well documented.[18] One of the first tasks in reforming such systems is precisely to delegate authority downward through incentive reform in order to remedy these problems.

Theoretical Reprise

It is important to emphasize that *all* authoritarian systems are vulnerable to the problems associated with the monopolization of political authority, including both the temptation to predation and the risk of ossification. There is no clear theoretical answer to the question of why some authoritarian regimes respond effectively to economic crises and perform well while others succumb to these vulnerabilities. Nonetheless, we have made three arguments about how the organizational characteristics of authoritarian rule might affect the *capacity* for governments to resolve economic crises and pursue coherent economic strategies. We noted that, in principle, one-party regimes enjoy an advantage that military regimes lack: the existence of organizational means for mobilizing and coopting social support. However, we have also argued that exploiting this advantage depends on two further features of the one-party system: the concentration of executive authority and the institutionalization of some checks on it. We have stressed two such checks: the existence of a private sector and the delegation of policymaking authority to technocratic teams. In the following sections, we show how these institutional factors help explain patterns of economic development in Taiwan and Mexico.

THE POLITICAL ECONOMY OF DEVELOPMENT IN TAIWAN

The KMT had already forcefully established its authority vis-à-vis local Taiwanese social forces prior to 1949.[19] Following its full-fledged retreat to Taiwan in that year, the party initiated a series of internal purges that further strengthened Chiang's authority within the party and gave the sys-

[18] For an introduction to the issues, see Janos Kornai, *The Socialist System: The Political Economy of Communism* (Oxford: Oxford University Press, 1992).

[19] For an analysis of the process of political consolidation on Taiwan, see Edwin A. Winckler, "Elite Political Struggle 1945–1985," in Winckler and Susan Greenhalgh, eds.,

tem its "leaderist" qualities. The immense size of the KMT relative to the island, the subethnic split between the mainlander government and the Taiwanese populace, the relative weakness of local social organization, and tight control over the coercive apparatus allowed the party to establish thorough, top-down control of all social organizations, including unions, farmers, and student groups.

The KMT's total political dominance and sociological distance from the local elite allowed for a sweeping land reform.[20] Motivated by the political lessons of the civil war on the mainland, the reform had the political effects of equalizing assets and creating a tacit base of rural support. The legacy of this reform, and the government's high investment in education, has proven long-lasting; despite some deterioration in the 1980s, Taiwan's income distribution remains extremely equal even by developed country standards. At the same time, the KMT built on farmers' organizations established under Japanese rule to penetrate the countryside and to extract the food required to feed the island's swollen population of refugees.

Because of the devastating political as well as economic effects of the great Chinese hyperinflation, stabilization was a priority issue for the party leadership. With American support and an aggressive policy effort, inflation was virtually halted early in Taiwan's postwar history. In the mid-1950s, macroeconomic stability was buttressed by the formation of a highly independent and powerful Central Bank. Both during the 1950s and in subsequent decades, state-owned enterprises and government spending played an important role in the economy; the KMT government was by no means small. However, conservative fiscal and monetary policy and rapid adjustment to external shocks have remained hallmarks of Taiwan's economic policy until this day.

The formation of a strong Central Bank was indicative of a broader pattern of policymaking. Despite the concentration of political power in Chiang's hands, he delegated substantial authority to technocratic centers of decision-making. Two such agencies, the Committee on United States Aid (CUSA) and the Joint Committee on Rural Reconstruction (JCRR), provided opportunities for collaboration between American advisers and a nascent group of Chinese technocrats;[21] a third, the Industrial Development

---

Contending Approaches to the Political Economy of Taiwan (Armonk, N.Y.: M. E. Sharpe, 1988), pp. 151–74.

In general, this section draws on Stephan Haggard, Pathways from the Periphery: the Politics of Growth in the Newly Industrializing Countries (Ithaca, N.Y.: Cornell University Press, 1990), chap. 4. A useful overview of Taiwan's development is Thomas Gold, State and Society in the Taiwan Miracle (Armonk, N.Y.: M. E. Sharpe, 1986).

[20] See Anthony C. Y. Koo, The Role of Land Reform in Economic Development: A Case Study of Taiwan (New York: Praeger, 1968); Martin M. C. Yang, Socio-Economic Results of Land Reform in Taiwan (Honolulu: East-West Center Press, 1970).

[21] For studies of these organizations, see Neil H. Jacoby, U.S. Aid to Taiwan: A Study of Foreign Aid, Self-Help, and Development (New York: Praeger, 1966); and Joseph A. Yager,

Bureau, forged selective ties with the emerging Taiwanese private sector. The CUSA and JCRR were highly insulated from political interference and became important players in the reforms of the 1950s.

The gradual shift in economic strategy toward export-led growth from 1958 to 1962 was precipitated by sagging economic performance, short-term pressure from the United States, and a projected reduction in U.S. assistance.[22] The subsequent combination of rapid growth, macroeconomic stability, and equity has become the subject of a large literature.[23] Though sharp debates continue about the precise role played by industrial policy, there is an emerging consensus on the core features of Taiwan's policy regime beginning in the 1960s:

1. conservative fiscal and monetary policies;

2. flexible labor markets;

3. maintenance of a stable and competitive exchange-rate regime;

4. relatively free trade in inputs for exporters and designated import-substituting activities, primarily intermediate and capital goods, coupled with continued protection of the domestic market for final goods;

5. relative openness to foreign direct investment;

6. a cautious industrial policy that targeted both exports and import-substituting activities, but which generally managed to link any subsidies to performance, even when state-owned enterprise was the chosen instrument of policy.

The economic success of the policy experiment, not fully anticipated at the time, rested both on institutional features of the government itself and on the government's relationship to the private sector. As Chalmers Johnson argues, the key feature of the "developmental state" is a clearly defined division of labor between political elites and bureaucrats charged with managing the economy.[24] Chiang and the mainlander elite dominated the party apparatus, though the KMT gradually coopted increasing numbers of Taiwanese. Mainlander and Taiwanese technocrats rose quickly within a meritocratic government apparatus; by the end of the 1960s, technocrats dominated the principal agencies of economic decision-making and imple-

---

Transforming Agriculture in Taiwan: The Experience of the Joint Commission on Rural Reconstruction (Ithaca, N.Y.: Cornell University Press, 1988).

[22] See Dennis Fred Simon, "External Incorporation and Internal Reform," in Winckler and Greenhalgh, Contending Approaches, pp. 138–50.

[23] Among the standard works are Walter Galenson, ed., Economic Growth and Structural Change in Taiwan (Ithaca, N.Y.: Cornell University Press, 1979); Ching-yuan Lin, Industrialization in Taiwan, 1946–72 (New York: Praeger, 1979); Samuel Ho, Economic Development of Taiwan, 1860–1970 (New Haven, Conn.: Yale University Press, 1978); Wade, Governing the Market. A comprehensive survey of the political economy literature is contained in Cal Clark, Taiwan's Development: Implications for Contending Political Economy Paradigms (New York: Greenwood Press, 1989).

[24] Johnson, "Political Institutions and Economic Performance."

mentation. The large state-owned enterprise sector operated somewhat independently of these arrangements, and provided one channel for state patronage, including to the military. Yet state firms were generally held to hard budget constraints, and in any case declined in relative size as the government first tolerated, then encouraged, the rapid growth of the private sector.

The second pillar of the strategy was the tolerance for a rapid expansion of the Taiwanese private sector. It is important not to mischaracterize this relationship as involving a close alliance of the KMT and the private sector. As Chu emphasizes, the KMT did not depend on the business community for political support, and business had little formal representation in the tightly organized ruling party.[25] Technocrats were also generally insulated from business interests, and the state-corporatist organization of business actually limited the private sector's access to decision-making, though clientelistic relationships did develop between political leaders, technocrats, and the largest firms.[26] Ethnicity constituted an additional barrier between the mainlander government and the local Taiwanese economic elite. Nonetheless, by allowing the private sector's share of total economic activity to expand, the KMT created a check on its own policies, which were broadly favorable to the private sector.

The results of this strategy in the two decades following the reforms have been widely documented:[27] rapid growth of both GDP and manufacturing output, fueled by a combination of extraordinarily high export growth and investment. Conservative fiscal and monetary policy contributed to low inflation, with the exception of sharp price increases during the two oil shocks. High levels of savings and strong export growth generated current account surpluses by the end of the 1970s; balance-of-payments difficulties were virtually unknown. Finally, growth took place in a context of steadily rising real wages and a highly egalitarian distribution of income.[28]

Given some broad similarities in their histories and subsequent economic development strategies, the contrast between Korea and Taiwan is useful in isolating the effects of single-party rule. Both countries have Japanese colonial histories. In both countries, external events and civil war altered traditional agrarian class relations and opened the way for land reform and centralized state support for the private manufacturing sector. In both cases,

[25] Yun-han Chu, "The Realignment of State-Business Relations in Taiwan's Regime Transition," in Andrew MacIntyre, ed., *Business-Government Relations in Industrializing East and Southeast Asia* (Ithaca, N.Y.: Cornell University Press, 1994), pp. 113–41.

[26] See also Wade, *Governing the Market,* p. 295.

[27] A cogent summary that places Taiwan in comparative perspective is contained ibid., pp. 34–51.

[28] On income distribution, see Shirly W. Y Kuo, Gustav Ranis, and John C. H. Fei, *The Taiwan Success Story: Rapid Growth with Improved Distribution of Income in the Republic of China, 1952–79* (Boulder, Colo.: Westview Press, 1981).

the withdrawal of U.S. aid was a factor in prompting the reforms that led toward an export-oriented growth strategy; in both cases, that strategy was reinforced by military as well as political and economic ties with the U.S. In both countries, economic management was at least partly delegated to independent and powerful technocratic agencies.

Notwithstanding these similarities, there remained important differences in policy style and performance.[29] Throughout its history, Korea pursued a more expansionist macroeconomic policy. Inflationary pressures were related in particular to the aggressive use of the financial sector and credit subsidies as an instrument of industrial policy. This strategy contributed to the accumulation of a substantial external debt and more severe adjustment problems in the late 1970s and early 1980s.

Differences between the two countries were not solely macroeconomic but extended to key features of industrial organization. Korea's industrial strategy favored the development of large, diversified conglomerates. The high degree of concentration in the industrial sector, and ultimately the surplus capacity associated with the heavy industry drive, contrast with the less concentrated industrial structure and smoother, more gradual path of industrial upgrading in Taiwan.

Although no single factor can explain these differences, the contrast between party and military rule does appear to be significant, particularly given that both countries had strong leaders. In Taiwan, however, a powerful party organization provided the basis both for selective incorporation and for the penetration of the educational system, the unions, and the countryside—of civil society generally. These mechanisms obviated any possibility of serious political challenges to the government while at the same time permitting at least some opportunities for participation. For example, the party apparatus assisted the government in controlling local and provincial elections, which had the effect of draining off pressures for participation.[30] The organizational strength of the party and the fiscal capacity of the state also meant that the KMT was not dependent on business support to finance its political activities.

In Korea, the ruling party organization was weak and shallow, and even during the nominally democratic governments of Rhee (1948–61) and Park (1964–72), leaders relied extensively on coercion to disorganize opponents

---

[29] The following draws on the outstanding comparative study by Tun-jen Cheng, "Political Regimes and Development Strategies: Korea and Taiwan," in Gary Gereffi and Donald Wyman, eds., *Manufacturing Miracles: Paths of Industrialization in Latin America and East Asia* (Princeton, N.Y.: Princeton University Press, 1990), pp. 139–79.

[30] For a compelling exposition of the KMT's manipulation of local politics, see Yung-mau Chao, "Local Politics on Taiwan: Continuity and Change," in Dennis Fred Simon and Michael Y. M. Kau, eds., *Taiwan: Beyond the Economic Miracle* (Armonk, N.Y.: M. E. Sharpe, 1992), pp. 43–67.

and retain power. The combination of nominally democratic rule and continued reliance on coercion complicated the task of governance. Lacking strong organizational mechanisms for coopting mass support, governments faced recurrent protests from students and workers, as well as some serious electoral challenges. The construction of close relations with the private sector grew in part out of these challenges, as governments sought both to use growth as a legitimating formula and to secure financial support for their political efforts.

These characteristics of Korean politics were not limited to "democratic" periods; Park and Chun were not able to build coherent party organizations during authoritarian periods either, and thus continued to rely on a combination of coercion and material payoffs. The absence of strong organization and a legitimating authority formula was associated with the periodic political crises we have already discussed in chapter 3: in 1964–65 over normalization of relations with Japan; in the late 1960s over Park's efforts to run for a third term; in 1970–71 prior to the Yushin crackdown; in 1979–80 prior to and following Park's assassination; and again beginning in the mid-1980s.

These political challenges exerted an influence over economic policy, and gave rise to discernible policy cycles.[31] Following the political crisis and tightening of political controls in the early 1970s, Park Chung Hee sought to justify his Yushin constitution through increased social expenditures and the "big push" policies of the heavy industry plan. These policies were sustained through heavy borrowing, and by the end of the decade had contributed to serious inflationary pressures, growing income concentration, and deepening class conflict. These conditions help explain the political crisis of 1979–80 and the ascent of the Chun government. The new government sought to stabilize and liberalize the economy, but as we suggested in the previous chapter, these efforts contributed to the broader political pressures on the regime in the mid-1980s.

Whereas the Korean government leaned toward expansionary spending, financial overextension, and an aggressive industrial policy during the 1970s, Taiwan adopted a more cautious approach. With respect to macroeconomic policy, the increases in oil prices were passed on quickly to consumers, and the shocks managed through brief, but sharp, deflationary policies rather than external borrowing. Fiscal and monetary policy remained highly conservative, with the government running substantial surpluses; this was true even during the rapid political changes of the early 1980s. The success of these policies reduced the volatility of both inflation and growth in Taiwan when compared to Korea.

---

[31] See Stephan Haggard et al., *Macroeconomic Policy and Performance in Korea, 1970–1990* (Cambridge, Mass.: Harvard University Press, 1994), chaps. 1–4.

This conservatism was also visible in the country's industrial policy, which did not reflect the same pressing need to forge political relations with the private sector; for example, the government generally eschewed credit policy as an instrument of industrial development.[32] Though the government did pursue a selective industrial policy, it also moved more steadily toward the liberalization and deregulation of the domestic market in the 1980s.

THE MEXICAN SYSTEM: THE CRISIS OF THE 1980s

In Taiwan and the Communist countries, state and society were dominated by "vanguardist" parties formed prior to the seizure of governmental authority.[33] Mexico's dominant party, in contrast, was fashioned a decade after the bitter civil wars of 1911 to 1920. It was headed by a coalition of government officials, revolutionary generals, and local *caciques* seeking to contain political rivalries and consolidate state authority. Over time, the official party, now the PRI, evolved into an important pillar of presidential power and of corporatist control over working-class and peasant organizations. Nevertheless, governing elites have typically had to negotiate with both contending factions within the PRI and partially independent nonparty groups in the bureaucracy and civil society.

Unlike in Taiwan, this more loosely structured system was unable to contain distributive pressures that contributed to a severe macroeconomic and debt crisis at the beginning of the 1980s. Once the crisis hit, however, control of a dominant party allowed the government to respond with sustained fiscal adjustments and sweeping trade and other reforms that trans-

[32] Tun-jen Cheng, "Guarding the Commanding Heights: the State as Banker in Taiwan," in Stephan Haggard, Chung Lee, and Sylvia Maxfield, eds., *The Politics of Finance in Developing Countries* (Ithaca, N.Y.: Cornell University Press, 1993), pp. 55–92.

[33] See Melvin Croan, "Is Mexico the Future of East Europe: Institutional Adaptability and Political Change in Comparative Perspective," in Samuel Huntington and Clement Moore, eds., *Authoritarian Politics in Modern Societies: The Dynamics of Established One-Party Systems* (New York and London: Basic Books, 1970), pp. 451–83.

General discussions of the Mexican political system include: Wayne A. Cornelius, Judith Gentleman, and Peter H. Smith eds., *Mexico's Alternative Political Futures* (San Diego: University of California at San Diego, Center for U.S.–Mexican Relations, 1989); Daniel Cosío Villegas, *El sistema político mexicano* (Mexico City: Joaquín Mortiz, 1973); Pablo González Casanova, *Democracy in Mexico* (New York: Oxford University Press, 1977); Roger D. Hansen, *The Politics of Mexican Development* (Baltimore: Johns Hopkins University Press, 1971); José Luis Reyna and Richard Weinert, eds. *Authoritarianism in Mexico* (Philadelphia: Institute for the Study of Human Issues, 1977); Soledad Loaeza, *Clases medias y política in México* (Mexico City: El Colegio de México, 1988); and Ruth Berins Collier and David Collier, *Shaping the Political Arena* (Princeton, N.J.: Princeton University Press, 1991). pp. 407–20, and 574–608.

formed the structure of the economy. During the 1980s, only Chile instituted reforms with comparable consistency and comprehensiveness. In this section, we explore the political origins of the crisis; in the next, we examine the government's response to it.

An essential point of departure for this discussion is the political framework established during the era of so-called stabilizing development *(desarrollo establizador)* from the mid-1950s to the early 1970s. This was an unusually successful period of import-substituting industrialization, characterized both by high growth and comparatively low rates of inflation. Stabilizing development rested on institutional structures that linked the ruling party with three groups: organized labor, technocratic elites, and the private sector.

The labor movement was tied to the PRI through the corporatist organization of the party itself.[34] As interlocutors between the government elite and organized workers, official union leaders coopted into this framework retained considerable bargaining leverage compared to those in Taiwan or in communist systems. Ruling elites, however, controlled access to power and rewards within the labor movement, and could generally count on corporatist union representatives to collaborate in maintaining industrial peace and the political loyalty of the rank and file. As a result, Mexico witnessed neither the militant wage claims that characterized industrial relations in Argentina nor the ideological radicalism encouraged by Brazilian electoral rivalries in the late 1950s.

Large financial-industrial conglomerates and smaller import-substituting manufacturers gained both from the government's overall policy stance and from their ability to exploit particularistic links to the system. Business influence flowed at times through corporatist chambers, at times through informal and private negotiations with authorities; in either event, until the early 1970s, state-business relations were characterized by high levels of mutual accommodation and support.[35]

Finally, import-substituting industrialization in Mexico was carried out

---

[34] On labor and popular movements, see Ruth Berins Collier, *The Contradictory Alliance: State-Labor Relations and Regime Change* (Berkeley: Institute of International Studies, University of California at Berkeley, 1992); Barry Carr, ed., *The Mexican Left, the Popular Movements, and the Politics of Austerity,* Monograph Series, no. 18 (La Jolla, Calif.: Center for U.S.–Mexican Studies, University of California, 1986); Ilan Bizberg, *Estado y sindicalismo en México.* México: El Colegio de México, 1990); José Luis Reyna et al, eds. *Tres estudios sobre el movimiento obrero en México* (Mexico City: El Colegio de México, 1976); Raúl Trejo Delarbre, *Crónica del sindicalismo en México (1976–1988)* (México: Siglo XXI, 1990).

[35] See Sylvia Maxfield and Ricardo Anzaldúa, eds. *Government and Private Sector in Contemporary Mexico,* Monograph Series, no. 20 (San Diego, Calif.: Center for U.S.–Mexican Studies, 1987); Robert Shafer, *Mexican Business Organizations: History and Analysis* (Syracuse: Syracuse University Press, 1973); Roderic A. Camp, *Entrepreneurs and Politics*

within a framework of macroeconomic policy tightly controlled by conservative technocrats within the Central Bank and the Finance Ministry. With backing from Mexican presidents, technocrats within Mexico's financial bureaucracy acquired a position of influence that had no parallel in any of the other large countries of the region.[36] Throughout the stabilizing development period, they exercised virtually unchallenged authority over monetary and exchange-rate policy, and placed important limits on the struggle among rival groups for fiscal resources.

Challenges to these arrangements began to emerge in the late 1960s among factions of the political elite concerned about increasing income inequality, continuing rural poverty, and structural bottlenecks generated by rapid economic growth. An important turning point occurred in 1968, when the government brutally repressed massive student protests in Tlatlelolco Square in Mexico City. The event convinced many sectors of the political establishment that the system had entered a crisis of legitimacy that required extensive social and economic reforms. The policy responses under Presidents Luis Echeverría (1970–76) and José López Portillo (1976–82) effectively brought the old political-economic era to a close.

The initiatives launched in the 1970s covered a spectrum of economic and political issues. In response to growing concerns about rural violence, Echeverría began a controversial land-reform program and created a large distribution network for subsidized items of popular consumption. López Portillo increased spending on health and education, and implemented an electoral reform aimed at coopting small leftist parties.[37] Though less populist in style than Echeverría, López Portillo also nationalized the banking system in an effort to gain support during the last turbulent year of his term. Both presidents substantially increased public investment and the size of the public enterprise sector, and each tolerated substantial union militancy, particularly in the public sector.

These measures arguably helped to deflect potentially dangerous anti-system protests. Yet the costs included growing political polarization within

---

in Twentieth Century Mexico (New York/Oxford: Oxford University Press, 1970); Carlos Arriola, *Los empresarios y el Estado, 1970–1982* (Mexico City: UNAM/Miguel Angel Porrúa, 1988).

[36] Maxfield, *Governing Capital,* pp. 45–94. The Bank of Mexico, it should be noted, had been formed in 1925, prior to the formation of the dominant party itself, and sustained recruitment patterns and institutional orientations that remained separate from the party. Brazil lacked a central bank throughout the postwar period, while in Argentina, the independence of the central bank was destroyed under Perón.

[37] Kevin J. Middlebrook, "Political Change and Political Reform in an Authoritarian Regime: The Case of Mexico," in Guillermo A. O'Donnell, Philippe C. Schmitter, and Laurence Whitehead, eds., *Transitions from Authoritarian Rule in Southern Europe and Latin America* (Baltimore: The Johns Hopkins University Press, 1986), pt. 2, *Latin America,* pp. 123–27.

the system, increasing macroeconomic imbalances, and ultimately the crisis of the early 1980s. Much of the political protest came from the right. The main beneficiaries of electoral reforms proved to be the conservative National Action Party (PAN), rather than the left. With increased financial backing from business and support from middle-class groups and the Catholic Church, the PAN began to acquire a significant presence as a regional opposition in the northern states. Business elites constituted an even more powerful pole of opposition. Though they profited from public contracts and subsidies, they were frightened by the populist initiatives of the Echeverría administration and by the bank nationalization under López Portillo. In contrast to the stabilizing development period, relations between the state and private-sector organizations became increasingly politicized and confrontational.[38]

Caught between its reformist objectives and the reaction of conservative forces, the Mexican government found it increasingly difficult to maintain macroeconomic equilibrium. Early in the 1970s, business groups successfully vetoed proposed tax reforms, and Echeverría relied heavily on external borrowing and the inflation tax to reconcile growing political conflicts. This road, however, led directly to high deficits, inflation, and a balance-of-payments crisis in 1975–76. The onset of the oil boom from 1978 to 1981 appeared to offer a respite from these problems. But the López Portillo administration used the oil windfall to continue the expansionist policies of his predecessor: consumer and producer subsidies and state enterprise losses grew dramatically in the late 1970s and early 1980s, contributing to a recurrence of large fiscal deficits, a badly overvalued peso, and a run-up in short-term debt. By the end of the decade, the economy was highly vulnerable to the external shocks that hit all of the developing world: the sharp rise in interest rates, the collapse of commercial lending, and for oil producers, the sharp fall in oil prices.[39]

---

[38] Rogelio Hernández Rodríguez, *Empresarios, banca y Estado: El conflicto durante el gobierno de José López Portillo, 1976–1982* (México: FLACSO/Miguel Angel Porrúa, 1988); Blanca Heredia, "Politics, Profits, and Size: The Political Transformation of Mexican Business," in Douglas Chalmers, Atilio Borón, and María do Carmo Campello de Souza, eds., *The Right and Democracy in Latin America* (New York: Praeger. 1992), pp. 277–302.

[39] The literature on the origins and features of the 1982 crisis is voluminous. See Edward Buffie and Allen Sangines Krause, "Mexico 1959–86: From Stabilizing Development to the Debt Crisis," in Jeffrey D. Sachs, ed., *Developing Country Debt and the World Economy* (Chicago: University of Chicago Press, 1989), pp. 141–68; Jaime Ros, "Mexico: From the Oil Boom to the Debt Crisis. An Analysis of Policy Responses to External Shocks, 1978–1985," in Rosemary Thorp and Laurence Whitehead, eds., *The Latin American Debt Crisis* (London: Macmillan, 1987), pp. 68–116; and Carlos Bazdresch and Santiago Levy, "Populism and Economic Policy in Mexico, 1970–1982," in Rudiger Dornbusch and Sebastian Edwards, eds., *The Macroeconomics of Populism in Latin America* (Chicago and London: University of Chicago Press, 1991), pp. 223–63.

Given our emphasis on the institutional capabilities of dominant party regimes, it is important to explain why the Mexican system failed so badly. Conservative critics of the regime attribute the country's economic difficulties to the decline in the influence of the financial bureaucracy, and the unchecked "populism" and corruption of the Echeverría and López Portillo administrations.[40] Yet while it is clear that the idiosyncratic behavior of these two presidents did contribute to economic problems, this conservative interpretation underestimates the role played by broader distributive conflicts in the Mexican political system, conflicts that a relatively inclusive and pluralistic dominant party could not easily contain.

One powerful constraint came from the business elite itself; its successful resistance to tax reform coupled with its strong appetite for government contracts and subsidies constituted a major source of fiscal difficulty.[41] Also important were the claims of corporate groups within the party apparatus, particularly those within the official union movement. Despite the fact that such groups were subject to substantial political and institutional controls, they were also an important component of the governing coalition, and the political cost of suppressing public-sector wage demands was therefore high. Finally, the legitimacy of the PRI and of the entire Mexican political system rested on the ruling party's dominance of the electoral arena. Though small parties did not threaten to actually unseat the PRI, the erosion of electoral margins was viewed as a judgment on the ruling party's performance. Patronage constituted an important weapon in countering these electoral challenges, although with obvious economic consequences.

As in the cases discussed in chapter 6, the onset of severe economic crisis resulted not only in a political realignment within the Mexican political system, but in important institutional changes as well. However, the response to the crisis is noteworthy not only because adjustments were unusually deep and comprehensive, but also because they were implemented without systematic coercion. These adjustments can be traced directly to the capabilities of the dominant-party system.

THE POLITICS OF ECONOMIC REFORM IN MEXICO, 1982–1988

Three features of the regime were particularly important in facilitating economic adjustment.[42] The first was the flexibility associated with the centralization of power in the presidency. The man named as the PRI's

---

[40] See Heredia's discussion of the views of business elites and conservatives, "Politics, Profits, and Size."

[41] Leopoldo Solís, *Economic Policy Reform in Mexico: A Case Study for Developing Countries* (New York: Pergamon Press, 1981), pp. 67–78.

[42] The following draws on Robert R. Kaufman, *The Politics of Debt in Argentina, Brazil*

presidential nominee in November 1981 was Miguel De la Madrid, an official with close links to the financial bureaucracy. De la Madrid was more inclined than his predecessors toward market-oriented reform, but at the time of his nomination he was also viewed as a moderate who would be cautious in changing existing policies. When the new president assumed office in the following year, however, the country was in crisis and he used his authority to move far beyond initial expectations.

The core of technocrats within the Bank of Mexico and the Finance Ministry was a second crucial feature of the system. Though the influence of these agencies declined during the 1970s, they continued to provide career opportunities for economists committed to stabilization and the market. De la Madrid delegated substantial decision-making authority to such technocrats and exploited his appointment powers to remove the leading advocates of expansionist and interventionist policies from virtually all major positions of influence at the Cabinet and sub-Cabinet level.[43] The new elite was by no means fully united around a detailed strategy of reform, and there was considerable debate and improvisation over the next six years. However, the technocrats did share a common perspective about the urgency of fiscal and monetary retrenchment and became the principal agents in the initiation of the broader structural adjustments that followed.

Corporatist control over the union movement was the third important source of leverage available to the political elite. De la Madrid substantially reduced the slack granted the official labor organizations during the 1970s, and held firm against efforts to test the government's resolve with regard to wage restraint and plant closings. Though official union leaders did become increasingly critical of the government's adjustment initiatives, they could not engage in sustained confrontations without jeopardizing their access to the political and economic resources they needed to maintain their own positions of authority.[44] For the most part, union officials cooperated with the government in keeping their members in line.

This cooperation, it should be noted, occurred in an economic context that posed serious long-term challenges to the role of the PRI as the dominant party. Corporatist leaders provided important links to unionized

---

and Mexico (Berkeley: Institute of International Studies, University of California, 1988), pp. 78–104.

[43] Rogelio Hernández Rodríguez, "Los hombres del presidente De la Madrid." *Foro Internacional* 28 (1988), pp. 5–38. The strongest reservations came from the Ministry of Commerce and Industry (SECOFI), which had established close links to import-substituting industrialists. Even SECOFI, however, had been purged of its most radical protectionists in the first year of De la Madrid's term, and by the end of the 1980s, its cautious position on trade reform had been eclipsed by the more drastic approaches of its rivals in the financial bureaucracy.

[44] Collier, *The Contradictory Alliance,* pp. 80, 108; Kevin J. Middlebrook, "The Sounds of Silence: Organized Labor's Response to the Economic Crisis in Mexico," *Journal of Latin American Studies* 21 (1989): 195–220.

workers and peasant organizations, but they had little capacity to mobilize electoral support among the expanding number of urban informal workers who were not members of such groups. The economic crisis also deepened divisions within the party over the reform program. Ultimately, dissidents grouped around Cuauhtémoc Cárdenas defected and launched a serious opposition challenge in the 1988 presidential race, raising the salience of questions of political reform during the presidential term of Carlos Salinas (1989–95). Under De la Madrid, however, control of the ruling party provided a secure organizational foundation for the reform effort.

The reforms initiated under De la Madrid advanced through trial and error. Initial steps from 1982 to 1985 focused primarily on fiscal adjustment and rescheduling of the external debt. The stabilization measures were among the toughest in the region; in just two years, the ratio of the fiscal deficit to GDP dropped by almost half. Very tight conditions attached to the initial debt rescheduling provided little breathing space for the government, however, and failed to reopen access to private credit markets. After two years of severe fiscal austerity, inflation still remained at over 60 percent a year, and there were only limited signs of recovery (see Table 8.1).

In 1985, the situation deteriorated seriously. The collapse of petroleum prices and a devastating earthquake placed new pressure on fiscal resources and triggered a sharp recession. Even prior to these shocks, increasing deficits had strained relations with the IMF; in September the fund suspended disbursements on an Extended Fund Facility (EFF) loan, triggering a new crisis with external creditors. The Mexican government argued, with considerable plausibility, that mounting fiscal deficits were attributable not to flagging adjustment efforts but to factors beyond its control, most notably, the inflation premium paid on the servicing of the domestic public debt and the decline in petroleum revenues. For the next nine months, attempts to renegotiate an EFF agreement stalemated.

The deteriorating situation, however, produced a new round of reforms. The U.S. government provided important assistance on the international front. Increasingly concerned about the risks of financial and political turmoil in its southern neighbor, the Reagan administration pressed the IMF to reach a new agreement in June 1986. Private financing followed, and by the end of 1987, the build-up of reserves had created the basis for new stabilization and structural reform efforts that were to fundamentally transform the Mexican economy. The Pact for Economic Solidarity (PSE), as the new package was called, featured an intensified fiscal adjustment, a fixed exchange rate, and an incomes policy negotiated with business groups and the official union movement.[45] Trade reforms received new emphasis.

[45] On the PSE, see: Robert R. Kaufman, Carlos Bazdresch, and Blanca Heredia, "The Politics of Economic Reform in Mexico: The Solidarity Pact of 1987–1988," in Stephan Haggard and Steven B. Webb, eds, *Voting for Reform: Democracy, Political Liberalization, and Economic Adjustment* (Oxford: Oxford University Press, 1994), pp. 360–410; Nora

TABLE 8.1
Economic Developments in Mexico, 1980–1992

	1980	*1981*	*1982*	*1983*	*1984*	*1985*	*1986*
GDP Growth	8.4	8.8	−0.6	−4.2	3.7	2.7	−3.9
Inflation	26.4	27.9	58.9	101.8	65.5	57.7	86.2
Fiscal Deficit/GDP	−3.1	−6.7	−15.4	−8.0	−7.3	−8.7	−13.2
Current Account/GDP	−5.5	−6.4	−3.6	3.6	2.3	0.3	−1.4
Investment/GDP	27.2	27.4	22.9	20.8	19.9	21.2	18.3
Real Wage	−4.3	1.2	0.9	−22.7	−6.6	1.6	−5.6

	1987	*1988*	*1989*	*1990*	*1991*	*1992*
GDP Growth	1.8	1.2	3.4	4.5	3.6	2.8
Inflation	131.8	114.2	20.0	26.7	22.7	15.5
Fiscal Deficit/GDP	−13.6	−10.2	−5.4	−4.0	−0.4	1.6
Current Account/GDP	2.6	2.3	0.3	−1.4	2.6	−1.4
Investment/GDP	19.3	19.9	21.2	18.3	19.3	22.5
Real Wage	0.7	−6.6	1.6	−5.6	0.7	na

Sources: Economic Commission on Latin America, *Economic Survey of Latin America and The Caribbean,* various issues; World Bank, *Trends in Developing Economies,* various issues; International Monetary Fund, *International Financial Statistics Yearbook,* various issues; World Bank, *World Tables,* various issues.

Note: For definitions of the first five variables, see Table 2.1. Real Wage: Average manufacturing wages.

Between 1985 and 1987, the government had already reduced quantitative restrictions, entered the GATT, and established a five-year schedule of tariff reductions. In 1988, trade liberalization accelerated: quantitative restrictions were virtually eliminated and the average tariff level fell dramatically.

The PSE marked a major turning point in the larger process of adjustment, and brought the De la Madrid administration to a relatively successful conclusion. The inflation that had plagued the Mexican economy for most of the 1980s finally yielded to the combined effects of fiscal adjustment and incomes policy, dropping from 160 percent in 1987 to under 30 percent in 1988 and 1989. The trade reforms reinforced the credibility of these efforts, paving the way to the negotiation of the Brady Plan agreement in 1989, the NAFTA, and a major change in economic expectations.

As we have argued throughout this section, the implementation of these reforms occurred within institutional structures that not only enhanced the power of the executive, but increased the possibility of securing the cooperation of affected groups. This feature of the dominant-party system was particularly visible in the PSE. First, the control of a dominant party

Lustig, "El pacto de solidaridad económica," in G. Rozenwurcel, ed., *Elecciones y política económica* (Buenos Aires: CEDES, Ed. Tesis, 1991); Leo Zuckerman Behar, "Inflation Stabilization in Mexico: The Economic Solidarity Pact: December 1987–December 1988." (M.Sc. thesis, University of Oxford, 1990).

reduced the risks of initiating a stabilization program in an election year. Once Salinas was designated as the PRI's presidential nominee, he was assured of election and of a six-year tenure in office; as a result, the government and its economic team did not face the short-term risks that occurs in more competitive electoral systems or even in military authoritarian settings.

The advantages of a dominant-party structure were also visible in the tripartite bargaining over incomes policy, in which labor organizations continued to accept the lead of government officials. Through all of 1988, official labor unions acquiesced to a freeze in nominal wages, in spite of a sharp deterioration in real public-sector and minimum wage levels. The government's capacity to "deliver" labor and to meet its commitments on fiscal adjustment, in turn, played a crucial role in securing the cooperation of business with respect to price controls and its more grudging acquiescence to the acceleration of trade reform.

At a more fundamental level, the negotiation of the PSE marked the end of a long period of adversarial relations between the private sector and the state that had begun in the 1970s. From the onset of his term, De la Madrid sought to effect a rapprochement, but business elites continued to criticize the government and to provide support for the opposition PAN. The agreements reached through the PSE, however, reaffirmed the government's commitment to reform and provided an important incentive for business elites to throw their weight behind the plan as well. By the start of the Salinas administration, representatives of the major business groups had ceased to campaign against the concentration of power within the political system and had again begun to rely on negotiations conducted away from the public eye. Although the policy context had changed dramatically, the informal collaborative links between business elites and the state evoked comparisons with the stabilizing development period of the 1950s and 1960s.

The reforms outlined above provided the basis for an economic upswing in the early 1990s. De la Madrid's successor, Carlos Salinas, had been a member of the reform team as minister of budget and planning; as president, he moved quickly to deepen the adjustment process. The government privatized virtually all major state enterprises outside the oil sector, including the banks nationalized in 1982.[46] Agreements reached under the terms of the Brady Plan reduced the Mexican external debt by about one-third, and negotiations over the NAFTA promised to lock in De la Madrid's trade liberalization efforts. These measures further strengthened the government's links to the financial elite, which profited substantially from the

---

[46] PEMEX, the "untouchable" public petroleum giant, was spared from the auction bloc, but the government also relaxed restrictions on subcontracting new operations to foreign companies.

privatizations and the related stock-market boom. The economy was further buoyed by the repatriation of flight capital and substantial new foreign investment entering in anticipation of the NAFTA agreement. From 1989 through 1991, Mexico's GDP expanded at an annual rate of 3.8 percent and inflation dropped almost to single digits.[47] As we shall see below, these developments also had an important impact on efforts to institute political reforms.

POLITICAL REFORM IN DOMINANT-PARTY SYSTEMS

In confronting pressures for political reform, rulers in dominant-party systems have capabilities and incentives that differ in several ways from those available to military leaders. On the one hand, dominant parties potentially face a greater risk than militaries in the transition to a fully competitive electoral system. Unlike military establishments, the heads of dominant parties cannot claim a permanent role within the state apparatus that is independent of their privileged links to political office. Risking incumbency implies fundamental changes in party organization, and might well threaten its disintegration. On the other hand, party leaders have advantages that military leaders do not; they control an apparatus that facilitates the cooptation of support groups and the management of elections. These capabilities allow for more extended and incremental processes of political change, and open the prospect that the dominant party might maintain power through democratic means.

The willingness to run the risk of political opening will be a function of how party leaders—and contending factions within the party—evaluate their electoral and career chances under more competitive rules. In part, this will depend on noneconomic factors. In Taiwan ethnicity and relations with the mainland were important questions. In Mexico the legacy of "the Revolution" remained a key issue of contestation. However, economic conditions can play an important role in elite calculations. As we saw with reference to the non-crisis cases, successful economic performance creates an opportunity to bid for general electoral support and to control the pace and design of institutional reform. Weak performance, by contrast, increases the risks associated with political opening.

The underlying political capabilities of dominant-party systems are visible in the fact that both Taiwan and Mexico experienced processes of political liberalization that stretched over decades without an unambiguous transition to fully competitive and open electoral politics. However, the comparison between the two countries also provides evidence of the way economic factors influence the pace and nature of political reform. Though

[47] *Latin American Weekly Report,* 12 November 1992, 92–44, p. 4.

the KMT was initially far more centralized than the PRI, and the system more overtly authoritarian, sustained economic growth provided the context for a quite dramatic political liberalization in the late 1980s and early 1990s. In Mexico, the recovery from crisis also provided opportunities for the PRI. But the costs of adjustment were more profound and the recovery more fragile. As a result, the party relied to a greater extent on its monopoly advantages and coercive controls.

Democratization in Taiwan

Taiwan seems a paradigmatic case for the modernization approach to democratization.[48] Three decades of rapid economic growth and extensive social change contributed to the gradual emergence of a robust civil society and increasing demands for political liberalization. Initially, the government responded to these pressures through a gradual "Taiwanization" of the KMT and the civil service and an incremental expansion of the scope of electoral politics. In 1986, a second, more dramatic phase of political change began with the formation of a political opposition, to which the government responded through a series of constitutional reforms.

A closer examination reveals that this "bottom-up" approach to explaining liberalization in Taiwan has significant limitations, and must be supplemented with an understanding of the unique institutional capabilities of the KMT and the short-term economic circumstances against which political challenges unfolded. The KMT crushed an incipient opposition in the 1960s, but tolerated opposition study groups and nationalist demonstrations in 1971 over a territorial dispute with Japan (the Tiao Yu Ti islands) and over the Republic of China (ROC)'s expulsion from the United Nations. In 1972, Chiang Kai-shek's son, Chiang Ching-kuo, ascended to the position of premier and extended the process of Taiwanization of party and state that had previously been limited largely to the local level. These reforms aimed at widening the regime's base of support, and were motivated by concern over emerging signs of domestic dissent as well as fears that rapprochement between the United States and the People's Republic of China (PRC) would leave the ROC government—and thus the KMT—diplomatically and politically isolated.

By coopting Taiwanese, Chiang Ching-kuo sought to create a cadre of

---

[48] See, for example, Hung-mao Tien, *The Great Transformation: Political and Social Change in the Republic of China* (Stanford, Calif.: Hoover Institute Press, 1989).

For overviews of the process, see Tun-jen Cheng, "Democratizing the Quasi-Leninist Regime in Taiwan," *World Politics* 42 (1989): 471–99; Cheng and Haggard, *Political Change in Taiwan;* and particularly Yun-han Chu's *Crafting Democracy in Taiwan* (Taipei: Institute for National Policy Research, 1992).

younger leaders with a stake in the party's image and performance. Main-landers continued to dominate the upper ranks of the party during the 1970s, but by the early 1980s, this had begun to change as Taiwanese who had risen through administrative and party ranks assumed cabinet posts and top positions within the KMT. In 1985, Chiang Ching-kuo announced that his succession would follow constitutional rules, implying that his hand-picked Taiwanese vice president, Lee Teng-hui, would ascend to the presi-dency. This occurred smoothly in 1988, and in that same year, Taiwanese achieved a majority in the Central Standing Committee for the first time. In 1993, Lee appointed a Taiwanese premier—the country's first—and was overwhelmingly endorsed as the head of the party in the Fourteenth Party Congress. By the early 1990s, the higher military ranks remained the last bastion of unambiguous mainlander dominance in the state apparatus, and that dominance will undoubtedly erode as lower-ranking Taiwanese officers are promoted.

Along with changes in recruitment policies, Chiang also began to rely more extensively on elections as a means of legitimation. Provincial, county, city, and township elections had been a regular feature of Taiwan's politics since 1950, but these contests necessarily centered on local issues and factional politics. Individual independents were sometimes allowed to become candidates, but the process was closely controlled by the KMT.[49] During the 1970s, however, the electoral process provided opportunities for a significant expansion of political contestation. In the provincial and local elections of 1977, individual dissidents for the first time challenged the government by forming a loosely organized opposition "camp," joining with several prominent liberals who bolted from the KMT. To the embar-rassment of the ruling party, the new movement succeeded in winning 35 percent of the seats in the provincial legislature and established itself as an important presence on the political scene.

The next decade was marked by growing divisions within both the op-position and the ruling elite. The split within the opposition between radicals and moderates grew particularly intense after the bloody Kaohsi-ung riots of 1979. Given that economic growth was generally robust and the distribution of income relatively equal, the issues turned less on eco-nomic performance than on questions of ethnicity, foreign policy and tactics. Radicals were willing to exploit ethnic resentment, and in the early 1990s were even to press the touchy issue of Taiwan's independence. They also pushed for more direct confrontations, including in the streets, with

[49] "Supplemental" elections were held for the National Assembly in 1969, 1972, 1980 and 1986, and for the Legislative Yuan in 1969, 1972, 1975, 1980, 1983, 1986, and 1989, providing additional opportunities for recruitment. These two bodies had been elected in 1948, but on the basis of the fiction that the KMT ruled all of China; mainland districts had representatives, and as these representatives became inactive or died, the two bodies atrophied.

the regime over the pace of political reform. Though the moderates also sought support from ethnic Taiwanese, they sought to work within the system to negotiate gradual political reform. They were, however, willing to challenge the ban on the formation of electoral groups; after the 1983 legislative elections, they moved to form a proto-party, the Association of Public Policy Studies, in defiance of KMT injunctions against doing so.

The apparent success of the opposition put moderates within the ruling elite on the defensive, particularly following the Kaohsiung riots. By 1983, however, the removal of General Wang Sheng and the scandal surrounding the involvement of the intelligence apparatus in the execution of dissident author Henry Liu in the United States signalled a weakening of the hard right. Despite several major scandals and slowed economic performance, the KMT managed to do well in provincial and local elections held in November 1985.[50] KMT victories demonstrated that the party was capable of winning substantial electoral support even under relatively inauspicious circumstances.[51]

In the year following these victories, three key decisions taken by Chiang marked major turning points in the transition process. The first was his announcement that the succession would follow constitutional provisions; this anointed Lee Teng-hui as Chiang's successor, and ruled out a dynastic bid from within the Chiang family and the destabilizing succession conflicts such a bid would necessarily entail. The second major step came in June 1986, when Chiang announced the formation of blue-ribbon commission to study political reform. Virtually all issues were placed on the table: a restructuring of the National Assembly; local autonomy; martial law; civic organizations; social reform; and further reforms of the party itself.

The third most important breakthrough came in September and October. Indirect negotiations had been taking place between the KMT and opposition over the transformation of the Association of Public Policy Studies from a research to a campaign organization. When these negotiations broke down, a group of opposition leaders announced the formation of the Democratic Progressive Party (DPP). The government chose not to suppress the new illegal entity. Within months, the government lifted martial law. The ban on political associations, including parties, also fell and the DPP was retroactively legalized.

It is beyond our scope to provide a history of the dizzying changes that followed, but it is clear that they involved major transformations in the Taiwanese political system. By the late 1980s, press freedom was extensive

---

[50] The two cases were the murder of Henry Liu in California, in which the military apparatus appeared to have participated and the Cathay Group Scandal, which showed weaknesses in the government's regulation of the financial sector.

[51] The KMT secured nearly 70 percent of the popular vote in the provincial assembly elections, and 62 percent of the votes—and 81 percent of the seats—in the elections for country magistrates and mayors.

and the DPP had been acknowledged as a legitimate opposition. In 1991, Lee suspended the last vestiges of martial law powers and returned the country to normal constitutional rule. In 1991, the Supreme Judicial Court, clearly with the nod of the party, ordered the complete renewal of all three legislative branches: the Legislative and Control Yuans and the National Assembly itself, all of which were dominated by aging members elected in 1947 and representing districts on the mainland, despite so-called supplemental elections.[52] Internal splits within the KMT delayed a resolution of the central issue of whether the president would be elected directly or indirectly, but that issue was resolved in mid-1994 as well, and the opening appeared both extensive and irreversible.

In their management of this controlled process of opening, KMT elites relied both on the privileged institutional position of the dominant party and on its capacity to mobilize support. Once the KMT committed itself to some form of political change, its overwhelming dominance and the absence of significant mass protest permitted the party to make piecemeal concessions and to tie the transition to already scheduled events, such as regular elections. Both the coercive power of the government and its commitment to gradual reform also allowed the KMT to set limits to the range of tolerable debate. Initial acceptance of the DPP as a legal party was contingent on the opposition accepting three conditions: no use of violence; no advocacy of separatism, and no support of communism.

The government also enjoyed a number of more specific institutional advantages. The KMT's large majority in the National Assembly, which has responsibility for constitutional reform, permitted it to dominate the process of changing the institutions of government. The party was able to write the electoral rules as it saw fit, to further expand the powers of the National Assembly over constitutional revision, and to increase the appointment powers of the executive over other branches of government.

The KMT was also well positioned with respect to the electoral arena. Control over the state-owned mass media was a plus, but so was party organization. Extensive party organization provided advantages in playing the complicated political game associated with the country's unusual electoral laws, the single-vote multimember constituency, also known as the single nontransferable vote (SNTV) system. Under this system, parties must be able to allocate or spread votes so that they are not wasted on the top candidates. Despite some decline in the capacity to discipline its own ranks, only the KMT has the organizational capability to do this.[53]

As in the non-crisis cases discussed in the previous chapter, strong

---

[52] See above, n. 49.

[53] The role of the SNTV in the KMT's electoral dominance was first noted by Edwin Winckler, "Institutionalization and Participation on Taiwan: from Hard to Soft Authoritarianism," *China Quarterly* 99 (1994): 481–99. See also Andrew J. Nathan, "The Legislative Yuan Elections in Taiwan," *Asian Survey* 33 (1993): 432.

economic growth and the regime's success in managing the economy buttressed these organizational advantages (see Table 8.2). During the late 1980s, the government did face some difficult policy problems, including an appreciating exchange rate and pressure from the United States to liberalize trade. Yet policy adjustments were undertaken in the context of a strong economy, robust growth in consumption, and only moderate inflation. Moreover, in contrast to virtually all of the other countries discussed in this volume, the government enjoyed substantial current-account surpluses.[54] These surpluses and the build-up of foreign reserves did pose complications for the management of monetary policy and inflation, but the political implications of adjusting to surpluses are quite different than those of adjusting to balance-of-payments deficits. For example, the government came under growing pressure to *increase* government spending, which had the advantage of providing the government with numerous political goods to dispense. Of course, such policies ran few risks only because of the government's continuing ability to control both fiscal and monetary policy; and when it became apparent that the goals of the six-year plan were too ambitious, the government moved quickly to scale it back.

As in the non-crisis cases, good economic conditions also had an important influence on the alignment of political forces. As the transition unfolded, it became clear that the interests of the KMT and the private sector converged at a number of points. To remain a viable electoral force, the KMT needed both direct funding and financially viable Taiwanese candidates. To secure these objectives, the party's identification with and links to the private sector became more open at both the national and the subnational levels, with corresponding charges of corruption and "money politics" from the opposition.[55] Business sought to free itself from burdensome regulations, and particularly from restraints on the range of its investment activities and restrictive land use policies, while also maintaining the advantages that flowed from the stability and competence of KMT rule. In a perceptive characterization, Yun-han Chu concludes that the KMT and the private sector "both see the need for the involvement of an active state in the process of industrial upgrading, both put economic growth before environmental considerations, both favor a slow growth in social welfare spending, and both support a state-orchestrated exclusion of organized labor from the economic policy-making."[56] However, the KMT's popularity with respect to economic policy is not limited to the private sector; a detailed analysis of public opinion at the time of the 1992 legis-

[54] Only Korea experienced similar current-account surpluses, but only briefly in the mid-1980s; in Taiwan, such surpluses were virtually chronic since the early 1970s.

[55] See for example, *Far Eastern Economic Review,* November 12, 1992, pp. 20–21.

[56] Yun-han Chu, "The Realignment of State-Business Relations and Regime Transition in Taiwan," p. 136.

TABLE 8.2

Economic Developments in Taiwan, 1980–1992

	1980	1981	1982	1983	1984	1985	1986
GDP Growth	7.3	6.2	3.6	8.4	10.6	5.0	11.6
Inflation	19.0	16.3	3.0	1.4	0.0	−0.2	0.7
Fiscal Surplus/GDP	4.8	0.3	−0.2	0.1	0.6	0.5	0.1
Current Account/GNP	2.2	1.1	4.6	8.4	11.7	14.5	21.1
Investment/GDP	33.8	30.0	25.2	23.4	21.9	18.7	17.1
Real Income	2.8	2.5	2.7	7.4	10.4	4.1	15.9

	1987	1988	1989	1990	1991	1992	
GDP Growth	12.3	7.3	7.6	4.9	7.2	6.6	
Inflation	0.5	1.3	4.4	4.1	3.6	4.5	
Fiscal Surplus/GDP	1.4	2.9	3.7	0.9	0.5	0.3	
Current Account/GNP	17.4	8.1	7.6	6.7	6.7	3.9	
Investment/GNP	20.1	22.8	22.3	21.9	22.2	23.9	
Real Income	12.2	10.9	14.6	13.5	11.0	5.0	

Sources: Republic of China, Council for Economic Planning and Development, *Taiwan Statistical Data Book 1993* (Taipei: CEPD, 1993); Central Bank of China, *Financial Statistics Monthly* (Taipei: Central Bank of China), various issues; Executive Yuan, *Quarterly National Economic Trends: Taiwan Area, Republic of China* (Taipei: Executive Yuan), various issues; Republic of China, Executive Yuan, *Statistical Yearbook of the Republic of China 1993* (Taipei: Executive Yuan, 1993).

Note: For definitions of the first five variables, see Table 2.1.

lative elections also shows substantial majorities of respondents scoring the KMT as more pro-growth and pro-development than the opposition.[57]

The KMT's position on highly charged foreign policy issues also played well with the electorate. In 1991, the DPP Party Congress called for a plebiscite on the previously forbidden question of the establishment of a Republic of Taiwan. This position was at least one factor in the opposition's resounding defeat in the important National Assembly elections of December. At the same time, the KMT gradually distanced itself from the hawks on the party's right who emphasized the utopian theme of reunification and moved toward a position quite close to that of the moderate opposition: acceptance of two separate sovereign entitites, each with jurisdiction in its own territory.

Electoral data show an unmistakable erosion of voter support for the KMT during the period of political liberalization that begins in the late

[57] Emerson Niou and John Fuh-sheng Hsieh, "Issue Voting in the Republic of Taiwan's 1992 Legislative Election," Duke University Program in Political Economy, Working Papers in International Political Economy no. 183, December 3, 1993, pp. 10–11.

1970s (Table 8.3). However, viewed comparatively, the most striking finding to emerge from Table 8.3 is the gradualness of that erosion and the continuing power and viability of the KMT as an electoral machine. Following setbacks in the December 1992 Legislative Yuan elections, the party showed its continued dominance in the local elections of December 1993. At the more important national level, the party is forging a center-right coalition around a combination of particularistic goods, the perceived advantages of stability, and the economic and foreign policy status quo.[58]

By the mid-1990s, the key question was less whether the KMT could compete effectively for votes in a more open political system, than whether it could resolve growing internal disputes associated with expanding pluralism and the peculiarities of the electoral system. Internal party conflicts have centered primarily on the growing disaffection of the "non-mainstream," that is, the mainlander anti-Lee faction. These factional disputes found reflection in sharp internal conflicts at party congresses in 1988 and 1993, and within the government in a debate in 1991 over the respective powers of the president and the premier in a mixed system.[59] In late 1993, portions of the non-mainstream faction broke away to form the New Party, an undeniable loss to the KMT. Yet the party has also seen increasing factionalism of a less ideological sort, as races attract a larger number of candidates than the party can expect to accommodate while pursuing a rational electoral strategy.

This fracturing of the KMT constitutes one of the most substantial challenges to the party, and could have implications for its strongest card, the management of the economy. Despite the continued strong performance of the economy, increases in public spending and charges of corruption in the conduct of economic policy have accompanied the liberalization of politics. But these political and economic developments do not necessarily diminish the party's chances of operating effectively on the electoral scene. By splitting the opposition, the KMT could gain as the dominant centrist force, a possibility that also exists for the PRI in Mexico. Meanwhile, factions could become institutionalized within the party as with the Liberal Democratic Party in Japan.

By mid-1994, certain important elements in the transition toward a fully

[58] The KMT's positive image with respect to stability is a particularly strong finding, ibid. See also Yun-han Chu, "The Process of Democratic Consolidation in Taiwan: Social Cleavage, Electoral Competition and the Emerging Party System," paper prepared for the Sixteenth International Political Science Association World Congress, Berlin, August 21–25, 1994.

[59] Formally, the system is a premier-presidential one in which the president is elected indirectly by the National Assembly, and then appoints a premier who is accountable to the legislature. Formally, the powers of the president—beyond the appointment of the premier—are limited, while the premier runs the government, but is accountable to the legislature. In practice, the country functioned as a presidential system under the Chiangs, in part through the president's creation of a national security bureau that functioned like an inner cabinet and took all crucial policy decisions not made by the president himself.

TABLE 8.3

Kuomintang Share of Votes and Seats in Elections to Legislative Bodies, Taiwan,
1977–1993 (Percentage)

	Offices Contested	Popular Vote	Seats
1977	Provincial Assembly	64.1	72.7
1980	National Assembly, Supplementary	66.4	80.3
	Legislative Yuan, Supplementary	72.1	80.0
1981	Provincial Assembly	70.3	76.6
1983	Legislative Yuan, Supplementary	70.7	80.2
1985	Provincial Assembly	69.8	76.6
1986	National Assembly, Supplementary	68.3	81.0
	Legislative Yuan, Supplementary	69.9	80.8
1989	Legislative Yuan, Supplementary	60.1	71.3
	Provincial Assembly	62.1	70.1
1991	National Assembly	71.2	78.1
1992	Legislative Yuan	53.0[a]	59.6

Sources: Through 1990, Fei-Lung Lui, "The Electoral System and Voting Behavior in Taiwan,"
in Tun-jen Cheng and Stephan Haggard, eds., *Political Change in Taiwan* (Boulder: Lynne Rienner,
1992), pp. 168–172; Jürgen Domes, "Taiwan in 1991: Searching for Political Consensus," *Asian
Survey* 32 (1992): 49; Jürgen Domes, "Taiwan in 1992: On the Verge of Democracy," *Asian Survey*
33 (1993): 60.

[a]Total for nominated KMT candidates. If KMT candidates who ran without party support are
included, the popular vote total increases to 60.5 and the share of seats to 64.0.

competitive system in Taiwan remained incomplete. Though the presidential election of 1996 will provide a test of how open the system is, a KMT
victory would still raise doubts about whether a full transition had occurred.
Yet regardless of the outcome of that election, the capacity of the KMT to
dictate the pace and scope of institutional change and to effectively limit
the opposition's room for maneuver has been clear. This in turn can be
attributed to the two factors we have emphasized: the advantages of a
dominant-party structure and the capacity to manage the economy efficiently.

Political Reform in Mexico, 1988–1994

As in Taiwan, long-term economic development and the expansion of
middle-class demands for participation constituted a central challenge to
the political dominance of the PRI in Mexico;[60] the growth of the PAN as

[60] This section draws upon Leopoldo Gomez and John Bailey, "La Transicíon política y
los dilemas del PRI," *Foro Internacional* 31 (1990): 57–87; Collier, *The Contradictory
Alliance;* Miguel Angel Centeno and Deborah A. Kaple, "Salinastroika or Gorbymania? A
Comparative Perspective on Two Transitions," unpublished ms. Princeton University, n.d.;

a significant regional opposition during the late 1970s and 1980s reflected such challenges. In addition, however, Mexico's highly unequal distribution of income and the prolonged economic stagnation of the 1980s left the PRI more exposed than the KMT to the distributive appeals of populist oppositions. Such an opposition materialized during the 1988 presidential campaign, led by Cuauhtémoc Cárdenas, who made enough of an electoral showing to call into question the probity of Salinas's victory.

During the De la Madrid period, the ruling elite focused primarily on the management of the economic crisis. The government devoted relatively little attention to the question of political reform and relied heavily on traditional corporatist structures to manage relations with labor and business groups. The outcome of the presidential campaign was shocking, however, because it highlighted a deterioration in the capacity of the PRI to legitimate its control of the presidency with credible electoral victories. At the same time, reliance on fraud and force was becoming increasingly costly, particularly given the priority attached to expanding commercial and political ties with the United States.

Thus while economic reforms continued to receive the highest priority, the emphasis attached to political liberalization increased substantially during Salinas's term (1988–94).[61] The political reform process consisted of several interrelated components. Constitutional amendments in 1990 and 1993, both passed with the support of the PAN, substantially reduced the capacity of the PRI and allied government officials to manipulate registration and election procedures, providing new opportunities for the opposition to gain representation in the legislature, and at the state and local level. The PRI also initiated an effort to strengthen its own electoral and coalitional base, mainly through the creation of a massive antipoverty bureaucracy, PRONASOL (or National Solidarity). PRONASOL was to serve both as a new link between the government and the urban and rural poor and as a political counterweight to the old-guard politicians within the PRI.[62]

The concurrent pursuit of economic and political reform created some

---

José Luis Barros Horcasitas, Javier Hurtado and Germán Pérez Fernández del Castillo, eds., *Transición a la democracia y la reforma del estado en México* (Mexico City: UNAM/FLACSO /Miguel Ángel Porrúa, 1991); Juan Molinar Horcasitas, *El tiempo de la legitimidad: Elecciones, autoritarismo y democracia en México* (Mexico City: Cal y Arena, 1991).

[61] Among the first steps were arrests of two highly visible public figures with reputations for corruption, the head of the petroleum workers' union and a prominent financial speculator. These were only symbolic moves against corruption, but helped to establish the personal authority of the president and to divert attention from his tainted electoral victory.

[62] Denise Dresser, "Bringing the Poor Back In: National Solidarity as a Strategy of Regime Legimation", in Wayne Cornelius, Ann Craig, and Jonathan Fox, eds., *Transforming State-Society Relations in Mexico: The National Solidarity Approach* (La Jolla, Calif.: Center for U.S.–Mexican Studies, University of California, 1994), pp. 143–66.

profound dilemmas for the government. The government's assumption was that political reform would create a more legitimate institutional setting for the continuation of the economic reforms pursued under De la Madrid and Salinas. This strategy, however, was contingent on both aggregate performance and the distribution of benefits. Faltering support for the adjustment program would imply increasingly difficult trade-offs between the credibility of the electoral process and the continuity of hard-won economic reforms.

This dilemma persisted throughout the Salinas period and intensified substantially during the turbulent presidential campaign in 1994, which was marked by a peasant uprising in Chiapas and the assassination of Luis Donaldo Colosio, the initial choice to be Salinas's successor. In managing the tensions between economic and political reform, the Salinas administration followed a pattern that had long characterized the Mexican system, making incremental concessions to opponents, but also deploying the resources of the government and the ruling party to retain the upper hand. We examine this pattern first with respect to the reform of electoral institutions and the expansion of multiparty competition, and then with respect to the organization of PRONASOL and the ruling party.

The electoral reforms of 1990 and 1993 significantly reduced opportunities for the type of blatant vote rigging that had marred the 1988 presidential elections, principally by establishing a more independent supervisory agency, the Federal Electoral Institute, and a new electoral court.[63] Nevertheless, the credibility of the process remained seriously compromised by the extensive access that the official party had to government patronage and to the media. As the 1988 results showed, there was no reason to assume that the governmental elite would refrain from using these resources when they faced losses in crucial election contests (Table 8.4). Moreover, central party officials could not always restrain the behavior of local officials and PRI politicians seeking state and municipal offices. Finally, the doubts raised by the PRI's overwhelming political predominance provided an incentive to the opposition to attribute their losses to fraud even when this was not necessarily the case.

In this political context, the expansion of multiparty competition at the state and local level depended not only on the distribution of votes but on prudential choices by the president about when and how much to cede to opposition protests. Predictably, the left-of-center Democratic Revolutionary Party (PRD) encountered tougher treatment than the more conservative PAN, although it did increase its representation in the legislature. PAN

---

[63] Molinar Horcasitas, *El tiempo de la legitimidad;* José Woldenberg, "Democracia y sistema electoral," in Barros Horcasitas, Hurtado, and Perez Fernandez del Castillo, *Transición a la democracia.*

TABLE 8.4

PRI Election Results, 1970–1994

		President	Chamber of Deputies	
	Candidate	Vote Share[a]	Vote Share[a]	Share of Seats[b]
1970	Luis Echeverría Alvarez	86.0	83.3	83.6
1973			77.4	81.8
1976	José López Portillo	100.0	85.0	82.3
1979			72.8	74.0
1982	Miguel De la Madrid Hurtado	74.3	65.7	80.4
1985			63.3	73.0
1988	Carlos Salinas de Gortari	50.7	51.0	52.0
1991			61.4	64.0
1994	Ernesto Zedillo Ponce de León	50.2	50.3	60.0

Sources: Dieter Nohlen, ed., *Enciclopédia electoral latinoamericana y del Caribe* (San José, Costa Rica: Instituto Interamericano de Derechos Humanos, 1993), pp. 440–41, 444, 449–50. Vote share 1994: Instituto Federal Electoral, *Elecciones Federales 1994* (Mexico City: Instituto Federal Electoral, 1994). PRI share of seats 1994: *La Jornada* (Mexico City), October 13, 1994, p. 6.

[a]Percentage of valid votes cast.

[b]Percentage.

activists also encountered harassment and intimidation, but the government was more inclined to adopt a flexible position with them in disputed state and local elections. Between 1989 and 1992, PAN governors were allowed to take office in Baja California, Guanajuato, and Chihuahua after large scale protests against voting fraud had called the honesty of the elections into question. These were the first times since the formation of the ruling party in the late 1920s that an opposition party had been permitted to fill such high positions.

Like earlier patterns of cooptation in Mexico, these policies helped throw the opposition off balance. By 1993, both the PAN and the PRD had become deeply divided over whether to pursue confrontational tactics or to negotiate over further opportunities for office and electoral reforms. The decision to tolerate the seating of PAN governors, however, indicated that the Salinas government was willing to expose the ruling party to electoral defeats. To retain control of the reform process, therefore, the government also had to find ways either to reverse the declining electoral strength of the PRI or to establish substitutes for it.

The PRONASOL program, launched in 1990, was the centerpiece of these efforts. Although the antipoverty bureaucracy was officially a non-partisan agency of the state, it sought to develop new linkages between the government and the informal sector, where Cárdenas had gained considerable support in 1988. Management of the program was entrusted to thirty-one regional directors and state-level coordinators, appointed directly by the president. The officials in turn allocated funds among thousands of local committees which were expected to design and implement community projects. By 1992, over 150,000 such committees had been formed, providing the president and his advisers with a major new political resource.

From a political point of view, the high point of this organizational effort came in the midterm elections of August 1991. Buoyed by economic expansion as well as by the popularity of the PRONASOL program, the PRI won 62 percent of the vote in a contest that most neutral observers agreed was comparatively free of fraud. This was a 12 percentage-point increase over the more questionable official totals of 1988. The PRD, conversely, received only 8.3 percent of the total votes cast, as compared with the official figure of 31 percent in 1988. According to one estimate, approximately one-fifth of the Cárdenas voters in 1988 returned to the PRI fold three years later.[64] Molinar and Weldon provide evidence of the role played by PRONASOL in these results. Controlling for regional and sociological variables, their regressions show a significant correlation between PRONASOL expenditures and the improvement in PRI electoral performance from 1988 to 1991.[65]

Despite the political payoffs derived from the program, relations between the PRONASOL organization and PRI politicians were ambiguous and tense. In many instances, state governors and local party officials did build alliances with regional directors or took control of local PRONASOL committees. But PRONASOL also bypassed traditional patronage hierarchies, and as a consequence, it often encountered considerable opposition from elected leaders and corporatist officials within the party.

The electoral victories in 1991 gave rise to a number of hypotheses about how such conflicts would be resolved. One scenario was that PRONASOL would form the nucleus of an electoral organization that would ultimately split from, and compete with, the PRI. A second was that it would succeed in mobilizing a pro-reform constituency to which all parties would have to appeal, thus lowering the stakes of multiparty contests. A third, more plausible hypothesis was that PRONASOL would be used as an organizational weapon through which the reformist elite would reform the structure of the ruling party itself, reducing the influence of its corporate sectors and making it more responsive to geographic representation.

To an important extent, all of these scenarios rested on the assumption that economic recovery would help to sustain the resurgence of political

---

[64] Craig and Cornelius, "Houses Divided," p. 387.

[65] Juan Molinar Horcasitas and Jeffrey A. Weldon, "Electoral Determinants and Consequences of National Solidarity," in Cornelius, Craig, and Fox, *Transforming State-Society Relations in Mexico,* pp. 123–42.

support for the PRI evident in the 1991 elections. By 1992, however, the economy had begun to slow again substantially. Macroeconomic decision-makers faced especially serious problems with respect to the appreciation of the exchange rate, which had anchored the stabilization program since 1988. Because of the risks posed to domestic price stability, officials had chosen to avoid a large devaluation. This choice, however, meant slow export growth and substantial trade deficits, and required very high interest rates to sustain the inflow of foreign capital. By the second half of 1992, domestic businesses were feeling the strain of both the credit squeeze and the influx of competitive American imports associated with the liberalization of trade. The growth rate flattened.

For government leaders, these developments increased the importance of maintaining decision-making autonomy and magnified the risks associated with the opening of the political system. As in previous periods of Mexican history, reliance on the dominant party seemed the safest way to guarantee the presidential succession and the continuity of economic policy. Thus, as the 1994 presidential race approached, speculation about the renovation of the ruling party faded, and the government moved to heal the breaches that had opened between the reformers and the old guard.

A key role in this process of reconciliation was assigned to Luis Donaldo Colosio, one of Salinas's closest aides. During the period from 1989 through 1991, Colosio served as head of the PRI. In 1992, he was placed in charge of PRONASOL in an effort to moderate its conflicts with the PRI and to provide greater coordination between the two hierarchies. These appointments provided Colosio an opportunity to build extensive personal networks of support within both the PRI and PRONASOL, and put him in an excellent position to engage in his fatal bid for the presidency in 1994.

The emphasis attached to political consolidation and organizational retrenchment was even more evident in subsequent personnel changes within both the government and the PRI. In January 1993, Patrocinio Gonzalez Blanco Garrido, a party hardliner and former governor of Chiapas, was named to head the Interior Ministry. As interior minister, he adopted a tougher position with respect to opposition political protests; despite vigorous PAN and PRD campaigns in a number of subsequent local elections, the government yielded no significant ground to the opposition throughout the rest of 1993. Efforts to draw closer to the old guard were also evident within the PRI itself. The party chairman, Genaro Borrego Estrada, was summarily replaced on the second night of the PRI's Sixteenth General Assembly in March 1993 after having delivered a keynote address on the importance of internal reform. Borrego's replacement was Fernando Ortiz Arana, a moderate politician with closer links to the corporatist sectors of the party.

The effort to close ranks was severely tested by the violence surrounding the 1994 campaign. The first shock was the dramatic Chiapas uprising in January 1994. Tough military counterattacks produced a quick suspension of the armed phase of the peasant rebellion, but the widespread sympathy that the movement received from urban as well as rural groups prompted at least some prominent leaders within the elite to urge more extensive democratic reforms.[66] A second severe shock came with the assassination of Colosio, which reopened the difficult question of the succession to Salinas. Conflicts with the old guard that had been smoothed over under Colosio resurfaced with the choice of Ernesto Zedillo, an economist without close ties to the party apparatus.

The electoral pressures of the 1994 campaign forced internal compromises, however. Technocratic factions, now headed by Zedillo, needed the old guard to continue in power; the old guard, as had been the case for many years, had little future outside of the framework of the PRI. The result of this accommodation was an impressive electoral victory for the ruling party. Despite very high voter turnout, which was presumed to work to the advantage of opposition candidates, and a strong showing by the PAN's Diego Fernández de Cevallos in a nationally televised debate, Zedillo won just over half of the valid popular vote. Fernández placed a distant second (27 percent) and Cárdenas a disappointing third (17 percent). Just as important were the PRI victories in Congressional races. PRI candidates ran well throughout the country, providing the ruling party (and thus the new president) with a strong legislative majority.

Continued pressures from opposition groups and widening debates over political reform within the elite itself made it almost certain that there would be important political changes during Zedillo's term. The PAN's strong electoral showing in the cities, particularly among younger middle-class voters, indicated the PRI's continuing vulnerability to protest votes within the urban areas. Nor could a resurgence of more populist protests be ruled out, despite Cárdenas's poor showing.

Dealing with such challenges implied the need to expand the process of political liberalization and to resume the modernization of the PRI. On the other hand, divisions within the ruling party remained deep. One indication was the assassination in September of yet another party moderate, José Francisco Ruiz Massieu, allegedly at the hands of disgruntled old-guard politicians. For the time being, however, the PRI had once again provided a pivotal instrument of political management and control. The party had continued to serve as a framework for bargaining among reform and

---

[66] The most visible was Manuel Camacho, who had been passed over as the PRI's presidential candidate, but was later placed in charge of negotiations with the Zapatistas.

conservative groups and succeeded in channeling its immense financial and organizational resources toward electoral victories and the maintenance of political continuity.

CONCLUSION

This chapter has combined the analytic focus on regime change in Part One with the question of effective economic management that is the subject of the other chapters in Part Two. Though dominant-party systems have potential weaknesses, we found that they also enjoy organizational advantages that can facilitate both the initiation and the consolidation of economic reform. The evidence from Taiwan in this regard is unambiguous. Despite the fact that Mexico experienced severe economic difficulties in the 1980s, both the earlier period of stabilizing growth and the government's striking ability to adjust are also testimony to these advantages.

From a normative perspective, the "advantages" of single-party dominance with respect to managing political change are much more ambiguous; the features of one-party systems that allow them to manage the economy effectively also provide them the ability to control the process of political reform. However, our analysis also shows that economic context matters. In Taiwan, good economic performance and a relatively equal distribution of the benefits of growth reduced the risk to the KMT of liberalizing the polity. Over the late 1980s and early 1990s, the KMT began to rely more and more on its capabilities as an effective electoral machine to maintain power and legitimacy.

In Mexico, by contrast, economic performance was more problematic. We have already emphasized how the uncertainty of the recovery placed the PRI in a bind with respect to the compatibility of economic and political reform. In addition, Mexico also presents a contrast to Taiwan in that the distribution of income is much more unequal and the wrenching reform process of the 1980s has generated a substantial set of losers.

Mexico thus raises questions quite similar to those raised by Chile and Turkey in the last chapter: what happens to economic reforms when the institutional constraints on opposition are lifted? A reformed PRI might allow Mexico to enjoy the stabilizing effects of a strong centrist party, even if its monopoly position is eroded. However, there are also risks associated with the PRI's center-right strategy and its tough stance toward the left, particularly given the country's skewed distribution of income. The events of 1994 are a reminder of the threat posed by antireform forces and social as well as political polarization. It is to these problems of consolidating economic and political reform that we now turn.

Part Three

THE CONSOLIDATION OF DEMOCRACY AND ECONOMIC REFORM

CHAPTER NINE

Economic Reform and Democratic Consolidation

As THE RECENT wave of democratization crested in the 1980s, skeptics questioned the capacity of new democratic governments to manage the daunting political challenges of economic reform. Though these doubts remain salient for some countries, the problems facing many others looked somewhat different from the perspective of the mid-1990s. As we have seen in Part Two, new democratic regimes facing severe crises were eventually able to launch wide-ranging reform programs. For these governments, the pressing issue was no longer whether policy changes could be initiated, but what their effects would be on economic performance and democratic consolidation over the longer run; these questions are the subject of this chapter.

Critics of neoliberalism have mounted a vigorous challenge to recent stabilization and structural adjustment efforts both on theoretical grounds and in response to the preliminary empirical evidence that is available. First, they argue that stabilization and adjustment efforts have adversely affected the capacity of the state to promote economic recovery and growth over the long run. Second, they express reservations about the implications of these reforms for the alleviation of poverty and the distribution of income. Finally, they argue that these combined failures will ultimately impinge on the prospects for democracy itself. Bresser Pereira, Maravall, and Przeworski summarize the case against orthodoxy most boldly: "Whenever democratic governments followed neo-liberal tenets, the outcome has been stagnation, increased poverty, political discontent, and the debilitation of democracy."[1]

Since many of the democracies under consideration here are so new, it remains impossible to fully confirm or disconfirm these claims by extending our comparative case analysis to the post-transition period. Though we believe that a number of criticisms of neoliberalism are exaggerated in important respects, we concur with the critics that the transition from crisis to sustained and equitable growth requires a rehabilitation and expansion of the state's capacities to manage the economy and deliver services. Moreover, we strongly agree that the failure to achieve stable growth can have

---

[1] Luiz Carlos Bresser Pereira, José María Maravall, and Adam Przeworski, *Economic Reforms in New Democracies: A Social Democratic Approach* (Cambridge: Cambridge University Press, 1993), p. 199.

devastating consequences for the consolidation of democracy. There have been surprisingly few authoritarian reversals during the past decade, but the fact that most new democracies have survived poor economic performance should not be a source of complacency; survival is not the same as consolidation, and it is altogether possible that faltering performance could, once again, place the legitimacy of existing political institutions at risk.

The reconstruction of the state and the formulation of a coherent growth strategy under democratic auspices ultimately hinge on whether political institutions allow for effective management of a market economy while remaining accountable to the interests and aspirations of competing social and economic interests. These institutional issues are the subject of the next chapter. We review a number of different solutions to the problem of democratic accountability, including corporatism and parliamentary vs. presidential forms of executive authority, and examine their consequences for economic policy and performance over the long run. As in earlier chapters, however, we pay particular attention to the way party systems structure the distributive conflicts and bargains that determine the stability of democratic capitalism.

NEOLIBERAL REFORM, THE RECONSTRUCTION OF THE STATE, AND THE PROSPECTS FOR GROWTH

In countries facing severe macroeconomic instability, the controversy over orthodox adjustment strategies centered initially on the speed with which governments should act to control inflation and re-equilibrate the balance of payments, and the emphasis that should be given to the traditional means of fiscal, monetary, and exchange-rate policies in doing so. Virtually all orthodox analyses emphasized that high and variable inflation was inimical to investment and growth and argued that, despite the short-term costs, rapid stabilization of prices constituted a prerequisite for other reforms.[2] Critics questioned the effectiveness of traditional instruments of stabilization when used alone, and placed greater emphasis on coordination problems, domestic incomes policy, and the need for international financial support.[3]

[2] For analyses along these lines, see Vittorio Corbo, Morris Goldstein, and Mohsin Khan, eds., *Growth-Oriented Adjustment Programs* (Washington, D.C.: International Monetary Fund and World Bank, 1987).

[3] See for example Lance Taylor, *Varieties of Stabilization Experience* (Oxford: Clarendon Press, 1988), and *The Rocky Road to Reform* (Cambridge: MIT Press, 1993), particularly pp. 39–94; Jose Maria Fanelli, Roberto Frenkel, and Guillermo Rosenwucel, "Growth and Structural Reform in Latin America: Where We Stand," in William C. Smith, Carlos H. Acuña, and Eduardo A. Gamarra, eds., *Latin American Political Economy in the Age of Neoliberal Reform* (New Brunswick, N.J.: Transaction Publishers, 1994), pp. 101–127.

Where inflation remained high, political debates over these issues persisted into the 1990s; countries in this category included Brazil and a number of the former socialist countries, as well as others in which the durability of stabilization efforts remained open to question. For those countries that had succeeded in achieving a modicum of macroecomic stability, however, two other questions began to command greater attention. How did governments move from stabilization and initial reform efforts to a sustainable growth strategy? And what was the appropriate role for the state in that process?

Critics of orthodox stabilization and liberalization programs have been concerned not only with their short-term costs in terms of output and employment, but with their longer-term effects on the capacity of the state to implement a coherent development strategy. Particular attention has been paid to the high costs of rapid fiscal adjustment. Spending cuts generally fell heavily on public investment, much of which was complementary to private-sector activity.[4] Basic services also suffered, with important implications not only for equity, but for the health and education of the work force. Drastic cuts in government salaries and payrolls had a demoralizing effect on public employees and drove the most competent workers out of the public sector. Guillermo O'Donnell, among others, has argued that "the extent to which the state was destroyed was enormous and unnecessary," and that adjustment strategies of the 1980s were "too simplistically addressed to short-term economic goals" and too strongly motivated by "intensely anti-statist ideologies. . . ."[5]

In many instances, no doubt, reforms were precipitate and might have been made in a way that would have, in O'Donnell's words, "left the state in much better shape for the tasks ahead."[6] Any evaluation must, however, take initial conditions into account. For most of the crisis cases discussed in this volume, the criticism of neoliberal reforms underestimates the extent to which the inflationary crises that preceded these adjustment efforts had already devastated the state. Governments faced profound fiscal and balance-of-payments problems; not adjusting aggressively also carried high political costs.

Failure to take initial conditions and constraints into account can lead to irrelevant comparisons and misleading prescriptions. An example is the invocation of the Spanish experience as an illustration of the virtues of a

---

[4] See Thomas Biersteker, "Reducing the Role of the State in the Economy: A Conceptual Exploration of IMF and World Bank Prescriptions," *International Studies Quarterly* 34: (1990): 477–92.

[5] Guillermo O'Donnell, "Some Reflections on Redefining the Role of the State," in Colin I. Bradford, ed., *Redefining the State in Latin America* (Paris: Organization for Economic Cooperation and Development, 1994), p. 252.

[6] Ibid.

more moderate policy path. However, the Franco government consistently ran budget surpluses; unlike many new democratic governments of the 1980s and 1990s, his democratic successors did not confront the difficult task of fiscal adjustment or the burden of a large public debt.[7] In addition, the post-Franco governments also benefited from a large net inflow of capital from foreign investors, tourism, and direct assistance associated with Spain's accession to the European Community. Both the internal and the external financial position of the government provided the space for the expansion of the social safety net, which in turn proved pivotal to the political consolidation of the Spanish reforms.

Strengthening the fiscal position of the state and achieving macroeconomic stability were also crucial to earlier economic reforms in the non-crisis cases. The Kuomintang government halted a hyperinflation with U.S. support in the late 1940s and early 1950s, and Korea undertook substantial fiscal reforms in conjunction with its shift to an export-oriented growth strategy the early 1960s. The combination of macroeconomic stability and a sound fiscal base provided the foundation not only for a consistent exchange-rate stance but for activist industrial policies as well. In Chile, the brutal adjustment policies of the Pinochet years laid the fiscal foundation for a gradual and selective rebuilding of welfare state commitments under Aylwin.

In much of Latin America, Eastern Europe, and the former Soviet Union in the recent period, economic reform has been akin to what Jeffrey Sachs has termed "life in the economic emergency room."[8] Packages of fiscal adjustment, privatization, and trade liberalization were, to be sure, sometimes embedded in a neoliberal ideological discourse; in the Southern Cone dictatorships of the 1970s, for example, radical economic reform was but one component of more comprehensive efforts to reorder state-society relations. In new democracies such as Argentina and Peru, however, such programs were motivated less by a broad faith in the market than by the urgent need to deal with runaway inflation and the fiscal collapse of the state. Severe balance-of-payments constraints and the need to attract foreign capital made it crucial to reassure foreign investors and the international financial institutions.[9]

We do not mean to suggest that there was only one way to adjust to the

[7] Richard Gunther, *Public Policy in a No-Party State* (Berkeley: University of California Press, 1980), pp. 46–110.

[8] Jeffrey Sachs, "Life in the Economic Emergency Room," in John Williamson, ed., *The Political Economy of Policy Reform* (Washington, D.C.: Institute for International Economics, 1993), pp. 501–24.

[9] See Dani Rodrik, "The Rush to Free Trade in the Developing World: Why So Late? Why Now? Will It Last?" in Stephan Haggard and Steven B. Webb, eds., *Voting for Reform: Democracy, Political Liberalization, and Economic Adjustment* (New York: Oxford University Press, 1994), pp. 61–88.

crises of the 1980s; the merits of a number of neoliberal reforms are open to debate. With respect to fiscal adjustment, there are crucial controversies about the weight to be given to raising taxes as opposed to cutting expenditure, particularly where the state's ability to provide basic services is being decimated. Privatization may reduce the state's fiscal burden, but its contribution to efficiency may be exaggerated. Trade liberalization and deregulation can strip the state of instruments that have proven effective in promoting growth elsewhere. Nor should the international context be forgotten; more official assistance and prompter debt relief would have made it easier for committed governments to reform.

For countries facing the manifold constraints outlined above, however, the benefits of radical reform programs appeared to outweigh their costs. In Bolivia, Argentina, Peru, and also Poland, radical programs succeeded in ending hyperinflation, reversing the breakdown of both public and private finances, and securing external support. These were not inconsiderable achievements. By halting the free-fall of their respective economies, the reforms established the conditions for the reconstruction of badly damaged states. By contrast, those countries that failed in these initial adjustments, such as Ukraine, faced not only debilitating economic problems but severe threats to the integrity of democratic rule as well.

Moreover, it should be emphasized that many neoliberal reforms have in fact been aimed explicitly at strengthening the state.[10] These include the establishment of a broader tax base, more effective tax collection, and reorienting public spending priorities toward investment and the provision of basic services. The organization of a competent civil service and the creation of economic decision-making agencies resistant to particularistic demands are reforms that are useful regardless of the economic strategy pursued. These steps are not only consistent with the pursuit of a more interventionist economic policy, but are prerequisites for it.

Assuming that such formidable challenges can be met, the question remains of how the state might most effectively intervene to promote long-term growth; reestablishing the fiscal integrity of government and achieving a sustainable balance-of-payments position may be necessary to achieve this objective, but they are by no means sufficient. To what extent is the contemporary emphasis on deregulation, privatization, and trade liberalization likely to generate recovery? What are the advantages of a more active state role, not only through regulation but through more active intervention to counter the pervasive market failures that are typical of backwardness?[11]

These are very old questions, and after a decade of market-oriented

---

[10] See Hector E. Schamis, "Re-forming the State: The Politics of Privatization in Chile and Britain" (Ph.D. diss., Columbia University, 1994).

[11] For a concise summary, see Albert Fishlow, "The Latin American State," *Journal of Economic Perspectives* 4 (1990): 61–74.

reforms there are still no unambiguous answers. Clearly, there are alternatives to the Anglo-Saxon model of the market economy. An accumulating body of evidence on the East Asian cases suggests the positive role the state can play through a variety of targeted industrial policies: from preferential credit policies to selective protection, direct subsidies, the use of state-owned enterprises, and government support for private-sector cartels.[12] Even the World Bank has cautiously endorsed some components of the East Asian model, particularly active government intervention in support of exports.[13]

As we have noted, however, government promotion of exports in Korea and Taiwan was accompanied by cautious macroeconomic policies, realistic exchange rates, and some import liberalization for exporters; unlike in Latin America, the incentive system was not weighted heavily in favor of domestic production. In these respects, the East Asian cases vindicate important components of the neoliberal story. Moreover, in several rapidly growing Southeast Asian countries, including Malaysia, Indonesia, and Thailand, export-led growth strategies have succeeded with much less emphasis on industrial policy than was the case in Korea and Taiwan.[14]

Systematic empirical evidence in support of the neoliberal faith, however, is also thin, both generally and with respect to the countries discussed in this volume. Signs of an economic turnaround were evident in a number of ex-Communist countries undertaking radical reform; the most notable example is Poland, where the "shock therapy" of the early 1990s initially attracted substantial criticism. Such experiences are too recent, however, to provide a clear basis for evaluation, and are hardly sufficient to resolve the debate about the mix between state and market that will be required for this part of the world to get on a sustainable-growth course. Similarly ambiguous findings have been advanced with respect to the daunting economic problems facing sub-Saharan Africa, where the transition to more market-oriented means of resource allocation hinge centrally on the rehabilitation of severely weakened states.[15]

Two of the most methodologically sophisticated attempts to provide broader comparisons of reforming and nonreforming countries—studies by Corbo and Rojas for the World Bank and by Mosley, Harrigan, and

---

[12] The two strongest statements of this position are Robert Wade, *Governing the Market* (Princeton, N.J.: Princeton University Press, 1990) and Alice Amsden, *Asia's Next Giant* (New York: Oxford University Press, 1989).

[13] See World Bank, *The East Asian Miracle* (New York: Oxford University Press for the World Bank, 1993), pp. 280–87, on the use of financial subsidies to promote exports.

[14] This puzzle is the theme of Andrew MacIntyre, ed., *Business-Government Relations in East and Southeast Asia* (Ithaca, N.Y.: Cornell University Press, 1994).

[15] See Michael Chege, "Sub-Saharan Africa: Underdevelopment's Last Stand," in Barbara Stallings, ed., *The New International Context of Development: Winners and Losers in the 1990s*, unpublished ms., University of Wisconsin, 1993.

Toye—find that structural adjustment programs increased the rate of growth of GDP and the ratio of exports to GDP, but that they also had the effect of decreasing the ratio of investment to GDP, at least in the short run.[16] The successful adjustment programs appeared to achieve their objectives through expanded exports that offset the contractionary effects of adjustment programs. But as Corbo and Rojas note, these positive effects were not universal. In some countries, "resources did not shift rapidly enough from non-tradable to tradable activities to increase growth, probably because of market distortions and institutional weaknesses."[17]

Williamson's review of Latin American countries for the late 1980s shows that the reforming countries did better than the nonreforming ones, but that the correlation was weak and that a number of reforming countries showed declining performance.[18] The outlook for Latin America appeared brighter in the early 1990s, as vigorous growth resumed in a number of countries. Yet a number of observers noted that this growth was extremely fragile, and was a function not only of economic reforms but of declining world interest rates and a resumption of capital flows to the region. These capital flows were arguably a response to economic reforms, but they were also easily reversible and created a number of problems including speculative bubbles in asset markets and overvalued exchange rates that undermined the effort to expand exports.[19]

The evidence from our sample of cases is mixed as well. If we exclude the experience of the East Asian countries, where reforms date to the very different international economic environment of the 1960s, several countries stand out as radical reformers, particularly Chile, Bolivia, Mexico, and Turkey. The clearest success story is Chile, where sustained growth

[16] Vittorio Corbo and Patricio Rojas, "World Bank–Supported Adjustment Programs: Country Performance and Effectiveness," pp. 23–36, and Paul Mosley's "Comment," pp. 37–39, in Corbo, Stanley Fischer, and Steven B. Webb, eds., *Adjustment Lending Revisited: Policies to Restore Growth* (Washington, D.C.: World Bank, 1992); Paul Mosley, Jane Harrigan, and John Toye, *Aid and Power: The World Bank and Policy-Based Lending* (London: Routledge, 1990). The methodological difficulties of conducting such studies are immense, however, particularly in measuring the extent to which policy reforms are actually undertaken. For example, the Corbo and Rojas study contains sophisticated controls for the influence of external shocks, but codes countries as adjusting on the basis of whether they received adjustment lending or not! On the general problem of measuring the effects of programs, see M. Goldstein and P. Montiel, "Evaluating Fund Stabilization Programs with Multicountry Data: Some Methodological Pitfalls," *IMF Staff Papers* 33 (1986): 314–44.

[17] Corbo and Rojas, "World Bank–Supported Adjustment Programs," p. 33.

[18] John Williamson, "The Progress of Policy Reform in Latin America," in Williamson, ed., *Latin American Adjustment: How Much Has Happened?* (Washington, D.C.: Institute for International Economics, 1990), p. 406.

[19] See Moises Naim, "Latin America: Post-Adjustment Blues," *Foreign Policy* 92 (1993): 133–50; Mario Damill et al., "Latin American Growth Prospects: News Stemming from Recent Experience," unpublished ms., CEDES, Buenos Aires, April 1993.

has continued into the 1990s and contributed to a relatively stable democratic transition. In that experience, however, more targeted support for export activities supplemented the basic market-oriented approach adopted under Pinochet. In Bolivia, the economy also began to grow in the late 1980s, with small but steady increases in per capita income from 1989 through 1992. This was the first time since the early 1970s that the country had experienced so many consecutive years of real per capita growth.

In other countries undertaking radical reform, however, prospects for recovery remain far more uncertain. Turkey has maintained robust export growth, but never tamed its macroeconomic policy and is thus still subject to destabilizing crises, as became evident in the spring of 1994. The Mexican case is in some ways the most troubling. As we saw in the last chapter, the stabilization and trade reform of the late 1980s did result in some modest growth. But the recovery must be seen as disappointing given the depth and consistency of the adjustment effort, and in 1993, growth ground to a halt. Though there were grounds for hope about future economic performance, important uncertainties existed with respect to exchange-rate policy and growing trade deficits, complicated by the complex political maneuvering of the election year.

It is more difficult to judge the reforms in Argentina and Peru, which at the time of this writing are much more recent. In Argentina, the economy expanded dramatically during 1991 and 1992, the first two years following the reforms, and positive growth rates returned to Peru in 1991 and were sustained through 1993. As in Mexico, however, the economic picture has been clouded by large trade deficits, high real interest rates, and overvalued currencies, conditions that raised questions about whether earlier stabilization efforts had been consolidated.

The most plausible conclusion that can be drawn from the "success stories" in our sample—Korea, Taiwan, Chile, and Thailand—is that as long as countries achieve and sustain a reasonable degree of macroeconomic stability and do not grossly distort prices, a variety of combinations of orthodox and heterodox policy interventions can yield sustainable growth. There are multiple high-growth equilibria, and the viability of any particular strategy will vary depending on international conditions, factor endowments, domestic political alignments, and the institutional capabilities of the government. Few reform experiences, if any, justify the dogmatic confidence that neoliberal ideologues place in the "magic of the market," but it is also difficult to discard the hypothesis that elements of the neoliberal menu can contribute to resumed growth.

For this reason, much of the debate between neoliberals and their critics has obscured rather than illuminated the controversies within the respective camps as well as the policy options that are actually available to new democracies. Mainstream economists have often expressed caution about the sequence and pace with which reforms should be introduced, and even about components of the neoliberal package itself.[20] Theoretical developments in two areas—endogenous growth theory and strategic trade theory—have placed greater emphasis on the role of government in stimulating growth.[21]

At the same time, most social democratic and heterodox critics now emphasize the importance of sound fiscal and exchange-rate policies. They are perfectly aware of the policy failures in the developing and socialist countries in the postwar period, and none would advocate a return to the status quo ante; the question is the appropriate path to stability and growth.[22] The advocacy of industrial policies also takes a wide variety of forms, from greater emphasis on general support for technological innovation, to broad financial support for exports, to more selective incentives to particular economic activities and industries.

General agreement on the importance of sustaining macroeconomic and balance-of-payments equilibrium can provide the basis for a vigorous and meaningful debate on these other issues of economic strategy, a debate that can be altogether salutary for economic policymaking itself. Pluralism can assist governments in correcting course as economic conditions change, and by airing a wide spectrum of plausible policy options, such debates in turn are likely to enhance the legitimacy of the political system as a whole.

The resolution of these normative issues will ultimately depend on the nature of underlying social cleavages and how they are organized politically. We would expect that contending views of the state will constitute one, if not the major, line of cleavage over economic policy; in the following chapter we explore how alternative institutional arrangements process these conflicting demands.

---

[20] For skeptical views of particular neoliberal reforms, see Paul Krugman and Lance Taylor, "Contractionary Effects of Devaluation," *Journal of International Economics* 8 (1978): 445–56; Dani Rodrik, "How Should Structural Adjustment Programs Be Designed?" *World Development* 18 (1990): 933–47; Carlos Diaz-Alejandro, "Good-bye Financial Repression, Hello Financial Crash," *Journal of Development Economics* 19 (1985): 1–24.

[21] "Endogenous" because traditional neoclassical growth models relied on exogenous population growth and technological change. See Robert Lucas, "On the Mechanics of Economic Development," *Journal of Monetary Economics* 22 (1988): 3–42; Paul Romer, "Endogenous Technical Change," *Journal of Political Economy* 98 (1990): 71–102; Robert Barro, "Government Spending in a Simple Model of Endogenous Growth," ibid., pp. 103–25.

[22] A recent study directed by Lance Taylor collects a number of country studies by specialists critical both of austerity-based stabilization programs and the emphasis on liberalization and deregulation that is characteristic of the "Washington consensus." However, as Taylor himself summarizes, "they do not go to the opposite extreme of rejecting all such policies, especially the need to maintain fiscal balance. They generally support activist but restrained state intervention in the economic system." Taylor, *The Rocky Road to Reform*, p. 2.

PROBLEMS OF EQUITY AND POVERTY

Even if new democratic governments succeed in reigniting economic growth, they also confront problems of poverty and income inequality. The effect of neoliberal reforms on these issues has also been controversial, though difficult to gauge because of the profound effects of the crisis itself. In countries experiencing economic downturns, real per capita income fell, real wages declined, and unemployment and underemployment increased. Two comprehensive reviews of income distribution in Latin America in the 1980s concur that poverty virtually always increased during economic crises, as it did in the Philippines in the early 1980s.[23] There is also evidence of a substantial worsening of the distribution of income in Argentina, Brazil, Mexico, and Peru during the decade, and of little improvement in Bolivia, the Philippines and Uruguay (Table 9.1).[24]

The effects of economic reforms on poverty and inequality are more difficult to measure because a tricky counterfactual is required: the relevant comparison is what would have happened to real incomes under an alternative adjustment program, or under none at all. It is plausible, however, that some adjustment measures exacerbated the effects of the crisis in the short run, particularly with respect to urban workers in both the formal and informal sectors. The elimination of subsidies on food, fuel, and transportation had negative consequences for the poor, and expenditures on social services declined in both absolute and relative terms during the crisis in a number of Latin American countries.[25]

A World Bank study that attempted an explicit comparison between countries that adjusted aggressively and those that did not found that the wage share of GDP and the wage share of total value added in manufacturing fell more precipitously in those countries that adjusted aggressively. Those countries also experienced sharper deterioration in wages and employment in the public sector, and a sharper fall in expenditures on social

---

[23] See Samuel A. Morley, "Poverty and Distribution in Latin America: Evidence from the Past, Prospects for the Future," unpublished ms., Inter-American Development Bank, April 1994; Nora Lustig, "Coping with Austerity, Poverty and Inequality in Latin America," unpublished ms., Brookings Institution, February 1994; Robert Dohner and Stephan Haggard, *The Political Feasibility of Adjustment in the Philippines* (Paris: Organisation for Economic Cooperation and Development, 1994).

[24] The reasons why this would occur are somewhat less obvious. One reason is that unskilled workers are the first to lose their jobs during downturns; a second focuses on the distributional consequences of inflation on the poor, who tend to hold larger cash balances and are less able to shield themselves from fluctuations in prices than the well-to-do.

[25] See Joan Nelson, "Poverty, Equity, and the Politics of Adjustment," in Stephan Haggard and Robert Kaufman, eds., *The Politics of Adjustment* (Princeton, N.J.: Princeton University Press, 1992), pp. 222–31; World Bank, *World Development Report 1990: Poverty* (New York: Oxford University Press, 1990), p. 116.

TABLE 9.1

Poverty and Income Distribution in the 1980s

	Urban Poor	National Poor		Gini Coefficients	
Argentina					
1980	7.6			.40[a]	
1989					
1990	28.5			.47[a]	
Bolivia					
1986	51.1			.52	
1989	54.4			.53	
Brazil					
1979		39	34.1		
1981	29.1			.58	
1983	38.2				
1989			40.9		
1990	28.9	43		.63	
Chile					
1980	40.3			.53[b]	
1985		45.0			
1987	48.6	38.1		.53[b]	
1990		34.8			
Korea					
1980		10		.39	.39
1982					.41
1985				.35	.41
1988				.34	
Mexico					
1977		32			
1984	23	30	16.6	.51	
1989			22.6	.55	
Peru					
1979	35				
1981				.34[c]	
1985/6	45	52			
1989				.44[c]	
The Philippines					
1985		59		.45	
1988		49.5		.45	

TABLE 9.1 *(continued)*

	Urban Poor		National Poor	Gini Coefficients
Taiwan				
1980				.30
1985				.32
1987				.33
Thailand				
1981			17.5	.43
1986			22.4	.47
1988			16.1	.47
1990			15.0	.49
1992			10.9	.51
Turkey				
1978				.51
1983				.52
1986				.50
Uruguay				
1981	9	6.2		.44[d]
1986	14			
1989	10	5.3		.42[d]

Sources: For Latin America, data are from Nora Lustig's compilation of national studies in her "Introduction" to *Coping with Austerity: Poverty and Inequality in Latin America,* unpublished ms., The Brookings Institution, 1994. Where series are available providing data for the same years, headcount ratios and Gini coefficients are averaged. For the Philippines, Robert Dohner and Stephan Haggard, *The Political Feasibility of Adjustment in the Philippines* (Paris: Organisation for Economic Cooperation and Development, 1994), Tables 1.3 and 3.2. For Taiwan, Harry Oshima, *Strategic Processes in Monsoon Asia's Economic Development* (Baltimore: Johns Hopkins University Press, 1993), pp. 201–2, 214. For Thailand, Yukio Ikemoto, "Income Distribution and Malnutrition in Thailand," unpublished ms., Center for Southeast Asian Studies, Kyoto University, March 1994, Tables 1 and 3; Turkey, Süleyman Özmucur, "Regional Distribution of Income," in Committee on Economic and Social Studies, *Regional Policies in Turkey* (Istanbul: Acar Matbass, 1989), Table 1 (In Turkish). For Korea, D. M Leipziger et al., *The Distribution of Income and Wealth in Korea* (Washington, D.C.: World Bank, 1992), Table 1–5, p. 10.

Note: Urban and national poor are poverty headcount ratios—the share of the population living below the poverty line. Two sets of figures in the same column are based on data from different surveys.

[a]Buenos Aires.
[b]Santiago.
[c]Lima.
[d]Urban.

services.[26] An OECD study of income distribution during the adjustment process also found an increase in urban unemployment and in the size of the informal sector, which in turn placed downward pressure on prices and incomes in that sector.[27] However, these studies do not consider the counterfactual scenario in which inadequate adjustment efforts were made; the failed heterodox stabilization efforts in Argentina, Brazil, and Peru had devastating effects on the poor.

Whatever the short-term costs of stabilization and structural adjustment, it is increasingly clear that if the reforms succeed in promoting economic growth, they are likely to reduce absolute poverty over the long run even if the distribution of income worsens. In the past, there was considerable skepticism about the idea that the benefits of growth would "trickle down" to poor households and individuals, and some speculation about the possibility that it would make them even poorer.[28] Where growth has been robust, however, absolute poverty has generally declined, even where the initial distribution of income was unequal.[29] This is evident in Thailand, Taiwan, and Korea, the countries in this volume that have consistently maintained high levels of economic growth for the longest period.[30]

The long-term consequences of successful structural adjustment for the distribution of income are much less clear: growth can either improve or worsen the distribution of income.[31] In Korea and Taiwan, the prototypical "structural adjusters," the rapid expansion of labor-absorbing, export-oriented industries during the 1960s, contributed to the growth of manufacturing employment and a reduction of poverty and income inequality. The evidence with respect to the 1980s is controversial; however, even if there was some deterioration in the distribution of income in the 1980s, both countries remained relatively equal, Taiwan among the most equal in the world.[32] Thailand, where both employment and real wages grew rapidly through the 1980s, also showed signs of improving income distribution.

---

[26] Anne Maasland and Jacques van der Gaag, "World Bank–Supported Adjustment Programs and Living Conditions," in Corbo, Fischer, and Webb, *Adjustment Lending Revisited* pp. 40–63.

[27] See François Bourguignon and Christian Morrisson, *Adjustment and Equity in Developing Countries* (Paris: OECD Development Centre, 1992), pp. 31–52.

[28] See for example Hollis Chenery et al., *Redistribution with Growth* (London: Oxford University Press, 1974).

[29] For a review of these arguments, see Stephan Haggard, "Markets, Poverty Alleviation and Income Distribution: An Assessment of Neoliberal Claims," *Ethics and International Affairs* 5 (1991) pp. 175–96.

[30] See Harry T. Oshima, *Strategic Processes in Monsoon Asia's Economic Development* (Baltimore: Johns Hopkins University Press, 1983), pp. 201–7.

[31] Gary S. Fields, "Growth and Income Distribution," in George Psacharopoulos, ed., *Essays on Poverty, Equity and Growth* (Oxford: Pergamon Press, 1991), pp. 1–52.

[32] See Oshima, *Strategic Processes,* pp. 201–7.

Yet the distribution of income in East Asia was relatively egalitarian even before the transition to export-led growth, largely as a result of extensive land reforms in Korea and Taiwan and a relatively equal distribution of land in Thailand. Moreover, the governments in Korea and Taiwan maintained and deepened their commitment to education during the reform process. Relative income equality benefited from the rapid growth associated with outward-oriented policies, but these distributional outcomes were not a function of the shift to outward-oriented policies alone.

The evidence from the other countries that have had prolonged experiences with structural adjustment—Chile, Turkey, Mexico, and Bolivia—is much more mixed. These reforms aimed at reversing biases in the structure of incentives that favored owners of capital, public and private firms in manufacturing, and unionized workers over agriculture, labor-intensive production, and workers in the informal sector. The actual impact of these reform efforts remains uncertain, however, and is likely to be strongly influenced by the prior distribution of assets, natural resources, and other structural features of the economy.

In Chile, employment and real wages grew rapidly in the early 1990s as a consequence of the extremely rapid expansion of labor-intensive exports in agriculture, fishing, and forest products. Moreover, there is evidence that poverty fell and the distribution of income improved.[33] This experience has not been repeated elsewhere, however. In Turkey, exports boomed but real wages fell. In Bolivia, unlike Chile, there are few natural resources outside the mining sector, and export-oriented policies have been far less effective in stimulating growth in investment and employment. In Mexico, agricultural liberalization will negatively affect peasant producers of corn and grain, and the positive distributional consequences of expanding manufacturing exports have been inhibited by exchange-rate appreciation and tight-money policies. In Mexico and Turkey, as well as in Argentina, privatization and financial liberalization provided segments of the business elite with tremendous windfalls and opportunities for corruption.

Data on poverty and income distribution in these countries are thin, and suffer from the difficulty of disentangling the effects of crisis from the effects of adjustment policies that we have noted above. Nonetheless, the results of existing studies are not encouraging. Poverty increased in Mexico and Bolivia during the adjustment phase, and though national-level poverty fell in Chile, urban poverty increased sharply in the 1980s and did not reverse itself until the 1990s. With respect to the overall distribution of income, there was no improvement in Chile until the 1990s, no change in

[33] Mario Marcel and Andres Solimano, "Developmentalism, Socialism and Free Market Reform: Three Decades of Income Distribution in Chile," The World Bank, Policy Research Working Paper no. WPS 1188, September 1983.

Bolivia and Turkey, and a deterioration of equity in Mexico. In all four, the top 20 percent of households maintained or increased its income share during the 1980s. In Bolivia, Mexico, and Chile, the income share of the bottom 20 percent declined; again, this trend was only reversed in Chile under Aylwin. In Turkey there is some evidence of an improvement in the poorest quintile, but that occurred in a context in which other indicators suggested that the adjustment process had high social costs: real wages fell steadily over most of the 1980s.[34] In Bolivia and Chile, the share of the bottom 20 percent experienced a larger decline than that of any other quintile. In Mexico, as well as Argentina and Brazil, the middle 40 percent lost disproportionately, probably as a result of reductions in public-sector wages and services.[35]

The most important point to emphasize, however, is that these ambiguous results occurred in national contexts in which poverty was high to begin with and the overall level of inequality in the distribution of both income and assets was extremely skewed. Though differences in the scope of the surveys on which the data are based do not permit precise comparisons across countries, Brazil and Mexico rank among the most unequal countries in the world. Levels of inequality are also extremely high in Bolivia, Turkey, and Chile. National income surveys are not available for Peru—the Gini coefficients are based on a survey of households in Lima—but income inequality in Lima worsened dramatically during the 1980s and levels of poverty are extremely high. Poverty and inequality are also high in the Philippines, where land ownership remains highly concentrated.

Democracy is unlikely to reverse these deeply entrenched patterns of inequality quickly; indeed, democracy is in many respects inimical to radical redistribution. But it is possible to conceive of specific policies that could have a significant effect in softening the short-term costs of adjustment and reducing inequalities over the long run. The World Bank has for some time advocated targeted antipoverty programs aimed at the poorest and vulnerable sectors of the population, including subsidies for poor children and women, and public employment schemes and compensations for laid-off workers;[36] such programs were implemented by governments pursuing market-oriented reforms in Bolivia, Mexico, and Chile under both Pinochet and Aylwin. Though success was uneven, these efforts have had some positive impact even in situations of recession and fiscal constraint.

---

[34] We are thankful to Süleyman Özmucur for providing data on the Turkish case from his papers (in Turkish) "Regional Distribution of Income," in Committee on Economic and Social Studies, *Regional Policies in Turkey* (Istanbul: Acar Matbass, 1989), pp. 9–68, and "Pricing and Distribution in an Economy with an Important Public Sector," Boğaziçi University Research Papers, ISS/Ec 92–12, Boğaziçi University, Istanbul, May 1992.

[35] Lustig, "Coping with Austerity," pp. 4–5.

[36] *World Development Report 1990*, pp. 117–20.

Broader steps to reduce inequality are also compatible, in principle, with the market-oriented growth strategies advocated by mainstream economists. Reallocating fiscal expenditures toward basic health services and primary education occupied a prominent place in John Williamson's well-known effort to summarize the "Washington consensus" on adjustment.[37] There has also been increasing emphasis placed on the fact that education, health policy, and land reform not only alleviate suffering and provide opportunities for the poor, but are determinants of growth as well.

The politics of such policies are likely to be quite complex under democratic rule. As Joan Nelson argues, attempts to implement antipoverty programs can generate serious distributional conflicts related to coverage of benefits and reallocation of resources.[38] The political incentives to target antipoverty programs narrowly are limited by the fact the poor are generally among the least organized sectors of the population. Cutting subsidies has proven one of the most politically difficult policy measures, even for authoritarian regimes: blue-collar and middle-class groups are likely to be important opponents of an emphasis on the lowest-income groups.

In some circumstances, it may be possible for a "progressive" coalition of low-income and middle-sector groups to press for broader social services financed by increased taxes on wealthier groups. Arguably, this could provide the political and economic bases for more ambitious programs of education and health reform, or even redistribution of agricultural land. A resumption of growth could increase the political and economic viability of such an alliance, since this would ease the trade-offs associated with financing broader social services.

As we discussed in the preceding section, however, building the state's capacity to deliver such services implies major economic and political challenges, which are compounded by the still fragile economic circumstances that continue to exist in many of the crisis cases we have examined. Even with substantial external financial assistance, enlarging the scope of public services to encompass a broad range of low- and middle-income groups would involve either the construction of a more comprehensive and progressive tax system or a reversion to the macroeconomic populism that has been so costly in the past.

Politically, there is no doubt that progressive tax reforms would encounter strong opposition from upper-income groups and would be difficult to enforce. And even if public revenues can be expanded, administrative reorganization of health and education services is likely to involve sharp conflicts within progressive coalitions, especially between potential low-in-

---

[37] John Williamson, "What Washington Means by Policy Reform," in *Latin American Adjustment,* pp. 10–12.

[38] Joan Nelson, "Poverty, Equity, and the Politics of Adjustment," pp. 233–44.

come consumers of such services and public-sector unions and other professional groups that have benefited from existing arrangments.[39]

Over the long term, the opportunities that democratic institutions provide for debate and contestation offer the best hope for finding durable compromises for the social conflicts and economic policy dilemmas sketched in the preceding section. As we suggest below, however, democracy itself can be undermined if governments are incapable of implementing a coherent, and equitable, growth strategy.

ECONOMIC GROWTH, SOCIAL WELFARE, AND DEMOCRATIC CONSOLIDATION

How much does the survival and consolidation of new democracies hinge on policies that can regenerate growth and move toward a reduction of poverty and income disparities? What are the dangers posed for democracy if current reforms fail to make progress toward these goals? Since the late 1970s, the importance of economic factors has been downplayed in much of the research on both democratic breakdowns and consolidation. Socioeconomic explanations were widely criticized, for example, in a series of influential studies edited by Juan Linz and Alfred Stepan on the breakdown of constitutional regimes in interwar Europe and Latin America.[40] In a similar vein, Linz and Stepan's more recent work on democratic consolidation has emphasized the role of such noneconomic factors as ethnicity, gender, territorial boundaries, and political institutions.[41]

While these factors are clearly significant, there are simple yet compelling reasons why economic performance, and particularly economic growth, might also be important for long-term democratic stability and consolidation. Growth eases the trade-offs associated with the organization of political support, in part by permitting compensation to negatively affected groups. More generally, growth can reduce the frustrations and conflicts resulting from inequality or other social cleavages, and can thus mute the tendency to political alienation and destabilizing social violence.[42]

[39] Ricardo Hausmann, "Sustaining Reform: What Role for Social Policy?" in Colin I. Bradford, *Redefining the State in Latin America,* (Paris: Organization for Economic Cooperation and Development, 1994), pp. 173–95.

[40] See Guillermo O'Donnell, *Modernization and Bureaucratic Authoritarianism: Studies in South American Politics* (Berkeley: Institute of International Studies, University of California, 1973), and the critical essays in David Collier, ed., *The New Authoritarianism in Latin America* (Princeton, N.J.: Princeton University Press, 1979).

[41] Juan Linz and Alfred Stepan, *Problems of Democratic Transition and Consolidation: Southern Europe, South America and Eastern Europe,* unpublished ms., pp. 83–94.

[42] This supposition is implicit in quite contending theoretical approaches to social violence. For empirical tests and reviews, see W. H. Flanigan and E. Fogelman, "Patterns of Political

TABLE 9.2
Survival Rates for Democratic Regimes, 1960–1990

	Years of Positive Growth	First Year of Negative Growth	Second Consecutive Year of Negative Growth
1960–1982			
Survived	319	27	10
Breakdown	13	5	4
Percentage Surviving	96	84	71
1982–1990			
Survived	130	22	16
Breakdown	0	0	2
Percentage Surviving	100	100	88
1960–1990			
Survived	449	49	26
Breakdown	13	5	6
Percentage Surviving	97	91	81

Sources: GDP data are from International Monetary Fund, *International Financial Statistics,* various years. Countries and coding of democratic breakdowns are from Stephan Haggard, Robert Kaufman, Karim Shariff, and Steven B. Webb, "Politics, Inflation, and Stabilization in Middle-Income Countries," manuscript, World Bank, Washington, D.C., 1990.

This argument is supported by data presented in Table 9.2 on forty-seven countries in the World Bank's "middle-income" category, all of those with populations of over two million.[43] On the one hand, democratic regimes rarely collapsed during periods of growth. Between 1960 and the onset of the debt crisis in 1982, the survival rate among democratic regimes—meas-

---

Violence in Comparative Historical Perspective," *Comparative Politics* 2 (1970): 1–20, and A. A. Goldsmith, "Does Political Stability Hinder Economic Development?: Mancur Olson's Theory and the Third World," ibid., 19 (1987): 471–80. See, however, Mancur Olson's argument that rapid growth can be destabilizing because it produces shifts in the relative position of different economic sectors and income groups. Mancur Olson, "Rapid Growth as a Destabilizing Force," *Journal of Economic History* 23 (1963): 529–52. We return to the argument about the distributional effects of growth and recession below.

[43] This method of calculating survival is derived from Adam Przeworski, *Democracy and the Market* (New York: Cambridge University Press, 1991), p. 32. These findings are very close to the survival rates calculated by Przeworski for all South American regimes—democratic and authoritarian—between 1946 and 1988. His calculations show survival rates of 91.6 percent for years of positive growth, 81.8 percent for one year of negative growth, and 67 percent for two consecutive years of negative growth. John Londregan and Keith Poole find that the level of economic development is more significant in explaining coups than growth itself, though growth does have a statistically significant effect. "Poverty, the Coup Trap and the Seizure of Executive Power," *World Politics* 42 (1990): 151–83.

ured as the share of years in which democratic governments were not overthrown—was 96 percent during years of positive real GNP growth. On the other hand, the survival rate fell to 84 percent among democratic regimes experiencing one year of negative growth, and to 71 percent among those experiencing two consecutive years of economic decline.

It does not follow, of course, that poor economic performance automatically leads to democratic breakdown. A substantial majority of the regimes in our sample survived one year, and even two years of negative growth, a fact that supports the contention that political as well as economic factors are likely to play into the explanation of regime change. Yet it seems difficult to deny that poor economic performance weakens democratic rule when other institutional and political weaknesses are present.

A review of the South American experience by Rueschemeyer, Stephens, and Stephens, for example, confirms the basic insights of the political economy approach to the demise of democratic regimes. They conclude that "acute economic problems" played at least some role in all but two of the democratic breakdowns occurring between the early 1920s and the mid-1970s, the exceptions being Venezuela in 1948 and Colombia in 1949. Although political factors were also important in the collapse of democracy elsewhere, all of the other cases experienced serious strains related to crises of the export sector, particularly during the 1920s and 1930s, or to problems associated with import-substituting industrialization. These include Chile in 1924 and 1973, Argentina in 1930, 1955, 1966, and 1976, Uruguay in 1933 and 1973, Brazil and Bolivia in 1964, Ecuador in 1961, and Peru in 1948 and 1968.[44]

This finding has some resonance with the non–Latin American cases in our sample as well. Economic difficulties contributed to the collapse of democracy in Korea in 1961 and the passing of the brief democratic moment there in 1980. Poor economic performance clearly contributed to the military interventions in Turkey in 1980 and in Thailand in 1976, as well as Marcos's coup d'état in the Philippines in 1972.

During the 1980s and 1990s, the relationship between economic performance and democratic survival appeared to vanish: despite the deepest crisis in the developing world since the Great Depression, only two of the 24 democratic breakdowns in our 47-country sample occurred during this period. This outcome did not necessarily imply increasing legitimation and acceptance of democracy, however; rather, other factors have helped sustain democracy in the face of economic adversity.

New democratic regimes benefited in the first place from the the decline and collapse of the Soviet Union and the end of Cold War politics. As

---

[44] Dietrich Rueschemeyer, Evelyne Huber Stephens, and John D. Stephens, *Capitalist Development and Democracy* (Chicago: University of Chicago Press, 1992), p. 210.

perceptions of the Soviet threat diminished, the United States and European governments were less willing to back dictatorial clients against opposition challenges, and more inclined to punish groups seeking to overthrow their constitutional successors. Even where authoritarian reversals occurred, international pressures played a significant role in preventing the consolidation of authoritarian rule (for example, Peru and Haiti), or in forcing a relatively rapid return to electoral politics (in Thailand and Guatemala).

A second reason for the survival of new democratic regimes in the face of crisis is the relatively short duration of the democratic revival and the lingering memory of military rule. Though crises occurred on the watch of many new democratic governments, they could credibly attribute these difficulties to ineffectual authoritarian predecessors. As a result, the domestic political support for authoritarian options remained weak, though as we will see, it was not altogether absent.

Yet even though economic deterioration has not yet lead to widespread authoritarian reversals, there is evidence that it has seriously jeopardized prospects for democratic consolidation. It does so in part by causing increased social violence and in part by creating the raw material for polarizing populist and antidemocratic political movements.[45]

The most politically troubling distributional questions center not on the poorest of the poor, but on middle-income employees and formal-sector workers. As discussed in the preceding section, the middle sectors have born a disproportionate share of the cost of adjustment in a number of countries in our sample, including Argentina, Brazil, and Mexico. Historically, downwardly mobile white-collar and small-business groups have been inclined to back right-wing or populist movements that not only are opposed to economic reform but have periodically expressed hostility toward democratic institutions as well.

Additional political challenges are also raised by the increasing urbanization of poverty. Typically, the urban informal sector is much more capable of exerting pressure on the government through strikes, riots, and demonstrations than are the poorest of the poor in the countryside. Indications of political alienation, increasing social tension, and civil violence are evident in many new democracies in the developing and former socialist worlds.

Finally, the rise of the Shining Path movement in Peru indicates the possibility that peasants themselves can in certain circumstances be mobilized into destabilizing terrorist organizations. The Shining Path leadership appealed to ethnic and regional antagonisms as well as to economic grievances, but the movement originated in the poorest regions of the country and then spread into the slums of Lima. During the past decade, civil vio-

---

[45] For a review, see Alex Hadenius, *Democracy and Development* (New York: Cambridge University Press, 1992), pp. 77–90.

TABLE 9.3
Death Toll and Economic Performance in Peru, 1980–1991

	Death Toll	GDP Growth	Inflation	Real Wage Growth
1980	3	2.9	59.2	
1981	4	3.0	75.4	
1982	170	0.9	64.4	2.3
1983	2,807	−12.0	111.2	−16.7
1984	4,319	4.8	110.2	−15.5
1985	1,359	1.6	163.4	−15.0
1986	1,268	8.5	77.9	26.7
1987	697	7.0	104.9	6.7
1988	1,986	−11.2	2,775.3	
1989	3,198	4.8	7,649.6	
1990	3,452			
1991	3,180			

Source: Cynthia McClintock, "Democracy and Civil Society in the Context of Economic Decline: Peru, 1980–1992," paper prepared for the Project on Economy, Society, and Democracy, Hoover Institution, 1992.

lence related to the movement has been closely linked to overall economic performance. Data collected by Cynthia McClintock show that deaths from conflict with the Shining Path peaked during the debt crisis of 1983–84, the hyperinflation of 1989–90, and the "Fuji shocks" of 1991—the sharp policy adjustments taken prior to Fujimori's suspension of the Peruvian Constitution (the "autogolpe") (see Table 9.3).[46]

Among the countries discussed in earlier chapters, the syndrome of democratic decay was most evident in Peru, where economic difficulties remained extraordinarily severe into the 1990s. Besides the civil violence associated with the Shining Path rebellion, opinion surveys also reveal widespread popular alienation within Peru's general public. Table 9.4 reports data on attitudes toward democracy and government performance in a number of new democratic regimes; the data from Peru were gathered during 1991, prior to Fujimori's "autogolpe." When asked which form of government they preferred, almost three Peruvians in ten chose a military regime, a share well above those answering similarly in Colombia and Bolivia, and slightly higher than in Ecuador, which also experienced substantial economic distress during the late 1980s. In a second survey conducted subsequent to the Fujimori coup in November 1992, support for democracy

---

[46] Cynthia McClintock, "Democracy and Civil Society in the Context of Economic Decline: Peru, 1980–1992," prepared for the project on "Economy, Society, and Democracy," Hoover Institution, 1992.

TABLE 9.4

Attitudes toward Democracy (Percentages of Survey Sample)

	Democracy Best for Country[a]	Prefer Military[b]	Dissatisfied with Democracy[c]	Believe Radical Change Needed[d]	Believe Things Going Poorly[e]
Bolivia					
7/91	74	11	58	34	70
10/92	77	11	40	71	
Colombia					
7/91	84	8	38	43	62
11/92	72	16	62		92
Ecuador					
7/91	63	25	64	42	91
11/92	66	26	43		79
Peru					
7/91	59	28	58	61	89
11/92	77	10	40		73
Venezuela					
1/92	76	na	43		88
Uruguay					
1991	73	10			
Chile					
1992	79				
Brazil					
1992	42	22	59		
Thailand					
3/93			22		23
Philippines					
11/92			28		29

TABLE 9.4 (*continued*)

	Democracy Best for Country[a]	Prefer Military[b]	Dissatisfied with Democracy[c]	Believe Radical Change Needed[d]	Believe Things Going Poorly[e]
Spain					
1985	70	10			
Portugal					
1985	61	9			
Greece					
1985	87	5			

Sources: Juan J. Linz and Alfred Stepan, *Problems of Democratic Transition and Consolidation: Southern Europe, South America and Eastern Europe,* unpublished ms.; "Andeans Favor Democracy Despite Dissatisfaction with Current Conditions," United States Information Agency, Research Memorandum, Feb. 7, 1992; "Fujimori and His Actions Are Widely Endorsed, but Peruvians Ultimately Want Democracy," Research Memorandum April 27, 1992; "Filipino Public Opinion on Democracy," Opinion Research Memorandum, March 19, 1993; "Andean Publics Prefer Democracy," Opinion Research Memorandum, April 8, 1993; "Urban Thai Opinion on Democracy," Opinion Research Memorandum, June 18, 1993.

[a]For Bolivia, Ecuador, Peru, Columbia, and Venezuela, response to question: "In your opinion, which type of government is best for (survey country)—a democratically elected government, a military government, or a revolutionary government?" Percent responding "democratically elected government." For Uruguay, Chile, Brazil, Spain, Portugal, and Greece, percent agreeing with the statement "Democracy is best for a country like ours."

[b]For Bolivia, Ecuador, Peru, Columbia, and Venezuela, response to question: "In your opinion, which type of government is best for (country in question)—a democratically elected government, a military government, or a revolutionary government?" Percent responding "military government." For Brazil, Uruguay, Spain, Portugal, and Greece, percent agreeing with the statement, "In some cases, a nondemocratic government could be preferable to a democracy."

[c]Response to question: "All things considered, are you satisfied or dissatisfied with the way democracy is functioning in (survey country)? Very satisfied, somewhat satisfied, somewhat dissatisfied, very dissatisfied." Percent responding "somewhat dissatisfied" and "very dissatisfied."

[d]Response to question: "Thinking for a moment about (survey country) as a whole, which of the following comes closest to your opinion: our society should be radically changed from the way it is now; our society is basically OK, but widespread reforms are required; our society is fine and neither revolutionary changes nor widespread reforms are necessary." Percent agreeing with statement that radical change is necessary.

[e]Response to question: "In general, how would you say things are going in our country—are they going very well, fairly well, fairly poorly, very poorly?" Percent responding "fairly poorly" or "very poorly."

in Peru increased. This did not reflect nostalgia for the old order, however, as much as it did terminological confusion. Over half of the respondents continued to consider Fujimori's government a democracy and 60 percent rejected the argument that he had violated the Constitution. Large majorities also supported the dissolution of Congress (78 percent), restructuring the Supreme Court (82 percent), and the closing of the Office of the Comptroller (70 percent).

Opinion surveys also indicated widespread political alienation in Brazil. Data collected by Stepan and Linz in 1992 showed that only 42 percent of the Brazilian respondents expressed a preference for the "democratic alternative," by far the lowest of any of the countries for which comparable data were available (Table 9.4). The preference for democracy dropped to only 36 percent among the large majority of respondents who perceived their income as extremely inadequate. The level of dissatisfaction with democracy, reported in other polls conducted in 1993, was also quite high, at 59 percent.[47]

These signs of political alienation appeared less widespread in most of the other countries for which comparable survey data are available, but there were also indications that support for democratic institutions remained tentative and unstable. Substantial majorities in most countries—between 70 and 80 percent—answered positively when asked if they preferred democracy to alternative forms of government; besides Peru and Brazil, Ecuador was the only South American country in which positive responses fell below 70 percent. When asked if they were satisfied with how democracy was working in their countries, however, large portions of the population in the Latin American countries (from 40 to 60 percent) answered negatively. This dissatisfaction appeared to vary closely with assessments of the performance of the incumbent president (Table 9.5).

Though a variety of factors shaped these opinions, erratic economic performance is clearly a major contributing factor. The lower rates of dissatisfaction reported in the two Asian cases for which there is comparable data are partly attributable to the timing of the surveys: immediately following the restoration of elected government in Thailand and the inauguration of the new Ramos government in the Philippines. But the difference

---

[47] European Society for Opinion and Marketing Research and Brazilian Institute for Public Opinion, as reported in James Brooke, "Inflation Saps Brazilians' Faith in Democracy," *New York Times,* July 25, 1993, p. 10.

Extensive survey research conducted by José Alvaro Moises indicates that while Brazilian democracy may still count on a "reservoir of legitimacy" that is independent of performance, there is also an empirical connection between diffuse support for democracy and satisfaction with the way government works. See "Democratization, Mass Political Culture and Political Legitimacy in Brazil," Research Center on International Relations and Comparative Politics, University of São Paulo, Brazil, Working Paper 1993/44, February 1993.

TABLE 9.5

Attitudes toward Democracy and Government Performance: Bolivia, Colombia,
Peru, and Ecuador (Percentages of Survey Sample)

	Bolivia	Colombia	Peru	Ecuador
Believe things going well, but dissatisfied with democracy	44	31	35	49
Believe things going poorly and dissatisfied with democracy	66	48	65	68
Unfavorable opinion of president, but satisfied with democracy	27	34	24	56
Unfavorable opinion of president, and dissatisfied with democracy	74	66	76	70

Sources and notes: see Table 9.4.

also reflected economic circumstances and expectations. Questions included in the Philippines survey indicated that fully 71 percent of the respondents saw their personal situation as "good" or "fairly good," and Thailand had the best economic performance over the 1980s of any country in our sample.

It is easy to sketch a stylized model of political decay in which prolonged economic deterioration undermines support for representative government and drains institutions of their democratic content. Such a cycle would begin with developments already evident in Brazil, Peru, Russia, Ukraine, and a number of other developing and formerly socialist countries: an increase in political cynicism and apathy, a decline in effective political participation, and an inability on the part of the political system to generate representative ruling coalitions. In a next stage, crime, civil violence and organized revolutionary or antirevolutionary ("death squad") activity contribute to a gradual erosion of the substance of democratic rule through intermittent repression of opposition groups, emergency measures, and a decline in the integrity of legal guarantees.

At a final stage—still short of a formal transition to authoritarian rule—electoral institutions are rendered a facade. Elected officials could be subject to the veto power of military elites, as happened in 1990 in Pakistan, or could become little more than fronts for them. This was the case with the highly repressive Uruguayan model from 1973 to 1985 in which civilians formally held the presidency for extended periods.

We can by no means rule out the possibility of open reversals of democratic rule. It is at least theoretically possible that authoritarian reversals would result from the military triumph of revolutionary movements spawned by the crisis, though given the changed international environment, this seems highly unlikely at present. A more likely scenario is that a general erosion of faith in the capacity of democratic governments to manage the economy would increase the appeal of authoritarian solutions to the crisis, not only among elites but among mass publics.

The erosion of support for democratic institutions could lead to the election of leaders or parties with plebiscitarian or openly authoritarian ambitions. More likely, however, is that economic crisis would reverse democratization through a more indirect route. Sustained poor performance or sudden economic deterioration lead to an increase in crime, strikes, riots, and civil violence. Rapid social changes and downward mobility for members of the middle and working classes increase the appeal of political movements on the extreme left and right. The deterioration of social order and increasing social polarization provide the classic justification for military intervention. In more extreme circumstances, the state could even collapse entirely as an organization with a credible claim to a monopoly of force.

CHAPTER TEN

Institutions, Democratic Consolidation, and Sustainable Growth

THE CONSOLIDATION of democratic rule depends not only on economic growth and a broad distribution of benefits; it also depends on the development of political institutions that can effectively mediate policy debates and coordinate the relations among contending social and economic interests. The construction of such institutions implies conditions quite different from the "politics of initiation" discussed in the preceding parts of this volume. As with the consolidation of economic reform, the consolidation of representative government implies a reduction in the personal discretion enjoyed by executives and greater accountability to elected representatives and interest-group leaders.

At various times, all democracies experience a tension between the need for rapid executive decision-making on the one hand and principles of participation and negotiation on the other. This tension is likely to be particularly acute in newly established regimes in which difficult economic adjustments have pulled governments toward centralized or even autocratic styles of decision-making.[1] Where economic crises are deep, democratic institutions may well be undermined by the failure to take swift and effective action; pressing challenges of economic reform thus create both opportunities and incentives for executives to augment their power. Over the longer term, however, executive authority must eventually be depersonalized and made accountable if both democracy and economic reform are to be institutionalized.

We have already highlighted this dilemma in Part Two. In the extreme crisis cases, stabilization and adjustment efforts were initiated by presidents who bypassed normal legislative procedures, often through reliance on emergency powers that were of unclear and contested constitutionality. Whatever the economic merits of such action in the short run, there are obvious risks that such centralization can degenerate into an autocratic style

---

[1] We have developed this theme at greater length in "The State in the Initiation and Consolidation of Market-Oriented Reform," in Dietrich Rueschemeyer and Louis Putterman, eds., *State and Market in Development: Synergy or Rivalry?* (Boulder, Colo.: Lynne Reiner, 1993), pp. 241–42, and in "Introduction: Institutions and Economic Policy," in Stephan Haggard and Robert Kaufman, eds., *The Politics of Economic Adjustment.* (Princeton, N.J.: Princeton University Press, 1992), pp. 18–20.

of decision-making that is inimical not only to democracy but to stable economic policy as well. The economic situation in the non-crisis cases was different, but the political problem was similar. Authoritarian governments pushed through reforms that provided relatively favorable economic conditions for new democratic governments. But the consolidation of democratic rule was jeopardized by continuities in the powers claimed by the executive agencies of the state, including by the military itself, and in continuing restrictions on participation.

It is difficult to predict precisely how the new democratic systems we have analyzed will manage these issues as they move beyond the initial phases of political transition and economic reform. Current institutional arrangements cannot be taken as fixed, and further constitutional changes may occur as the economic situation and the balance of power among contending interests shift. As in the previous chapter, however, it is possible to draw on a combination of theory and the experiences at hand to advance some conclusions about the relationship between institutional design, economic governance, and the consolidation of democracy.

We begin by examining the constitution of executive authority and its effects on the capacity for economic management. We then address three debates about alternative modes of interest representation and political accountability: the merits of direct representation of interest groups in economic decision-making, either through social pacts or corporatism; the advantages of parliamentary versus presidential systems; and alternative ways of structuring party competition.

THE DILEMMA OF EXECUTIVE ACCOUNTABILITY

In most democracies, either the Constitution or informal understandings provide executives with some emergency powers to respond to national crises in ways that bypass normal legislative procedures. Most constitutions also endow executives (and particularly presidents) with more routine forms of legislative authority, or what Shugart and Carey have labeled "entrenched presidential power."[2] Such authority includes vetoes, the power to introduce legislation, and the power to issue decrees subject to Congressional approval. In addition to their legislative powers, prime ministers in some parliamentary systems can also dismiss parliament and call for new elections.

It is crucial to distinguish these emergency and entrenched constitutional powers from executive authority that derives from the explicit legislative

[2] Matthew Soberg Shugart and John M. Carey, *Presidents and Assemblies* (New York: Cambridge University Press, 1992), p. 132.

delegation of decision-making responsibility in specified policy areas. Such authority may be delegated to the executive directly, or it may be vested in independent agencies or commissions. For example, central banks and quasi-judicial policymaking agencies in the trade area have played an important role in economic policymaking in the advanced industrial states as well as in successful cases of reform in the developing world.

Such delegation can be interpreted either as a rational response by politicians to the presence of collective action problems or as a device for institutionalizing changes that favor a particular policy coalition.[3] It should be underlined, however, that this form of explicit and delimited delegation does not necessarily reflect a decline in democratic oversight or an abdication of legislative responsibility. As Kiewit and McCubbins have argued most forcefully, legislatures maintain a variety of mechanisms through which they can delegate while maintaining effective monitoring of executive behavior.[4] Such delegation therefore does not pose the same risks as the high level of discretionary authority associated with the emergency or "entrenched" powers that are the concern of this section. To the contrary, we interpret delegation of this sort as evidence of the institutionalization of rules and policymaking processes that are likely to survive changes of political leadership; in short, as evidence of consolidation.

Entrenched powers can also help overcome collective action and aggregation problems and thus contribute to the successful initiation and consolidation of politically difficult economic reform measures.[5] During the 1980s and 1990s in Chile, Korea, and Thailand, for example, executives maintained the right to set limits on government spending unilaterally, tying the hands of legislatures with respect to fiscal policy. In chapter 5, we suggested that the power of the president in Uruguay to limit fiscal expenditures and to set public wages contributed to the avoidance of extreme macroeconomic instability.[6]

Emergency powers are much more controversial. Such powers have typically been written into constitutions to manage severe external and

---

[3] Robert H. Bates and Anne O. Krueger, "Generalizations Arising from the Country Studies," in Bates and Krueger, eds., *Political and Economic Interactions in Economic Policy Reform* (Cambridge, Mass.: Basil Blackwell, 1993), pp. 463–67.

[4] Roderick Kiewit and Mathew McCubbins, *The Logic of Delegation* (Chicago: University of Chicago Press, 1991).

[5] In presidential systems, the veto is typically one of the most important legislative powers granted to the president. Where extraordinary majorities are required for an override, it is a powerful instrument for blocking Congressional initiatives. As such, however, it is more important for preserving the continuity of existing policy than for instituting changes. We are grateful to Matthew Shugart for clarifying our thinking on this point.

[6] See also Jennifer McCoy, "The Collective Dilemma of Economic Reform: Uruguay in Comparative Perspective," presented to the Instituto de Ciencia Política, Universidad de la Republica, Montevideo, Uruguay, September 1992.

internal security challenges and have had their most pronounced effect on the integrity of the judicial process and individual political rights. In some instances, however, broad interpretations of the constitutional powers of the executive during emergencies have been used to authorize major economic policy initiatives, as with the "need and urgency decrees" issued under Alfonsín and Menem. And even where open-ended emergency powers are not already specified by the Constitution, they have at times been granted to the president by legislative majorities to deal with economic as well as political crises; this was the case in Argentina, Bolivia, and Peru.

Whether claimed through constitutional interpretation or through legislative delegation, such broad grants of emergency powers by definition permit heads of government to supersede the normal channels of representation and decision-making that new democracies seek to institutionalize. Such steps may be justified in some cases by the dangers posed by prolonged immobilism and severe economic deterioration. In Bolivia, for example, decree powers used to tame hyperinflation in 1985 were accompanied by substantial repression of union opposition, yet the actions arguably saved democracy by breaking the impasse over economic policy and by preempting military intervention.

Regardless of its advantages in economic crises, however, the exploitation of broad emergency powers carries far more serious implications for democratic consolidation than does the routine and circumscribed delegation of decision-making authority in particular policy areas. The potential for abuse is obvious. Most directly, claims to emergency authority can provide the opening for the assumption of dictatorial power. Yet it is just as important to emphasize, as Guillermo O'Donnell has done,[7] that strong executive authority can have important indirect effects on the effectiveness and legitimacy of representative institutions.

First, endowing the executive with extensive legislative discretion, particularly in presidential systems, can undermine the incentives of party leaders to reach compromises on economic issues. This is particularly dangerous where the party system is characterized by sharp ideological cleavages. Valenzuela has argued persuasively that during the 1950s and 1960s in Chile, constitutional reforms that increased presidential powers over the budget contributed directly to increasing polarization, both by reducing legislators' opportunities for securing constituent benefits through Congressional logrolling and by increasing the stakes attached to winning the presidency.[8] As Shugart and Carey argue, "an assembly represents the diversity

---

[7] Guillermo O'Donnell, "Delegative Democracy?" Working Paper no. 172, Kellogg Institute, University of Notre Dame, 1992.

[8] Arturo Valenzuela, "Party Politics and the Crisis of Presidentialism in Chile: A Proposal for a Parliamentary Form of Government," in Linz and Valenzuela, *The Failure of Presidential Democracy*, vol. 2, *The Case of Latin America*, pp. 130–37. However, in some instances,

of a polity far better than an executive dependent on the president's whim is likely to do. Because of the diverse forces represented in an assembly, such a body has the potential for encompassing divergent viewpoints and striking compromises on them."[9]

Vesting strong discretionary powers in executives also increases the likelihood that they will seek broad popular mandates through media appeals and personalist movements, rather than relying on institutionalized consultation with legislators and interest groups. Guillermo O'Donnell has coined the expression "delegative democracy" to describe such situations; Bresser Pereira, Maravall, and Przeworski refer to "decretismo." Both concepts are closely akin to Weber's notion of "plebiscitarianism."[10] Such systems may continue to rest on electoral legitimation, but the style of decision-making serves to undermine representative institutions.

The grant of discretionary powers may be matched with adequate legislative oversight in established democracies, but the possibility that delegation will degenerate into abdication is greater in the developing world where the legal system remains underdeveloped, particularly with respect to judicial review; governments confront major adjustment difficulties; and nonelected officials in the military or bureaucracy continue to exercise independent control over resources. As we have seen in a number of the formerly socialist republics in particular, the commitment of elected politicians to democracy is by no means certain. Under these conditions, legislative majorities may be willing to grant broad powers that open the door to executive abuse but which cannot be effectively controlled by judicial or legislative oversight.

In the absence of consultation and oversight, decision-makers in the executive are also deprived of feedback that can be crucial both for the technical quality of policies and for the political support necessary to sustain them. Economic reforms are thus likely to be unstable and subject to reversal. In a typical sequence, an unaccountable leader—whether orthodox or populist in policy orientation—fails to deliver fully on promises with regard to economic policy and performance. Credibility and authority deflate rapidly, and support disintegrates. Opposition movements mobilize

---

as Shugart and Carey point out, such powers may actually facilitate system stability: where parties are organized primarily around regional interests, extensive presidential authority over economic policy can free individual legislators to service local constituencies, while also providing a check against particularism that might undermine the system as a whole. See Shugart and Carey, *Presidents and Assemblies*, p. 187.

[9] Ibid., p. 165.

[10] Luiz Carlos Bresser Pereira, José María Maravall, and Adam Przeworski, *Economic Reforms in New Democracies* (New York: Cambridge University Press, 1990), p. 208; Guillermo O'Donnell, "Delegative Democracy?"; Max Weber, *Economy and Society*, 2 vols. (Berkeley: University of California Press, 1978), 1:268–71, which contains several brilliant insights on the relationship between plebiscitarianism and economic management.

on the basis of a complete rejection of the government's approach, regardless of its merits. Counter-elites win office, but employing a style of governance that is little different from that which they replace.

We should not assume that democracies characterized by such erratic swings in policy will persist.[11] As we argued in the previous chapter, if reform initiatives fail or generate populist backlashes, then a cycle of political decay leading to the weakening or collapse of democracy is altogether possible. Yet even where the reform initiatives of plebiscitarian presidents yield positive economic results, there is substantial risk of a slide into a kind of "soft authoritarianism" in which economic success is used by the ruler to chip away at constitutional limits on his power.

FUNCTIONAL REPRESENTATION: THE PROSPECTS FOR SOCIAL PACTS AND CORPORATISM

One means of promoting greater accountability is through corporatism: the institutionalized participation of interest associations in policy formulation and implementation. The most important historical examples come from the societal corporatist arrangements that emerged in the smaller European countries during the 1930s and 1940s. These arrangements rested on two interrelated components: hierarchical, state-sanctioned, and monopolistic peak associations; and tripartite "concertation" between these peak business and labor groups and the government over economic policy questions, including macroeconomic management and particularly wage policy.[12]

As Terry Karl has argued, it is important to distinguish these "managerial" forms of concertation from the "foundational pacts" that accompanied some democratic transitions, including those in Colombia and Venezuela during the late 1950s and in Spain in the 1970s.[13] The explicit negotiation of mutual guarantees that characterized the transitions in these countries arguably contributed to the stability of democracy and has thus figured prominently in theorizing about regime change more generally.[14] With the

[11] O'Donnell reaches a similarly pessimistic conclusion in "Delegative Democracy."

[12] Though conceptually distinct, these two dimensions tend to be closely associated. Philippe Schmitter, "Reflections on Where the Theory of Neo-Corporatism Has Gone and Where the Praxis of Neo-Corporatism May be Going," in Gerhard Lehmbruch and Philippe C. Schmitter, eds., *Patterns of Corporatist Policy Making* (Beverly Hills: Sage, 1982), p. 264.

[13] Terry Lynn Karl, "Dilemmas of Democratization in Latin America," *Comparative Politics* 23 (1990): 1–21.

[14] See, for example, Guillermo O'Donnell and Philippe Schmitter, *Tentative Conclusions about Uncertain Democracies,* pt. 4 in O'Donnell, Schmitter, and Laurence Whitehead, eds., *Transitions from Authoritarian Rule: Prospects for Democracy* (Baltimore: Johns Hopkins University Press, 1986), pp. 37–47. The literature on corporatism bears a relationship to the study of "consociational" forms of rule in which representation is based on ethnic identifica-

partial exception of Spain, however, these foundational pacts did not resolve important economic policy issues, which remained the subject of considerable contestation. As we have shown in chapter 6, this was also true of the Uruguayan effort at pact-making in the mid-1980s.

In Spain, a detailed program of stabilization and structural adjustment was included in the famous Moncloa Pact of 1977, which helped to commit parties of the left to the democratic reform process at a moment of considerable uncertainty. But interest-group leaders were not signatories, and this pact and subsequent ones played only a limited role in influencing actual policy decisions.[15] Key provisions on tax reform, privatization, and financial liberalization were not implemented under Suarez. Trade liberalization, one of the major reforms of the Socialist years, was never included in any of the pacts, and the labor-market reform passed in 1984 was bitterly opposed by the unions. Agreements on wage restraint were an important component of the Spanish pacts and arguably contributed to the depoliticization of industrial conflicts. Yet given the slack Spanish labor market, it is not clear that the pacts had a major effect on wage growth, which would probably have been restrained in any event. Moreover, strikes increased substantially throughout the 1980s, in spite of the agreements.

In other parts of Europe, more institutionalized corporatist arrangements contributed directly to successful macroeconomic policy and efficient structural adjustment, at least into the early 1980s. But most developing countries face political and economic conditions that are far less favorable for such an option. The first difficulty is the organizational weakness of the relevant players, including both interest groups and parties. The essence of corporatist negotiation is that the most important economic actors are capable either of negotiating binding agreements on major policy variables directly, or of providing credible support for bargains struck on key government initiatives with respect to macroeconomic and incomes policies. Such capabilities will be greatest where the number of actors is small and each is internally cohesive. In most European countries where corporatism proved effective, strong social democratic parties played an important role. Moreover, centralized peak associations of both business and labor had acquired the capacity to speak authoritatively for their memberships and to guarantee a minimum level of compliance.

---

tion rather than functional position in the division of labor. See Arend Lijphart, *The Politics of Accommodation* (Berkeley: University of California Press, 1968).

[15] Nancy Bermeo and José García-Durán, "Economic Liberalization in New Democracies: Lessons from the Spanish Case," in Stephan Haggard and Steven B. Webb, eds., *Voting for Reform: Democracy, Political Liberalization, and Economic Adjustment* (New York: Oxford University Press, 1994), pp. 93–94; Eric Hershberg, "Transitions from Authoritarianism and Eclipse of the Left: Toward a Reinterpretation of Regime Change in Spain," (Ph.D. diss., University of Wisconsin, Madison, 1989).

Though such conditions have been approximated in a few cases such as Chile, most of the countries in this volume lack such organizational capabilities at present. Peru, Bolivia, Thailand, and the Philippines are characterized by both weak political parties and weak labor organizations. In Korea and Turkey, emerging labor organizations have been hampered politically by the absence of ties to a strong center-left party. In Korea, recent labor reforms loosened the hold of the peak labor federation, which was (rightly) associated with the repressive labor regime of the Park and Chun years. In Latin America, business and labor have at times been represented in wage-setting agencies and other regulatory and administrative institutions in the past. But such corporatist practices were more likely to conform with what Schmitter calls "state corporatism" than the social democratic variant, and have typically involved substantial elements of top-down control. With the exception of Mexico's authoritarian regime, moreover, such arrangements have rarely dealt with general issues of macroeconomic management on a continuing basis.[16] Unions in Argentina, Brazil, and Uruguay have at times demonstrated strength in particular sectors or industries, but generally lack cohesive peak associations.[17]

The second broad barrier to concertation is economic. For reasons discussed in chapter 5, the relevance of European-style corporatism is especially questionable in countries experiencing very high inflation. Time horizons are short, the risks of making concessions are high, and severe constraints on fiscal policy make it extremely difficult for governments to organize the compensatory arrangements that typically cement such corporatist agreements. Even where such crises are brought under control, however, the organization of corporatist bargaining systems is likely to face important structural and institutional obstacles that were not generally present in the European countries.[18]

Corporatist politics in Europe initially evolved when capital was less mobile internationally and national economies were less open to trade. Since production could not easily be shifted abroad, employers in the traded goods sector had an incentive to back centralized wage and labor-market

[16] For the classic statement on this, see Philippe Schmitter, "Still the Century of Corporatism?" *Review of Politics* 36 (1974): 85–131. For discussions of corporatism in the Latin American context, see James Malloy, ed., *Authoritarianism and Corporatism in Latin America* (Pittsburgh: University of Pittsburgh Press, 1977), and Ruth Berins Collier and David Collier, "Inducements vs. Constraints: Disaggregating Corporatism," *American Political Science Review* 73 (1979): 967–86.

[17] See the discussion by Juan Carlos Torre, "Transición democrática y emergencia económica: El gobierno de la economia bajo la presidencia de Alfonsín," unpublished ms., Princeton University, 1992.

[18] For a parallel critique, see Adam Przeworski, *Democracy and the Market: Political and Economic Reforms in Eastern Europe and Latin America* (New York: Cambridge University Press, 1991), p. 185.

policies that would control wage pressures emanating from groups less exposed to international competitive pressures.[19] The continued existence of a large non-traded goods sector also made it possible for governments to use the tools of Keynesian demand management to sustain agreements on wages and social compensation.

During the 1980s and 1990s, the international economic milieu changed radically. Within Europe itself, increasing exposure to trade, highly integrated international financial markets, and the growth of foreign direct investment contributed to intensified sectoral conflicts within union peak organizations and made it more difficult to maintain solidaristic wage bargains. As Jonas Pontusson has argued with respect to Sweden, long considered the paradigmatic case of social democratic corporatism, "post Fordist" responses to increased international competition attached a higher priority to flexibility, with respect to both shop-floor arrangements and wage-setting procedures.[20] The combination of the internationalization of capital markets coupled with the move toward fixed exchange rates also weakened, if it did not undermine altogether, the ability of governments to use the traditional instruments of fiscal and monetary policy to sustain corporatist bargains.

These economic constraints are likely to affect the prospects for institutional innovation along corporatist lines in developing countries as well. In the export-oriented countries of East and Southeast Asia—Korea, Taiwan, and Thailand—concerns about the maintenance of competitiveness are arguably similar to the ones that motivated the organization of centralized bargaining arrangements in Europe in earlier decades.[21] Yet even if the political and organizational barriers to the formation of such systems could be overcome, the prospects are also affected by the same trends that have jeopardized social democratic corporatism in Europe: the trend toward financial market and import liberalization, increasing international competition in wage-sensitive sectors, the explosion of foreign direct investment, and the global trend toward more flexible production processes.

Other countries in our sample face even more difficult obstacles to successful corporatism. Their economies have typically been characterized by large income disparities between the urban and rural sectors, high levels of under- and unemployment, and large informal sectors that are intrinsically difficult to organize. The most organized segments of the union

[19] Peter Swenson, "Bringing Capital Back In, or Social Democracy Reconsidered: Employer Power, Cross-Class Alliances, and Centralization of Industrial Relations in Denmark and Sweden," *World Politics* 43 (1991): 513–44.

[20] Jonas Pontusson, "At the End of the Third Road: Swedish Social Democracy in Crisis" *Politics and Society* 20 (1992): 305–32.

[21] For an analysis of recent trends in unionism in the Pacific Basin, see Stephen Frenkel, ed., *Organized Labor in the Asia-Pacific Region* (Ithaca, N.Y.: ILR Press, 1993).

movement in Latin America, moreover, remain located in the non-tradables sector, in import-substituting industries, and in the public sector and state-owned enterprises, all activities that stand to lose from current structural adjustment efforts.

Under these circumstances, it is not surprising that efforts to forge centralized economic pacts have not generally been successful. Though the viability of a social corporatist model has been debated extensively among intellectuals in Korea and Turkey, these proposals have made little headway in the political system.[22] As we saw in chapter 7, a corporatist structure for representing business interests did emerge in Thailand in the early 1980s, but labor interests were explicitly excluded and the consultative body was not central to overall economic policymaking. Brief moves in the direction of corporatist accommodation with labor in the more open political environment under Chatichai in the late 1980s, but these were reversed by the coup. In the Philippines, there have been no moves in the direction of either pact-making or corporatism, and in Taiwan, democratization has spawned efforts by both labor and capital to break free of state-corporatist arrangements.

The most important initiatives at concertation have come in the Latin American cases, in part perhaps because of their cultural ties with Europe. However, these have generally failed to accomplish their purpose. Shortly after Sarney's inauguration in Brazil, for example, talks were initiated between business, government, and representatives of one of the major labor federations, but these quickly broke down in the face of opposition from the more radical labor confederation. In 1986, the government launched the Cruzado Plan by decree, attempted a new round of pact negotiations when this collapsed in early 1987, then decreed a new program under Bresser Pereira a few months later.[23]

Similar stories can be told for most of the other Latin American countries. In Argentina, Alfonsín moved toward a policy of "concertación" with the General Confederation of Labor (CGT) in May 1984, after earlier conflicts over reform of the labor law, promulgated the Austral Plan by decree in 1985, then again attempted to build an alliance with labor by appointing a prominent union official to the Cabinet in 1987. Throughout this period, however, both business and labor representatives adopted neo-Keynesian stances resisted by officials in the Finance Ministry, and as in Brazil, the fragmentation within the union movement meant that "there would always be some section of organized labor which would refuse to

[22] See, for example, Ziya Öniş and Steven B. Webb, "Turkey: Democratization and Adjustment from Above," in Haggard and Webb, eds., *Voting for Reform*, pp. 145–47; Hagen Koo, "The State, *Minjung*, and the Working Class in South Korea," in Koo, ed., *State and Society in Contemporary Korea* (Ithaca, N.Y.: Cornell University Press, 1993), pp. 158–60.

[23] Ian Roxboro, "Organized Labor: A Major Victim of the Crisis," in Stallings and Kaufman, eds., *Debt and Democracy in Latin America* (Boulder, Colo.: Westview Press, 1989), pp. 91–108.

be bound by any agreement."[24] In Peru, a more limited form of concertation with the major business association disintegrated when Alan García unilaterally decided to nationalize the private banking system.

Because systematic cooperation among interest groups and state officials is important for the effective long-term management of the economy, there will certainly be further efforts to institutionalize new modes of consultation. The broad difficulties sketched above, however, suggest that concerted agreements brokered among peak associations and government leaders are not likely to be a viable means for accomplishing these objectives in most countries.

More promising possibilities may lie in the evolution of more limited forms of corporatist representation within the context of the regulation of particular issues or sectors.[25] Such "meso-level" forms of concertation also pose difficulties for economic management and democratic accountability, however. In contrast to "macro" corporatism, such arrangements are necessarily less encompassing both in the nature of the issues they address and in the interests represented. For example, countries pursuing import-substituting growth strategies had such intermediate forms of representation that became the locus for rent-seeking, capture, corruption, and the institutionalization of rigidities in the allocation of resources and income across groups and sectors. Such arrangements can also be characterized by secrecy and the absence of accountability and oversight.

Though we are skeptical about the prospects for both macro and meso levels of corporatism in the new democracies of the developing world, it is clear that the functioning of both will depend heavily on the relationship between these structures and the legislatures that create and oversee them. For those countries lacking the prospects for effective corporatism, the legislative arena becomes even more important in determining the effectiveness of economic policy.

LEGISLATIVE REPRESENTATION: THE
PRESIDENTIAL-PARLIAMENTARY DEBATE

A central issue in recent debates on the design of democratic institutions is the relative merits of parliamentary and presidential systems of government.[26] Quite surprisingly, there has been little direct reference in this

---

[24] Ibid., p. 200.

[25] During 1993 and 1994, for example, wage, investment, and tax agreements forged through tripartite agreements in the Brazilian automobile sector had attracted considerable attention as a possible means of industrial modernization and expansion.

[26] A number of the more important pieces have been collected in Larry Diamond and Marc F. Plattner, eds., *The Global Resurgence of Democracy* (Baltimore: Johns Hopkins University Press, 1993), including Juan Linz, "The Perils of Presidentialism" pp. 108–26, and "The

debate to the crucial economic issues that dominate the political agenda of many new democracies. Yet a brief review of several major points of contention suggests that the debate is highly relevant to the question of combining democratic rule with coherent and stable economic policy.

"Parliamentistas" argue that the two core features of presidential systems—separate and independent election of the executive and legislature and fixed terms—both pose significant difficulties for the stability and efficiency of democratic rule. The first feature, "dual democratic legitimacy," is claimed to be the source of the tendency to stalemate between the branches. Executives with an independent electoral base and separate powers have fewer incentives to seek enduring coalitions, or even to negotiate compromises, and may be more inclined than prime ministers to engage in plebiscitarian appeals.[27] For their part, independently elected legislators have strong incentives to focus on their constituents' interests and are less likely to cooperate with the president where it cuts against those interests.[28] This is true even when the president's own party holds a legislative majority, and will be particularly marked when executives are limited to a single term or when the president's agenda includes difficult adjustment measures. In the crisis cases, for example, Alfonsín, Menem, and Siles all faced serious difficulties in containing dissent within their own parties in the legislature. The possibility for stalemate is even greater under conditions of divided government.

The separate electoral mandate for executives in a presidential system can complicate relations with the legislature in other ways as well. Direct elections for the president provide greater opportunity for outsiders to gain executive power; where many candidates are in the race, there are also greater possibilities for politicians appealing to narrow interests or the extreme ends of the political spectrum.[29] Donald Horowitz and others have suggested that it is possible to reduce these risks by geographical distribution or runoff requirements that encourage the formation of broad electoral

---

Virtues of Parliamentarism," pp. 138–45; Donald L. Horowitz, "Comparing Democratic Systems," pp. 127–33; and Arend Lijphart, "Constitutional Choices for New Democracies," pp. 146–58. See also Scott Mainwaring, "Presidentialism in Latin America," *Latin American Research Review* 25 (1989): 157–79; Matthew Shugart and John M. Carey, *Presidents and Assemblies* (New York: Cambridge University Press, 1989), pp. 28–54; Juan J. Linz and Arturo Valenzuela, eds., *The Failure of Presidential Democracy*, 2 vols. (Baltimore: Johns Hopkins University Press, 1994), vol. 1, *Comparative Perspectives;* and Scott Mainwaring and Matthew Soberg Shugart, eds., "Presidentialism and Democracy in Latin America," unpublished ms., University of California, San Diego.

[27] See for example, Juan J. Linz, "Presidential or Parliamentary Democracy," in Linz and Valenzuela, *The Failure of Presidential Democracy*, vol. 1, *Comparative Perspectives,* pp. 6–8.

[28] Shugart and Carey, *Presidents and Assemblies,* p. 33.

[29] Ibid.

coalitions.[30] Nevertheless, if countries such as Brazil and Peru had had parliamentary systems during the 1980s, it is unlikely that a Collor or Fujimori would have come to power, or that leaders like Lula or Brizola could have been serious contenders for the Brazilian presidency.

If outsiders or extremists come to power without the backing of broadly based party organizations, they are poorly positioned to develop the legislative support required to sustain their programs. This weakness compounds the tendency to executive-legislative stalemate, and thus increases the temptation for the executive to bypass the legislature through the exploitation of decree powers, or even by extraconstitutional means.

In parliamentary regimes, by contrast, executive and legislative authority are fused, creating clearer lines of decision-making authority. In majoritarian systems, legislators have a greater incentive to cooperate with the executive and to maintain party discipline, if for no more complex reason than that the fall of the government could lead to the calling of new elections. In multiparty systems in which coalition government is more typical, defenders of parliamentarism find the process of coalition formation itself a salutary one that involves negotiation and compromise among diverse interests. Executives are less likely to be outsiders in parliamentary systems; parliamentary leaders normally ascend to office as a result of extensive party and legislative experience. Moreover, since their tenure depends on their capacity to maintain legislative majorities, they must consult with supporters to retain those majorities, whether backbenchers within their own parties or coalition partners. For these reasons, they are also more likely to be able to forge coalitions of support for their programs.

A second cluster of defects in presidential systems arises from the existence of fixed terms. It is extremely difficult to change governments when the legislature, but more particularly the president, has lost political support and exhausted leadership potential. Presidentialism served to prolong crises in Brazil and Peru, for example, where presidents Sarney, Collor, and García outstayed their effectiveness. In Bolivia and Argentina, lame-duck presidents were forced to resign before the expiration of their terms. Arguably, the transition would have come earlier and more smoothly under parliamentary rule, under which votes of no confidence can lead to new elections when governments have failed.

Advocates for parliamentarism have not gone unchallenged, and many of the counterarguments are pertinent for understanding the prospects for coherent economic management under different governmental forms. First, it is important to note that the entire debate over presidential and parlia-

---

[30] Donald L. Horowitz, "Comparing Democratic Systems," in Larry Diamond and Marc F. Plattner, eds., *The Global Resurgence of Democracy* (Baltimore and London: Johns Hopkins University Press, 1993), pp. 127–34.

mentary forms of rule may be moot. Opportunities for a comprehensive redesign of presidential constitutions are rare, and may have already passed in Latin America, the Philippines, and Korea. When such opportunities have arisen, as in the Brazilian plebiscite of 1992 or the extensive debates on the issue in Korea in the late 1980s, they have encountered powerful opposition from groups with interests in the existing system, usually including the incumbent president and those backing the leading aspirants for the office.

Even in circumstances where presidential regimes might be replaced by parliamentary systems, it is unclear that the change would result in coherent agreements on such crucial issues as thresholds of representation, provisions governing votes of confidence, and relations between the head of government and the head of state. It is quite possible that constitutional negotiations, which would necessarily involve groups linked to the older institutional arrangements, would produce hybrid outcomes that leave lines of accountability unclear and combine the worst of both systems. Under such circumstances, incremental reforms of the presidential system may be a wiser course than a shift to parliamentarism.

We are also skeptical, however, that parliamentarism per se is inherently superior to presidentialism for meeting the challenges of economic management that we have highlighted in the preceding chapters. In both the crisis and non-crisis cases, some of the central difficulties of policymaking had less to do with the executive's relationship with the legislature than with the difficulty of securing the cooperation of business and unions. Parliamentarism offers no guarantees that these relationships would be handled more effectively. Indeed, if consultation is seen as an important component of reaching bargains over major adjustment issues, it is not clear that a parliamentary form is necessarily superior. In majoritarian systems, or where ruling coalitions are cohesive, prime ministers in parliamentary systems have greater discretionary latitude than presidents, who must necessarily negotiate with legislatures to achieve their objectives.[31]

It is also important to emphasize that "executive-legislative" stalemates are possible in parliamentary as well as presidential systems, though they naturally take a different form. Under parliamentary systems with proportional representation, fragmentation of the party system and patronage demands from party leaders can create dangerous stalemates not only in making policy but in the formation of governments. At least one study of European parliamentary systems shows that stabilization initiatives are more difficult as the number of parties in the governing coalition grows

---

[31] For this reason, defenders of parliamentarism tend to favor a proportional representation system that encourages coalition governments over the Westminister form. See Mainwaring and Shugart, "Presidentialism and Democracy."

larger because of the increase in the number of side payments required.[32] Among our cases, Turkey in the late 1970s stands out as an example of a parliamentary government in which economic policymaking was exceedingly incoherent because of the difficulty of negotiating compromises within coalitions and the instability of governments themselves.

The political upheavals in Japan and Italy in 1993 showed that pork-barrel politics and corruption can flourish just as well in parliamentary systems as in presidential ones, particularly where parties are constructed around patronage networks. Though such systems did not slow growth in those two cases, the costs of patronage are arguably higher in the developing world, and parliamentarism per se does not provide a solution.

Finally, we note that the statistical evidence is mixed as to whether parliamentary systems are any less vulnerable than presidential ones to usurpation of power, the suspension of constitutional norms, or the assumption of executive powers by the military. Shugart and Carey survey all regimes in the twentieth century that have had at least two consecutive elections, and find the rate of breakdown among developing countries to be about 52 percent for presidential systems and just over 59 percent for parliamentary ones.[33] Not included in this tally, moreover, is the wave of parliamentary breakdowns that occurred during the 1920s and 1930s in Eastern and Southern Europe, or in Japan.

Stepan and Skach, by contrast, find greater durability for parliamentary systems. In one test among several, they examine the set of all countries that achieved independence between 1945 and 1979. Grouping them on the basis of their constitutional form at the time of independence, they find that the only countries to still have continuous democratic rule between 1980 and 1989 were to be found among the parliamentary regimes (36 percent of those that were parliamentary "at birth"). Of the 52 countries in the nonparliamentary category—presidential, semipresidential, and monarchical governments—none managed to achieve or sustain continuous democratic rule into the 1980s.

However, the vast majority of these survivors were former British colonies that had adopted the Westminster model of majoritarian rule, many of them small island states that are of highly dubious comparative significance. Moreover, these governments all approximated two-party systems;

---

[32] Nouriel Roubini and Jeffry Sachs, "Economic and Political Determinants of Budget Deficits in the Industrial Economies," *European Economic Review* 33 (1989): 903–33.

[33] Shugart and Carey, *Presidents and Assemblies,* pp. 38–43. The criterion of two consecutive elections is aimed at eliminating "ambiguous cases in which one election was held under the watchful eye of a departing colonial power or as a mere 'demonstration' for foreign consumption. Breakdowns excluded cases of 'reequilibration' in which brief lapses of democratic authority were followed by new constitutions or a return to the preexisting one." ibid., p. 39.

among the survivors, only Israel and Papua New Guinea had more than 2.5 effective parties.[34] This raises the crucial question of whether it is characteristics of the party system or parliamentarism that is the source of political stability,[35] not to mention the question of whether small ex-British colonies are relevant for understanding the more industrialized and socially heterogeneous middle-income countries that are the concern of this volume.

There are many technical and data barriers to assessing the economic effects of parliamentary versus presidential rule in the countries of interest to us here. Many democracies have been founded very recently and it is premature to assess current adjustment efforts; as a result, standard statistical modeling will not necessarily yield meaningful results. Nonetheless, some tentative observations can be drawn by sorting democracies according to the simple typology presented in Table 10.1. We situate the twelve countries examined in this book in the context of all other developing countries classified by Shugart and Carey as having held at least two successive democratic elections without breakdown as of 1991.

The table differentiates governments along two axes. The first is whether they have presidential, parliamentary, or "mixed" systems. Along the second axis, countries are ranked by the number of effective parties in the legislature. We distinguish between those characterized by dominant parties or two-party competition (1.5–2.5 effective parties), those characterized by moderate multipartism (2.5–3.0 parties), and those with over 3.0 effective parties. We also show average growth and inflation rates for the second half of the 1980s (1986–90), a period of adjustment in most developing countries, recognizing that these data are not necessarily good measures of the underlying variable we are trying to explain: effective economic management.

The table reveals that our sample is biased toward the presidential cell; only two of our twelve cases are classified as parliamentary, and two more are classified by Shugart and Carey as "mixed types," because the legislature is involved in the choice of the president (Bolivia) or in the formation of the Cabinet (Peru). Given contemporary preferences for presidentialism throughout the developing world, however, this distribution is not as skewed as it appears. Parliamentary systems based on proportional representation are rare in the developing world, and thus we have surprisingly little evidence as to how such systems would actually perform there. Those parlia-

---

[34] Alfred Stepan and Cindy Skach, "Presidentialism and Parliamentarism in Comparative Perspective," in Linz and Valenzuela, *The Failure of Presidential Democracy,* vol. 1, *Comparative Perspectives,* pp. 119–36. The survivors were: Bahamas, Barbados, Botswana, Dominica, India, Israel, Jamaica, Kiribati, Nauru, Papua New Guinea, St. Lucia, St. Vincent, Solomon Islands, Trinidad and Tobago, and Tuvalu.

[35] This is a central point of both Lijphart, "Constitutional Choices for New Democracies," and Horowitz, "Comparing Democratic Systems."

TABLE 10.1

Types of Democratic Systems and Economic Performance, 1986–1990

Effective Number of Parties[a]	Presidential[b]	Mixed[b]	Parliamentary[b]
1.5–2.3	Senegal: 1.3 Growth: 2.1 Inflation: 0.2		Botswana: 1.3 Growth: 9.3 Inflation: 10.2
	Korea: 1.8[c] Growth: 8.3 Inflation: 7.5		Malaysia: 1.3 Growth: 10.2 Inflation: 5.4
	Chile: 2.0[d] Growth: 5.9 Inflation: 17.7		Jamaica: 1.5 Growth: 3.5 Inflation: 13.3
	Colombia: 2.1 Growth: 4.6 Inflation: 25.0		Bahamas: 1.6 Growth: 2.3 Inflation: 5.1
	Dominican Republic: 2.3 Growth: 2.1 Inflation: 35.0		Trinidad and Tobago: 1.7 Growth: -1.7 Inflation: 9.7
			Barbados: 1.7 Growth: 2.3 Inflation: 3.8
			India: 2.1 Growth: 6.1 Inflation: 8.4
2.4–3.5	Argentina: 2.9 Growth: 0.3 Inflation: 1191.6		Solomon Is.: 2.5 Growth: -3.7 Inflation: 13.0
	Venezuela: 2.6 Growth: 3.2 Inflation: 38.8		
	Uruguay: 3.2 Growth: 3.6 Inflation: 79.0		

TABLE 10.1 *(continued)*

Effective Number of Parties[a]	Presidential[b]	Mixed[b]	Parliamentary[b]
3.5 +	*Brazil:* 5.5 Growth: 2.1 Inflation: 1,056.4	*Peru:* 3.9 Growth: -1.3 Inflation: 2,342.2	*Turkey:* 3.9 Growth: 6.0 Inflation: 54.5
		Bolivia: 4.4 Growth: 1.7 Inflation: 67.7	Papua N.G.: 4.0 Growth: 1.2 Inflation: 5.1
		Ecuador: 5.8 Growth: 2.1 Inflation: 47.0	*Thailand:* 6.6 Growth: 9.9 Inflation: 3.9

Sources: Political data are from Alfred Stepan and Cindy Skatch, "Parliamentarism in Comparative Perspective," in Juan J. Linz and Arturo Valenzuela, eds., *The Failure of Presidential Politics,* 2 vols. (Baltimore: Johns Hopkins University Press), vol. 1, *Comparative Perspectives,* p. 122 and Table 4.3; for Chile, unpublished data from the UN Commission for Latin America and the Caribbean, Santiago, Chile, 1994; for Malaysia, *Keesing's Record of World Events* (Cambridge: Longham), various years; and for Senegal, Samba Ke and Nicolas Van de Walle, "Senegal: Stalled Reform in a Dominant-Party System," in Stephen Haggard and Steven B. Webb, *Voting for Reform: Democracy, Political Liberalization, and Economic Adjustment* (Washington, D.C.: World Bank, 1994). Data on growth (GDP) and inflations (CPI) are from International Monetary Fund, *International Financial Statistics,* 1992.

Notes: Names of countries discussed in this volume are in italics. Excluded from the table are the countries directly affected by the wars in Central America: El Salvador, Guatemala, and Honduras.

[a]Calculated on the basis of seats in the lower chamber.

[b]Figures following country names show average number of effective political parties for 1979–89 for Bahamas, Barbados, Botswana, Colombia, Dominican Replubic, India, Jamaica, Malaysia, Papua and New Guinea, Senegal, Solomon Islands, Trinidad and Tobago, and Venezuela. For the remainder of the countries, which underwent transitions after 1979, the figures following the names show the average effective number of parties for the post-transition period. Growth and inflation figures are average annual percentage changes for 1986–90, except as noted.

[c]Effective number of parties reflects the formation of the "Grand Coalition" in 1990. Economic data are for the Roh administration, 1988–92.

[d]Effective number of parties is for competing blocs. Economic data are for 1990–93.

mentary systems that do exist have largely been based on the Westminster model, combining parliamentarism with plurality electoral rules. Ironically, this form has generally not been favored by advocates of parliamentarism because of the limited representativeness of two-party systems!

The main conclusion that can be drawn from this limited sample of cases is that there is no clear pattern differentiating presidential and parliamentary systems with respect to their capacity to manage the economy or undertake economic reform. Among the countries discussed in this volume,

Korea and Chile continued their high-growth trajectories under presidential auspices, and the Philippines at least avoided the tragedies of the other crisis cases. In Colombia and Costa Rica, presidential regimes instituted moderate adjustment policies and maintained positive growth rates. On the other hand, performance in the Dominican Republic was highly erratic, and the Venezuelan regime did not address major structural problems until the end of the decade; when it did, it experienced the most profound political upheaval since the inception of its contemporary democratic structure in 1959. All of the severe cases of hyperinflation discussed in this volume also occurred under presidential or mixed systems.

In our two examples of multiparty-parliamentary regimes, Thailand and Turkey, we do find some capacity to sustain adjustments undertaken under authoritarian auspices. But Thailand's political system was only semidemocratic for most of the 1980s, and its successful adjustment was arguably in spite of, rather than because, of the parliamentary nature of its democratic rule. Moreover, as we argued in chapter 7, the country experienced a decline in the coherence of economic policy and ultimately a coup precisely as political parties gained in influence during the Chatichai period. Turkey performed reasonably well when compared to the crisis cases. Yet among the non-crisis transitions, Turkey stands out as having the most difficulty in managing inflation; Korea and Chile, both presidential systems, have clearly done better in this regard.

Economic performance in a number of the pure Westminster systems is relatively good, particularly with regard to rates of inflation. But this may be due less to parliamentarism than to other British institutional inheritances, such as strong currency boards. Moreover, most of these cases do not provide particularly enlightening comparisons for the large, middle-income countries that are the core of this study. The highly open nature of the very small island economies and their dependence on tourism means that their economic performance is driven to an unusual extent by external developments, which in the late 1980s and early 1990s included sluggish performance in the United States and Europe.[36] Trinidad and Tobago is somewhat larger, but its record is not encouraging; the country experienced profound policy drift and seven straight years of economic decline in the late 1980s.

India's economic performance showed a mixed record: growth during the period examined here was higher than in the past, but budget deficits and inflation increased as well. Moreover, the country showed disturbing signs of increasing ethnic and regional polarization; its political stability

---

[36] Inter-American Development Bank, *Economic and Social Progress in Latin America, 1992 Report* (Washington, D.C.: Distributed by the Johns Hopkins University Press, October 1992).

was more tenuous than at any time in its history. It could be argued that these forces have been contained by a strong parliamentary heritage. Yet it is just as plausible to argue that it was the dominance of the Congress Party and federalism, rather than parliamentarism, that mattered in this regard.

Differences among the cases in the table appear to turn as much on the number of parties as on the distinction between parliamentary and presidential systems. Whether presidential or parliamentary, the countries characterized by high growth and relatively low inflation all approximated two-party or dominant-party systems: Korea, Chile, Colombia, and Costa Rica in the presidential column, Malaysia and Botswana in the parliamentary one. Most of the "two-and-a-half" party systems (Argentina, Uruguay, Venezuela, and Jamaica) had significantly greater problems, but were able to implement macroeconomic and structural reforms that helped to stave off economic collapse.

The table does provide considerable support for Scott Mainwaring's contention that the combination of presidentialism and polarized multiparty competition can be especially devastating.[37] As noted above, the presidential and mixed systems with the most fragmented party systems have had the greatest difficulty in combining democratization with macroeconomic stability and growth. Only Bolivia can be argued to have successfully implemented and sustained adjustments under democratic auspices. In most of the others, prospects for sustained growth and democracy appeared highly problematic. Brazil continued a pattern of policy immobilism and economic decline, and Peru encountered major difficulties on both the economic and political front.

On the other hand, as we have also suggested, party fragmentation has also posed serious problems for parliamentary regimes. We have already noted how the management of the economy in Thailand became less coherent as constraints on multiparty competition were relaxed in the late 1980s. Along with Peru, it was also the only country in our sample to revert to authoritarian rule since its recent democratization. Similarly, Turkey in the late 1970s demonstrates that multiparty parliamentary systems are not immune from either economic crisis or political breakdown; indeed, the parliamentary nature of the system was arguably a contributing factor in the breakdown of democracy in 1980.[38]

Party fragmentation and polarization are, of course, often a consequence as well as a cause of poor economic performance. Nevertheless, the cross-sectional data presented here are consistent with the arguments presented in Part Two that the nature of the party system is a crucial variable in

[37] Scott Mainwaring, "Presidentialism, Multipartism, and Democracy: The Difficult Combination," *Comparative Political Studies* 26 (1993): 198–228.

[38] Stephan Haggard and Robert R. Kaufman, "The Political Economy of Inflation and Stabilization in Middle Income Countries," in Haggard and Kaufman, *The Politics of Economic Adjustment*, pp. 270–315.

understanding the possibility of reconciling democratic consolidation and economic reform. It is possible that a constitutional change toward parliamentarism might provide incentives for politicians to strengthen their organizations and broaden the range of legislative alliances. In many fragmented and polarized systems, however, the institution of parliamentarism would carry serious risks if it were not accompanied by reform of the party system and the electoral rules on which it is based.

ECONOMIC REFORM, DEMOCRATIC CONSOLIDATION, AND THE ORGANIZATION OF PARTY SYSTEMS

Economic crisis and reform efforts have significantly altered the context of party politics in the developing world. The social base of traditional parties has been changed by the weakening of labor unions, the increasing political assertiveness of business, and the emergence of new grass-roots groups and social movements organized around neighborhoods, environmental issues, gender, and ethnicity. At the same time, the opportunities for traditional political competition over patronage and the provision of social services has been severely limited by a scaling back of the size and responsibilities of the state.

Despite these changes in social structure and the capacities of government, party competition in new democracies will continue to be strongly influenced by the distributional issues surrounding the economic adjustment process and the shift to more market-oriented means of resource allocation. The nature of that competition cannot be deduced from social structure and the policy issues alone, however; much will depend on the incentives in the party system and how individual parties organize themselves internally.

It is possible to conceive of a number of different party systems that might provide stable support for the functioning of capitalist democracy and avoid the problems of political polarization and fragmentation explored in Part Two. We focus on four: two-party systems, consociationalism, and multiparty systems dominated by either the center-left or the center-right. In each case, we consider some of the socioeconomic and political conditions under which these alternative party systems might arise, their likely orientation with regard to the management of the economy, and the characteristic political and distributional conflicts that affect their performance and stability.

Two-Party Systems

A two-party system based on roughly balanced catchall parties is likely to emerge where there is a relatively high degree of elite consensus on the appropriate economic model and a weakly mobilized or controlled left. The development of such systems might be facilitated by the weakening of popular-sector forces during long periods of economic crisis and reform, particularly where ethnic or class conflicts are not highly politicized. Interestingly, however, most new democracies have not opted for electoral rules that would support such a party system.[39] These include plurality voting with single-member districts, regardless of whether the system is presidential or parliamentary, though similar centripetal tendencies can also emerge under "moderate" proportional representation systems that discourage small parties.[40]

Among established developing country democracies, this system has been characteristic of presidential regimes in Colombia, Venezuela, and Costa Rica, and the ex-British colonies that inherited Westminster-style parliamentarism. Among the new democracies under consideration here, the electoral rules in the Philippines might encourage the reemergence of such a system, which characterized Philippine party competition from the colonial era to Marcos's coup. It is also approximated by the competition between the Peronists and Radicals in Argentina, and to a lesser extent, in Uruguay, where the Colorados and Blancos continue to dominate the presidency in spite of the presence of an important third force within the party system.

Such a system would provide some role for labor, left and other minority interests, but as distinctly junior partners to elite-dominated centrist parties that compete for overlapping cross-class constituencies. Competition between center-right and center-left parties might provide the basis for a kind of mild reformism similar to that envisioned by the Alliance for Progress. As we have argued elsewhere in more detail, these two-party systems appear to have had a good long-term record in maintaining stable macroeconomic policies, a record that is not irrelevant to the maintenance of electoral democracy as well.[41]

On the other hand, these systems are not without characteristic problems. First, parties in such systems may become little more than elite-dominated machines, with the risk both of undermining coherent economic policy and of taking on exclusionary features that can weaken support for the political system as a whole. The exclusionary side of such parties accounts in part for the widespread alienation evident in the Venezuelan riots of 1989, and even more fundamentally, for the ongoing guerilla warfare that has characterized both the Philippines and Colombia.

---

[39] For reflections on why this might be the case, see Barbara Geddes, "Democratic Institutions as a Bargain among Self-Interested Politicians," paper prepared for the American Political Science Association meeting, San Francisco, 1990.

[40] We are thankful to Matthew Shugart for this last point.

[41] See Haggard and Kaufman, "The Political Economy of Inflation."

The challenge in such systems is to find ways to broaden participation and extend social compensation without recourse to the large state sectors that were characteristic of developmentalism in the 1960s and 1970s or to extensive patronage. Costa Rica probably comes closest to this objective, but projects of this sort demand an extremely delicate balancing act. Jamaica's experience under Manley in the 1970s provides a good illustration. Manley's goal was precisely to broaden the political and economic base of an elite-dominated two-party system, but the expansion of the role of the state coincided with the collapse of the bauxite market and the first oil crisis. The inability of Manley to reverse his political commitments contributed to a deterioration in economic performance, which in turn fueled a dramatic increase in political polarization. During the 1980s, both electoral pressures and economic constraints pushed the political system, and Manley personally, back toward the center. The reestablishment of elite consensus, however, has once again substantially reduced the scope for participation available to the Jamaican left.

Consociationalism

Multiparty systems, encouraged by proportional representation, are more likely to emerge in ethnically divided societies, where political movements on the left succeed in winning the loyalties of substantial portions of the working class, or where previous patterns of two-party competition have produced destabilizing polarization. A shift to proportional representation may occur when a dominant party or coalition, typically on the right, recognizes that it will lose its advantage in the future and seeks to defend its ability to secure some representation; this pattern was visible in the negotiations over electoral rules in the new East European democracies.[42]

In ethnically plural societies, democratic consolidation might rest on consociationalism and/or federalism. Power-sharing agreements could be negotiated among the major contending ethnic or regional groups, or power might devolve to the regional level in the name of "autonomy." Arend Lijphart has been most closely associated with the argument that such agreements can provide an effective base for governance in advanced industrial societies characterized by ethnic pluralism, but their stability in developing countries is much more problematic.[43] Malaysia arguably provides a positive model, though it should be remembered that this system has institutionalized Malay dominance over the political system, contrib-

---

[42] Geddes, "Democratic Institutions," p. 16.

[43] Arend Lijphart, *Democracy in Plural Societies* (New Haven, Conn.: Yale University Press, 1977).

uted to extensive patronage to "indigenous" Malays in the 1970s and 1980s, and showed signs of creeping authoritarianism in the 1990s. Other examples once held up as models, particularly Lebanon and Cyprus, have met appalling fates.

The problem with such systems derives directly from the fact that distributional issues are framed not along a left-right axis but along ascriptive lines given by the ethnic and regional structure of the country. Unlike the growth-oriented class compromises that are theoretically possible between right and left, political mobilization is more likely to center on distributive claims that take on a zero-sum character. Where one group is dominant, it will be tempted to exploit its position to monopolize the political gains of office; this is arguably what occurred in Malaysia and Sri Lanka. Where ethnic or regional divisions are more evenly balanced, the political bargains required to sustain the system are likely to deepen fundamental economic problems; Nigeria presents an example.

For these reasons, there has been a growing interest in electoral rules that would force ethnically or regionally based parties to form broader constituencies, for example, by demanding that parties achieve thresholds of support in all regions.[44] While such rules might help to stabilize democratic politics, it would do so precisely by pushing the principle of party organization and competition away from consociationalism toward one of the other alternatives discussed in this section.

Center-Right Dominance

Democratic consolidation might also be achieved in an electoral system in which parties or coalitions on either the social democratic left or the center-right are capable of establishing dominance over the electoral system. From a sociological point of view, this pair of alternatives is most likely to emerge in societies such as Chile, Korea, or perhaps Brazil, where ideological divisions have been sharpened by histories of strong partisan loyalties, working-class subcultures, or the recent mobilization of working-class movements. In such circumstances, the shape of the party system will turn heavily on the political allegiances of the middle classes and rural sector. Rural and/or middle-class alignment with the right would create the basis for the dominance of conservative coalitions, as in Japan. Long-term alliances of these groups with working-class movements—such as the Swedish "Red-Green" alliance—would contribute to the formation of relatively stable, European-style social democratic coalitions. Either model could

---

[44] See, for example, Donald L. Horowitz, *A Democratic South Africa: Constitutional Engineering in a Divided Society* (Berkeley: University of California Press, 1991), chap. 7.

conceivably form a viable basis for the electoral legitimation of democratic capitalism, though of very different sorts. Yet as with the other alternatives, both face characteristic problems.

The increasing political activism of business elites in many new democracies, along with the weakening of traditional labor movements and left forces, provides the conditions for the emergence of a "Japanese model" dominated by a strong center-right party or coalition. This is likely to be predicated on an economic model that emphasizes the prerogatives of business, investment over consumption and transfers, and an instrumental legitimating formula based on the promise of rapid growth. In Japan, this system was buttressed by a highly institutionalized system of pork-barrel politics and corruption, though one disciplined by strong central controls on fiscal and monetary policy.[45] Organized labor and the left would be relegated to a position of long-term opposition, perhaps even through legal and political provisions that provide checks on their freedom of maneuver. Examples might include electoral rules that limit the entry of small leftist parties, or systems of industrial relations that restrict the political activities of unions.

Whatever the presumed advantages of this model in terms of providing support for growth-oriented policies, its exclusionary features pose greater problems for democratic consolidation than the two-party option discussed above. These systems would require governments to produce high rates of economic growth, substantial opportunities for upward mobility, and at least a modicum of welfare concessions to the opposition. All of these might be undermined by economic forces beyond the government's control.

A second dilemma of the center-right model is more explicitly political. The conditions likely for this outcome to emerge in the first place are characteristic of several of our non-crisis cases, including Turkey, Thailand, and Korea, as well as the two dominant-party regimes in our sample, Mexico and Taiwan: a labor movement weakened by some combination of market conditions and legal restraints, an ideologically coherent and politically strong rightist bloc, both inside and outside the state apparatus, and middle-class groups that are disinclined to ally with the left. If these conditions are coupled with political alienation and marginalization among "radicals," they could lead to political polarization, the pursuit of anti-system politics on the left, and the emergence of quasi-authoritarian "solutions" in response. These risks were clearly present in Korea during the Roh administration, during the prolonged transition in Taiwan, in the Özal years in Turkey, and most recently in the events in Chiapas in Mexico.

---

[45] For different expositions of the "Japanese model" of party politics, see Gerald Curtis, *The Japanese Way of Politics* (New York: Columbia University Press, 1988), particularly pp. 45–79; and Kent E. Calder, *Crisis and Compensation: Public Policy and Political Stability in Japan, 1949–1986* (Princeton, N.J.: Princeton University Press, 1988).

The Social Democratic Option

The social democratic model is in many respects the mirror image of the "Japanese" alternative.[46] The principal elements in this model would be strong, if not dominant, center-left parties with a policy emphasis on social welfare, employment, and equity. Such parties originated in working-class movements and governed by forging alliances first with agriculture and then with the middle class.[47] The core economic bargain was that capitalists would gain consensual decision-making, predictability in the overall business and macroeconomic environment, and wage restraint, in exchange for accepting welfare state policies and the involvement of labor in the formulation of macroeconomic, social, and industrial policies.

A large literature has documented that such bargains have proven effective not only with respect to social welfare and unemployment, but with respect to traditional indicators of growth and inflation as well. Alvarez, Garrett, and Lange, for example, have shown that European social democratic governments with strong links to centralized and encompassing union organizations were able to pursue activist investment and labor policies while at the same time maintaining macroeconomic stability.[48] The foundation of this performance was the "rational restraint" of the labor movement.[49]

As Peter Katzenstein has argued for the small European states, social democracy is not antithetical to the maintenance of open markets either;

[46] For an exposition centered on the small, open European economies that might have relevance for some developing countries, see Peter J. Katzenstein, *Small States in World Markets: Industrial Policy in Europe* (Ithaca, N.Y.: Cornell University Press, 1985), particularly pp. 80–135. For broad overviews, see also Adam Przeworski, *Capitalism and Social Democracy* (New York: Cambridge University Press, 1985); Adam Przeworski and John Sprague, *Paper Stones: The History of Electoral Socialism* (Chicago: University of Chicago Press, 1986); Gösta Esping-Andersen, *The Three Worlds of Welfare Capitalism* (Princeton, N.J.: Princeton University Press, 1990); Gregory M. Luebbert, *Liberalism, Fascism or Social Democracy* (New York: Oxford University Press, 1991).

[47] Ibid.

[48] R. Michael Alvarez, Geoffrey Garrett, and Peter Lange, "Government Partisanship, Labor Organization and Macroeconomic Performance," *American Political Science Review* 85 (1991): 539–56. For other arguments along these lines, see Colin Crouch, "Conditions for Trade Union Wage Restraint," in Leon N. Lindberg and Charles Maier, eds., *The Politics of Inflation and Economic Stagnation* (Washington D.C.: The Brookings Institution, 1985), pp. 105–39; Lars Calmfors and John Driffill, "Bargaining Structure, Corporatism and Macroeconomic Performance," *Economic Policy* 3 (1988): 13–61; Michael Bruno and Jeffrey Sachs, *Economics of Worldwide Stagflation* (Cambridge: Harvard University Press, 1985). For a skeptical view, see John R. Freeman, *Democracy and Markets: the Politics of Mixed Economies* (Ithaca, N.Y.: Cornell University Press, 1989).

[49] The theoretical foundation for this argument is spelled out in Peter Lange, "Unions, Workers, and Wage Regulation: The Rational Bases of Consent," in John H. Goldthorpe, ed., *Order and Conflict in Contemporary Capitalism* (Oxford: Oxford University Press, 1984), pp. 98–123.

to the contrary. Such political systems were forged in part because of their exposure to external shocks, and are likely to invest in labor mobility and training that facilitates openness.[50] Precisely for this reason, this variant of market-oriented social democracy has been held out as a desirable one for countries seeking to make a transition to a more open, export-oriented development strategy. Compared to center-right systems and possibly even to the two-party model, inclusionary features of the social democratic outcome could provide it with a relatively broad base of legitimacy and support.

Among our cases, there are several in which parties with social democratic leanings and working-class support have emerged or reemerged in the post-transition period; these include Argentina, Brazil, Chile, and Turkey. In both "postindustrial" Europe and these countries, however, the small size of the industrial working class has raised two questions about the viability of the social democratic model. First, can social democratic parties win elections? And if they do, can they govern?

In Europe, social democratic parties have faced difficult ideological and strategic choices between continued appeals to a declining blue-collar base of support, and efforts to construct a broader "post-materialist" constituency. In many developing countries, blue-collar workers constitute an even smaller share of the total work force and the electoral challenges faced by social democratic movements are therefore even greater. To compete effectively, they will have to incorporate small businesses, the informal sector, or new social movements whose interests with respect to gender, employment issues, and the environment often conflict with the claims of the working-class base. The traditional means of reconciling such conflicting interests is through populism, an electoral and policy strategy that has not only been discredited, but is itself arguably inimical to the consolidation of both economic reform and democracy.

Within Europe, there are some indications that the socialist parties that made the most effective electoral adaptations to the shifting social environment were those in which declining blue-collar unions had relatively limited financial and organizational influence and were thus unable to block programmatic changes that ran against their traditional concerns.[51] Spain's Socialist Party is the most relevant example for our purposes. The unions included only about 13 percent of the active work force and had only

---

[50] Peter Katzenstein, *Small States in World Markets* (Ithaca, N.Y.: Cornell University Press, 1985), pp. 39–79; and David Cameron's influential article linking the size of government to openness, "The Expansion of the Public Economy: A Comparative Analysis," *American Political Science Review* 72 (1978): 1243–61.

[51] Thomas A. Koelble, "Recasting Social Democracy in Europe: A Nested Games Explanation of Strategic Adjustment in Political Parties," *Politics and Society* 20 (1992): 51–69; Herbert Kitschelt, "Class Structure and Social Democratic Party Strategy," *British Journal of Political Sociology* 23 (1993): 299–377.

limited representation within party decision-making bodies.[52] For party leaders seeking to broaden the socialists' electoral appeal, this made it easier to deemphasize the traditional goals of full employment and state protection. During the 1980s, solid socialist majorities in the parliament backed a controversial package of ambitious market-oriented reforms. Though coupled with extensive unemployment compensation, these reforms included a sweeping deregulation of the labor market.

This aspect of the "Spanish story" provides some intriguing parallels to the experiences of Chile and Argentina, where unions have provided an important, but still limited base of core support for parties in power. Ironically, however, the highly orthodox trade and macroeconomic policies pursued by these governments raise the question of whether such parties can offer approaches to issues of equity and welfare that would distinguish them programmatically from their more conservative competitors. As Geoffrey Garrett and Peter Lange ask in the European context, "what's left for the Left?"[53]

Garrett and Lange have shown that from 1974 to 1987, some European social democratic governments were able successfully to combine cautious fiscal and monetary policies with activist labor and investment policies, but only in countries where strong links to centralized and encompassing union organizations facilitated wage restraint and cooperation from the labor movement.[54] They suggest that the worst of all possible worlds from the perspective of stable policy is the combination of center-left parties with weak labor organizations.

For reasons that should be evident, such findings are not encouraging for the countries examined in this volume, or for many others in the developing world. Few social democratic movements have the kinds of organizational ties to unions that Garrett and Lange argue were successful in Europe. In Brazil, the Labor Party constitutes a partial exception; the party grew directly out of the labor movement and continues to be closely linked to it. It remains highly uncertain, however, whether the party could overcome strong left-wing resistance to cautious macroeconomic policies were it to assume power.

In most other instances, center-left parties have had much looser organizational ties to the labor movement, and as a result might be expected to

---

[52] Koelble, "Recasting Social Democracy," p. 59. Membership data are from Robert Fishman, *Working Class Orgnization and the Return to Democracy in Spain* (Ithaca, N.Y.; Cornell University Press, 1990), as cited in Nancy Bermeo, "Sacrifice, Sequence, and Strength in Successful Dual Transitions: Lessons from Spain," *Journal of Politics* 56 (1994): 609.

[53] Geoffrey Garrett and Peter Lange, "Political Responses to Interdependence: What's 'Left' for the Left?" *International Organization* 45 (1991): 539–63.

[54] Ibid.

have a difficult time managing industrial relations in the context of highly open economies and substantial pressures to contain wage costs. In Chile (and also Spain), center-left governments did provide welfare benefits to low-income constituents, but received only resigned acquiesence from organized labor to their overall policy approach. In the absence of more active forms of collaboration, these programs remained vulnerable to destabilizing wage pressures over the long run. Such uncertainties applied with even greater force to Argentina under Menem, where the social safety nets eroded badly during the reform period, or under Demirel in Turkey, where coalitions with center-left participation were unable fully to control macroeconomic or wage policy.

A final and even more daunting problem with the social democratic model has no current parallel among the European democracies. In many developing countries, a consolidation of the model implies a reconciliation between the left and military and business elites, which remain relatively strong and hostile to the compromises on which such a system must rest. The sources of right strength might include the continuing presence of external threats, a memory of "disorder" associated with political openings to the left, or middle classes disinclined to play the role of a swing force because of the factors just cited. In countries such as Brazil and the Philippines in which landed interests remain a significant social and political force, they are also likely to constitute a barrier to this solution.

CONCLUSION

The political and economic transformations occurring in the developing world and ex-socialist countries have breathed new life into a long-standing intellectual tradition that sees a natural affinity between democracy and the market.[55] In fact, these two principles of social organization have often been in conflict. In his classic study *The Great Transformation,* Karl Polanyi chronicled the revolt against the liberal utopianism of early Victorian radicalism.[56] This revolt consisted of successive political efforts to protect the individual from the dislocations associated with the market. Some of these efforts, namely Leninism and fascism, were explicitly antidemocratic.

In the advanced industrial democracies that were spared these extremes, a key feature of political stability was support from the middle sectors for the gradual incorporation of the working and lower classes into the political

---

[55] One of the most comprehensive philosophical statements in this vein is Friedrich van Hayek's *Law, Legislation and Liberty,* vol. 1: *Rules and Order* (Chicago: University of Chicago Press, 1973), particularly pp. 124–44.

[56] Karl Polanyi, *The Great Transformation: The Political and Economic Origins of Our Time* (Boston: Beacon Press, 1957).

system and the development of some forms of social compensation and protection. This process of political and economic incorporation occurred through a variety of mechanisms: the expansion of the franchise and public education, the creation of institutions for regulating industrial relations, networks of social security, and policies for alleviating poverty. As John Ruggie has argued, it also rested on a broadly liberal, but by no means laissez-faire posture toward integration with the world economy, a stance Ruggie labeled "embedded liberalism."[57]

Arriving at some sort of political and socioeconomic compromise that likewise "embeds" liberalism is also essential for the consolidation of newer democracies. As our brief survey of institutional mediations and alternative party systems makes clear, however, none are fully likely to escape the central political tension between democracy and the market, or to offer an unambiguous response to the warnings raised by Polanyi. Yet this finding may also be read in a hopeful way. Though the options for managing this tension creatively—of striking the compromise of embedded liberalism—are not completely open-ended, they are multiple. To the extent that these different party systems imply alternative ways of organizing a market economy, our study of them buttresses other recent work that has emphasized the continuing variety of national economic systems.[58] In the conclusion, we explore briefly both the theoretical and normative implications of these multiple pathways to the consolidation of democratic capitalism.

[57] John Gerard Ruggie, "International Regimes, Transactions, and Change: Embedded Liberalism in the Postwar Economic Order," in Stephen D. Krasner, ed., *International Regimes* (Ithaca, N.Y.: Cornell University Press, 1983), pp. 195–232.

[58] Rogers Hollingsworth, Philippe Schmitter, and Wolfgang Streeck, eds., *Comparing Capitalist Economies: Variations in the Governance of Industrial Sectors* (New York: Oxford University Press, 1992).

Comparing Democratic Transitions

SINCE the beginning of the third wave of democratization, debate on the subject has traversed a path that, in retrospect, appears highly predictable. The work of the early years of the democratic resurgence—the late 1970s and early 1980s—was absorbed with the contingency and uncertainty of the process; this is perhaps best captured by the title of a well-known essay by O'Donnell and Schmitter that reaches "tentative conclusions about uncertain democracies."[1] Nonetheless, the emphasis on possibilities rather than probabilities had a hopeful, even expectant quality.

This was followed by a moment of liberal triumphalism, when the ascent of democracy seemed both widespread and assured.[2] With triumphalism came teleology. Democratization seemed an inevitable trend, and a variety of factors were invoked to explain why what had happened was necessary.

By the early 1990s, the debate had shifted once again. The pressing analytic issue was not the dynamic one of democratization, but the comparative analysis of the structure and performance of new democracies. With that new focus came a more reserved, even pessimistic, assessment. Mere survival meant neither good health nor a fulfillment of all the unrealistic expectations that democracy was forced to carry. Nor was the survival of democracy itself any longer taken for granted.

This study is clearly a product of this third stage of debate. We are more concerned with the differences among democracies—including the existence of manifest policy and economic failures in some of them—than we are with the fact of transition per se. And we have concerns about the fate of democracy in particular countries.

A central theoretical motivation for this study was our dissatisfaction with the choice-based approaches that animated the early transitions literature and have remained a theme in discussions since. We took from this early literature the crucial insight that the process of democratization had to be understood as a series of strategic interactions between incumbent

---

[1] Guillermo O'Donnell and Philippe Schmitter, *Tentative Conclusions about Uncertain Democracies,* pt. 4 in O'Donnell, Schmitter, and Laurence Whitehead, eds., *Transitions from Authoritarian Rule: Prospects for Democracy* (Baltimore: Johns Hopkins University Press, 1986).

[2] See for example Francis Fukuyama, "The End of History?" *The National Interest,* Summer 1989, pp. 3–20.

authoritarian rulers and oppositions, as well as among factions within both camps; Part One was based on this premise. Our theoretical purpose, however, was to introduce more structure—both economic and institutional—into the analysis of democratic transitions and the performance of new democracies. We believed that actors should not be identified and differentiated exclusively in terms of political orientations and strategies. With the perspective provided by the crises of the 1980s, it is painfully obvious that economic constraints figured much more centrally in determining the political agenda, the interests and capabilities of the central protagonists in the democratization drama. In many countries, the rising demand for democratization was virtually indistinguishable from the demand for more effective economic management. Moreover, the strategic interactions that were at the heart of the choice-based approach cannot be understood without reference to the institutional context; this was true both in examining the politics of the transition and in understanding the political economy of new democracies.

Our approach to the relationship between the economic and political dimensions of the transition process grew out of an extensive comparative literature on the politics of economic reform. This literature emerged in the wake of the debt crisis of the 1980s, and focused primarily on policy choices rather than political change. But it raised issues highly relevant to the study of democratic transitions, issues that did not receive systematic attention until quite recently.[3]

In this study, we have addressed three such questions. The first is the effect of both economic crisis and adjustment efforts on the stability and transformation of authoritarian rule. Second, we considered how alternative sequences of economic reform and political change affected policymaking in new democracies. Finally, we examined how the institutions that aggregate the preferences of social actors and represent them in the political arena, particularly parties, affect the prospects for market-oriented reform and the consolidation of democracy.

Our method was to combine some orienting theoretical insights from

---

[3] See Adam Przeworski, *Democracy and the Market: Political and Economic Reforms in Eastern Europe and Latin America* (New York: Cambridge University Press, 1991); Luiz Carlos Bresser Pereira, José María Maravall, and Adam Przeworski, *Economic Reforms in New Democracies: A Social Democratic Approach* (Cambridge: Cambridge University Press, 1993); Robert H. Bates and Anne O. Krueger, eds., *Political and Economic Interactions in Economic Policy Reform* (Cambridge, Mass.: Basil Blackwell, 1993); William C. Smith, Carlos H. Acuña, and Eduardo A. Gamarra, eds., *Latin American Political Economy in the Age of Neoliberal Reform: Theoretical and Comparative Perspectives for the 1990s* (New Brunswick, N.J.: Transaction Publishers, 1994); John Williamson, ed., *The Political Economy of Economic Policy Reform* (Washington, D.C.: Institute for International Economics, 1993); Stephan Haggard and Steven B. Webb, eds., *Voting for Reform: Economic Adjustment in New Democracies* (New York: Oxford University Press, 1994).

contemporary political economy with a comparative historical analysis of a number of middle-income countries. The absence of compelling theory on which to draw and the complex and variegated nature of the political and economic transformations we examined posed major challenges for both research and exposition. Comparisons did, however, permit the identification of some general causal patterns that applied across a range of cases. We here summarize our contribution and findings, identify further research questions, and speculate on how our arguments might be extended to the analysis of other countries not covered in this volume, particularly the post-socialist societies. We conclude with some speculation on the prospects for democracy in the developing world.

ECONOMIC CRISES AND AUTHORITARIAN WITHDRAWALS

The political challenges that have confronted authoritarian regimes since the late 1970s have been closely related to economic crises and the efforts—often unsuccessful—to adjust to them. There is broad comparative evidence that economic circumstances influenced the extent of political support that authoritarian governments could mobilize, the nature and scope of the political opposition they faced, and the internal cleavages within the leadership itself. The importance of these factors was either ignored or denied outright by the early literature on transitions, despite the longstanding assumption that authoritarian rule was vulnerable in the face of poor performance.

Not all authoritarian regimes were equally vulnerable to crisis, however; the institutions of rule mattered. Those best suited for managing political and economic crises were those in which authority was concentrated. The defection of business elites and mass protest are undeniably important to the transition process, but the group that ultimately determines the likelihood that an authoritarian government will maintain office is the political and coercive apparatus itself. Those regimes that fell in the face of crisis were those in which external pressures fragmented the ruling coalition. Collective leaderships or diffuse and decentralized lines of authority were more likely to result in such increased factional conflict and immobilism. Those regimes that survived had developed centralized organizational means for controlling internal dissension, primarily by concentrating both political and military authority in the hands of a single individual. We also found that dominant-party authoritarian systems in middle-income countries proved more adept than military regimes at managing conflicts within the government and controlling and coopting broader political challenges.

These institutional configurations were relatively uncommon, however. For most authoritarian governments, economic crises increased the probability of regime change and shaped the terms on which the transition occurred. Incumbent governments unable to avoid or adjust to crises were in a weaker position vis-à-vis domestic opponents and were thus less able to influence the contours of the new democratic order than those rarer cases in which economic policy was successful.

CRISIS AND NON-CRISIS TRANSITIONS AND THE NEW DEMOCRATIC ORDER

The economic and political forces that influenced the end of the old regime also conditioned the new one. A central question addressed by the book is whether there were systematic differences in the political economy of those democratic governments that came to office amidst crises and those countries in which economic policy adjustments had already been undertaken by the outgoing authoritarian regime and in which economic performance was robust.

New democratic governments in the non-crisis cases inherited both relatively favorable economic circumstances and a policy regime that had been successful in promoting macroeconomic stability and growth; those factors alone facilitated their ability to sustain past policy and to make further economic adjustments as required. Coalitional alignments, particularly the relative strength of groups favored by the old economic model, also constituted a force for continuity. The political legacy of the non-crisis transitions was more ambivalent, however, and included institutional restrictions on full democratic contestation that privileged segments of the old authoritarian coalition. These legacies have lingered and continue to cloud the prospects for full democratic consolidation.

Transitions occurring under crisis conditions produced fewer restrictions on contestation. But new democracies in these countries faced politically difficult decisions with respect to stabilization and structural adjustment that themselves posed challenges to democratic governance. High inflation, low growth, and macroeconomic instability constituted challenges not only because they increased distributional conflicts and demands on the state, but because of the incentive to "solve" these latter, fundamentally political problems through an autocratic decision-making style. The crisis countries typically faced trade-offs between the concentration of authority required to launch reforms and the institutionalization of effective representation that is necessary both for the consolidation of democracy and for a stable market economy.

There are several possible objections to our focus on crisis. For purposes of exposition, we have treated the distinction between crisis and non-crisis cases as dichotomous, when economic performance is obviously a continuous variable. Moreover, there are important differences within each category that are not solely a result of differences in economic performance. Poor economic performance was important in the collapse of authoritarian rule in the Philippines, but the outgoing authoritarian government successfully stabilized the economy prior to leaving power; this distinguished that case from other crisis countries and had implications for the policy alternatives facing the Aquino government. In Turkey—which we classify as a non-crisis case—the military failed to consolidate fiscal adjustment; this constituted a troubling legacy for the Özal government. The policy problems confronting the crisis and non-crisis cases must therefore be disaggregated.

A second objection is that our definition of crisis focuses on macroeconomic policy and performance to the exclusion of the structural changes associated with crisis and market-oriented reform.[4] How, for example, are civic association and political organization affected by economic liberalization, deregulation or capitalist industrialization more generally? Such a focus would appear to be particularly important in the formerly socialist countries, where fundamental property rights and institutions are undergoing change.

There are two justifications for our focus on macroeconomic variables. The first is that they had been ignored. Virtually all of the literature on the economic underpinnings of democracy concentrated on the effects of growth in the long run, for example, by focusing on the emergence of middle classes. Second, our study suggests that the macroeconomic setting has a powerful influence on the politics of market-oriented reform and structural change. Inflation, growth, and employment were key determinants of political protest in the cases that we have examined, more important in our view than the distributional effects of policy that have been the focus of some accounts.[5] The fiscal position of the state was a key determinant of the ability of governments to respond to these protests. For these reasons, the focus on macroeconomic factors seems a reasonable point of departure, even if structural economic factors also play a role in the politics of adjustment.

POLITICAL PARTIES, DEMOCRACY, AND ECONOMIC GOVERNANCE

Although analyses of democratization have often attached considerable importance to the institutional choices made during transitions, there has been little work on the way institutions affect economic policy and per-

[4] Dietrich Rueschemeyer, Evelyne Huber Stephens, and John D. Stephens, *Capitalist Development and Democracy* (Chicago: University of Chicago Press, 1992), pp. 41–51.

[5] See for example, Jeffry A. Frieden, *Debt, Development and Democracy* (Princeton: Princeton University Press, 1991).

formance during such periods. Our work begins to explore that issue. The weight we attach to political institutions is broadly in line with contemporary work in political economy. Though an analysis of the social and political consequences of economic performance is the starting point for any political economy, political and policy outcomes cannot be understood as a simple vector of social interests. We do not make the strong claim that institutions affect the underlying preferences of social actors, but they do affect their strategies and capabilities, and thus the likelihood that they will achieve their objectives.

We attach special emphasis to the role of political parties in this process, although other institutional arrangements are also significant and constitute important areas for future research. As in the advanced industrial states, these include the myriad of formal and informal institutions that link interest groups directly to the state: corporatist arrangements, regulatory or quasi-judicial agencies in which interest groups are represented, and other lobbying and consultative relationships. More attention should also be paid to the quasi-public regulatory functions frequently assumed by private associations.

The countries examined in this study suggest, however, that these institutional relationships will be strongly influenced by the broader party system and legislative-executive relations in which they are nested. Because of their role in aggregating interests and mobilizing consent, parties are particularly important when there is contestation over broad changes in development strategies or in the rules of the political game itself. In fragmented and polarized party systems, executives can sometimes initiate economic reforms by reliance on military backing, direct plebiscitarian appeals, or the exploitation of constitutional powers. In the cases we have examined, however, fragmented and polarized party systems have posed major impediments to sustained implementation of reform. In short, we concur with an insight of Samuel Huntington's *Political Order in Changing Societies*: the capacity to organize stable political rule—whether authoritarian or democratic—in the modern context of broad social mobilization and complex economic systems ultimately rests on organized systems of accountability, and these in turn rest on political parties.[6]

We are clearer about the effects of parties on policy outcomes than about the way party systems are established and evolve during the transition process. As we argue in chapter 4, the initial party configurations are a function of both the pre-authoritarian history of party organization and the political and economic circumstances at the time of the transition. The conditioning effects of the transition itself are most evident in the non-crisis

---

[6] Samuel Huntington, *Political Order in Changing Societies* (New Haven, Conn.: Yale University Press, 1968), pp. 1–92.

cases. In these countries, outgoing elites retained greater direct and indirect control over the rules of competition and the institutions of governance in the new democratic system. In Chile, for example, political parties drew on loyalties and identifications formed prior to the Pinochet era. But economic and political changes under the dictatorship created the possibility of a fundamental realignment in the party system—an alliance between the center and the left—that marked a complete departure from the cleavages of the 1960s and 1970s.

In the crisis cases, both the rules of the political game and key elements of economic policy were contested by a wider array of groups. In the re-democratization of societies dominated by military regimes, evolving party systems were more likely to reflect patterns of political organization and cleavages that existed prior to the authoritarian period, even where, as in Brazil, political elites regrouped under new party labels. This tendency reflected the inability of authoritarian governments in the crisis cases to permanently restructure the pre-authoritarian polity.

The political institutions established during the transition were not fixed for all time; they continued to evolve in response to the policy and political challenges inherited from the old regime. Nonetheless, it is important to note that the extent of post-transition constitutional revision in our cases is surprisingly limited and that the initial political bargains struck at the time of the transition had important implications for the subsequent path of political development. For example, in all of the Latin American crisis cases except Uruguay, fragmentation and/or polarization of the party system contributed to profound policy failures. These failures, in turn, motivated changes in the powers granted the executive and in party alignments. The links between the initial institutional arrangements agreed at the time of the transition, the policy choices of the new democratic government, and the demand for further institutional change are difficult to trace, but constitute an important avenue for future research.

IMPLICATIONS FOR SOCIALIST TRANSITIONS

In designing this study, both prudence and questions of comparability decided us against extending our analysis to the socialist countries of Eastern and Central Europe and the Soviet Union. First, international political factors, both in the Soviet Union and within the Western bloc, played a more decisive role in shaping political change in the region than was the case in the countries examined in this volume. Withdrawal of Soviet backing for incumbent Eastern European governments must be seen as the single most important factor driving political change in the region. Political change was also complicated by ethnic and nationalist rivalries, as well as by intense conflicts over definitions of citizenship and national territory that were, for the most part, absent from the countries we survey in this book. Finally, the new democracies of the region face very different economic challenges than the countries we have examined, including fundamental changes in property rights and the development of basic market institutions.

These factors make comparisons difficult and guarantee that patterns of economic and political change will differ in important respects from the experiences of the developing capitalist economies that are the subject of this study. Notwithstanding these differences, our analysis does raise a number of questions relevant to comparative research both on transitions in socialist countries and on the performance of their democratic successors.

The first point to note is the centrality of poor economic performance in the transition process. The most severe shocks to the region came *after* the fall of the Berlin Wall, with the end to Soviet oil subsidies and the collapse of the regional trading system, the Council for Mutual Economic Assistance (CMEA), in 1990 and 1991. Yet Soviet bloc economies had been experiencing severe economic difficulties since the late 1970s. Even relatively "good" performers such as Czechoslovakia and the German Democratic Republic had been characterized by overcentralized command economies, stagnating output, and shortages of consumer goods. Poland, Hungary, and Romania experienced profound balance-of-payments and debt crises and recessions. These difficulties did not translate directly into political change, but they created grievances that could be exploited, weakened regimes that had come to depend heavily on the distribution of material surpluses to maintain legitimacy and control, and contributed to splits within the leadership itself.[7]

The political and organizational capabilities of dominant parties constitute a second point of comparison. On the one hand, as discussed in chapter 8, adjustment to mounting economic difficulty was impeded by the ideological preferences of the central leadership and by the strength of conservative interests within the ruling parties; in contrast to Taiwan and Mexico, the failure to engineer an economic recovery eventually contributed to a loss of control over the process of political change.

Compared to the military governments we analyzed, however, the one-party states of the Soviet bloc were relatively durable. In the Soviet Union itself, the Communist Party remained a central pillar of stability throughout the political and economic decay of the Brezhnev years. Eastern European parties were arguably weaker, and owed their continued dominance to

---

[7] Arguably, the economic difficulties in the Eastern bloc also affected the Soviet Union, which was forced to shoulder increasing burdens in terms of trade subsidies and credits in order to stave off domestic unrest within its empire. Valerie Bunce, "The Empire Strikes Back: The Evolution of the Eastern Bloc from a Soviet Asset to a Soviet Liability," *International Organization* 39 (1984–85), esp. pp. 13–23.

Soviet backing. Nonetheless, dominant parties in the Eastern European countries provided ruling elites with a crucial instrument of political coordination and social control until the late 1980s.

The capacity of the ruling coalition to maintain its power in the face of economic decline varied cross-nationally according to the centralization of authority within the party apparatus and the extent of the "limited pluralism" that had been tolerated under the old regime. Social and political structures of Poland and Hungary bore the closest resemblance to the middle-income capitalist societies, and it is in these societies that we see the strongest parallels to the crisis-induced political transitions discussed in previous chapters. Civil society, which included a limited private sector in agriculture, was generally stronger and better organized than in neighboring countries, and there was also greater independence for industrial managers. In both societies, mounting external debt and conflicts over the appropriate adjustment strategy generated widening conflicts within the ruling elite. In Poland, where policy stalemates were combined with particularly severe economic distress, there was also significant mass protest.

The strains produced by these divisions had important implications for the Soviet imperial system as a whole. The initial stages of the transition in these countries were marked by round-table discussions between government and opposition forces in mid-1989. The purpose of these discussions had been to coopt opposition to Communist rule and enlist broader social support for necessary economic reforms, while managing the process of political change from above. As in the crisis cases discussed in this volume, however, the collapse of the regional economy eliminated the chance that "softliners" would be able to control the process of change.

In Poland, plans to form a coalition government were undermined by the loss of control over macroeconomic policy during the second half of 1989.[8] Solidarity seized the opportunity to form a government, but was left with daunting adjustment tasks. Crises hit Hungary somewhat more slowly, and as we would predict, better economic performance was associated with more restrained demands by the government's principal negotiating partner, the Hungarian Democratic Forum, for political and economic reform. By the time of the first parliamentary elections, however, the economic shocks of 1990 were becoming increasingly evident, and the forum began to compete with other opposition parties in its demand for sweeping political changes in the old regime.[9]

Unlike in Hungary and Poland, the ruling parties in Czechoslovakia and the German Democratic Republic had remained relatively closed to reformist influences and excercised far more centralized control over economic

[8] Simon Johnson and Marzena Kowalska, "Poland: The Political Economy of Shock Therapy," in Haggard and Webb, *Voting for Reform,* pp. 196–218.

[9] Nigel Swain, "Hungary," in Stephen White, Judy Batt, and Paul G. Lewis, eds., *Developments in East European Politics* (Durham, N.C.: Duke University Press, 1993), pp. 72–73.

and social life. The suddenness and totality of the political collapse in these societies at the end of 1989 revealed the fragility of the loyalties and ideological convictions that underlay party rule. Nevertheless, the fall of the Czech and German "dominoes" was closely related to earlier events in Hungary and Poland. Rulers withdrew in the face of mass protest only after the political changes in Poland and Hungary made it clear that they could not count on the backing of Soviet troops.

Ruling parties proved most durable, finally, in the poorer, more rural societies of Eastern Europe—Romania, Albania, and Bulgaria—where power had been concentrated in the hands of personalist leaders, and opposition groups had few opportunities to mobilize prior to the transition. As the Soviet empire disintegrated, incumbent leaders were replaced in palace coups, and their successors were impelled to relinquish their formal monopoly of power. Nevertheless, the old Communist parties in these tightly controlled systems still commanded formidable political resources. Unlike in Central Europe, "unreformed" Communist parties retained control of financial assets, buildings, government records, and patronage. Their leaders were able to hold onto office during the first round of competitive elections in 1990, and they remained important political forces thereafter.

The politics of adjustment in post-Communist regimes offers a third axis for comparison, particularly with the experiences of the crisis cases outlined in chapter 6. The nature of the economic changes required was far more complicated and wide-ranging than anything confronted by the developing world. The widespread rejection of the command economy and the appeal of an idealized market system provided a strong initial groundswell of popular support for radical economic reforms. As in Southern Europe a decade earlier, moreover, the domestic political incentives to undertake reform were reinforced by the prospect of entry into the European Union and the promise of extensive Western aid. Post-Communist governments generally initiated stabilization and market-oriented reforms more quickly and comprehensively than in any of the new developing country democracies.

An important parallel with our cases, however, is that the initiation of reform appeared to depend on whether leaders at the head of broad popular movements were in a position to concentrate authority sufficiently to dislodge interests embedded within the old ruling party. The groundswell of popular support for Solidarity provided the initial momentum for radical reform in Poland, even though the blue-collar base of the movement eventually bore much of the cost and the movement quickly disintegrated into competing factions.[10] In Czechoslovakia, similarly, a sweeping victory of the Civic Forum in the June 1990 parliamentary elections contributed to the ascendency of radical reformers who eventually implemented broad

---

[10] Johnson and Kowalska, "Poland: The Political Economy of Shock Therapy," pp. 196–200.

economic changes in the Czech Republic.[11] Ironically, the relatively centralized and disciplined state bureaucracy that the Czech reformers inherited from the Communists facilitated the process of economic reform.

A somewhat slower pace of economic reform in post-Communist Hungary was in part attributable to the influence of independent managerial elites that had emerged during earlier reform efforts.[12] At the same time, although Communists were decisively defeated in the parliamentary elections of 1990, the incoming government of József Antall lacked the broad popular support initially enjoyed by Solidarity and by the Civic Forum. As a consequence, it was inclined to move more cautiously in its economic policy, although the costs were arguably a slower economic recovery than in the Czech Republic and Poland.[13]

Economic reforms moved most slowly, finally, in the poorer countries to the east, where continuing control over patronage resources allowed Communist Party officials to acquire strong bases of support in legislatures, local governments, and within portions of the government bureaucracy itself.[14] In a number of these countries, executives have attempted to bypass recalcitrant legislatures and initiate reforms through decree powers similar to those discussed elsewhere in this volume. Nevertheless, several cases, including former Soviet republics such as Russia and Ukraine, provide virtual textbook examples of the consequences of fragmented and polarized party systems: prevarication, legislative stalemates, failed initiatives, and the continuing lure of quasi-authoritarian "solutions."

Political processes that have followed the initiation of reform also bear resemblance to those discussed elsewhere in this volume. Policy changes overlapped with crises, and were accompanied by demands for relief from labor unions in state enterprises, pensioners, farmers, and *nomenklatura*-cum-"owners" of appropriated state assets. In Central Europe, the backlash against reform from at least some of these groups contributed to the rapid disintegration of the Solidarity movement in Poland and to the even more fundamental division between the Czech Republic and Slovakia.

[11] Gordon Wightman, "The Czech and Slovak Republics," in White, Batt, and Lewis, eds., *Developments in East European Politics,* pp. 53–56.

[12] László Bruszt and David Stark, "Transformative Politics in East Central Europe," *East European Politics and Societies* 6 (1992): 52–70.

[13] Ben Slay, "Rapid versus Gradual Economic Transition: Some Lessons from an Old Debate," paper presented at conference on The Social and Political Bases of Economic Liberalization, sponsored by the Social Science Research Council and the Polish Institute for International Affairs, Warsaw, Poland, September 23–26, 1994.

[14] See the discussion of Bulgarian reform by Ekaterina Nikova, "The Bulgarian Transition: A Difficult Beginning," in Joan M. Nelson, ed., *A Precarious Balance: Democracy and Economic Reforms in Eastern Europe* (San Francisco: International Center for Economic Growth, the Overseas Development Council, and the Institute for Contemporary Studies, 1994), pp. 125–63.

Even where radical reform programs have produced substantial changes in macroeconomic, price, and trade policy, it has become increasingly evident that governments will be unable to reform property relations or to restructure labor and capital markets without enlisting the organized cooperation of at least some of these groups. Our analysis would predict that without such support, the capacity to sustain these initial reforms would be in jeopardy.

The upsurge of antireform opposition, finally, raises the question about the institutional mechanisms that might contribute to the consolidation of coherent economic policies. In the Polish case, it is striking that reforms have been maintained on the whole, despite numerous changes of government, considerable electoral instability, and a resurgence of support for reformed Communist parties. This can be attributed in part to noninstitutional factors, such as the pull of the European Union, discussed above, which has helped to narrow the ideological gaps over reform issues.

Our study would suggest, however, that institutions are likely to be significant factors as well, and the variety of institutional arrangements within the former Soviet bloc offers important new opportunities for empirical research. In contrast to the Asian and Latin American countries discussed in this volume, for example, post-Communist societies feature a wide array of parliamentary and semipresidential systems. Both intra- and cross-regional comparisons can thus provide new evidence about the way the rules governing executive-legislative relations affect electoral politics and economic management. In Poland, Russia, and Ukraine, presidents have at times played important roles in initiating reforms or keeping them on track. On the other hand, it is arguable that parliamentary constitutions have permitted Hungary and the Czech Republic to avoid the divisiveness evident in the presidential systems of the region.

The emerging party systems of post-Communist societies offer similar opportunities for comparative research. In most parts of the region, parties remain unstable, without roots in society, and prone to extremist appeals. In Central Europe, on the other hand, there are some signs that parties are responding to electoral rules and competitive pressures by consolidating into a smaller number of more cohesive organizations.[15] In Poland, higher thresholds for representation substantially reduced the number of parties in the legislature after the second round of parliamentary elections. In the parliamentary regimes of Hungary and the Czech Republic, the interdependence of governments and legislators may also have encouraged greater internal party discipline and more stable governing coalitions.

---

[15] For a general discussion of party system consolidation in Eastern Europe, see Herbert Kitschelt, "Emerging Structures of Political Representation in Eastern Europe," presented at the conference on The Social and Political Bases of Economic Liberalization.

Finally, the recent election of "reformed" Communist governments in Poland and Hungary raises important issues for future analysis. Clearly, the resurgence of the post-Communist parties raises worrisome political and economic questions. It reflects broad dissatisfaction with the pace and scope of economic reform and for this reason has been greeted with concern within segments of the Western business and diplomatic elite. On the other hand, as we have seen in several of our cases, reforms have sometimes been more effective when they are implemented by "left" parties that can provide some possibility of political influence and compensation to those negatively affected by the reform process. Thus, a hopeful interpretation of party politics in Central Europe is that we are seeing a new phase of the reform process: a turn away from the radical reformism of the early transition years, but also a reduction in the degree of polarization over economic issues, a stabilization of expectations around a more gradual reform path, and thus better prospects for both economic and political consolidation.

THE FUTURE OF DEMOCRACY IN THE DEVELOPING WORLD

As we turn to the question of the consolidation of democratic institutions, the experiences of advanced industrial democracies provide important historical points of reference. The stability of postwar welfare states provides evidence that it is possible to manage the tensions between the egalitarian logic of democracy, and economic systems based on private property and initiative that imply inequality of both income and wealth. Such societies have not been immune to severe social conflicts and political breakdowns, but there appears to be no inherent contradiction between these two forms of social organization, as both Marxists and property holders once assumed. On the contrary, the historical correlation between democracy and capitalism suggests that market economies have at times contributed to the expansion of human freedom by strengthening the distinction between public and private domains of power.

The compatibility of capitalism and democracy in advanced industrial societies should be reassuring to those now attempting to implement market-oriented economic reforms and to institutionalize democratic government. But the existence of such a possibility does not necessarily mean that there are feasible paths toward the desired end state at this particular historical juncture. In the poorer developing countries and in many of the new republics of the former Soviet Union, new democratic governments face fundamental problems of state-building that resemble those confronted in Western Europe in the early modern period; it is sobering to remember that in these historical cases the consolidation of central government power involved centuries of royal absolutism, civil war, and revolution. Even where the problems are less profound, the reconstruction of the state in the wake of debilitating fiscal crises remains a central challenge for the possibility of a democratic politics.

Second, our analysis of the politics of the initiation and consolidation of economic reform shows that governments may be unable to mobilize the support for the initiation of reform. Political systems with weak executives and fragmented party systems, divided government, and decentralized political structures responded poorly to crises, and may well continue to do so. These weaknesses with respect to policymaking can, in turn, have implications for democracy itself. If the current, young wave of democratization begins to reverse, we expect the first casualties to be those countries that are incapable, in the face of crisis, of achieving adequate executive authority to overcome crippling institutional and political divisions.

Third, it is possible that societies that initiate reform will continue to experience poor economic performance, either because the reforms were poorly conceived or implemented, or because of forces beyond the control of the government. Even if reforms are successful in generating growth, moreover, inequality and shifts in class structure may make it difficult to consolidate support for the reform effort.

Finally, it is important to underline that even if economic reforms are successful, democratic projects can still fail. Such failures could result from ethnic conflicts only indirectly related to economic issues. It is also possible that leaders who successfully extricate their societies from economic crisis will exploit their political advantage to resist the depersonalization of power and the institutionalization of checks on their authority. The costs to democratic institutions associated with *decretismo* and the exploitation of emergency powers should not be underestimated.

These multiple impediments to economic and political reform suggest that—as in earlier waves of democratization—some societies now seeking to consolidate democratic institutions will be unable to do so. On the other hand, there is some hope to be derived from our observations in the last two chapters concerning the varieties of economic strategies that have successfully generated growth, and the range of institutional arrangements in which these might be embedded. The existence of multiple equilibria—of a variety of possible combinations of the market and democracy—necessarily means that there is a variety of possible transition paths. Combinations among these are not open-ended, and the multiplicity of paths by no means implies that they are available to all comers. But countries do have a number of different models they might follow while still managing to combine the benefits of representative government and market means of resource allocation.

Equally important are the uncertainties institutionalized in the process of democratization.[16] We have argued that democracies are unlikely to be consolidated if there is wide divergence of preferences with respect to fundamental assumptions about economic policy. This does not imply, however, that there is no room within each evolving system for contestation about both policy and modes of representation; indeed, within the broad parameters of a market economy and political pluralism, such debate is an essential component of democratic development.

We might venture more: democratic debate and contestation are themselves a form of collective learning in which citizens acquire the capacity to reject what fails and to attempt something new. The capacity to learn means that the unexpected is possible, that neither politics nor policy is simply a game of repeating what has become before. It is on this fundamental characteristic of democracy that we pin our hopes.

[16] This is the central theme of Adam Przeworski's penetrating essay, "Some Problems in the Study of the Transition to Democracy," in O'Donnell, Schmitter, and Whitehead, eds., *Transitions from Authoritarian Rule,* pt. 3, *Comparative Perspectives,* pp. 47–63.

About the Authors

STEPHAN HAGGARD is Professor of Political Science in the Graduate School of International Relations and Pacific Affairs at the University of California, San Diego. ROBERT R. KAUFMAN is Professor of Political Science at Rutgers University. They are the co-editors of *The Politics of Economic Adjustment* (Princeton).